CASS SERIES: STUDIES IN AIR POWER
(Series Editor: Sebastian Cox)

COURAGE AND AIR WARFARE

CASS SERIES: STUDIES IN AIR POWER
(Series Editor: Sebastian Cox)

COURAGE
AND
AIR WARFARE

*The Allied Aircrew Experience
in the Second World War*

MARK K. WELLS

FRANK CASS
LONDON

First published in 1995 in Great Britain by
FRANK CASS & CO. LTD
Newbury House, 900 Eastern Avenue,
London IG2 7HH, England

and in the United States of America by
FRANK CASS
c/o ISBS
5804 N.E. Hassalo Street, Portland, Oregon 97213-3644

British Library Cataloguing in Publication data

Wells, Mark K.
  Courage and Air Warfare: Allied Aircrew
  Experience in the Second World War. –
  (Studies in Air Power)
  I. Title   II. Series
  940.544

ISBN 0-7146-4618-0 (cloth)
ISBN 0-7146-4148-0 (paper)

Library of Congress Cataloging in Publication data

Wells, Mark K., 1953–
    Courage and air warfare : the Allied aircrew experience in the
  Second World War / Mark K. Wells.
      p.   cm. — (Cass series—studies in air power)
    Includes bibliographical references (p.) and index.
    ISBN 0-7146-4618-0. — ISBN 0-7146-4148-0 (pbk.)
    1. World War, 1939–1945—Aerial operations, British. 2. World
  War, 1939–1945—Aerial operations, American.   3. Great Britain.
  Royal Air Force—Airmen.   4. United States. Air Force—Airmen.
  5. Great Britain. Royal Air Force. Bomber Command—History.
  6. United States. Air Force. Air Force, 8th—History.
  7. Bombardment.   I. Title.   II. Series.
  D786.W44   1995
  940.54'4941—dc20   95-3290
                                                         CIP

Typeset in 10½/12 Imprint by
Regent Typesetting, London
Printed in Great Britain by
Bookcraft (Bath) Ltd, Midsomer Norton

Contents

List of Illustrations

The author and publisher are grateful to the USAF Academy Library Special Collections for permission to reproduce photographs 7, 11, 14, 18, 19, 20, 22, 23, 24, 25, 26, 27, 28, 29, 30, 32, 33 and 34, and to Don Stull for photographs 21 and 31. The remaining photographs are from the author's own collection.

Editor's Foreword

IN WRITING this study of human factors in air warfare, and the military policies which sprang from them, Colonel Mark Wells is following in some distinguished footsteps, from ancient historians such as Thucydides, through Carl von Clausewitz and Ardant du Picq in the nineteenth century, to S. L. A. Marshall, Lord Moran and John Keegan in more recent times. Clausewitz's marvellously understated comment on the novice's reaction to coming under fire for the first time – 'even the bravest can become slightly distracted' – might serve as a suitable *leit-motif* for this book.[1]

Colonel Wells's specific concentration on the Anglo-American experience in the Combined Bomber Offensive quite literally extends these earlier works into a new dimension, that of air warfare. The additional pressures, both psychological and physiological, which fighting in the air exerts is explored for the first time. By including in the study not only the nature of air combat, but also the way in which aircrews were recruited, and the treatment of those who proved to be incapable of meeting the demands imposed, the author has extended our knowledge into some neglected or badly obscured areas. In particular he has produced the first detailed study of the emotive and controversial subjects of morale and 'Lack of Moral Fibre', subjects which other historians have touched upon but not studied in great depth.

Colonel Wells offers historians, psychiatrists, military officers and sociologists a much greater insight into the motivations of military airmen in the most sustained and intensive air battle ever fought. His study sheds much greater light on the operation of the military bureaucracies, especially with regard to recruitment, leadership and psychological reaction to and treatment of combat-induced stress. These are all questions that are of as much concern today as they were half a century ago. To illustrate the point, the modern Royal Air Force Officer and Aircrew Selection Centre at RAF Cranwell still refers to some of its current battery of aptitude tests as Stanines (see pages 7–11), betraying both their origin, and the continued relevance today of much of the subject matter in this book.

SEBASTIAN COX

NOTE

1. Carl von Clausewitz, *On War*, edited and translated by Michael Howard and Peter Paret (Princeton: Princeton University Press, 1976), p. 113.

Foreword

THE TASK of the historian has been defined by many critics as having three main components. First is the need to assemble and describe the facts accurately and in as much detail as needed to give a true picture of the events under discussion. Second is the effort to combine these facts into a broad perspective that sees the forest as well as the trees. Finally there is the need to draw conclusions from these events, which, helped by hindsight, may help in formulating policies that will optimize decisions in similar circumstances in the future.

That Colonel Wells has met these goals admirably will be readily apparent to readers of this volume. He has researched the facts meticulously, not only the written records but, of even more significance, the reports of many of the survivors of the air war, both in England and in the United States. He has assembled these facts in a way that provides a global picture of events not possible at the time they were happening, in part because of wartime censorship and in part because those of us involved were so concerned with our own tasks and responsibilities that we had little time to ponder the larger picture. Finally, Colonel Wells analyzes the issues that were troubling all those involved in the monumental task of keeping men flying under extremely hazardous conditions, and distills the crucial conflict that underlay the various official decisions concerning the disposition of flyers who were unable or unwilling to fly further combat or training missions.

As one of three psychiatrists assigned to the Eighth Air Force Central Medical Establishment in January 1943, I was initially detailed to do psychiatric evaluations of aircrew members who were referred by the squadron or group flight surgeons for examination. The conflict between one's duty and one's fears, so ably and fully described by Colonel Wells, gave rise to an astonishing variety of symptoms. These ranged from various psychosomatic complaints to serious psychological problems. The complex issues involved in the identification and disposition of these men have been accurately portrayed in this volume, both in the RAF Bomber Command and in the Eighth Air Force. The real conflict in philosophies, in both organizations, was a three-way affair. One one side were the combat commanders, many of whom tended to favor the attitudes of the old line neuropsychiatrists who, drawing from First World War experiences, tended to stress the organic, neurological roots of the symptoms. This was one of the elements leading to the use of the term 'Lack of Moral Fibre'. These same elder statesmen of medicine were in constant struggle with their younger, more dynamically orientated colleagues, who tended to view the airmen's problems as a reaction to the extreme stresses to which they were subjected.

These issues were highlighted for me, when, as a fairly young medical officer, I was detailed to accompany Air Commodore R. D. Gillespie, one of the newer breed of psychiatrists, on a tour of Eighth Air Force bomber bases to see how the Americans were dealing with these problems. From my recollections of discussions with Air Commodore Gillespie, I feel that Colonel Wells has captured very accurately the issues that command and medical personnel were struggling with in both air forces.

Modern air warfare has changed so radically, with the introduction of electronic and computerized wonders, that it is difficult to extrapolate many of the lessons of the Second World War. I would hope, however, that the clear presentation of the problems arising in flying personnel, and the solutions considered – as detailed in this volume – might have an impact on future decisions about selection criteria, tours of duty, and disposition of problem cases. If the conclusions Colonel Wells draws are considered seriously by 'the Brass', then his very fine effort will have been rewarded.

BERNARD C. GLUECK
Flight Surgeon, Major
Medical Corps, U.S. Army Air Forces

Acknowledgements

THIS BOOK would not have been possible without the support of many people. It is based on my doctoral thesis for King's College, London, and I am deeply indebted to Dr Mike Dockrill, my supervisor, for his continued assistance, critical suggestions and kind encouragement throughout the course of my studies. I received similar unflagging support from all members of the War Studies Department, especially from Professor Lawrence Freedman and Professor Brian Bond. My frequent requests were always met with great flexibility and kindness.

A number of institutions were very helpful during my work. I offer the staffs at the Air Historical Branch, Public Record Office, Imperial War Museum, RAF Museum, US National Archives, Library of Congress, US Air Force Historical Research Agency and Special Collections at the Air Force Academy Library my heartfelt thanks.

Among scores of individuals who deserve particular accolades for their warm and expert assistance are Sidney Brandon, David Chandler, David Stafford-Clark, Sebastian Cox, Urban Drew, Gavin Edwards, Lynn Gamma, James Hill, John Huston, Richard Holmes, Brad King, Richard Kohn, David MacIsaac, Phillip Meilinger, Richard Overy, Douglas Radcliffe, Duane Reed, Edward Spiers, Edgar Spridgeon and Hub Zemke.

I need to thank personally Colonel Carl W. Reddel, Professor and Head of the Department of History at the US Air Force Academy, for setting in motion my entire course of study in London. It nevertheless took the aid of General John A. Shaud, USAF (retired), to convince the Air Force of the value of a doctorate for this flying officer. General Shaud's inspirational example and superb leadership were powerful motivators to finish the job.

Once committed to the project, I quickly discovered the same spirit of co-operation that had been so much a part of the Allied wartime effort. I gratefully received the selfless assistance of innumerable British and American veterans on both sides of the Atlantic. Hundreds of aircrew responded to my queries with detailed and very personal recollections on sensitive and almost forgotten topics. Scores more spoke frankly about their experiences during face-to-face interviews. Many of these communications are referenced in end-of-chapter notes. All of the participating veterans deserve full credit by name here; regrettably, space precludes such a listing. Members of the following American bomb group associations were tremedously helpful: 34th, 92nd, 95th, 96th, 100th, 303rd, 306th, 351st, 379th, 385th, 392nd, 401st, 448th, 482nd, 486th, 487th, and 490th. I also heard from several members of the American Fighter Aces Association, the 364th fighter group and Class 41-F. Furthermore, the fact that I cannot list them all does nothing to diminish my immense gratitude and great respect for all the veterans of the Daedalians, the Eighth Air Force Historical Society, the Air Crew Association and Bomber Command Association. I shall always remember them.

My parents, Major and Mrs Maurice L. Wells, also deserve special credit for their prompt responses to all my frantic long-distance logistics requests. Whether it was computer supplies, car parts or research materials, they never failed to find and ship things quickly.

Finally, and most importantly, I want to thank my wife Donna and two children, Nathan and Emily. Their love, support, and encouragement allowed me to carry on. Moreover, without their strength to overcome the 'operational fatigue' associated with six family moves from 1986 to 1992, none of this would have been possible.

Mark K. Wells

Abbreviations

AAF	Army Air Forces
ACRC	Air Crew Receiving Centre
AFHRA	Air Force Historical Research Agency
ARMA	Adaptability Rating for Military Aeronautics
ATC	Air Training Command
CMB	Central Medical Board
CME	Central Medical Establishment
DGMS	Director General of Medical Services
FEB	Flying Evaluation Board
FPRC	Flying Personnel Research Committee
HMSO	His/Her Majesty's Stationery Office
ITW	Initial Training Wing
LMF	Lack of Moral Fibre
MO	Medical Officer
NCO	Non-commissioned officer
PNB	Pilot, navigator and bomb-aimer
RAF	Royal Air Force
USAAF	United States Army Air Force
USSAFE	United States Strategic Air Forces in Europe

Introduction

Countless minor incidents – the kind you can never really foresee – combine
to lower the general level of performance, so that one always falls far short of
the intended goal. Iron will-power can overcome this friction; it pulverizes
every obstacle, but of course it wears down the machine as well.

Carl von Clausewitz, *On War*

FEW MILITARY campaigns in modern times have attracted as much
historical attention as the Second World War's Combined Bomber
Offensive. Considerable controversy still exists regarding its strategic
aims, conduct, costs, results and morality. Historians, politicians, public
figures, veterans and religious leaders have argued over these issues
almost non-stop since 1945. If anything, the rhetoric has become ever
more heated, especially as various reunions, memorials, and dedications
continue to mark the Anglo-American campaign's 50th anniversary.

On one subject, however, there seems to be less debate and acrimony.
When it comes to remembering the contribution and sacrifice of
thousands of American, British and Commonwealth aircrew and ground-
support veterans, few people disagree. The Allied servicemen and women
who participated in the world's first combined, and most sustained,
strategic bombing campaign are widely acknowledged to have endured
more hardship and made greater sacrifices than almost any group of combatants in modern warfare. Moreover, they carried the war offensively to
Nazi Germany at a time when the Allies lacked any other means of defeat-
ing the enemy and they would do so almost alone for two full years.
Stepping away from the moral issues, which frankly seem far more
prominent now than they did at the time, and considering only the
efficacy of the campaign, it would seem indisputable that air power played
one of the decisive roles in the outcome of the war. Even if it failed to live
up to the more hopeful projections of its prominent pre-war and wartime
advocates, it nevertheless devastated German cities, all but halted oil production, disrupted transportation, hampered armaments production, tied
down millions of men, cleared the air of the Luftwaffe and ultimately

paved the way for the victorious advance of Allied armies. A strong argument can therefore be made that it measurably shortened the conflict. Significantly, after the war, very few of the top German officials underestimated the impact of the Allied strategic air offensive on the Nazi war effort.

All these achievements came at terrific cost, however. Men from the United States Eighth Air Force and the Royal Air Force's Bomber Command sustained combat casualties which exceeded 50 per cent of their aircrew strengths. More than 18,000 Allied aircraft were lost and about 81,000 British, American and Commonwealth airmen gave their lives. At least 6,000 lie in unknown graves or in the sea.

However dramatic or tragic, statistics alone cannot possibly tell the whole story of the Allied air offensive. The air war over Europe was not won merely by the number of sorties generated, bomb totals, targets destroyed or victory tallies in air-to-air combat. Although this was a war which employed scientific and technical means to a greater extent than had ever been seen previously, its results nevertheless still rested on the individual courage, stamina and determination of thousands of men and women. These were the human qualities, above all others, that air war seemed to demand.

The reasons for this are apparent from the nature of the conflict. If we accept the Clausewitzian notion that countless minor and unpredictable factors can cause things to go wrong in war, it follows that courage, determination and stamina, which together might be characterized as willpower, help overcome these impediments to success. According to Clausewitz, however, attempts to overcome the friction of war eventually take their toll on combatants.

Understanding the human stresses of combat is therefore a useful way to frame any investigation of the Strategic Bomber Offensive. Too often campaign summaries, personal memoirs, biographies and aircraft monographs tell us little about the real nature of air combat or its impact on its participants. Vivid and graphic recollections of dog-fighting at 25,000 feet, stories of individual heroism, or descriptions of crashing aircraft and exploding bombs make riveting reading. But, in a very real sense, they do not reveal the full picture, which requires consideration not just of the physical but also of the mental world of air battle. Historical attention needs to be more closely focused on the psychological dimension of the campaign, especially topics relating to aircrew selection and classification, reaction to combat, adaptability to stress, morale, leadership and combat effectiveness.

All too often the strategic bombing offensive against Germany is regarded as two separate campaigns. In fact, it was very much a common enterprise. Officially initiated with the Casablanca directive of January 1943, but for practical purposes already underway, the Allied campaign featured two air forces, two different organizational and philosophical concepts and two distinct approaches to essentially the same problem. Both forces were committed to a central objective.

The study which follows responds to questions which might very broadly be categorized as all relating to aircrew stress, morale and combat effectiveness. Unlike other investigations, it exploits sources such as medical evidence, disability statistics and psychiatric records. Despite much that has been written about the revolutionary aspect of air war, air and ground combat are fundamentally similar in respect of the human dimension. Even so, the terrific demands placed on aerial combatants – danger, physical exertion, uncertainty and chance – can rightly be seen as greatly magnified in the air. It should be noted that the principal focus is on bomber missions, both day and night, as well as American fighter operations. Obviously, there were other important elements of the air war, but it was success or failure in these main endeavours which largely determined the outcome of the Combined Bomber Offensive.

Comparisons between the Eighth Air Force and the Royal Air Force Bomber Command in the human dimension offer illuminating insights, especially since the aims of both forces were essentially similar, while their approaches to the task were often so radically different. The different philosophical, institutional and medical approaches taken by the Allied air forces in the Combined Bomber Offensive led to recognizable human factor consequences. By comparing the two it is possible to gain some real insight into the nature of air combat and its impact on aviators.

1

Choosing the Best: Selection and Classification of Aircrew

FROM THE earliest days of aviation, airmen have been regarded as members of an élite group, largely as a result of the dangers associated with flying. In the early part of the twentieth century, flimsy machines, unreliable engines, and inadequate preparation caused scores of accidents.[1] Aircraft and flying were considered novelties and pilots were often seen as daredevils. In the view of many, it took a special type of man to brave the obvious perils.[2]

This image became even more exaggerated during the First World War, especially in the popular perception. Circumstances combined to generate the favoured notion that aviators were somehow 'supermen', who not only had nerves of steel, but were also physically and mentally superior. The air combat arena appeared far more antiseptic, and certainly more captivating, than the daily grind of trench warfare. Heroes were easier to identify as individuals and, with their youthful, mostly handsome faces, less difficult to glamorize.[3]

The reality was very different, of course, but elements of this attitude were common even inside military services. Long before the war most countries began laying down minimum physical standards for airmen. Good eyesight was an obvious requirement, as was a modicum of muscular co-ordination.[4] Often these standards were related to characteristics associated with sportsmen, hunters or cavalrymen. Naïve notions relating to the social and cultural background of flyers were similarly popular, especially in Britain,[5] but it was the war itself which served to give the biggest impetus to more rigorous and realistic selection criteria.

During the First World War, many military commanders and aviation medical authorities settled on the necessary prerequisites for successful flyers. The intensity of combat operations and rapidly advancing aircraft technology made it clear that, at an absolute minimum, a robust emotional constitution was necessary for an aviator's success and survival. Fixed physical standards were therefore supplemented with detailed personal characteristics which gave clues to a flyer's temperament.[6] Eagerness to fly counted for much, as did youth, resolution, tenacity and a willingness to take risks. Each of the war's belligerents adopted this formula in some form to help select suitable candidates.

In America, the desire to identify good men – and eliminate the unsuitable – received special impetus from US War Department figures. The conflict brought 50,000 battle deaths but more than double that number of soldiers were admitted to hospital on psychiatric grounds.[7] There was considerable surprise at the rate at which ground soldiers broke under the strain of combat; so much so, that in the summer of 1918 General John J. Pershing demanded a screening examination to reduce the intake of those who might succumb to what was then termed 'shell shock'.[8] By war's end no fewer than 48,888 individuals had been rejected for service for reasons based on indications of mental disorder.[9] Despite this, more than 125,000 mentally afflicted veterans would eventually apply for monetary compensation under the War Risk Insurance Act.[10] In an attempt to control alarming statistics like these, army psychiatrists joined the staffs at all induction centres, and would remain a permanent fixture of the American military selection process.

In Britain, due largely to cultural and economic factors, there was more reluctance to rely on psychiatric explanations for breakdown. This was also partly explained by the great faith the British maintained in traditional methods of classification and selection of recruits. Even after the events of 1914-18 there was no great inclination to add any kind of psychological or psychiatric examination to the process. It was not until early in the Second World War that the system was modified to include psychiatrists and a psychiatric examination. Even so, under ordinary circumstances psychiatric specialists would only be called in to examine especially suspicious or obvious cases of disorder.[11] In the case of the RAF, as we shall see, this step was taken for aircrew candidates only reluctantly.[12] Most often, British selection boards relied on their own internal and essentially non-professional expertise. For the British, the underlying notion was that airmen with no aptitude for flying could be 'weeded out' without too much difficulty by general observation and practical appraisal.

Thus, as will become apparent, at the beginning of the Second World War, both the Royal Air Force and the US Army Air Corps (in 1941 renamed the US Army Air Forces) had functional systems for finding qualified aircrew members for training. At a fundamental level the goal was essentially the same: to find the best candidates for flying duty. But the approaches taken by the two air forces would reflect quite different techniques and, especially for the Americans, were aimed not only at singling out the men best suited to withstand the rigours of training, but also at identifying those who would succeed in combat.

AIRCREW IDENTIFICATION AND TESTING IN THE USAAF

The American approach to aircrew selection and classification reflected a strong faith in the scientific method of evaluating human capabilities. During the first year of US involvement in the Second World War, the US Army Air Forces (USAAF) had relied on a system which emphasized the traditionally high educational and physical standards set for aircrew during the interwar years.[13] Reception centres subjected new recruits destined for aircrew enlisted duties to a series of tests designed to measure general intelligence, mechanical aptitude and probable speed of learning. Despite the best intentions, the psychiatric examination at the time was best characterized as 'intuitive and haphazard'.[14] Men were ostensibly interviewed to reveal civilian skills or experiences which might be easily related to military specialities. Scores were assigned and candidates divided into five categories according to the result. For most of the period, Air Corps training programmes received a larger percentage of the top rated men for enlisted duty than did the other branches of the army.[15]

Potential officers were similarly culled. From 1927 to 1942 there was an educational requirement which called for a minimum of two years of college. Physical standards for pilots, navigators and bombardiers were already high.[16] Moreover, it was intended that every aspiring officer would have a comprehensive interview with an experienced flight surgeon or an aviation medical examiner.[17] The US Army School of Aviation had developed a guide to be used in the evaluation of the personality of potential pilots.[18] Unfortunately, many examiners, a high proportion of whom were old flying instructors, smugly believed themselves particularly adept at picking prospective candidates,

I can observe a boy as he drives a car, plays tennis, or even as he walks across the street, and tell you whether or not he will make a flier![19]

As the need for qualified candidates grew exponentially, it became clear that the AAF would need a better way to screen volunteers. The scientific community was prepared to provide help.[20] Various schemes were investigated, some quite novel, but some with questionable scientific validity.

One of the more dubious approaches was based on an examination of a candidate's facial features. The theory was that a man's face could be used as an indicator of his mental, physical and emotional capability and stamina. The size and shape of particular parts of a face were carefully measured and charted. These areas were thought to correspond to particular skills. By comparing the results with a composite picture drawn from 20 outstanding aviators, a man's potential was measured. Not surprisingly, practical experimentation proved that this 'test' was of no value in determining success in flying training.[21]

After January 1942, under wartime manpower pressures, the AAF dropped the college requirement in favour of an aviation cadet qualifying examination for all volunteers.[22] This written qualifying examination, lasting three hours, was frequently altered in the hope of improving its predictive quality. Likewise, its pass marks were occasionally changed to meet varying manpower requirements.[23]

A 1943 experiment directed solely to test the efficacy of this AAF qualifying examination allowed a group of 1,000 applicants to enter training regardless of their marks. Of those admitted who would have nominally failed the exam, fully 88.9 per cent were subsequently eliminated from flying training. Moreover, two-thirds of those who passed were also eliminated. So while the experiment validated the qualifying examination as a tool to screen those with almost no potential for flying service, it also showed that further testing was necessary to find men who could fly. In short, although generally effective at preventing blatantly unqualified men entry into the technical environment of the air forces, the aircrew qualifying examination was an inadequate tool for identifying actual aircrew aptitudes.[24]

As a result, it was supplemented by a series of 20 tests, both written and physical, known as 'the classification battery', or 'stanine tests'. The latter term arose as a result of the words '*sta*ndard *nine*', and referred to the scores assigned to men ranging from one (low) to nine (high). Individual scores were weighted and cited as composites which measured potential for the three major aircrew positions of pilot, bombardier and navigator. The higher the score in a particular category the man earned, the better his chances of success in training in that speciality.[25]

For these tests to work properly it was obviously necessary for military and medical authorities to predict what kind of skills would be necessary for successful pilots, navigators and bombardiers. Psychologists worked closely with training officials and instructor pilots to create such a list. Among the most important predictors of success for pilots were the ability to perceive and react to stimuli, adequate muscular co-ordination, the skill to visualize mechanical movements and adeptness at discriminating between visual objects. Some of these characteristics could be measured by 'psychomotor' equipment. Typically simple wooden devices of various configurations with pulleys, lights and rudimentary controls, these apparatuses were designed to be centrally produced. Delays in production and the large number of men to be tested often forced the reception centres to use locally devised tests of questionable value.

I do remember trying to hold a stylus in a small round hole while they were trying to distract me with marbles falling on a tin pan over my head and yelling at me 'You are going to crash!'[26]

Physical stanines were complemented by written examination and a similarly scored interview designed to investigate a candidate's background and interests. There was much publicity at the time about the value of 'ink-blot' tests and word association quizzes. It was obviously intended that every man be adequately examined, but, largely as a result of the huge number of men to be screened, most veterans apparently received only a very cursory interview with a psychiatrist.[27] For aircrew candidates the results became part of the 'Adaptability Rating for Military Aeronautics' or ARMA. The interview's purpose was to review their family histories and screen them for blatant clues of emotional disorder. Accordingly, much weight was assigned to traits which might be easily spotted or casually admitted: loudness, timidity, excessive nervousness, bed-wetting, nail-biting, and sexual preference.[28] Men who appeared effeminate, 'unmanly', or were suspected of outright homosexuality were quickly rejected. Generals Arnold and Eaker opined that 'the frank, open-faced, pleasant-mannered, serious-minded, and co-operatively-inclined boy' was the one wanted and selected in nine out of ten cases.[29]

As a result of feedback coming from various theatres of combat, by late 1944 the School of Aviation Medicine began developing a programme which emphasized a longer and more intensive psychiatric evaluation. By that time aircrew manpower requirements had eased somewhat, and more psychiatric specialists were available to do the screening. However, the objections of some local commanders – many of whom always regarded psychiatrists with scepticism and suspicion – and the end of the war led to the programme's abandonment.[30]

For much of the war an overall ten or 15 per cent rejection rate on the original psychiatric interview was about the average. Altogether about 40 per cent of all rejections at the induction centres were made on neuro-psychiatric grounds.[31] Moreover, depending on manpower requirements, air force authorities could use the expedient of lowering or raising the overall stanine scores required for flying specialities to decrease or increase the flow of men to training units. Usually pilot candidates required a composite of at least six to enter training. Navigators, who had to show more proficiency at calculation, needed a seven. Bombardiers had to be doubly qualified and needed to score six on the bombing stanine and at least a five on the navigator scale.[32]

Ultimately, for the entire programme to work, it was important to determine the accuracy of all examinations by going back to compare successful aircrew training graduates and their training records with their test scores.[33] The goal was constantly to improve the predictive quality of the overall qualifying examination and subsequent stanine tests and thereby save training costs and improve efficiency.

At various times statistical data from across the United States was correlated to test the validity of the stanine scores. As part of this continuing process, one such review occurred in 1943 for all classes carrying the designation '44-E'. Under that designator a total of 7,164 cadets had entered pilot training nationwide. One thousand five hundred and eighty-five, or 22 per cent, were eventually eliminated either because of flying deficiency, fear or at their own request. Analysis indicated that the wash-out rate for men with stanine scores of seven or eight was significantly lower than the class average, and of the men who had scored a nine on the pilot's stanine, only about one in ten did not complete the training course. In stark contrast stood those with the low stanines of two or three. These men suffered an attrition rate in training of more than double their class-mates. At the lowest level – where a mark of only one had been assigned – fully half the men failed.[34] Subsequent experiments reinforced these results. In fact, as the stanine tests were continually refined, their accuracy seemed to increase. Late in the war one such repetition showed that fewer than one-third of men with stanines under seven would graduate from pilot training if accepted. Accordingly, few authorities disputed the predictive quality of the stanine tests, at least in so far as training was concerned.[35]

Statistical analysis aside, there were inevitable problems with this scientific attempt to select and classify so many people. Some men, who might otherwise be perfectly suitable, were rejected for what might be considered trivial reasons.[36] Intellectual capabilities notwithstanding, some had understandable difficulty involving simple testmanship. Certainly, few had undergone anything which compared with the intensive 18 or 26-day classification routine. In addition, intangible factors like motivation, background and interests were difficult to quantify. Many veterans have only the vaguest memory of the details of the psychiatric examination, largely because of its brevity. However, a significant number of these men also recall bitterly how important it seemed to their futures. Given the importance of interviews in the process, it is not hard to imagine the nervousness of the candidates. When probed for information on essentially private matters, some quite naturally became defensive, possibly even evasive. Most probably were simply afraid to say something wrong. Men who had hoped for years to become pilots were sometimes arbitrarily rejected for any number of minor excuses. Occasionally the logic of rejection appeared nonsensical. One pilot candidate, for example, told that he was 'too nervous' for flying, was promptly classified for training as a left-waist gunner where the stresses were every bit as great if not greater. Subsequently winning his commission and pilot's rating, he successfully flew combat missions in two later wars.[37]

From time to time it was made clear that the ultimate goal of the selection and classification programme was to identify pilots (fighter and bomber), navigators, bombardiers, gunners and other aircrew who would best perform in combat. On this score the results of the stanine test and selection process are more difficult to assess. One reason, of course, is that, unlike training criteria, valid signals of success in combat were not easy to identify and measure. The accuracy of bombing – a traditional measure of combat effectiveness – was not just a function of aircrew proficiency, but also depended on aircraft altitude, the weather, enemy defences, the quality of equipment and scores of other factors. Similarly, in fighter aviation, success could not be predicted solely on pilot proficiency because shooting down an enemy was related, among other things, to the number of opportunities afforded a man, the opponent's skill, luck, timing and aircraft capability. In sum, the myriad of circumstances which made combat itself so chaotic and unpredictable likewise rendered attempts to forecast an airman's proficiency unreliable at best.[38]

The recognition of these facts, even at the time, did not prevent medical officials from continuing their attempts to validate their data scientifically. Under the direction of the Psychological Branch, Research Division, Office of the Air Surgeon, no less than three detachments went to advanced training bases in the United States and combat stations in Europe between 1943 and 1945 in hopes of correlating classification tests with actual combat results.

The preliminary results of the investigations came from transition and advanced training bases where, unlike at airfields concerned only with flying fundamentals, techniques closer to actual combat were practised. Indeed, statistics demonstrated that aircrew who enjoyed higher scores on the stanine tests consistently performed better while handling the more complex requirements of operational aircraft. Measured by a constant weeding-out process, higher stanine pilots, navigators, bombardiers, not to mention enlisted crewmen, were far less likely to be re-evaluated for ineffectiveness. Practice bombing appeared more accurate, fixed gunnery results more positive, and navigation far more precise. Additionally, the accident rate – always a concern in an air force which had lost more aircraft in training than in combat – was lowest for high stanine crews.[39] In short, the correlations seemed to justify the air force's faith in its classification and selection process.

However, the evidence coming from combat in the Eighth Air Force was less persuasive. When interviewed in theatre, squadron commanders often stated that a pilot's performance had less to do with his predicted abilities than with his interest and enthusiasm for the job.[40] For all their value, stanine tests failed to give sufficient weight to a person's preferences. There were frequent cases of dissatisfaction with the type of aircraft assigned by a training process which paid more attention to instructor recommendations, height and weight restrictions, and quota requirements than it did to long-held personal desires.[41] An often heard complaint in the Eighth Air Force was,

The men in my class who wanted to be pursuit pilots got four-engine assignments and the men who wanted four-engines got pursuit.[42]

True or not, the popularity of such a sentiment seriously undermined the confidence which aircrew might have had in the system and, according to the same report, 'substantially' decreased the efficiency of air force combat groups.[43]

More detailed studies of fighter and bomber pilots actually in operational units in the Eighth Air Force led superficially to more encouraging conclusions. Most of the airmen were about half way through their combat tours when observed. It was therefore possible to evaluate their performance directly and also collect the subjective observations of their commanders. By comparing the results with their scores on the classification battery (which, for most of the subjects, had been taken at least one or two years previously) it was hoped to demonstrate a correlation between high stanines and combat success.

Investigators found that pilots with the lower stanines of four, five, or six were in fact frequently rated by their commanders as 'having doubtful value to their group'. Additionally, these same men more often went missing in action as compared to those officers with the relatively high stanines of seven, eight, or nine.[44] But absolute proof of any connection nevertheless eluded the investigators.

The reasons for this were many. By the time airmen got to operational units, training attrition alone had reduced the numbers of less qualified men. Quite apart from the difficulty in measuring combat effectiveness itself, personnel turnover was so rapid that it was tough to measure any airman's contribution accurately. Significantly too, there was some disagreement over just what traits were most important for the stanines to identify, largely because the optimum characteristics of bomber pilots and fighter pilots were considered to be so different. Finally, many commanders and medical officials were sceptical about the value of trying to predict combat success altogether.[45] This view is repeated in the history of the Personnel Distribution Command, compiled during the months before the war's end, which stated categorically, 'there was no correlation between the pre-combat selection tests, as expressed in stanines, and success in combat, as exemplified by the criterion, whatsoever'.[46] In the end, the most useful finding on the whole subject was that there was a general benefit from raising selection standards for all airmen.

Whatever the conflicting evidence, there were those who believed that the stanine test battery had proved its validity convincingly. At the senior level of the US Army Air Force – perhaps where it counted the most – there was considerable satisfaction with the programme:

The Aviation Psychology programme has paid off in time, lives, and money saved, and through its selection of the raw material has aided in the establishment of an effective combat air force. This has been done at a total cost of less than five dollars per candidate tested.[47]

AIRCREW SELECTION IN BRITAIN

During the Second World War the Royal Air Force's approach to aircrew selection and classification was noticeably different from that of the US Army Air Force. In the United States there was greater faith in the ability of psychologists and psychiatrists to assess human potential accurately, whereas in Britain there was an institutional bias towards more traditional methods. There was correspondingly much less reliance on the scientific method. Although it is true that British Aircrew Reception Centres eventually used a number of examinations, similar to their American counterparts, to measure a recruit's general intelligence, mathematical skills and motor co-ordination, among other things, more weight was placed on the practical aspects of a candidate's performance during selection and subsequent training. A review of the RAF's selection and classification process shows that British methods gradually evolved away from educational and intellectual standards and more towards measurement of natural aptitude. Furthermore, despite their own strong efforts, psychiatrists played a lesser role in personnel selection in the RAF than they did in any other British service.

It is possible to plot these changes in the RAF selection procedure. At the very beginning of the war selection for aircrew training depended entirely on a non-standardized interview. At the time it was widely accepted that the RAF's selection of pilots and aircrew was very much based on socio-economic factors.[48] Recruiting materials did not minimize the fact that the goal was to find as many public school boys as possible, and there was a heavy emphasis on desirable traits like leadership, sportsmanship and knowledge of hunting. Expressing what must have been a fairly typical view, a medical officer commented on the qualities of a successful aviator this way:

This question of background is really important . . . Breeding very definitely is of great importance. It is unlikely that the son of a coward would himself become a hero, for it is remarkable how heroism often runs in families.[49]

Underscoring this kind of philosophy is the idea that the 'correct' sort of men could be identified and selected by recruiting boards, without too much difficulty.[50] Language and regional accent must have been used as immediate discriminators for the right sort of selection. Defining standards of character by the public school criteria was another. No flying personnel even attended as voting members of these early selection boards.[51]

Inevitably there were inequalities within the system. How many men, otherwise qualified, might have been turned down simply due to prejudice will never be known. It cannot be excluded, however, that some of those rejected had only themselves to blame.[52] It was, after all, easier to find fault with a collection of 'Colonel Blimps' or the 'old school tie' outlook than to admit one's shortcomings.[53]

Predictably, however, the spiralling requirements for aircrew during wartime quickly outstripped the available supply of public school candidates. This not only explains the RAF's willingness to open its aircrew ranks to others, but also sheds light on the motivation of many to serve. Thousands of enthusiastic young volunteers from further down the economic scale showed up at recruiting stations in the hope of winning a training slot. Occasionally the irony of the situation was not lost on those with the highest hopes,

The Selection Board were very Top Brass. Three of them, asking questions such as 'Can you drive a car?' and 'Can you drive a motorbike, ride a horse?' Few English boys with a working-class background could do any of these things in 1941, if only because of monetary reasons. There were only two cars in our street of about one hundred houses – one owned by a retired publican from World War One, the other by an insurance man. I clearly wasn't the type to make a pilot, but they took me on just the same. The standards were much lower than they had been before the war![54]

It was about this time that more effective psychometric – or motor coordination – tests were introduced to help the selection boards. For the most part, these made use of similar sorts of mechanical devices to those used in the United States, and were aimed at evaluating a potential airman's physical aptitude. As early as 1937 a machine had been available which measured a recruit's ability to manipulate a turret, checked his finger dexterity, and calculated his reaction times. Called the 'Sensory Motor Apparatus Number 3', or SMA3, it was widely employed and the results validated.

The aircrew classification method in use throughout 1941 might best be called 'survival selection'. In any group of 100 volunteers arbitrarily classified as pilots 'under training' by the Selection Boards, 25 would not make it to solo in the Elementary Flying Training Schools. The rest, no matter what their relative skills, were then sent on to the next higher stage at Service Flying Training Schools (SFTS). Some of these pupils were very good. Others, however, might be considered only average or poor flying prospects, but because the RAF had already invested some months of expensive training in them, they were sent forward in the hopes they would eventually reach minimum proficiency. To some extent the training system was therefore filled to capacity with scores of men whose major achievement was only that they had managed to survive their first solo.[55]

During the middle of 1942 the Air Ministry decided that the system needed overhaul. It instructed the Aviation Candidate Selection Boards to classify recruits into the broad categories of 'PNB', or pilot, navigator and bomb-aimer. As before, medical testing was thorough and focused much on athletic prowess as well as physical strength. Although a candidate's general health history was documented by the widespread use of a special sheet (RAF Form 87), emotional evaluation was still not sophisticated and much depended on what the candidate was willing to reveal about himself.[56] One veteran recalled:

... it was carried out by observation and assessment of answers to questions such as: 'Why do you want to fly?' Simple tests were given which amounted to sorting out various shapes for various slots in a given time and being asked, 'Do you consider yourself normal?' I replied words to this effect: 'What is normal?' I was one of only two out of fifty who were passed as fit aircrew, and we two at first glance looked like the nuts of the pack but we had the eyesight, the hearing, the heart and the plumbing to be accepted.[57]

Men were occasionally interviewed without their clothes on under the dubious premise that their general embarrassment would render them less likely to withhold information. The results must often have brought a smile to some faces:

The final examination took place with the candidates standing naked before a panel of three medical officers seated at a table. They asked us to do simple jumping, leg-spreading and arm-raising exercises. The candidate in front of me was instructed to turn around and bend over. He said, 'I hope I can trust you fellas'. The panel chairman immediately said, 'Unsuitable!' and the examination ended at that point.[58]

The major innovation to the system at this juncture was the inclusion of practical flight testing before actual formal flying training. It was considered so effective that in modified form it remained the final basis for pilot selection in the RAF to the end of the war. Starting in 1942, all PNB candidates were given 12 hours of flight time during which their aptitude for flying would be evaluated twice.[59] Those who did the best were identified as full pilot candidates and proceeded to training. Others with perhaps slightly less aptitude for controlling aircraft took their place on an order-of-merit list. This list, in turn, provided names for filling the navigator and bomb-aimer quotas.[60] As with the US forces, individual preferences were often overridden by the specialized manpower needs of the RAF. Candidates outside the PNB categories, which included wireless operators, air-gunners, and flight engineers, were still classified according to the recommendation of an interviewing board.[61]

Having thus arranged the candidates by practical aptitude, the RAF was able to start at the top and reach down as far as it needed to fill its fly-ing training requirements. By grading roughly twice as many candidates as was required to fill pilot quotas, the RAF was in a position to select the best half of all candidates for training. Moreover, this was based on demonstrated aptitudes and not purely on the subjective evaluation of the Aircrew Selection Boards.

Coincidentally with these developments, British neuropsychiatric specialists worked to get more involved in the selection process. In the beginning, much of the activity was carried out by Wing Commander R. D. Gillespie, who, along with Air Commodore Sir Charles P. Symonds and Air Commodore Hugh L. Burton, shared duties involving all aspects of neuropsychiatry.[62] Gillespie's background in psychiatry convinced him that scientific methods could be used to improve aircrew selection. This opinion was reinforced by the increasing numbers of neuropsychiatric casualties which were appearing as a result of combat operations.

Gillespie shared a view common to many of his psychiatric contempo-raries. For practical purposes, they struggled to convince the executive to accept a model of emotional failure which held that predisposition (or internal factors) plus stress (external factors) equalled breakdown.[63] Predisposition was a term used for measuring those personality factors, or 'neuroses', which each man carries with him into any situation and which might render him unable to carry on. In some measure all people have neurosis of one sort or another. Defined, in part, as thoughts, feelings of anxiety or compulsive behaviours which help shape personality, these ordinarily cause little problem. But in the high-stress world of air combat operations, Gillespie accepted the notion that a man's neuroses might give him a greater predisposition to breakdown. Traits which seemed to relate closest to predisposition were timidity, lack of aggression, immaturity or previous breakdown.[64] According to the formula, by minimizing pre-disposition, the emotional breakdown rate could be reduced.

If this model was accepted, it appeared to follow that careful psychiatric interview could identify and eliminate those aircrew training volunteers with the greatest predisposition for failure. This would not only save valuable training time by not wasting it on the hopeless, but would also result in combat-ready airmen best suited to withstand the rigours of combat.

Gillespie's earliest experiments were conducted at RAF Hospital, Matlock. His method was to use psychiatric interview to test operational airmen already identified as suffering from emotional disorder. If a significant level of predisposition was found the hypothesis would seem confirmed. As it turned out, fully two-thirds of the men he interviewed showed strong evidence of predisposition. Moreover, he observed that these same predisposed individuals, besides being more liable to emotional breakdown in combat, were less effective in the air than their less predisposed comrades.[65] These results were promising enough for Gillespie to seek the further support of his superior, Air Commodore Symonds.

Symonds, whose background in neurology doubtless convinced him that many aircrew emotional problems were organic in origin, was at first sceptical that psychiatric interviews would be practical or cost effective with regard to selection and classification. Furthermore, like most of the RAF's establishment, he felt that selection procedures were reasonably adequate. At least early on, he shared the conviction that the three most important things for any potential airmen to have were 'courage, confidence and character' and that these were usually being successfully identified.[66] Commenting on Gillespie's efforts, he wrote that instructor pilots at initial training wings or operational training units were in a better position than psychiatrists to watch for examples of 'nervousness or unsatisfactory behaviour'. He was nevertheless flexible enough to allow the investigation to proceed.[67]

Gillespie was further supported by Air Commodore Burton, the RAF's senior psychiatrist, in a letter to the Director General of the Medical Service. Like Symonds, Burton urged that Gillespie be allowed to continue, lest the RAF fall behind in psychiatric research. By this time Burton, among others, was well aware that the Americans were using psychiatric testing and interview to identify flyers. Moreover, he knew that the British Army had similarly employed a multistep procedure for screening recruits. As early as 1941, British Army officer candidates had been given special leadership tests and subjected to psychological interviews on the German model.[68]

While thus concerned that 'the Army has ranged ahead of the Air Force', Burton was not completely convinced that Gillespie's statistical proof was enough to justify widespread employment of the interview procedure.[69] He expressed his reservations regarding the value of psychiatric evaluation this way:

Such an assessment may be found to correlate with ability to learn to fly, but I think there is another important psychiatric aspect to be considered. From experience of selection over the past 20 years I believe that it is of greater importance to attempt the assessment of a candidate's potential to stand up to the nervous stress of flying, particularly of operational work, without the risk of breakdown.[70]

The first large-scale test of Gillespie's views took place during the first six months of 1942. Between February and August an analysis was made of all of the RAF's aircrew emotional casualties. Based on the criteria previously established, which measured each man against ten traits related to neurotic predisposition, 67 per cent of men were so identified.[71] When, during the following year, the experiment was repeated with a larger sample, an even greater correlation was found. Of the 2,200 airmen suffering from psychological disorder in 1943, three-quarters showed evidence of predisposition in a single psychiatric interview. Moreover, one-fifth of them were considered so heavily predisposed that, according to the neuropsychiatrists, they should have been rejected at entry.[72]

As this last fact came to light, it became clear that it was important to test non-operational men as well. Accordingly, Gillespie and others simultaneously undertook an inquiry at an Initial Training Wing near Matlock to try to determine whether healthy recruits could be screened for predisposition, thereby reducing the heavy wastage during flying training.[73] Despite their best intentions, the doctors were limited by man-power and time and only 12 minutes could be devoted to each interview. Even so, about one-quarter of 608 volunteers were found to have at least some neurotic predisposition.[74]

Even before these numbers were fully reported, the evidence was enough finally to convince Air Commodore Symonds and his superior, Air Commodore Whittingham, that psychiatrists were indeed useful in the selection of aircrew. Moreover, by the middle of 1943, there was enough data to move even the Air Ministry, albeit reluctantly. A sub-committee was appointed to review the whole question. Various officials, including Symonds, Whittingham and Air Commodore D. V. Carnegie, the Director of Flying Training, Air Ministry, were in attendance at its first meeting on 5 May. After evaluating the American system, including the use of stanines and interview, they decided it was generally good, even if it resulted in a ten per cent psychiatric rejection rate, which was slightly too high.[75]

From the British point of view, the other problem with such a system was that it required large numbers of well-trained medical officers, if not outright psychiatric specialists. In Britain these were in extremely short supply.[76] So even had the committee been in a position to change the RAF's aircrew selection philosophy entirely – and it certainly was not – the resources to implement a wholly new system simply did not exist.

Predictably, the committee settled on the next best thing, which was to recommend further tests to check the validity of psychiatrically examined recruits.[77] They also went so far as to support the introduction of a general mental health questionnaire for RAF ground staff.

Developed by the office of the Director-General of Medical Services (DGMS) in consultation with Gillespie, this questionnaire was designed to signal the potential for emotional problems in recruits destined for various ground trades. It was a simple written form and was administered along with standard intelligence tests. Devised to be 'graded' by specially trained WAAF (Women's Auxiliary Air Force) officers, the test's questions asked about family history, schooling, health, hobbies and employment.[78] Only when a man's responses seemed to signal something which could be a problem was he referred to a psychiatrist for an interview.[79] About one-third of these referred men were subsequently eliminated on psychiatric grounds, and, although the overall rejection rate varied from centre to centre, it generally averaged between seven and eight per cent.

At various times there were concerns that people were being rejected out of hand, or that poor categorization would cost the RAF much needed ground trade manpower. As a result, in 1943 a few of the men who nominally would have been rejected on psychiatric grounds were admitted, trained and followed up. Not surprisingly, 79 per cent were eventually discharged for unsatisfactory service. Whether or not this was a valid test of the entire ground staff selection process or simply a case of a self-fulfilling prophesy remains an open question. But Gillespie was convinced of the questionnaire's efficacy, and wrote to Whittingham that the ground staff selection programme had been 'exceptionally successful in picking out unsuitable individuals'.[80] He clearly hoped that a similar questionnaire be instituted for all aircrew candidates.

It is significant that such a test was not adopted, however. The Air Ministry's position was that the aircrew selection and training process in the RAF, more than in any other service, was continuous and extended from the recruit's first day all the way to his arrival at an operational unit. The nature of flying made the system rigorous, and subjected a potential flyer to plenty of scrutiny.[81] Because provisions had been made to have medical officers and psychiatrists available for referrals during every step of the process, this was considered sufficient. From the Air Ministry's vantage point, it was unnecessary for every single candidate to be psychiatrically evaluated. Moreover, it was not considered economical, either in time or money, to have psychiatrists involved in interviewing men who gave 'normal' responses to aircrew selection boards.[82] In other words, and quite apart from the difficulties of implementing a complex psychiatric interviewing process, it was felt that there was no overwhelming need to adopt a system like Dr Gillespie and others seemed to be recommending.

At about this time the DGMS issued a memorandum to all flying instructors which advised instructors and commanders how to recognize the symptoms of excessive nervousness or emotional disorder, and re-emphasized the importance of eliminating those with no realistic chance of success.[83] The executive had long held that the flight instructor during training, and later the unit commander in operations, was a principal agent in identifying those men who were temperamentally unsuitable.[84]

Thus, by the spring of 1944 the RAF would have in place an aircrew selection and classification system which it would use for the rest of the war. Reconfirmed on 1 April by the Director of Flying Training, the programme's goals were to bring together all aircrew volunteers during a period of common appraisal, measure their practical aptitudes, and provide the RAF with candidates with a good chance of completing training. At every step of the process candidates were kept advised of their status. This was because it was recognized that much of an airman's success in any category of training – whether pilot, navigator, bomb-aimer, flight engineer or air gunner – rested on his enthusiasm and willingness to be part of the team; but candidates were also cautioned that the wartime requirements of the air force took precedence.[85]

The existing procedures at the Aircrew Candidate Selection Boards were not changed by the 1944 programme. As had been the practice from the beginning of the war, candidates were still screened and tentatively classified by boards without benefit of direct psychiatric or psychological testing. Similarly, however, examining officers were empowered to refer questionable cases to psychiatric specialists to see if unusual symptoms or questionable behaviour had mental origins.

As with the 1942 system, after the selection boards identified and selected men into PNB categories, these potential aircrew were sent on to Air Crew Receiving Centres (ACRC).[86] They were advised that their selections were provisional – some used the term 'shadow' selections – and that much depended on the needs of the service and their aptitudes as demonstrated on written and practical examinations. Permitted to wear a distinctive white flash on their caps, all candidates received a general intelligence examination, a mathematics test, a mechanical comprehension battery, and were required to demonstrate their muscular co-ordination and reaction times.[87]

On completion of all the testing at the ACRC, candidates were shipped to one of several Initial Training Wings (ITW) where up to three months of basic military training followed. As with all newcomers to the military, RAF recruits practised rudimentary skills in dress, deportment and drill. They were also exposed to the basics of meteorology and the principles of flight, and spent hours in physical fitness training. Basic military training was often derided as 'square-bashing' and 'corporals were exalted to celestial status'. It was only endurable for many because flying training beckoned. Despite efforts on the part of officials to make the training worthwhile, it was inevitable that airmen would chafe and grumble. Any unforeseen delays which prevented moving to the next stage of the process had a serious impact on morale.[88]

One feature of the 1944 scheme was quite different from previous versions. After allowance for physical criteria and age, only those PNB cadets demonstrating the most promising potential at the original selection board and through ITW were tentatively identified as pilot candidates and earmarked for flight 'grading'.[89] These fledgeling aviators were sent to basic flying schools where they were given rudimentary instruction in small biplanes and expected to solo after eight or ten hours of flying time. Those who managed to solo inside the allotted period, and were therefore considered most likely to become full pilots after training, proceeded into the formal training scheme, and were posted to any one of the training bases in the United Kingdom, Canada, the United States, South Africa or Australia.[90] Identification as fighter or bomber pilots came later.

After filling the requirements for pilot candidates with the most promising material, the system then sifted the remainder of the volunteers for those best qualified for the navigator and bomb-aimer positions. Only after manpower requirements in these categories had been satisfied with the best alternatives, were the other aircrew categories addressed. It is important to keep in mind, however, that although the process appeared to 'cream off' the best men for the pilot or navigator positions, some effort was directed to identifying specific aptitudes and placing men accordingly.[91]

SOME DIRECT COMPARISONS

Having thus examined the two systems for selecting and classifying air-crew destined for duty with the US Eighth Air Force and the RAF's Bomber Command, it is worth summarizing their salient characteristics. Such a review must begin with the assertion that both the British and American authorities were successful in finding suitable candidates for aircrew flying duties. Despite quite different institutional and medical approaches to the considerable task of selecting the very best men available, both services managed to do so in a deliberate and systematic way.

The American system owed much to the lessons learned from the First World War. The impact of that conflict on the US military selection system was profound. Most important was the fact that it led American medical and military officials increasingly to rely on a systematic and scientific method of evaluating human potential. This approach, in turn, rested heavily on a faith in the abilities of psychologists, who largely predicted and measured 'normal' human abilities, and psychiatrists, who were judged able to find the best and eliminate the abnormal. The results of their co-operation, typified by the stanine tests and the ARMA, were representative of America's scientific and technological approach to warfare.

From the beginning of the Second World War, those who commanded the US Army Air Forces were confident that these scientific methods could be used to identify, select and categorize the very best men for aircrew training. So confident were many in the system, that they also believed it could successfully distinguish those men best able to perform in combat. Intelligence test scores, statistics, physical examination equipment and psychiatric interviews, however brief, were considered behavioural measurements so accurate that a huge number of men went to training with no true practical test of their aptitudes. It must be admitted that most of those with the higher scores did quite well in training, and if the data coming from combat theatres seemed to show much less correlation between a man's predicted performance and his actual combat effectiveness, it did little to undermine the widespread faith in the selection process.

The RAF's aircrew selection system was no less a demonstration of Britain's military heritage, but predictably reflected a traditional rather than a scientific bias. Forced by manpower requirements to widen the selection criteria beyond a purely public school boy basis, the RAF jealously defended the prerogative of its Aircrew Selection Boards. There was more than sufficient evidence to indicate that a psychiatric interview for each candidate might improve the quality of selectees. But putting such a system in place would not only have cost much in terms of time, money and energy, but was not deemed feasible due to a lack of trained specialists. Additionally, the executive had long held that selection boards – even manned as they were with non-expert, but veteran military men – were perfectly capable of recognizing those candidates who were weak or temperamentally unsuitable. Flexibility, such as it was, extended so far as to allowing flying officers eventually to take part and, later, for psychiatrists to be available for consultation.

In fairness, it should be noted that the RAF, like the USAAF, used a rigorous series of physical and mental examinations to test everything from muscular co-ordination to general intelligence and mathematical ability. Few physically unhealthy or intellectually impaired men slipped through the net and entered aircrew training. Moreover, the RAF placed a clear emphasis on aptitudes which could be tested in a practical way. Few would argue that putting men through actual flying exams or, in the case of 1944 pilot candidates, requiring them to solo, was an ineffective technique. In fact, such measures made eminent sense and worked quite well, given that resources were too scarce to permit a more scientific approach.

Arguably, even had RAF psychiatrists been more a part of the process, their focus on predisposition would probably have limited their value to identifying men at risk of emotional failure. In other words, unlike American psychiatric specialists, many of whom were busy with psychologists trying to identify the men best suited for training and combat, British doctors concentrated on a negative goal. Rather than wanting to select the best, they hoped to eliminate the worst. This is quite a different thing.

Although a comparison of the two selection systems seems to beg the question which was better, no real answer can be given. They both worked in their own ways. And although at times the results seemed arbitrary, occasionally unfair, or might rightfully be criticized for inefficiency, in the main, both the British and American selection procedures produced thousands of reasonably healthy and enthusiastic volunteers for aircrew duty. How these men subsequently performed in combat and what sustained them there are legitimate questions requiring further investigation.

NOTES

1. The toll was so high it prompted one American exhibition pilot to remark, 'We were killing them off so fast that I was beginning to fill everybody else's dates'. See Glenn H. Curtiss and Augustus Post, *The Curtiss Aviation Book* (Frederick A. Stokes, 1912), pp. 1–5.
2. Claude Grahame-White, a dashing motor-car racer, personified the gallant aviator in the years before the war. In constant demand as an exhibition pilot, he was gushingly referred to as the 'daring and spectacular young man who has won the title of matinée idol of the aviation field'. See *The New York Times*, Picture Section 1, 6 Nov. 1910.
3. Arguably the Germans were the best at this. See Manfred von Richthofen, *Der Rote Kampfflieger* (Berlin, 1918), pp. 60–65.
4. The first physical requirements for American military aviators were prescribed on 2 Feb. 1912. 520.7411–9, Air Force Historical Research Agency (hereafter AFHRA).
5. Captain T. S. Rippon and E. G. Mannell, 'Report of the Essential Characteristics of Successful and Unsuccessful Aviators', *The Lancet* (28 Sept. 1918), pp. 411–15.
6. Colonel Thomas R. Boggs, Medical Consultant, AEF, to the Chief of the Air Service, 28 Dec. 1918, AFHRA.
7. See Richard A. Gabriel, *No More Heroes: Madness and Psychiatry in War* (New York: Hill and Wang, 1987), p. 73 and Leonard P. Ayres, *The War With Germany: A Statistical Summary* (Washington, DC: US Government Printing Office, 1919), p. 122.
8. Twenty-five years after the First World War, nearly half the 67,000 beds in Veteran Administration hospitals were occupied by the neuropsychiatric casualties of the war. The care of the men had cost the US government about one billion dollars. See 'The Psychiatric Toll of Warfare', *Fortune* (Dec. 1943), pp. 141–49.
9. G. O. Ireland, 'Neuropsychiatric Ex-Serviceman and his Civil Re-establishment', *American Journal of Psychiatry* 2 (1923), p. 685.
10. J. J. Kindred, 'Neuropsychiatric Wards of the United States Government; their Housing and other Problems', *American Journal of Psychiatry* 1 (1921), p. 183.
11. Privy Council Office, *Report on the Expert Committee on the Work of Psychologists and Psychiatrists in the Services* (London: HMSO, 1947), pp. 50–1.
12. British attitudes towards psychiatrists, especially in the Second World War, often reflected a mixture of hostility, mistrust and uncertainty. At the very top, Churchill's doubts were well known. Lord Moran, his personal physician and a famous author on courage and morale, was clearly not a strong supporter of psychiatry and did little to dissuade Churchill. Similarly, senior military officers, many of whom were quick to dismiss the opinions of 'trick cyclists', were anxious to prevent what they considered to be an easy escape from military service. See F. M. Richardson, *Fighting Spirit: Psychological Factors in War* (London: Leo Cooper, 1978), pp. 94–5; Wing Commander F. MacManus, RAF, 'Flying Stress in RAF aircrew', lecture at the Defence Medical Services Military Psychiatry Course, 17 Oct. 1991, London. For a defence of the psychiatric contribution to the RAF's war effort see Expert Committee on the Work of Psychologists and Psychiatrists in the Services, Meeting minutes, 17 Sept. 1942, AIR 2/5998.
13. In the 16 years between 1923 and 1939 only 3,505 rated pilots were trained. Figures available from the *Army Air Force Statistical Digest, World War II* (Washington, DC: US Government Printing Office, 1945) and History and Research Division, Headquarters, Air Training Command, Randolph AFB, Texas.
14. The Army Regulation which covered neuropsychiatric criteria was AR 40–110. See Mae M.

Link and Hubert A. Coleman, *Medical Support of the Army Air Forces in World War II* (Washington: US Government Printing Office, 1955), p. 320.

15. Wesley F. Craven and James L. Cate (general eds), *The Army Air Forces in World War II*, 7 vols. (Chicago: University of Chicago Press, 1958), Vol. VI, pp. 538–42.

16. See War Department, 'Standards of Physical Examination for Flying', 1942, Army Regulation 40–105; and War Department, Army Regulation 40–100. Copies may be found at the Air University Library, Maxwell AFB, Alabama.

17. Office of the Air Surgeon, *Stanines, Selection, and Classification for Air Crew Duty* (Washington: US Government Printing Office, 1946), p. 1.

18. R. F. Longacre, 'Personality Study', *The Journal of Aviation Medicine* 1 (1929): pp. 33–50.

19. Quoted in Henry H. Arnold and Ira C. Eaker, *This Flying Game* (New York: Funk and Wagnalls Company, 1943), p. 109.

20. About the same time the Air Surgeon's office assumed overall responsibility for aircrew selection and classification. See Brig. Gen. David N. Grant to Commandant of the School of Aviation Medicine, 23 March 1942, 141.28, AFHRA.

21. Howard N. Cappel to Chief of the Air Corps, Subject: The Merton Method, 27 May 1940, AFHRA. See also Major Joseph F. Dorfler, *The Branch Point Study: Specialized Undergraduate Pilot Training* (Maxwell AFB: Air University Press, 1986), p. 4.

22. Statistical evidence measured then and subsequently also showed that a man's level of education bore little relation to his success in primary pilot training. See Office of the Air Surgeon, 'Selection and Classification of Aircrew Officers', Feb. 1944, 141.28F, AFHRA.

23. Frederick B. Davis (ed.), *The AAF Qualifying Examination*, Army Air Forces Aviation Psychology Program Research Reports, Report No. 6 (Washington, DC: US Government Printing Office, 1947), pp. 2–12.

24. The AAF qualifying examination might therefore rightly be considered only a minimum first hurdle for aspiring aviators. Well over one million young men took the examination. About 650,000 succeeded in passing. See Office of the Air Surgeon, 'Stanines Selection and Classification for Air Crew Duty', 141.28–20, AFHRA.

25. Lt. Col. J. C. Flanagan and Major P. M. Fitts, Jr., 'Psychological Testing Program for the Selection and Classification of Air Crew Officers', *The Air Surgeon's Bulletin* I (June 1944), pp. 1–5.

26. William W. Thompson (351st Bomb Group) to author, 9 May 1989.

27. Medical statistics show that for the entire US Army more than 15 million men were examined. One psychiatrist recalled having time for only four questions per candidate and interviewing as many as 512 men per day. See Eli Ginzberg, John L. Herma, and Sol W. Ginsburg, *Psychiatry and Military Manpower: A Reappraisal of the Experiences in World War II* (New York: King's Crown Press, 1953), p. 13.

28. Similar criteria had been used before the war. See Lt. Col. R. C. Anderson, MC, 'Psychiatric Training of Medical Officers in the Army Air Forces', Record Group 112, Box 1331, National Archives.

29. Arnold and Eaker, *Flying Game*, p. 110.

30. Link and Coleman, op. cit., p. 321.

31. Office of the Surgeon General of the Army, Memorandum for the Director, Training Division, Record Group 112, Box 1328, National Archives.

32. Candidates with lower scores were not 'lost' by any means. Frequently they ended up in radio-operator, flight engineer or gunner positions.

33. 'The Aviation Psychology Program of the Army Air Forces', *Psychological Bulletin* 40 (Dec. 1943), pp. 759–69.

34. Similar results were obtained for navigators and bombardiers. See Office of the Air Surgeon, 'Stanines Selection and Classification for Air Crew Duty', 1141.28–20, AFHRA.

35. Aircrew training attrition rates varied during the war as standards were periodically relaxed or toughened. They also varied according to crew position. For pilot training the overall attrition rate, including fatalities, averaged 40 per cent. For navigators it was 20 per cent and for bombardiers 12 per cent. See Craven and Cate, op. cit. Vol. VI, pp. 575, 585, 589.

36. One veteran, whose comments mirror the views of many, wrote, 'The psychological tests were an insult to an average person's intelligence'. General Lewis B. Hershey, the director of the American draft system, who was alarmed at the number of rejections, protested at one point that men were being turned down who 'were no queerer than the rest of us'. See Allen J. Bandy (351st Bomb Group) to author, 22 April 1989 and Hershey Papers, Box 58, US

Army Military History Institute, Carlisle Barracks, Pennsylvania.

37. Letter from Carter Hart, Jr., (385th Bomb Group) to author and interview with Major M. L. Wells, USAF (retd), 20 April 1992.

38. A more complete discussion of the air combat environment and combat effectiveness is presented in the next chapter. For a discussion on the predictive value of stanines see Office of the Air Surgeon, 'Stanines Selection and Classification for Air Crew Duty', 141.28–20, AFHRA, and General Henry H. Arnold, 'Report of the Commanding General of the US Army Air Force to the Secretary of War', 27 Feb. 1945, AFHRA.

39. Office of the Air Surgeon, 'Selection and Classification of Aircrew Officers', Feb. 1944, 141.28F, AFHRA.

40. Office of the Air Surgeon, 'Analysis of the Duties of Aircrew Personnel, Descriptions of Aircrew Performances from Theaters of Combat', 5 May 1943, 141.28D–10–19, AFHRA.

41. In a fairly typical case, approximately 95 per cent of the graduates of Class 41–F at one base were made instructors. Brig. Gen. George H. Wilson, USAF (retd) to author, 9 Nov. 1992.

42. Office of the Air Surgeon, 'Report on Survey of Aircrew Personnel in the Eighth, Ninth, Twelfth, and Fifteenth Air Forces', April 1944, 141.28B, AFHRA.

43. Ibid.

44. Ibid.

45. 'It can be accurately stated that the final criterion of selection for the military aviator is combat flying.' See Donald W. Hastings, David G. Wright, and Bernard C. Glueck, *Psychiatric Experiences of the Eighth Air Force: First Year of Combat* (New York: Josiah Macy Jr. Foundation, 1944), p. 39.

46. US Army Air Forces, 'History of the AAF Personnel Distribution Command', v.3, 254.1, 1945, AFHRA.

47. General Henry H. Arnold, 'Report of the Commanding General of the US Army Air Force to the Secretary of War', 27 Feb. 1945, AFHRA.

48. The Air Ministry never gave up the notion that public school 'gentlemen' made the best officers and aircrew. Max Hastings, *Bomber Command* (London: Michael Joseph, 1979; London: Pan Books, 1981), p. 254. See also AIR 2/6146.

49. Victor Tempest, *Near the Sun: The Impressions of a Medical Officer of Bomber Command* (Brighton: Crabtree Press, 1946), pp. 49–50.

50. Lord Moran, *The Anatomy of Courage* (London: Constable and Company, 1945; reprint edn, Garden City Park: Avery Publishing Group, 1987), pp. 151–4, 160.

51. Wing Commander C. E. Morse to Air Ministry, 5 May 1943, AIR 2/8236.

52. For the first three years of the war the RAF rejected approximately 21 per cent of the volunteers it examined for aircrew duty. AIR 2/4620.

53. A similar state of affairs existed in the British Army. Even so, the Army moved quicker than the RAF to modernise its selection system. See E. S. Turner, *Gallant Gentlemen: A Portrait of the British Officer 1600–1956* (London: Michael Joseph, 1956), pp. 300–1.

54. Geoff Parnell (Stirling veteran) to author, 15 April 1990.

55. Air Ministry, Air Member for Training, 'Flying Training', Aircrew Training Bulletin No. 12, Aug. 1943, p. 9. RAF Museum, Hendon.

56. Candidates accidentally admitting to migraines, insomnia, bed-wetting, head-injury or fainting spells were routinely disqualified. Lt. Col. Neely C. Mashburn, MC, and Major Frank A. Marshall, MC, 'Aviation Medical Standards, British RAF vs. US Army, Air Corps', 141.28N, 1942, AFHRA.

57. W. T. MacFarlane (Halifax pilot) to author, 18 July 1989.

58. R. F. Pritchard (Lancaster mid-upper gunner) to author, 25 June 1992.

59. 'Flying Training', Training Bulletin No. 12, p. 10.

60. AIR 2/4620.

61. Air Ministry, Air Historical Branch, *Flying Training*, Vol. I: *Policy and Planning* (London, 1952), pp. 66–7.

62. Burton held the Diploma in Psychological Medicine, Symonds was a Harley Street neurologist with long service in the RAF Volunteer Reserve; Gillespie was a psychiatrist. See AIR 2/5998.

63. Training films on the subject were aimed at educating commanders that men who broke down did not necessarily have 'yellow streaks in them'. See US Army, 'Field Psychiatry for the General Medical Officer', Film No. 1167, USAF Motion Media Records Center, Norton AFB, California. Copy in author's possession.

64. Charles P. Symonds and Denis J. Williams, 'Investigation into Psychological Disorders in Flying Personnel, Review of Reports submitted to the Air Ministry since the outbreak of the war', FPRC 412(d), April 1942, AIR 2/6252.
65. Ibid. It should be noted, however, that for this first report Gillespie interviewed only 31 total cases of psychological disorder.
66. Interview with Dr David Stafford-Clark, 19 Jan. 1992.
67. Charles P. Symonds, 'Note on the predictability of breakdown by use of aircrew interview', 21 May 1941, AIR 2/6345.
68. The overall psychiatric rejection rate for the British Army was 2.2 per cent. The American rate was more than three times this figure. See Robert H. Ahrenfeldt, *Psychiatry in the British Army in the Second World War* (London: Routledge & Kegan Paul, 1958), p. 258 and Turner, op. cit., pp. 302–3.
69. H. L. Burton, 'Report on Gillespie's visit to the Army Initial Training Centre', 21 April 1943, AIR 2/6400.
70. Burton to Whittingham, 27 Dec. 1941, AIR 2/6345.
71. Symonds and Williams, 'Statistical survey of the occurrence of psychological disorder in flying personnel in six months (3 Feb. to 3 Aug. 1942), FPRC 412(g), AIR 2/6252.
72. It should be borne in mind, however, that the investigation was carried out on men who had already been withdrawn from combat. Various examinations of 'healthy' airmen – those still flying – showed that only 15 per cent were found to have evidence of predisposition. Symonds and Williams, 'Clinical and statistical study of neurosis precipitated by flying duties', Aug. 1943, FPRC 547, AIR 2/6252.
73. Whittingham to AOC in C, Flying Training Command, 3 March 1942, AIR 2/6345.
74. About 18 per cent were moderately to very considerably predisposed. See Privy Council Office, *Report of an Expert Committee on the Work of Psychologists and Psychiatrists in the Services* (London: HMSO, 1947), p. 74.
75. RAF Sub-committee on Assessment of Temperament in Connection with Aircrew Selection, meeting 5 May 1943, AIR 2/6345.
76. Numbers fluctuated slightly, but at the end of 1943 there were only 37 RAF medical officers engaged in neuropsychiatric duties. Significantly, only three of these were at Recruit Reception Centres. See AIR 2/5998.
77. By this time Gillespie and those who shared his views must have expressed considerable frustration over the inertia of a system unable or too slow to adapt to change. See Symonds and Williams, FPRC 412(d), AIR 2/6252 and Interview with Dr David Stafford-Clark, 19 Jan. 1992.
78. AIR 2/6400.
79. The number of cases referred to a psychiatrist varied from centre to centre. The average for the RAF was seven per cent. See AIR 2/6400.
80. Gillespie to Whittingham, 10 Jan. 1944, AIR 2/6400.
81. Air Historical Branch, *Flying Training*, pp. 66–8.
82. There were many officials in the Air Ministry, as elsewhere, who felt that psychiatrists were unfit to judge normal people because they spent so much of their time with the abnormal. See Richardson, op. cit., p. 97 and AIR 2/5998.
83. 'Notes for Instructors on the Recognition of Nervousness in Pilots', June 1943, AIR 2/6252.
84. Regarding the duties of a commanding officer, a key Air Ministry memorandum admonished that, 'it is he who should know his men more intimately than anyone else and he may in certain cases by more careful handling enable an individual to recover morale and become a sound member of an operational crew'. See S.61141/S.7.c(1), 19 Sept. 1941, AIR 20/10727.
85. 'The Selection, Classification and Initial Training of Air Crew', 31 March 1944, AIR 15/53.
86. By 1945 the functions of the ACRC were confined to a few locations, among them London and Torquay. See Norman Longmate, *The Bombers* (London: Hutchinson, 1983; Arrow Books, 1988), p. 178.
87. Examples of these tests are preserved at the Public Record Office in AIR 2/5998.
88. Alan S. Gall (Lancaster navigator) to author, 23 April 1992. See also Roger A. Freeman, *The British Airmen* (London: Arms and Armour Press, 1989), pp. 11–12.
89. A change from the earlier procedure where all PNB candidates were allowed a brief flight test. See Air Historical Branch, *Flying Training*, p. 66.
90. The RAF had discovered that the number of hours required for a student's first solo bore a striking relationship to his subsequent performance in flying training. Fifty-two per cent of

men who were considered 'very fast' to solo were subsequently graded as 'superior' in flying ability at SFTS. Moreover, 70 per cent of them reached operations. See Air Historical Branch, *Flying Training*, p. 8.

91. Interestingly, any candidate who had made it as far as the ACRC, but who was then considered unclassifiable, was sent to the Combined Reselection Centre at Eastchurch. There, unlike elsewhere, psychiatric examination was generally a direct part of re-evaluation and assignment to other duties. But the psychiatrist was cautioned not to get too involved with 'reclaiming a doubtful case'. See Air Marshal P. Babington, AOC Flying Training Command to Air Ministry, 3 Oct. 1942, AIR 20/10727.

2

The Nature of Air Combat During the Combined Bomber Offensive

THE ULTIMATE aim of the Allied strategic bombing offensive was to destroy Germany's war-making potential and to help bring a speedy end to the war. To accomplish this goal it was necessary to redefine many of the traditional measures of success in conflict. For centuries victory in land warfare had been measured by territory seized and enemy ground forces killed or captured. On at least a theoretical level, it was felt that successful air war would alter these goals.[1] During the early years of the Second World War, Allied airmen spoke confidently about the ability of long-range bombers to penetrate deep into the Nazi homeland, strike accurately and return with minimum losses.[2] There were corresponding hopes that Germany's capability to wage war would be destroyed along with its willingness to resist.[3]

The reality of combat between 1939 and 1942 did much to damage these simplistic notions. Optimistic projections about the ability of air power to win the war by itself were painfully dispelled throughout the ensuing long months of the conflict. The idea that a swift, clean and relatively bloodless air campaign could be decisive in twentieth century industrialized warfare gradually gave way to the realities of mounting losses and indecisive results.[4] In the air war of attrition which inevitably developed, the Allies' vast reserves of manpower, equipment and resources were ultimately more important than German technological innovation, individual ability and tactical finesse.[5] In short, at the most fundamental level, war in the air proved to be not much different from war on the ground.

Yet there were obvious ways in which air war and ground war cannot be compared. The environment of air combat is largely unique. If we accept Clausewitz's view that all war takes place in an atmosphere of danger, physical exertion, uncertainty and chance, and that together these constitute 'friction', then in the air these factors seem magnified many times.[6] Because flight itself can be considered to be conducted in an essentially hostile environment, the concept of friction has a much expanded meaning for airmen.

A principal reason for this is that airmen, unlike most ground soldiers, are sustained in their 'fighting environment' by what are essentially artificial means. Without aircraft to carry men aloft, without life-support equipment to keep them warm and breathing, and without relatively sophisticated weapons, no fighting could take place in the skies above the ground. Such fundamental reliance on mechanical support only increased the potential that something could go wrong, and when it did airmen were often not 'safe' until returned to earth by parachute. Thus, airmen, more than many other wartime combatants, had to deal not only with the direct challenges of combat, but also faced the life-threatening hazards of their surroundings.[7]

This is the basis of any understanding of the human dimension of air combat during the Combined Bomber Offensive. In very real ways friction dominated the efforts of Allied airmen from the moment of take-off to the mission's end. It comes as no surprise that British and American military authorities, assisted by scientists, doctors, engineers, and manufacturers, expended considerable effort to minimize the impact of such friction on operations and, although rarely couched in Clausewitzian terms, these efforts were clearly directed at improving combat effectiveness.[8]

If, therefore, we are to understand fully the human dimension of air combat during the Combined Bomber Offensive, it is important to focus on those aspects which make air combat very much a singular experience conducted in a dangerous environment. This environment is not restricted exclusively to the physical surroundings of the sky, but also encompasses some of the hazardous elements on the ground affecting aircraft and airmen. The individual categories and elements of air-to-air combat must be identified and, to some extent dissected, in order to assess their impact on fighter and bomber crewmen. Finally, it will be important to elaborate on the traditional measures of success in air war. Only then will it be possible to determine how well the men produced by British or American selection methods performed in combat and withstood its stresses.

THE MULTIPLE DANGERS OF FLYING

It is self-evident to suggest that the British and American airmen of the Eighth Air Force and Bomber Command faced extraordinary dangers during their campaign service. Quite apart from the already considerable physical threats of violence, wounds or death that any combatant faces in battle, these airmen assumed the routine but serious risks of aerial flight. While not nearly so exciting, nor possibly even as glamorous, as fighting an identifiable enemy, the day-to-day hazards of flight operations took a steady toll of Allied airmen during the years of the Combined Bomber Offensive. Hundreds of factors combined to increase the atmosphere of danger within which they had to operate. Some factors were a natural result of technological advances designed to keep them aloft, alive and fighting in a hostile environment. Others were connected directly to the normal perils associated with flying and still more, related to the ground hazards of basing tens of thousands of heavily armed aircraft in a relatively small country like the United Kingdom.

Aircraft technology had advanced rapidly in the years just before the Second World War. Major advances in aeronautical design, metallurgy, engines, electronics and weaponry led to the swift introduction of newer, and far more sophisticated combat aircraft. The war itself brought the fastest rate of change, as improved models of aircraft were often introduced only months apart.[9] Aircraft became faster, flew higher, were capable of longer ranges and could carry heavier payloads.

All of this had a human price. More complicated aircraft systems called for better training and more intelligent operators. Higher altitudes forced aircrews to labour against the restrictions of bulky flight-crew clothing and oxygen-support equipment. Long-range missions, so much a feature of the Combined Bomber Offensive, put airmen at greater risk for a sustained period of time and required even more reliance on sophisticated aircraft control and navigation systems.

One look into the pilot's cabin of a B-17 will convince you that its flight is actually an engineering operation demanding manual and mental skills that put the driving of an automobile into the kiddy-car class. The compartment is lined – front, sides ceiling, and part of the floor – with controls, switches, levers, dials and gauges. I once counted one hundred and thirty. The co-ordinated operations of all these gadgets would be difficult in the swivel-chair comfort of your office. But reduce your office to a five-foot cube size, engulf it in the constant roar of engines, and increase your height to around five miles . . . that will give you an idea of the normal conditions under which these men worked out the higher mathematical relationships of engine revolutions, manifold and fuel pressures, aerodynamics, barometric pressure, altitude, wind drift, airspeed, groundspeed, position and direction.[10]

Despite the often nostalgic reflections of many veterans about the pleasant aerodynamic qualities of B-17s, B-24s, Lancasters, Stirlings and Halifaxes, these aircraft could be especially difficult to fly at times.[11] Furthermore, overburdened by bombs, full fuel loads, flight crews and defensive armament, they often barely managed to take off, and could be downright treacherous if they suffered engine failure.[12] Fighter aircraft similarly posed safety challenges, not the least of which was the torque produced by power-plants typically rated above 1,200 horsepower.

After equipment-associated problems, among the more dangerous

challenges to airmen were weather and general flying safety risks. The
weather over England and Western Europe had never been known for its
consistency. But the special risks it imposed on thousands of Allied aircraft were all-too-apparent to many.

If the weather at the target area was not suitable to bombing, then a whole
mission had been wasted and perhaps the lives of many crewmen had been
lost to no effect. If the weather on return to base was 'socked in', then disaster
could ensue. As any visitor to England and all members of the Eighth Air
Force will recall, England is occasionally hit by dense fog over large areas,
and that fog can be so dense that it is difficult to walk from the mess to the
operations office – to say nothing of finding hardstands and the airplanes . . .
It is quite possible that the entire Eighth Air Force could be lost on a single
afternoon by returning to England and finding all bases 'socked in'. And
bombing accuracy was heavily degraded by even partial cloud cover of the
target. The weather was actually a greater hazard and obstacle than the
German Air Force.[13]

Weather-related accidents were common to both the Eighth Air Force
and Bomber Command. The piston-powered aircraft of the day were
especially vulnerable to poor atmospheric conditions. Structural damage
due to turbulence or icing accounted for many of the losses. Cross-winds
on airfields caused innumerable crack-ups.[14] Among scores of other difficulties caused by the typically wet or cold weather, engines iced up, control surfaces would not operate, instruments froze and radios failed.

The principal problems in the winter were caused by freezing rain,
restricted visibility, ice, mist and fog. Even on days which started clear,
the variable nature of weather patterns brought unpredictable changes
and often tragic results.[15] Spring and summer promised only occasional
respite from cloud and rain. Strong winds, turbulence and thunderstorms
were not uncommon at any time. Similarly, good days or nights over
England did little to guarantee flyable conditions over Germany.[16]

At the human level, bad weather affected aviators in a number of
important ways. Sometimes it caused missions to be aborted or reduced
bombing accuracy.[17] Inevitably it scattered the bomber streams or made
formation flying almost impossible.[18] Most typically it restricted visibility
and forced pilots to rely on instrument flying to stay airborne. Flying
safely by these gauges required intense concentration, was physically
taxing, and a moment's inattention or distraction could lead to a loss of
control.[19] Moreover, in these conditions navigators were often unable to
use ground points to back up their calculations. If the rudimentary radar
or radio equipment failed to reveal locations accurately, it might be difficult to avoid an accident. How many crews were killed as a result of
blundering into high ground or being lost and going down over the sea
may never be known.[20] And, as if that was not hazard enough, without
visual reference aircrew sometimes got air-sick or suffered from various

forms of spatial disorientation. In laymen's terms, pilots sometimes could not tell which way was up and flew into the ground as a result.

In both air forces all accidents that occurred during operational training or during actual combat missions were investigated. Causes of accidents were classified in categories. Mechanical problems and technical faults accounted for many. It is not difficult to imagine the impact of even the smallest breakdown as aircraft, burdened with thousands of pounds of high explosives and gallons of volatile gasoline, hurtled down runways or clawed for altitude.[21] Engine failures, oil pressure problems, supercharger breakdowns, magneto fouling and runaway propellors were endemic to both air forces. Most aircrew gritted their teeth, spoke of 'gremlins' and 'hangar queens', and flew on.

Predictably, however, with thousands of young, relatively inexperienced airmen at the controls of complex multi-engine aircraft or speedy single-seat fighters, there were a huge number of crashes very likely due simply to pilot error.[22] Failure to follow operating procedures, over-confidence or downright recklessness took a steady toll of both British and American airmen.[23] The latter category of accidents were all the more tragic in the sense that they might easily have been avoided.

Bomber Command records show 2,681 accidents involving casualties in the two years between the start of 1943 and the end of 1944. Almost 6,000 airmen were killed and a further 4,400 were injured in these mishaps.[24] This toll was probably made worse by virtue of the fact that Bomber Command flew many of its training sorties at night. In the darkness aircrew struggled with restricted visibility, visual illusion and circuit density in overcrowded airspace. Crashes were inevitable.

The American accident rate likewise rose fairly constantly until continued efforts to bring it down took effect. For much of the bombing campaign it averaged almost 50 accidents per 100,000 flying hours.[25] In the 18 months between 1944 and the end of the war this resulted in a toll of 1,660 aircraft.[26] The introduction of newer, faster and more sophisticated airplanes inevitably brought an initial surge in accidental crashes. Sixty-five per cent of all non-combat deaths reported between July 1942 and June 1945 (a total of 1,806) were due to aircraft accidents.[27]

A large number of American accidents occurred during the rendezvous of the huge bomber formations. Because so many missions began in overcast sky conditions, it was often necessary for hundreds of aircraft to circle radio beacons in complicated timing patterns.[28] Only after breaking out on top of the clouds was it possible to conduct visual rejoins. Tragically there were scores of spectacular mid-air collisions.[29] Few crewmen would survive these kinds of mishaps.

Both air forces also suffered high ground accident rates that caused numerous casualties. Unwary maintenance personnel or unlucky aviators occasionally walked into turning propellors. Vehicles blundered onto active runways. Aircraft sometimes taxied into each other or into ground obstructions. Landing accidents were almost a daily occurrence, particularly if the runway was wet or icy.

With thousands of tons of high explosives and fuel stored in and around air bases, the potential for explosion and fire was high. Armourers and aircraft bowsers often worked in abysmal conditions against terrible time constraints. When mistakes were made the results could be truly spectacular, and the costs quite high, both in human and equipment terms.[30]

It comes as no surprise that both air forces went to considerable lengths to focus aircrews' attention on the importance of safety. Eighth Air Force airmen were bombarded with a constant stream of advice and information, some of it coming from local sources and some from headquarters. Handbooks designed to initiate newcomers to the dangers of a combat theatre were common. Containing a quaint mixture of homily, advice and directive, these pamphlets were designed to help crews avoid costly mistakes and assimilate quickly into the unit.[31]

British and Commonwealth aircrew were similarly supplied with training films, lecture notes and safety materials.[32] The most famous publication in this regard was 'Tee Emm', a training manual which was widely distributed. Its most enduring feature was a cartoon character called Pilot Officer Percy Prune, a creation of cartoonist Bill Hooper. Prune was made to survive disaster after disaster, in a humorous attempt to teach safety lessons and demonstrate mistakes to avoid.[33]

CHARACTERISTICS OF THE AIR BATTLEFIELD

The most obvious difference between air and ground combat is where each takes place. The characteristics of the atmosphere give air combat much of its unique nature and increase the impact of physical exertion and uncertainty. The salient feature of an air battle is its almost limitless size and scope. Bomber Command and Eighth Air Force missions from Lincolnshire and East Anglia, both fighter and bomber, often ranged more than 600 miles into Germany. The British bomber streams and American formations themselves could stretch for a considerable distance along the whole route.[34] Moreover, several thousands of feet might separate the highest aircraft from the lower flying ones. This was truly a three dimensional battlefield whose 'limits' extended from over Britain's airfields to the targets in Germany and back.

Another indicator of the size of the battlefield arises from aircraft spacing requirements. The trend in the Eighth Air Force was toward tighter formations for defensive purposes. Even so, by 1944 each grouping of 36 aircraft occupied a block of airspace more than 900 million cubic yards in size. Moreover, there were frequent raids featuring more than 400 aircraft.[35]

The difficulty of scanning so large a battlefield consumed much energy. A typical mission encompassed several thousand square miles of airspace. Depending on conditions, airmen had constantly to watch ahead, behind, above, below and to the sides of their aircraft. This requirement, combined with the sheer size of the envelope, made absolute knowledge of their situation and the enemy problematical.[36] In other words, combat flying was frequently characterized by tremendous uncertainty.

A striking feature of the air battlefield was its beauty. Veterans often speak and write of the wonder they experienced when surveying crystal-clear blue skies, sunlit vistas of clouds, or shiny moonlight reflecting off an undercast.[37] Because of the duration of most missions, and the variable nature of the weather, almost all airmen experienced, at one time or another, an incredible range of weather and visual phenomena. But these same beautiful elements could bring extreme danger. Bright skies made American formations visible for miles. German fighters often used an approach from the sun to blind American gunners. Beautiful moonlit nights silhouetted British bombers and made them easier targets for lurking defenders or anti-aircraft fire. Just as frequently, the gloomy conditions of cloud cover and darkness increased the chances for mid-air collision or navigation error.

Operating in an arena so vast also had several human consequences. First, the physical circumstances of flying often demand considerable exertion. It was not unusual for missions to extend past ten hours of flying time. For most aviators, but especially the pilots, there was virtually no time to relax during an actual operation. These normal physical demands were significant enough, yet they were made worse by physiological phenomena associated with noise, vibration and gravity forces.[38] For the most part, absolute attention was required just to fly the aircraft safely. This was tiring enough, but an additional burden was levied by the requirement to remain vigilant for enemy threats.

One of the more dynamic features of the air battlefield was the impact of chance on flight operations. Aviators had been subjected to considerable training from the very beginning of their service. British and American authorities went to great pains to ensure that the men they sent over Germany were the fittest and best trained that both nations could muster. Indoctrinated by a flying philosophy that rightly suggested that hard training makes for easier operational missions, most airmen worked diligently to improve their flying and combat skills. This attitude was underscored by the lessons learned early in the campaign. Time off between sorties in both the RAF and Eighth Air Force was frequently filled with practice flights, ground training sessions, lectures on weapons and tactics, or rehearsal for operations. All of this was designed to improve the quality of flying, gunnery, bombing and overall combat effectiveness. It was considered absolutely vital if losses were to be kept low.[39]

To a very real extent, however, many of the losses were strictly due to the misfortunes of war. Aircraft or equipment malfunctions claimed many aircrew who were absolutely on the top of their form. Likewise, German attacks could indiscriminately shred whole squadrons in split seconds and leave little time to react.[40] A British veteran had this to say:

Casualties appeared to strike at random, although many crews were lost in the first 5 or 6 trips. On the other hand, 15 October 1943 saw the loss of our Wing Commander – an experienced 2-tour man – and two nights later the acting CO was lost – also a 2-tour man. Although experience was a great help to avoid defended areas en route and combating bad weather, it was just a matter of bad luck if a fighter was directed on to your aircraft or a shell exploded too close to the target area.[41]

Many American veterans would have agreed with the previous sentiment and spoke in similar terms:

It seems to me that casualties were at random . . . I think that many of us thought we had some control over our destiny, and tried to behave in ways which would insure this control. Whether what we did had any effect, I don't know. I do know that losses came to all types of crew, regardless of the reputation – good, bad, or indifferent – that these crews enjoyed.[42]

The unpredictable meeting of two aircraft in thousands of square miles of airspace could often not be reckoned with. Even on nights when German defences were muddled or unco-ordinated, chance or unlucky encounters with German fighters and flak caused the loss of scores of Bomber Command's aircraft without a trace. British aircrews generally regarded maintaining higher altitudes as the safest bet for survival. Despite earnest discussions on the relative vulnerability of 'Purple Heart Corner' and 'Tail-end Charlies', inside American daylight formations, no single position was truly much safer than any other. Combat reports which meticulously investigated the formation position of downed aircraft, showed only small correlation.[43] With regard to the Americans, the only thing which seemed axiomatic was that the enemy fighters tended to concentrate on any aircraft which appeared damaged and was falling out of the formation.[44] British bombers which were illuminated by engine-damage or fire similarly became quick victims.

Aircrew rapidly became aware of the randomness of death and the heightened importance of chance. Some men responded with a fatalistic attitude and morosely calculated the odds against their survival. Others did everything they could to improve their chances.[45] The prevailing attitude seems to have been that an airman – whether flying a fighter or as a part of a bomber crew – might enhance the odds very slightly by hard training, teamwork and painstaking attention to detail.

Casualties did strike at random, but inferior crews had less of a chance of surviving in an emergency. Inferior crews could be spotted by their lack of discipline, lack of knowledge of the aircraft sub-systems, or air of bravado.[46]

In the grim circumstances, hard training and avoiding thinking about the worst were enough to keep many men going. Some of these worst moments were occasioned by events which took place on board aircraft immediately after battle damage. Few other situations were as stressful or more clearly demonstrated a greater impact of friction and chance on an airman's survival. Depending on the extent of damage inflicted during an attack, the occupants of a bomber aircraft might have only seconds to react to save their lives. The same was true of fighters. Some aircraft simply exploded instantaneously in balls of fire when hit. Others might be flown straight and level long enough to permit their crews time to bail out. Even while abandoning the aircraft men had to reckon with a multitude of unpredictable things which could go wrong. Riddled fuselage structures, or weakened and burning wings, might collapse and send bombers hurtling earthward with terrific centrifugal force, pinning crewmen helplessly inside. Because of their bulk, parachutes were frequently not worn during flight but required attachment before jumping. Moving even a few feet in a burning and wildly gyrating aircraft could be impossible. Hatches on some aircraft were poorly located, difficult to operate and, in at least one case, almost criminally too small for easy egress.[47] Parachutes themselves were not 100 per cent reliable, nor was it possible to predict with certainty how men would come out of damaged aircraft. Many were struck and killed by props, wings or tails as they made their exit.

Those who managed to survive the harrowing, and sometimes heroic, circumstances of leaving a damaged aircraft frequently faced the rigours of high altitude bail-out, which included oxygen deprivation and frostbite. Many had already been terribly wounded before coming out of their aircraft. Moreover, parachute landings – often in wooded or mountainous terrain – were extremely perilous. In many instances pure luck determined survival. Finally, those unfortunate enough to land among angry civilians were often killed despite negotiating all the earlier hazards.[48] In addition, while treatment by Luftwaffe personnel was generally in accordance with the Geneva Convention, some Allied airmen fell victim to the SS or Gestapo before making it to prisoner-of-war camps.

CATEGORIES OF COMBAT: FIGHTER AIR-TO-AIR

Second World War day-fighter aircraft were typically armed with fixed, forward-firing cannon or machine-guns. These weapons had maximum ranges which reached more than 2,000 yards, but were rarely effective at more than 800 to 1,000 yards.[49] Given the relatively high speeds of combat aircraft and the attendant difficulty of angle-off shooting, it was usually necessary for successful fighters to fly into a lethal cone, roughly corresponding to 30 degrees, behind their targets. Firing outside this area made the problem of deflection and estimating target speed and range too difficult for the majority of fighter pilots.[50] Even inside the best firing zone, aerial gunnery was still a complicated business. Both target and shooter were flying swiftly, and often erratically, in three dimensional airspace and could instantaneously be subjected to several times the force of gravity. These factors, as well as the ballistic qualities of bullets and cannon-shells, made hitting anything a difficult feat, despite technological advances in gun-sights.[51] As a result, training manuals admonished fighter pilots to open fire only at 500 yards or less.[52] Some veteran pilots even suggested withholding fire until the enemy aircraft filled the windscreen.[53]

Air-to-air fighter combat therefore consisted largely of seeing an enemy, deciding whether or not an attack was possible, closing by manoeuvre, firing and escaping. If the original attack was unsuccessful, further manoeuvre was necessary either to re-engage or to avoid attack and survive. All this very frequently took place in a matter of seconds, and at very high speeds. After the initial engagement, actions were most often taken instinctively, because pilots did not have time for reflection or deliberate decision-making.[54]

It might therefore be safely concluded that anything which reduced the uncertainty of the air battlefield, and increased the opportunity to detect the enemy, would reduce friction and enhance combat effectiveness and survival. But detecting the enemy was not the only problem which confronted combatants. After detecting an enemy, it was necessary for fighter aircraft to be manoeuvred into attack positions which promised a real chance of success. This sometimes required brute physical strength:

You needed strong arms and shoulders. Those controls weren't hydraulically operated, and at 400 mph they became extremely heavy. Without cabin pressurization, flying at high altitude wore you out. And so did pulling 'Gs' in sharp turns and steep dives. A two-hundred pound pilot weighs eight-hundred pounds during a 4-G turn. After a couple of minutes of dogfighting, your back and arms felt like you had been hauling a piano upstairs. You were sweaty and breathing heavily.[55]

No less important was a pilot's mental agility. Air combat demanded an almost intuitive sense of where the opponent was headed, because both aircraft were moving in space simultaneously. In short, a successful pilot had scant seconds to evaluate the situation and employ his aircraft's airspeed and manoeuvrability to achieve a position inside the effective range of his weapons.

The whole thing goes in a series of whooshes. There is no time to think. If you take time to think you will not have time to act. There are a number of things your mind is doing while you are fighting – seeing, measuring, guessing, remembering, adding up this and that and worrying about one thing and another and taking this into account and that into account and rejecting this notion and accepting that notion. But it doesn't feel like thinking.[56]

There is evidence, too, which supports the contention that firing itself required some preliminary psychological preparation, largely because of the knowledge that the target was not just an aircraft, but also had a human crew.[57]

Successful or not, firing on an enemy aircraft was usually followed by some form of disengagement and escape. Often this action was brief and only designed to allow detection and subsequent attack of further enemies. But just as often it might end the air-to-air engagement. Classic 'dog-fighting' – where a one-on-one situation led to lengthy manoeuvring for advantage – is generally considered to have taken place only infrequently.[58]

Fighter combat tactics were often carefully worked out to enhance combat effectiveness. For most of the war the basic Eighth Air Force fighting element consisted of two aircraft – a leader and a wingman. The leader's principal job was to be the attacker; the wingman was responsible for sticking to his leader and protecting his rear. Even when assigned to flights of four or more aircraft, as in the famous 'finger four' adapted from the Germans, this attacker-protector concept was not changed.[59]

In the confusion and chaos which so typically characterizes fighting in the air, anything which diverted a pilot's attention from the circumstances of combat could reduce his effectiveness and be potentially dangerous. For much of the Eighth Air Force's daylight campaign, for example, American bomber formations were escorted by large numbers of fighters. Occasionally they were met by sizeable German formations. Increasing the number of aircraft in any given amount of airspace tended to restrict the ability of individual pilots to keep track of them all. Such encounters, however fleeting, were largely free-for-alls because there was precious little time to manoeuvre for advantage. The 'normal' sequence of combat might be truncated to one which put a premium on avoiding collision, shooting when possible, and managing to survive.[60]

A careful reading of firsthand recollections of fighter pilots often reveals the keys to success and survival in any air combat situation. Given that flying itself was demanding, under combat conditions many men found themselves unable to react appropriately to events going on around them. Some were fully occupied merely keeping the aircraft under control. At best, they might devote only limited attention to events happening outside. These types, either poorly trained, brand new to combat or momentarily confused, often became the quickest victims. Paying attention to what was happening outside the cockpit and spotting enemy aircraft was the key to the subsequent events of air combat. Moreover, a decisive advantage was often gained by seeing the enemy before being seen.[61] The result was often surprise and quick victory.

The importance of surprise seems hard to overestimate. Post-war analysis of combat reports along with the reflections of veterans indicate quite strongly that the overwhelming percentage of fighter aircraft which were shot down in combat were lost as a result of being 'bounced' by undetected attackers.[62] In short, pilots who, for whatever reason, failed to monitor the skies around them usually did not last long.

Other pilots, even those who did not actually fly very well, were sometimes better able to stay on top of the combat situation because they directed enough attention outside. In very elementary situations they might perform perfectly adequately, but when they were forced to handle too much at any one time, their ability to react coherently would break down. Sometimes it was possible to notice the very moment of transition; when information overload proved too much for otherwise capable men and they would be shot down. Colonel Gentile's wartime memoirs graphically portray such an encounter with two German pilots who initially fought well:

But suddenly, I don't know, something happened in their minds. You could see it plainly. Their brains had dissolved away under the pressure of fear and had become just dishwater in their heads. They froze to their sticks and straightened out and ran right into their graves like men stricken blind who run, screaming, off a cliff.[63]

Modern analysis speaks of the ability of airmen to fly their aircraft and react to outside stimuli in terms of 'situational awareness'.[64] Second World War veterans more often spoke of 'being on top of the situation'.[65] The most successful airmen were able to maintain situational awareness – and avoid task saturation – despite the multiple mental and physical demands of a combat situation. Moreover, they were able to overcome the paralysing panic that sometimes came with being at a momentary disadvantage. Given the opportunity, these were the kinds of men who scored victories in the air. It should be noted, however, that virtually all men suffered lapses in their ability to react to the events taking place in a hostile environment from time to time. The fortunate ones survived. But many apparently made it through by virtue only of considerable luck:

. . . those who were marginal pilots, who lacked the necessary degree of aggressiveness, many of them were killed in their first 5 to 10 missions . . . some of them, however, made it all the way through, never contributing anything to the overall effort, but just filled a spot in a flight formation, they never saw anything happen around them, could barely keep their position in the formation, but somehow, made it through.[66]

CATEGORIES OF COMBAT: BOMBER VS. FIGHTER

In many ways the central feature of the Combined Bombing Offensive was the category of combat which pitted bombers against fighters. From the Allied point of view it was necessary to win this battle, and for the bombers to successfully hit their targets, if the entire concept of strategic bombing was to be validated. Not only did the bomber crewmen of the Eighth Air Force and Bomber Command consequently face some of the greatest risks, but it was clearly upon their shoulders that victory or defeat in the campaign rested.

By 1942 American bombers were generally heavily armed. By mounting an average of ten 0.50 calibre flexible machine-guns, these aircraft were initially considered self-defending, especially when flying in close formation with others. When arranged in multiple group formations of between 18 and 36 aircraft each, the volume of fire available to defend these bomber armadas appeared truly formidable. Fifty calibre machine-guns were each capable of about 700 rounds per minute, so 360 guns could theoretically fill the sky out to about 3,500 feet with more than a quarter of a million rounds in 60 seconds.[67] Flying into this fusillade must have required great determination.

Having said that, there were a number of mitigating factors – Clausewitz's 'friction' again – which dramatically reduced the effectiveness of this wall of lead. Many of these impediments were identified in an April 1943 report by the commander of the 306th Bomb Group, Colonel Claude E. Putnam. To begin with, Putnam's report noted the difficulty of seeing attacking aircraft in the vast expanse of sky. Moreover, even during daylight, it was practically impossible to identify accurately a fighter aircraft at ranges beyond 700 or 800 yards. This problem was especially critical if the bombers were being escorted.[68] American P-51s looked like German Me-109s and P-47 Thunderbolts might easily be mistaken for Fw-190s. How many bombers accidentally withheld their fire and were surprised by Germans will never be known. Nor will it be possible to determine how many Allied fighters were fired upon by jittery gunners.

German fighter tactics against American bombers were not complicated but nevertheless contributed to the difficulties of defensive gunnery. Typically, slashing attacks in the form of high-speed dives – employing various techniques from different angles – were made at the formations to damage individual aircraft and force the formation to disperse.[69] Despite their slower rates of fire, German cannon out-ranged American defensive armament.

The German shift toward heavier attack armament was clearly indicated by an analysis of damaged Eighth Air Force aircraft. In the last six months of 1942, for example, about 40 per cent of the gaping holes in returning battle-damaged bombers were caused by cannon fire. By the autumn of 1943 this had risen to 80 per cent, and by 1944, for every 100 machine-gun bullet holes there were 135 cannon punctures. The Germans calculated it took between 20 and 25 20mm cannon hits to bring down a B-17. Significantly, it took only four or five concentrated strikes from a 30mm cannon to do the same thing. This helps further to explain the increase in armament.[70]

Slashing tactics were not the only techniques employed. Fighter attacks from directly astern the bomber had the obvious advantage of reducing deflection angles and were frequently seen. However, such attempts were also more dangerous from the German point of view because overtaking a bomber could take some time, depending on airspeed differential, and occasionally left an attacker exposed for too long. A typical attack beginning at 1,000 yards to the rear of the bomber took almost 20 seconds to reach 100 yards. Searching for alternatives, the Germans discovered the relative vulnerability of B-17s and B-24s to head-on attack early in the campaign. As a result, wave after wave of specially armed fighters would often approach from this direction.[71] The collision dangers of this tactic were obvious. In such an attack the opposing aircraft might be converging at more than 200 yards per second. Moreover, it took a special fortitude for German pilots to overcome the psychological pressures occasioned by the sight of the huge American bomber formations.[72] An additional refinement, therefore, was the development of 21cm rockets, which, with their lethal 90lb warheads, could be released well outside the bombers' zones of fire.[73] Fired en masse, they could seriously disrupt a formation and make it easier for subsequent German attacks to succeed.[74]

Putnam rightly noted that the critical period of most attacks usually lasted only about two or three seconds. The high closing speeds of the aircraft, particularly if the attacks were coming from the front, were responsible for the brevity of this time. It is also important to remember that, because of the location of the machine-guns on the bombers, only a portion of the guns in any formation might physically be brought to bear during an attack. The result of all of this was that comparatively few bullets might actually be fired in the general direction of an enemy plane. Under the circumstances, and given the difficulty of spotting and aiming accurately, it comes as no surprise that only about ten per cent of gunners who might theoretically fire on an attacking plane did so during the critical time-span. Putnam further calculated that at least four gunners were required to fire on an attacking enemy in order to have at least a

50–50 chance of stopping his attack.[75] Even this did not necessarily mean shooting him down.

These factors also ignore the generally substandard state of gunnery which plagued many Eighth Air Force units. This was not the fault of the men, who by and large worked diligently to improve their skills. But the complexities of trying to hit rapidly moving targets while shooting from an unstable platform were never totally overcome.[76] There were constant calls for more training and much effort was directed to improving the efficacy of formation firepower. Some recommendations were comparatively radical, however:

I really felt that the gunners, in some cases, were more a hazard than they were protection. I do not think that we will ever know how many airplanes we shot down ourselves by this wild spraying of .50 calibre machine guns. I wasn't getting much support for this theory until well along in the war . . . Certainly, we got rid of the waist gunners, and I think practically everybody did that in due course. Those were two men and hundreds of pounds of ammunition that we got out of the airplane. I wanted to dump the ball turrets. I did not really think they did that much good either. I did not get much support there from the higher-ups or from my own people, who thought that I was taking chances.[77]

The chief problems thwarting more accurate results were inadequate gunsights, the almost insurmountable challenges of deflection shooting, the extremely cold temperature, and bulky life-support equipment which made swift reactions difficult. These did not prevent hard-pressed gunners from overestimating their success, however.

There was tardy recognition during the campaign that gunnery claims of enemy aircraft destroyed were widely inflated.[78] Well into 1944 the Luftwaffe continued to function at a strength which was in excess of Allied intelligence estimates. This was based, in part, on the over-estimation of victory claims. The problem was to balance the requirements for maintaining the morale of combat crews and the need for an accurate appraisal of the Luftwaffe's strength.[79] In many ways this dilemma was never really solved. Attempts to tighten reporting procedures and establish stricter criteria for awarding victory credit never seriously reduced the gap between Allied projections and the reality of German losses.[80]

Bomber Command's gunners faced all these difficulties and more. Compared with their American counterparts, British bombers were woefully underarmed. The standard machine-guns on Stirlings, Halifaxes, and Lancasters were Browning 0.303 inch weapons, firing 1,200 rounds per minute but lacking range and destructive power.

One of our difficulties was that enemy fighters were fitted with cannon which far out-ranged our puny 0.303 Browning guns in our own turrets, and so could shoot at us while still out of range from return fire, and often without having been seen at all by our gunners. Also, the Luftwaffe had developed a system of mounting a cannon in their twin-engine fighter which could be aimed vertically upwards, so they could creep right up underneath a bomber and well below, shielded by the dark background . . . thus achieving complete surprise for their attacks.[81]

British efforts were therefore principally directed at increasing the stealthiness of their bombers. As was the case with some Americans, recommendations to remove guns came from British sources, who noted that bombers without turrets would fly 50 mph faster and be more manoeuvrable.[82] Various measures, well documented elsewhere, were taken to overwhelm and confuse German defenders, including the use of aluminium strips, called 'windows', to blind German radars.[83] Bombers strained for altitude and some captains, convinced that the use of defensive machine-guns was useless and would only give away the bomber's position, even ordered their gunners to throw ammunition overboard.[84]

A British bomber's best defence was to spot a potential attacker first. Accordingly, vigilant crew-members strained to catch a glimpse of other aircraft in the darkened skies. From any vantage point this was difficult and, especially without ventral turrets, there were some terrible blind-spots. Cold and isolated in turrets or crew positions, subjected to noise and vibration, and occasionally even deprived of an adequate oxygen supply, crewmen and gunners struggled with reductions in visual acuity. It was obviously vital to keep perspex windscreens and bubbles free of dirt, oil, scratches or smudges.

Most of my trips were night operations and if you picked up a fighter getting into position to attack, quick evasive action usually took care of him. He too was looking for a soft target, ie, someone who had not seen him. This is one reason I insisted on immaculately clean windscreens. Over the target area I had my engineer, who had an astrodome over his head, to never mind the engines but keep his head out of the cockpit. It paid off twice.[85]

Some tail-gunners even removed the clear vision panels entirely and subjected themselves to the effects of a slipstream between 180 and 210 mph. In such conditions, wind-chill temperatures fell as low as −56 degrees.[86] If lucky enough to be alerted, a pilot could initiate a series of turns and altitude changes called a corkscrew. Some crews understandably preferred to do this type of manoeuvring almost from the moment they crossed enemy territory, although it took an obvious toll on physical stamina.[87]

In summarizing this section, it is possible to apply the same kind of analysis regarding situational awareness to bomber combat as it was in fighter combat. Bomber aircrew, either British or American, who maintained a greater awareness of what was going on around them were surprised less often, doubtless protected themselves more efficiently and, in the main, probably hit their targets better. If there was a major difference for bomber crews, it was that crew cohesion was far more critical to their survival. Clausewitzian friction notwithstanding, it was important for each man on a bomber crew to perform adequately. The most accomplished pilot and co-pilot, for example, could not compensate for a navigator unable to find the target or a bombardier unable to hit it. The best crews might be let down, or even killed, by a single member suffering a momentary lapse or inability to handle a situation.[88]

CATEGORIES OF COMBAT: AIRCRAFT VERSUS FLAK

The final major category of combat pitted Allied aircraft against German flak and small-arms fire. While statistical data tended to show that German fighters actually put British and American airmen more at risk, many Allied veterans preferred to face almost anything rather than the threat of anti-aircraft guns over their targets.[89]

It was true enough that flak accounted for a sizeable percentage of Allied losses. Germany expended a huge amount of resources on its anti-aircraft artillery branch. By 1944 the ground-based air defence personnel numbered more than 900,000.[90] These men and women directed 14,250 heavy guns, ranging from 88mm to 128mm, and almost 35,000 lighter weapons, mostly 20mm and 37mm. One estimate says German flak batteries could fire 5,000 tons of explosives every 60 seconds.[91]

Seventy per cent of all heavy flak batteries consisted of the famous Krupp designed 'Eighty-eight' anti-aircraft cannon. Various models of this multipurpose weapon were introduced during the war, but typically they fired between 15 and 20 20lb high-explosive shells into the air every minute. With radar or optical direction, these shells arced skyward as high as 40,000 feet, although 20,000 feet was the optimum effective range. When the shells exploded they sent 1,500 steel shards through an effective radius of about 20 yards.[92]

A direct hit by one of these weapons was enough to destroy any Allied aircraft. Usually, however, it was the aircraft's systems or aircrew which were struck and damaged by shrapnel. Fuel lines, hydraulics, oil systems and engines were especially vulnerable. The thin aluminium skin of wings and fuselages offered little protection and armour plating was too heavy to be used in more than a few critical areas. When hit and damaged, an aircraft's loss of airspeed and altitude or ignition of fuel tanks frequently led to subsequent attack and loss, mostly to fighters.

Flak shrapnel also subjected aircrew to personal injury. Body protection armour came into widespread use during the middle of the Combined Bomber Offensive, although with mixed results. Wound statistics clearly showed that serious flak wounds almost always occurred to head and thorax. Even so, many American crewmen too often refused to wear the steel helmets eventually issued and, convinced that flak was mostly a danger from below, sometimes preferred to sit on folded body-armour – called 'flak vests' – rather than wear it properly.[93]

Despite its potentially lethal effect on aircrew and airframes, in many ways flak was a psychological weapon. The difficulties of directly bringing down a high-flying bomber were great. Careful calculations of azimuth, range, timing and elevation were necessary to forecast where the aircraft's flight path was taking it. General Curtis LeMay, a civil engineer by academic background and given to figuring the odds, calculated that only one B-17 was hit for every 372 88mm flak shells the Germans fired.[94] Flak batteries were usually placed in concentric rings around potential target cities and important factories. The idea was not only to bring down attacking aircraft, but also to discomfort their crews and disrupt their aim and bombing patterns.[95] Later in the war the Germans began placing cannon in large batteries designed to fire a barrage or 'box' of shells into a predetermined spot.

Flak directed at night-flying British bombers was similarly radar-aimed but also relied heavily on the use of searchlights, star-shell illumination and visual target acquisition. Because Bomber Command's aircraft flew generally at lower altitudes, they sometimes came within range of far greater numbers of rapid-firing 37mm and even 20mm cannon. These weapons, capable of discharging thousands of rounds of smaller but still lethal shells, were often aimed by tracer trails.

The visual effects of flak at night could be dramatic, and even if it did not hit, it was terribly unnerving:

From the ground up to our bombing height of 20,000 feet was a varying patchwork of colour. Fire, smoke, cloud, marker flares, flak bursts, tracer, smoke from flak bursts like small clouds blending into one mass of light grey colour, movement, noise, and sudden death. Flames, smoke and bursting bombs on the ground were a background pattern for the searchlights and the light tracer flak up to 10,000 feet, with the heavy stuff between 15,000 and the height we were flying at. When you could see it winking at you when it burst, then it was too damned close for comfort, and the aircraft would shudder and thump, and make a noise like a colander full of ball bearings being shaken, and when the shrapnel tore through you, it varied in sound, sometimes a fearful shriek, other times a hissing sound, and big lumps would really make a noise.[96]

For all its limitations, light flak was especially dangerous to Allied fighter aircraft, particularly towards the end of the war when the Luftwaffe's inability and refusal to engage forced Allied airmen to low altitudes in search of targets. Originally these ground strafing missions had been performed only occasionally and by isolated units, as fighters were returning home from escort duties. Later, the attacks became commonplace and received sanction from the Eighth Air Force's commanders.[97] Scores of enemy aircraft were destroyed as a result, but few missions were more dangerous than strafing German airfields.[98] It was not unknown for derelict German aircraft to be parked in the open as decoys to lure Allied fighters into traps. Met by cross-fires of cannon, machine-gun and small-arms fire, many Allied planes fell victim to the perils of these operations. While the ledger of attrition was clearly in the Allies' favour – and hundreds of German planes were lost – it is significant that a sizeable number of Allied fighter aces were brought down in this manner.[99] At least one source indicates that only one USAAF ace, Lieutenant Ralph K. Hofer of the 4th Fighter Group, was lost in air-to-air combat; 'everyone else went down while attacking things on the ground'.[100]

The limitations of human reactions were largely responsible for this. Attacks close to the ground called for iron nerve, split-second timing and almost instantaneous physical reactions. Flying at tree-top level at more than 300 miles an hour was not for the faint-hearted or heavy-handed.[101] Furthermore, not only was the defensive environment more lethal, but pilots in damaged aircraft had precious little altitude to spare in the event that bail-out was necessary. Those aircraft which were hit and did not explode or crash almost instantly often belly-landed on the very fields they had been strafing.

COMBAT COSTS

Fortunate in some ways to survive long enough actually to make it to an operational sortie, an aviator then faced combat's obvious Clausewitzian 'frictions'. In this regard, the most prominent danger to British and American combat airmen was the potential for being killed, wounded or captured by enemy action. As subsequent chapters will detail, for much of the Combined Bomber Offensive, Allied bomber losses averaged over three per cent of sorties.[102] Bomber Command records cite 47,268 men missing in action later to be classified as killed. Nine thousand, eight hundred and thirty-eight were captured by the Germans, 4,200 returned wounded from operations and another 4,203 were wounded in ground or flying accidents in the UK. The US forces did not get off lightly either. About 26,000 Eighth Air Force airmen were killed. Another 20,000 were made prisoners.

Combat intensity and attrition at this level had obvious statistical implications for any one aviator's eventual survival. Both Bomber Command and Eighth Air Force suffered an overall casualty rate which exceeded 50 per cent of their crew forces. During the height of the air war, the records section of the Eighth Air Force put together a study of 2,085 combat airmen from six bombardment groups. All but 34 of these men started their combat tours – which at the time consisted of 25 missions – at the same time. Detailed information was recorded on each man until final disposition. Table 2.1 shows the number starting each mission, the number killed or missing in action, and the percentage of losses.

Table 2.1

Mission No.	Men starting	No. KIA and WIA	Per cent
1.	2,051	93	4.5
2.	1,927	139	7.2
3.	1,775	94	5.3
4.	1,651	46	2.8
5.	1,585	117	7.3
6.	1,451	74	5.1
7.	1,360	56	4.1
8.	1,291	75	5.8
9.	1,203	76	6.3
10.	1,117	60	5.3
11.	1,047	54	5.1
12.	990	36	3.6
13.	942	61	6.4
14.	873	28	3.2
15.	831	20	2.4
16.	794	37	4.6
17.	748	31	4.1
18.	708	20	2.8
19.	680	21	3.0
20.	654	20	3.0
21.	623	12	1.9
22.	605	6	0.9
23.	588	7	1.2
24.	564	3	0.5
25.	559	9	1.6

TOTAL: 1,195   Av. Percent: 3.9%

Although the table seems to show that the loss rate remained fairly constant until the last few missions, further analysis showed that crews were statistically most at risk during the first ten missions. Thereafter, the loss rates decreased at a moderately fast rate. This information underscored similar findings in the RAF. The human story revealed by these figures is grim. Of 2,085 individuals in the study, about 57 per cent were killed or went missing and 17 per cent were lost as a result of physical disability, emotional instability, or death through accident. Only 25 per cent survived their operational tours unscathed.[103]

Serious as these statistics seemed, there were other visible and daily reminders of the carnage. At various times during the bombing offensive between one-third and one-half of all aircraft limping back to England needed battle damage repair.[104] In the Eighth Air Force, a report in June

1944 confirmed that 38 per cent of all successful bombers returning to base carried battle damage. And these crippled aircraft often carried terribly injured men. For every ten bombers shot down – and 100 airmen missing in action – 11 more came back wounded and five more returned killed.[105] Of the men actually carried back on damaged aircraft between November 1942 and August 1944, the Eighth Air Force's senior surgeon listed 3,441 wounded and 299 killed.[106]

Just over half the dead men were killed by flak shrapnel. Another 36 per cent were mortally wounded by aircraft cannon shells. Twelve per cent were struck by machine-gun fire and one per cent died as a result of being hit by fragments from their own aircraft. Wounded men shared statistics similar in scope, except that by a wide margin more wounded men had been hit in the extremities. The dead had almost always been struck in the head or chest.[107]

British investigations told a similar story in Bomber Command. In 1 Group – typical of much of the rest of the force – between January 1943 and January 1944, 813 crews commenced either a first or second tour. Records showed that 455 crews, approximately 3,185 men, went missing and only 207 crews survived to complete their tours.[108] At RAF Station Woodbridge, one of Bomber Command's emergency airfields, an analysis of casualties showed that 516 killed and wounded men returned in 1,720 aircraft. The majority of wounded men had been hit in the arms or legs while the greater number of dead had been felled by injuries to head or chest.[109]

A REVIEW OF COMBAT EFFECTIVENESS

Tactics and technology notwithstanding, success in air combat rested on the human element. At the fundamental level it was aircrew intelligence, skill, willpower and endurance that helped compensate for danger, physical demands, uncertainty and chance, and decided the results of many individual actions. Moreover, in the collective sense, thousands of these individual battles determined the air war's outcome.

Combat performance was carefully monitored during the war by both the RAF and USAAF. Successful airmen were considered to have various characteristics. Not surprisingly, perhaps, given their dissimilar missions, the optimum traits of bomber aircrew were almost universally thought to be different from those of good fighter pilots.[110] The wartime picture of the ideal fighter pilot was of a young, aggressive and very fit aviator who was capable of quick and decisive actions. Moreover, his motivation for combat was very high. A spirit of youthful adventure was considered helpful, as was a certain devil-may-care attitude. Commanders considered the optimum age for fighter pilots to be about 22 years.[111]

Discussions between commanders and medical authorities in both

Bomber Command and the Eighth Air Force yielded a slightly different picture of the optimum bomber pilot. He was a more mature individual, who would be likely to remain steady and cool in combat. Reliability and dependability – making the right decision and using good judgement – were considered more important than doing something too quickly. Bomber pilots typically had more responsibilities than their fighter pilot counterparts. Answerable for their crews and aircraft, they needed the wherewithal to oversee training, safety and equipment. The complexities of flying multi-engine aircraft and co-ordinating the activities of up to nine other men demanded a steady and firm character. Mission lengths called for foresight and meticulous planning on the part of pilots.[112] Good navigators and capable bombardiers on bombers were likewise noted for their dependability, judgement and emotional control, as well as their powers of orientation and observation. Radio operators and gunners needed more mechanical aptitudes and were often considered better if they were older and more responsible.

As described in the first chapter, it would appear that finding such men was not an insurmountable difficulty. To some extent the real problem was to establish some useful criteria for success.

Fighter pilots, for example, were encouraged to use the traditional measurement of air combat success, which was shooting down an enemy aircraft. Fighter units went to extraordinary lengths to verify and record victories. The competitive nature of fighter combat sometimes led to an atmosphere of team rivalry between individuals and units.[113]

The identification of easy-to-spot personality characteristics and the simple tallying of scores could not account for certain, almost indefinable qualities which seemed to set some fighter pilots off from others. Based on the previous discussion of situational awareness, it seems clear that this factor was important. Yet even staying on top of a combat situation does not tell the complete story of combat effectiveness. A veteran of the 359th Fighter Group who had been given credit for destroying 10½ German aircraft noted the differences between men he observed in this way:

Having flown in excess of 155 combat missions over a one and one-half year time span, I came to the conclusion that given an opportunity, there were probably 20 per cent or so of our Group pilots on a mission that would aggressively seek combat. Another large block – 60 per cent – would, when conditions were right, prove to be moderately effective. Then there were those that were of little use in air-to-air combat *no matter what the conditions of encounter happened to be* [veteran's emphasis] . . . When the sporadic air-to-air encounters occurred, one could usually predict which pilots would have seen action and fired their guns.[114]

Another ace expressed a similar sentiment when he wrote simply, 'there were fighter pilots and then there were men who flew fighters'.[115] Combat statistics collected at the time showed pretty convincingly that a small percentage of men in any unit were accounting for the largest percentage of enemy aircraft shot down.[116] Eighth Air Force records of all 5,000 or so fighter pilots who flew against the Germans show that only 261, or about 5.2 per cent, ranked as aces with five victories. Surprisingly, this 'élite' accounted for a full 40 per cent of the 5,284 German aircraft claimed destroyed by the American Air Force. Another 1,031 American pilots were given credit for between one-half and one kill, while almost 3,700 scored no victories at all.[117]

It would be wrong, however, to assume that pilots who failed to score an aerial victory were ineffective. In fact, scoring a victory had as much to do with opportunity, timing and luck as with anything else. After 1944 in particular, most American fighter pilots had only scant chance to engage the increasingly grounded Luftwaffe. Data showed that German interception rates dropped by two-thirds between March and December. Engagement summaries and combat reports of the Eighth Air Force's Fighter Command indicate that an American pilot could expect to meet a German only once every 25 combat missions.[118] In the final analysis, it is important to remember that as long as American fighters flew their missions, protected the bombers and returned safely to base, they were, in a very real sense, combat effective. Their unchallenged presence intimidated the Germans, may have discouraged attack and clearly contributed to Allied air superiority. This was true whether or not they actually shot down any aircraft.

During the Combined Bomber Offensive the most significant measure of tactical accomplishment for bombers was considered the number of bombs which fell on target. Although modified criteria evolved during the almost constant search for accuracy, this yardstick never fundamentally changed. In other words, for bomber crewmen their daily or nightly mission performance was gauged almost solely against the number of bombs they had successfully released against the mark.

Statistics collected during the war painstakingly traced bombing accuracy. American data throughout showed a steady rise in the percentage of bombs dropped within 1,000 feet of their targets. During the painful and costly months of the autumn of 1943, for example, only 27 per cent of bombs did so. The introduction of American long-range fighter escort, and the resulting lowering of German defensive efficiency, helped raise bombing accuracy. Over 40 per cent of bombs fell within 1,000 feet of the target one year later. By the spring of 1945 about half of all bombs fell inside the circle.[119]

Bomber Command's crews had similar difficulties with accuracy. Early in the war a member of the War Cabinet Secretariat, Mr D. M. Butt, conducted a study to gauge the effectiveness of the RAF's night bombing. His report contradicted some of the more optimistic assertions of the Air

Ministry and showed that only one aircraft in three dropped its bombs within five miles of its target.[120] Subsequent improvements in accuracy, due in some measure to technical and tactical advances, nevertheless did not prevent occasional lapses. A March 1944 raid on Stuttgart, for example, cost 37 aircraft and essentially missed the city entirely.[121]

It would be incorrect, however, to measure the overall effectiveness of the Combined Bomber Offensive strictly against the figures on accuracy. The Anglo-American offensive dropped a total of 1,578,212 tons of bombs on targets within Germany. More than half of this total was delivered after August 1944. By any measure, their impact was devastating. Slightly more than 300,000 Germans were killed and 780,000 were wounded during the onslaught. Nazi oil production came to a virtual halt and the German transportation system was thoroughly disrupted. German cities were devastated and almost two million people lost their homes. Aside from tying down the efforts of more than four million military personnel and workers, and vast amounts of resources which would have been employed by the Nazis elsewhere, the air offensive also swept the Luftwaffe from the skies. A strong case can be made that the Allied victory could not have been gained without air power.[122]

If there is a problem with traditional approaches to combat success during the Second World War it is that they largely ignore the human element. Bombing accuracy and the destruction it caused was clearly important, but many bomber crewmen measured their personal success quite differently from bombs on target or aircraft shot down. Survival was obviously paramount in many minds. Virtually all veterans comment on the feeling of euphoria they experienced as they touched down after a long mission. With so many visible reminders of death around them, the idea that they had survived another mission, and were therefore measurably closer to living through the war, must have been almost intoxicating. For many, even if their bombs had fallen well wide of any target, just coming home was reward enough.

The leaders of Bomber Command and the Eighth Air Force obviously knew that many aircrew were not as efficient as they might have hoped. It was abundantly clear at the time that scores of bombs were dropped inaccurately and, despite widely-inflated claims, thousands of gunners never shot down a single enemy aircraft. But it is also a fundamental mistake to regard these bomber aircrew as less than effective. In fact, in many ways, just by participating in missions they contributed to the goals of the Strategic Bomber Offensive.

Consider, for example, some of the aircrew in the massive American bomber formations. Even those who missed the target entirely contributed in some measure to the defensive cohesiveness of the formation and added their firepower to the whole. Moreover, those who survived at least brought their aircraft back to be flown again: no small achievement in the late summer and autumn of 1943. It was obvious that many crews improved as they gained experience and bombing accuracy improved. Finally, even those, who, because of lack of skill or bad luck were shot down, may have prevented others, more capable of hitting the target, from becoming casualties themselves.

Although many of the circumstances of the British night bomber streams were different, this last point was clearly recognized, if somewhat coldly, by Sir Arthur Harris in a January 1943 communication to Sir Charles Portal. It is worth quoting in its entirety:

It is inevitable in war that the best are the keenest to go back to operations and they are the ones who, when they get there, hit the target. There are perhaps 20-25 in each 100 who can be classed as the best and the remaining 75-80 divert the enemy effort from the destruction of the best, and receive a certain number of casualties so saving the best from being picked off by the enemy. At the same time, the weight of bombs they drop, some of which hit the target some of the time, all help to add to the damage but to a smaller degree than the bombs of the best which will normally land on the target. This is true in any service in any war and in any operation, eg, in the infantry there are a certain number of the not-so-good who confuse the enemy and make it diffi- cult for him to pick off the best men only.[123]

In a very real sense Air Marshal Harris's comments leave us in a better position to continue an evaluation of the human element during the Combined Bomber Offensive. Clausewitz's ultimate definition of friction was that it distinguished real war from war on paper. Harris, with characteristic bluntness, was speaking to the same idea; on paper all air- men were the same but in actual combat some men did better than others. Sortie totals, bomb loads and targets might be identified by intelligence officers and staff planners with mathematical precision. There was an antiseptic, detached and seemingly scientific element which distinguished the doctrine of strategic bombing.[124] But during the days and nights over Germany thousands of British, Commonwealth and American airmen came face-to-face with the very real and magnified effects of danger, exertion, uncertainty and chance brought on by the unrelenting demands of air combat.

NOTES

1. Giulio Douhet, *Command of the Air* trans. Dino Ferrari (New York: Coward-McCann, 1941; reprint edn, Washington: Office of Air Force History, 1983), pp. 8–10. See also 'Bombardment Aviation', 1937–38, 248.101–9, AFHRA; and Captain Laurence Kuter, 'The Power and Effect of the Demolition Bomb', 1939, 248.2208A–3, AFHRA.
2. AWPD–1, tab 1, 'Intelligence', 145.82–1, 1941, AFHRA and AWPD–2, part 4, 'Report', 1942, Special Collections, Air University Library, Maxwell AFB, Alabama.
3. See 'The Aim in War', Haywood S. Hansell Papers, Box 20, Special Collections USAF

Academy Library and R. J. Overy, *The Air War 1939–1945* (New York: Stein and Day, 1980), pp. 1–3.

4. American advocates of airpower, like General Billy Mitchell and Alexander P. DeSeversky, held that modern industrialized nations were extraordinarily vulnerable to aerial bombardment. See William H. Mitchell, *Winged Defense: The Development and Possibilities of Modern Air Power* (New York: G. P. Puttnam's Sons, 1925), p. 16 and Alexander P. DeSeversky, *Victory Through Air Power* (New York: Simon and Schuster, 1942), p. 147. As late as July 1943, one Eighth Air Force Wing Commander wrote that he believed no invasion of the continent would ever have to take place. See 'Operational Letters', Vol. 1, 168.491, 21 July 1943, AFHRA.

5. The causes of the Luftwaffe's defeat are outside the scope of this work. For an excellent discussion see Williamson Murray, *Luftwaffe* (Baltimore: The Nautical and Aviation Publishing Company, 1985), pp. 282–96. A more direct view can be found in Adolf Galland's 'Defeat of the Luftwaffe: Fundamental Causes', *Air University Review* 6 (Spring 1953), pp. 16–36.

6. Clausewitz, op. cit., pp. 104–21.

7. A similar analysis might be extended to naval combatants, especially submariners, who, like airmen, are mechanically suspended in an environment incapable of sustaining human life by itself. It is especially striking too that of all Second World War combat forces, only German U-boat crews suffered casualties comparable to Bomber Command's airmen. See Timothy P. Mulligan, 'German U-boat Crews in World War II: Sociology of an Elite', *The Journal of Military History* 56 (April 1992): pp. 261–81.

8. Among others see Air Ministry, *Operational Research in the RAF* (London: HMSO, 1963), pp. i–xx; R. W. Clark, *The Rise of the Boffins* (London, 1962), pp. 117–73; Craven and Cate, op. cit., Vol. VI, pp. 299–331; Vol. VII, p. 428; and 'Report of Pursuit Board', 168.12–9, 1942, AFHRA.

9. Field modification was responsible for much of the innovation, but manufacturers were also working at a feverish pace. The North American P-51 Mustang, one of the most successful fighter-planes of the war, went from design to prototype in 117 days. See William H. Green, *Warplanes of the Second World War*, Vol. 4: *Fighters* (Garden City: Doubleday and Company, 1961), p. 136.

10. Major General David Grant, Surgeon General, USAAF (retd), 'A Day at the Office', quoted in Ian L. Hawkins (ed.), *B-17s Over Berlin: Personal Stories from the 95th Bomb Group (H)* (Washington: Brassey's, 1990), pp. 63–4.

11. Much depended on flying conditions and aircraft weight. Among other often repeated generalizations were that B-17s required excessive strength to fly in formation, B-24s had a heavy and sluggish control response, Stirlings were notoriously difficult to land and Halifaxes could slip into uncontrolled spins. Contemporary aircraft operating manuals contained numerous operating cautions. See, among others, 'Familiarization Manual for Operation of Model B-17F Bombardment Airplane', Seattle: Boeing, 1942; and Roger A. Freeman, *British Airmen*, pp. 82–3.

12. In a story which was far from unusual, one veteran remembers a dusk take-off during which the aircraft directly in front of his and the one immediately behind both crashed. E. L. Hay (Lancaster pilot) to author, 31 July 1989.

13. Brig. Gen. Haywood S. Hansell, Jr., USAF (retd), *The Air Plan that Defeated Hitler* (Atlanta: Higgins-McArthur Longino and Porter, 1972), p. 121.

14. Between April 1940 and March 1942 there was one landing accident for every 140 landings. See H. E. Whittingham to Air Commodore Vernon S. Brown, nd, AIR 20/10727.

15. One pilot recalls being advised that three weather fronts had transited England during a single mission to and from Germany. Lieut. Col. David W. Litsinger (351st Bomb Group) to author 6 April 1989.

16. Weather bad enough to hinder visual bombing prevailed, on average, 250 days per year. At least one-quarter of all days during the year were bad enough to prevent flying at all. See Report No. 2, 'Weather Factors In Combat Bombardment Operations in the European Theater', *United States Strategic Bombing Survey* (Washington: US Government Printing Office, 1945), p. 2.

17. 'Considering a theoretical daily potential effort for the Eighth Air Force, it is deduced that only about 55 per cent of that effort could be used on a monthly basis'. In short, according to post-war analysis, bad weather almost halved the effectiveness of American efforts. Ibid.

18. An unforecast jetstream was a major cause of Bomber Command's disastrous losses on the Nuremberg raid. See Brian D. Giles, *Meteorology and World War II* (Birmingham: Royal Meteorological Society, 1987), p. 56 and Summary of Events, No. 8 Group, 30–31 March 1944, AIR 14/450.

19. Air Vice-Marshal H. A. C. Bird-Wilson, RAF (retd), recalled a single mission in 1944 when two aircraft crashed on take-off, two had mid-air collisions, and two more were lost as a result of a snow storm. See Norman Franks, *Scramble to Victory* (London: William Kimber, 1987), p. 52.

20. Number 4 Group lost no fewer than eight aircraft to accidents during one winter night in 1942. For one of the best veteran accounts of weather-related problems see Group Captain Tom Sawyer, RAF (retd), *Only Owls and Bloody Fools Fly at Night* (London: William Kimber and Co., 1982; London: Goodall Publications, 1985), pp. 61–8.

21. Lancasters were loaded with 2,000 gallons of petrol, 150 gallons of oil, flammable hydraulics and about nine tons of bombs. During one two-month period alone in 1944, there were 33 accidents involving Lancasters, Halifaxes and Stirlings owing to tyre bursts on take-offs or landing. Sixteen of the 33 resulted in the complete write-off of the aircraft. See Air Ministry, 'One More Reason for Accident Increase', Air Crew Training Bulletin, No. 16, March 1944, RAF Museum, Hendon.

22. More than one-quarter of all accidents were categorized under 'pilot error'. But because of the large percentage of undetermined causes it is likely that even more could be attributed to it. See Eighth Air Force, 'Aircraft Accidents', 1943–1944, 520.742–7, AFHRA.

23. Buzzing towers and, as the RAF called it, 'beating up the field' were strictly prohibited but not infrequent occurrences. Predictably, there were also calls for 'stern discipline, inordinate attention to duty, and frequent inspections'. See General Ira C. Eaker to General Carl A. Spaatz, 25 Aug. 1942, Box 9, Spaatz MSS, Library of Congress and 'Note by I.G. II on Discipline and the fighting spirit in the RAF', 14 May 1943, AIR 20/3082.

24. Dr S. C. Rexford-Welch (ed), *The Royal Air Force Medical Services*, Vol. II: *Commands* (London, HMSO, 1955), p. 75 and Report No. S.77, 'Casualties Among Aircrew Personnel Directly Due to·Enemy Action', 12 March 1943, AIR 14/1803.

25. General Henry H. Arnold, 'Report of the Commanding General of the US Army Air Force to the Secretary of War', 27 Feb. 1945, AFHRA.

26. Eighth Air Force, 'Statistical Summary of Eighth Air Force Operations: European Theater 17 Aug. 1942–8 May 1945', 520.308–1, AFHRA.

27. Link and Coleman, op. cit., pp. 691–2.

28. See John J. Cochrane, Thames Television Interview, No. 002821/02/01–02, IWM and Roger A. Freeman, *The Mighty Eighth War Manual* (London: Arms and Armour Press, 1986), p. 19, 35.

29. Not rare by any means, the results of some accidents were captured by photographers. See GP–389–HI (Bomb), June 1943–May 1945; and GP–392–HI (Bomb), August 1943–June 1945, AFHRA.

30. Unit records are replete with scores of individual tragedies. One such occurred at Alconbury on 27 May 1943. A 95th Bomb Group B-17 was being loaded with 500lb bombs when one accidentally·detonated. The ensuing explosions destroyed four aircraft, damaged 11 others, killed 18 men and wounded 20 more. See GP-95-HI (Bomb), April 1943–Aug. 1945, AFHRA.

31. Major General Curtis E. LeMay, 'Combat Crew Handbook', 3rd Bombardment Division, nd, Command Papers, Box B4, LeMay MSS, Library of Congress.

32. See Air Ministry, 'Air Crew Training Bulletin', No. 14, Nov. 1943, pp. 24–26 and Air Ministry, 'Air Crew Training Bulletin', No. 16, March 1944, pp. 30–31. RAF Museum, Hendon.

33. So popular did Prune become that there were concerns that airmen needed a role model who was not quite so ludicrous and brainless. See Air Ministry, 'Minutes of meeting to consider training to improve morale and discipline', 6 Jan. 1944, AIR 20/4583.

34. Under normal conditions the 795 aircraft dispatched on the 30–31 March 1944 raid on Nuremberg would have taken up almost 70 miles of airspace. Winds and human error probably stretched it to nearly 100. See Air Ministry, War Room Manual of Bomber Command Operations, AIR 22/203 and Group Operation Record Books, 30–31 March 1944, AIR 25.

35. For a German pilot's reaction to seeing the Eighth Air Force's massive daylight formations

see Adolf Galland, *The First and the Last* (London: Methuen, 1955), pp. 265–6. On the size and structure of formations see Freeman, *War Manual*, pp. 37–44; US Army Air Forces, 'Pilot's Flight Operation Instructions for Model B-17', Wright Patterson Field, 1944; and 'Combat Crew Handbook', 3rd Bombardment Division, nd, Command Papers, Box B4, LeMay MSS, Library of Congress.

36. It might be argued that the vastness of the sky reflected the trend in warfare since the nineteenth century toward increasingly 'empty battlefields'. See Paddy Griffith, *Forward into Battle* (Novato, CA: Presidio Press, 1991), pp. 10–11, 116–17 and S. L. A. Marshall, *Men against Fire* (New York: 1947; reprint edn, Gloucester, MA: Peter Smith, 1978), pp. 44–5.

37. 'We would be the privileged spectators of scenes defying description in their beauty and impossible for the earthbound to picture and understand'. Roderick Chisholm, *Cover of Darkness* (London: Chatto & Windus, 1953), pp. 19, 42.

38. Chapter 6 provides more details of the stresses associated with flying and aviators' reactions to them. See H. G. Armstrong and M. Grow, *Fit to Fly: A Medical Handbook for Fliers* (New York and London: D. Appleton-Century Company, 1941), pp. 2–20.

39. Brig. Gen. Ira C. Eaker, HQ VIII Bomber Command, to General Carl Spaatz, Commanding General, Eighth Air Force, 25 Aug. 1942, Eaker MSS, Library of Congress.

40. During a 28 Sept. 1944 mission to Magdeburg the 303rd Bomb Group lost 11 of its B-17 aircraft in one devastating attack by German Fw-190 *Sturm* fighters. Such incidents were not uncommon. See William F. Miller (303rd Bomb Group) to author, 10 April 1992; GP-303-HI (Bomb), 28 Sept. 1944, War Diary; and SQ-Bomb-358-HI, SQ-Bomb-359-HI, SQ-Bomb-360-HI, Sept. 1944, AFHRA.

41. Wing Commander G. Cairns, RAF (retd), (Lancaster flight engineer) to author 5 July 1990.

42. Lieut. Col. William G. Ryan, USAF (retd), (91st and 482nd Bomb Groups) to author 19 Oct. 1989.

43. 'Purple Heart Corner' was the unofficial term Eighth Air Force airmen used to identify the location corresponding to the lowest and most rearward bomber squadron in a Group or Combat Wing formation. 'Tail-end Charlie', a position which actually varied depending on formation, was typically the most rearward airplane in the lowest element. These were regarded as the most hazardous positions. For detailed information and diagrams of Eighth Air Force formations see, Eighth Air Force and Army Air Forces Evaluation Board, 'Eighth Air Force Tactical Development, August 1942 – May 1945', 1945, AFHRA. On the dangers of formation locations see 'Summary of B-17s Lost', Box B6, LeMay MSS, Library of Congress.

44. Eaker to Spaatz, 25 Aug. 1942, Spaatz MSS, Library of Congress.

45. 'I'm sure that common sense, knowing your job, never falling asleep, keeping everybody on their toes, and never underestimating the opposition increased one's chances of survival'. C. P. Rudland (Lancaster flight-engineer) to author, 28 Aug. 1989.

46. Colonel Lester F. Rentmeester, USAF (retd), 91st Bomb Group, to author 16 May 1989.

47. British crews faced the terrifying difficulty of finding escape hatches in the dark. Operational Research statistics showed that about 50 per cent of Americans successfully bailed out of damaged aircraft. In contrast, only about one-quarter of British airmen made it safely out of Halifaxes and Stirlings. With a mere 15 per cent escape rate the Lancaster was worst of all; the width of the door was only 22 inches. For a firsthand recollection of this tragedy which caused unnecessary loss of life see Freeman Dyson, *Disturbing the Universe* (New York: Harper & Row, 1979), pp. 27–8.

48. Scores of post-war memoirs and mission histories contain riveting firsthand accounts of bail-out and survival. Among many others see Ian Hawkins, *The Münster Raid* (Blue Ridge Summit, PA: Tab/Aero Books, 1989), pp. 189–209; Martin Middlebrook, *The Berlin Raids* (New York: Viking Press, 1988; London: Penguin Books, 1990), pp. 54–9. The Special Collections section of the USAF Academy Library also maintains a large body of similar material collected from men who ended up as prisoners-of-war.

49. The tendency during the war was to increase both the explosiveness and weight of firepower carried by fighter aircraft. By 1945, German Fw-190s mounted two 20mm cannon and two 13mm machine-guns capable of loosing 26lb of metal in a 3-second burst. Even more remarkable, the Me-262 jet fighter could fire 96lb of explosive shell in the same period. Americans, confident in the accuracy and ballistic qualities of their 50-calibre weapon, standardized fighter armament at six or eight machine-guns. See Alfred Price,

Fighter Aircraft (London: Arms and Armour Press, 1976), pp. 60–8; Eighth Air Force, 'An Evaluation of Defensive Measures Taken to Protect Heavy Bombers from Loss and Damage', Nov. 1944, 520.520A, AFHRA; and 'The Development of German Aircraft Armament at War's End', 1957, K113.107–193, AFHRA.

50. Attacks delivered inside the 30 degree cone were statistically almost four times as successful as attacks made outside it. See Air Ministry, 'Armament Training', Air Crew Training Bulletin, No. 7, Dec. 1942, RAF Museum, Hendon.

51. In the USAAF a hit percentage of only five was required to pass gunnery school. See Robert S. Johnson, *Thunderbolt* (New York: Ballantine, 1959; New York: Bantam Books, 1990), p. 118.

52. Success in combat at less than 600 yards was three times greater than when outside that range. Ibid. and VIII Fighter Command, 'Combat Crew Training, Gunnery', 1943, Box 91, Spaatz MSS, Library of Congress.

53. According to one of the USAAF's top aces, estimating ranges and learning to withhold fire until close enough was a key to success. See Colonel Francis Gabreski, USAF (retd), *Gabby: A Fighter Pilot's Life* (New York: Orion Books, 1991), pp. 70–73. Another Eighth Air Force pilot, quoted in a British training advisory said, 'My shooting methods have one aim – dead astern at 50 feet'. Air Ministry, 'Armament', Air Crew Training Bulletin No 20, Oct. 1944, RAF Museum, Hendon.

54. In the words of one fighter ace, 'It was just second nature'. Urban L. Drew (361st Fighter Group) to author, 9 April 1989.

55. Brig. Gen. Charles E. Yeager, USAF (retd), *Yeager: An Autobiography* (New York: Bantam Books, 1985), p. 68.

56. This passage was written by one of the most successful American fighter aces of the war. See Don Gentile, *One Man Air Force* (New York: L. B. Fischer Publishing, Corporation, 1944), pp. 8–9; see also John R. Boyd, 'Aerial Attack Study', USAF Fighter Weapons School, Document No. 50-10-6C, Nellis AFB, Nevada, 1960, p. 49.

57. According to S. L. A. Marshall men had to overcome their 'inner and usually unrealized resistance toward killing a fellow man'. See Marshall, pp. 78–9 and Office of the Air Surgeon, 'Analysis of the Duties of Aircrew Personnel, Descriptions of Aircrew Performances from Theaters of Combat', 3 May 1943, 141.28D-10-19, AFHRA.

58. Mike Spick, *The Ace Factor* (Annapolis: The Naval Institute Press, 1988), pp. 12–15.

59. Major Barry D. Watts, 'Fire, Movement and Tactics', *Topgun Journal* 2 (Winter 1979/80), pp. 4–24.

60. For a detailed explanation of American fighter escort tactics from a quadruple ace and squadron commander refer to General John C. Meyer, USAF (retd), Thames Television Interview No. 002823/01, Imperial War Museum. For a description of multiple aircraft combat from another ace see Yeager, pp. 65–9.

61. VIII Fighter Command, 'Combat Crew Training, Air Fighting Principles', 1943, Box 91, Spaatz MSS, Library of Congress.

62. Lieut. Col. Mark E. Hubbard, commander of the 20th Fighter Group for a short period of time, estimated that, '90 per cent of all fighters shot down never saw the guy who hit them'. Quoted by William E. Kepner in an VIIIth Fighter Command report, 'The Long Reach: Deep Fighter Escort Tactics', 29 May 1944, AFHRA.

63. Gentile, op. cit., p. 11.

64. Spick, op. cit., introduction and pp. 1–14.

65. An ability, according to an ace with 34 victories, which comes with experience. Colonel James A. Goodson, USAF (retd), (4th Fighter Group) to author 21 June 1989.

66. Urban L. Drew (361st Fighter Group) to author 9 April 1989.

67. Along with the predictable safety risks of this large volume of machine-gun fire came the real hazards to lower flying aircraft in the formation. Wings, engines, turrets, and cockpits were often damaged by expended brass until steps were taken to keep most of it inside firing aircraft. General Ira C. Eaker to Commanding General Eighth Air Force, 25 Aug.1942, Box 9, Spaatz MSS, Library of Congress.

68. Lieut. Col. Claude E. Putnam to Commanding General, 1st Bombardment Wing, 5 April 1943, Box 91, Spaatz MSS, Library of Congress.

69. Combat reports show consistent similarities in German attack methods. Not surprisingly the Germans expended much energy on working out the most effective techniques. See, among others, Heinz Knoke, *I Flew for the Führer: The Story of a German Fighter Pilot*

(New York: Holt, 1953), pp. 88–9, 120–6; and, from among hundreds of combat reports, SQ-Bomb-365-SU-OP-S, Aug. 1944, AFHRA.

70. Faced with fighting multi-engine bombers, the chief of the German fighter arm had long argued for heavier armament. See Galland, op. cit., pp. 200–1; and Eighth Air Force, 'An Evaluation of Defensive Measures Taken to Protect Heavy Bombers from Loss and Damage', Nov. 1944, 520.520a, AFHRA.

71. An excellent analysis of German attack techniques can be found in US Army Air Forces, 'German Fighter Tactics Against Flying Fortresses', Special Intelligence Report No. 43–17, 31 Dec. 1943, Imperial War Museum.

72. One German Knight's Cross winner even ordered his younger pilots to close their eyes during approach and ignore US tracer fire which was used to frighten them. Werner Schroer, Thames Television Recorded Interview No. 002950/01/01, Imperial War Museum.

73. 'The Development of German Aircraft Armament to War's End', 1957, K113.107–193, AFHRA.

74. War Department, 'Handbook on German Military Forces', Technical Manual TM-E 30–451, 15 March 1945, p. X–43.

75. Lieut. Col. Claude E. Putnam to Commanding General, 1st Bombardment Wing, 5 April 1943, Box 91, Spaatz MSS, Library of Congress.

76. Compounding this difficulty was the fact that many American bomber pilots practised very limited evasion action within the confining constraints of their formations. This often amounted to rapid rudder inputs or slight variations on the control column. Of questionable value in throwing off German fighters and certainly detrimental to defensive aiming, it nevertheless boosted aircrew morale. See Brian K. O'Neill, *Half a Wing, Three Engines and a Prayer: B-17s over Germany* (Blue Ridge Summit, PA: Tab/Aero Books, 1989), p. 103.

77. General Theodore Ross Milton, USAF (retd), Commander 384th Bomb Group, Oral Interview, 9 July 1982, 239.0512–1339, AFHRA.

78. Fighter claims, largely because of the use of gun-camera film, were considered more accurate. But some cynics observed that higher scores were the result of liberal co-operation between wingmen, 'such as A confirming two for B, and B confirming 3 for A'. See Kepner, *Tactical Development*, p. 100, and on high claims, R. L. 'Dixie' Alexander, quoted in Laddie Lucas (ed.), *Wings of War* (London: Hutchison and Company, 1983), p. 348.

79. Major General James H. Doolittle, Headquarters Eighth Air Force, to Commanding Generals, 1st, 2nd, and 3rd Bombardment Divisions, 5 Feb. 1944, 527.674, AFHRA.

80. As an example, the Eighth Air Force claimed 983 German aircraft destroyed or probably destroyed in October 1943. A single mission, the famous 14 October Schweinfurt raid, saw 199 aircraft claimed. Yet German records – which admittedly do not always agree – show only about 284 losses for the month and between 27 and 39 on the ball-bearing mission. Almost six months later, during the Berlin raids, the claim rates were still almost 300 per cent too high. See 'VIII Bomber Command Narrative of Operations', 1943–1944, 519.332, AFHRA; 'VIII Fighter Command Narrative of Operations', 1943–1944, 168.6005–55, AFHRA; Headquarters, US Strategic Air Forces Europe, 'Statistical Data', 570.677A, AFHRA; *Auswertung der Einsatz bereitsch der fliegenden Verb. vom 1 August 1943 bis Nov. 1944*, 28 June 1949, 110.8–22, AFHRA; and 'German Air Force Losses in the West', Jan.–April 1944, 512.621 VII/133, AFHRA.

81. Sawyer, op. cit., p. 163.

82. Dyson, op. cit., p. 25.

83. For an excellent summary of the electronics war see Alfred Price, *Instruments of Darkness* (London: Macdonald and Jane's, 1977).

84. Various veterans in the Bomber Command Association have mentioned this in informal conversation from time to time. Their reflections are supported by an Operational Research report which indicated that too great a readiness to open fire actually increased the risk of attack by enemy fighters, and a significant percentage of British bombers were damaged by 'friendly fire'. See Air Ministry, *Operational Research*, p. 65.

85. W. T. MacFarlane (Halifax pilot) to author, 18 July 1989.

86. James B. Bage (Halifax gunner) to author, 25 April 1990.

87. Group Captain Hamish Mahaddie, RAF (retd), Thames Television Interview No. 002897/03/01–03, Imperial War Museum.

88. On the importance of crew co-ordination see Air Ministry 'Bomber Command Crew Co-operation', Air Crew Training Bulletin No. 7, Dec. 1942, RAF Museum, Hendon and Major General Curtis E. LeMay, 'Combat Crew Handbook', Eighth Air Force, 3rd Bombardment Division, nd, Box B4, LeMay MSS, Library of Congress. Fascinating evidence regarding the importance of crew co-ordination, teamwork, and cohesion can be derived from listening to a BBC recording made during an actual combat mission on 3 September 1943. Sadly, this aircraft was lost on a subsequent mission in January 1944. Refer to Wynford Vaughan Thomas and R. Pidsley, 'Raid on Berlin', BBC Broadcast, 3 Sept. 1944, Sound Recording No. 6454-8/2178, Imperial War Museum.

89. When asked what caused them the most concern many veterans respond with sentiments reflected by one who said, 'Having to helplessly watch flak and its results was very disturbing'. Thomas L. Hair (385th Bomb Group) to author, 12 March 1989.

90. Sir Charles Webster and Noble Frankland, *The Strategic Air Offensive Against Germany, 1939–1945* 4 Vols. (London: HMSO, 1961), Vol. II, p. 296.

91. 'Air Staff Post Hostilities Intelligence Requirements on the German Air Force', 1935–1945, 510.601B, Sec IIIA 1 and 2, AFHRA. The German Armaments Minister noted after the war that Germany produced 11,957 heavy guns between 1941 and 1943 and 'most of them had to be deployed for anti-aircraft purposes within Germany'. See Albert Speer, *Inside the Third Reich* (New York: The Macmillan Company, 1970), note 2, p. 278.

92. War Department, *Handbook on German Military Forces*, Technical Manual TM-E 30-451 (Washington DC: US Government Printing Office, 1945), pp. VII 42–8.

93. The details of the development and efficacy of US aircrew body-armour is well told in Link and Coleman, op. cit., pp. 617–35.

94. This statistic led him to argue against evasive maneuvre as a way to improve bombing accuracy. After the war a German General estimated even more pessimistically that it took 4,000 flak shells to down one bomber. See Thomas M. Coffey, *Iron Eagle: The Turbulent Life of General Curtis LeMay* (New York: Crown Publishers, Inc., 1986; New York: Avon Books, 1988), p. 35; and 'The Development of German Anti-aircraft Weapons and Equipment of All Types up to 1945', K113.107–194, AFHRA.

95. There is evidence too that the German population took a measure of psychological support from the sights and sounds of the flak firing at bombers. Hitler, the self-appointed expert in aerial warfare, was never very happy with German day fighters, and often ordered increases in anti-aircraft artillery production at their expense. During one tantrum on 11 August 1944 he even ordered all fighter production stopped in favour of flak. See Murray, p. 130, and Speer, p. 408.

96. James B. Bage (Halifax tail gunner) to author, 25 April 1990.

97. Major General William E. Kepner, VIIIth Fighter Command, Oral Interview, 15 July 1944, 524.0581, AFHRA.

98. German locomotives, staff cars, trucks, barges, hangars, railway stations, and flak towers were also frequently attacked. Almost anything that moved was fair game. Yeager suggested, 'we weren't always scrupulous about our targets'. Yeager, op. cit., p. 62.

99. As an example, German losses to strafing during just April and May of 1944 totalled 741 aircraft destroyed and 353 damaged. Conversely, Allied losses to light flak increased from 13 per cent of all downed aircraft in February, and 30 per cent in March, to 37 per cent in April, and to 44 per cent in May. No fewer than nine of the Eighth Air Force's top aces were shot down in this way. See Generalleutnant Josef Schmid, 'Aerial Warfare over the Reich in Defence of Vital Luftwaffe Installations and Supporting Services', 1 April 1944–6 June 1944, K113.107–160, AFHRA; 'Air Staff Post Hostilities Intelligence Requirements', Sec. IV I, Vol. 2, appendix 3, AFHRA; Stephen L. McFarland, 'The Evolution of the American Strategic Fighter in Europe, 1942–1944', *Journal of Strategic Studies* 10 (June 1987), p. 199; and Roger A. Freeman, *The Mighty Eighth* (London: Jane's, 1986), pp. 272–81.

100. Garry L. Fry and Jeffrey L. Ethell, *Escort to Berlin* (New York: Arco, 1980), p. 73.

101. Strafing 20 feet above the ground was considered too high. See Stephen L. McFarland and Wesley P. Newton, *To Command the Sky* (Washington: Smithsonian Institution Press, 1991), p. 234.

102. During the war Bomber Command lost 8,953 aircraft as a direct result of enemy action and another 1,368 written-off in operational accidents. Even the most conservative estimate

indicates that the Eighth Air Force suffered 4,200 battle losses and half again as many in accidents. See Eighth Air Force, 'Statistical Summary of Eighth Air Force Operations, European Theater, 17 August 1942–8 May 1945', 520.308–1, AFHRA; Air Ministry, War Room (Statistical Section), War Room Manual of Bomber Command Ops, 1939–1945, AIR 22/203; and Martin Middlebrook, *The Bomber Command War Diaries* (London: Viking Books, 1985; London: Penguin Books, 1990), p. 707.

103. Table and data from Lt. Col. Robert E. Lyon, 'Trend of Losses Related to Combat Crew Experience, Heavy Bomber Operations', *circa* Feb. 1944, 519.7411–1, 1943–1946, AFHRA.

104. William R. Emerson, 'Operation POINTBLANK: A Tale of Bombers and Fighters', *The Harmon Memorial Lectures in Military History 1959–1987* (Washington, DC: Office of Air Force History, 1988), p. 459.

105. Eighth Air Force, Operations Research Section, Report 8 June 1944. In AIR 14/1803.

106. Eighth Air Force, 'Wounded and Killed in Action', 519.7411–6, Nov. 1942–Aug. 1944, AFHRA.

107. Eighth Air Force, 'Location of Wounds Incurred in Action', Nov. 1942–1 Sept. 1944, Cumulative to Date', 519.7411–6, AFHRA.

108. Post-war analysis would show that only about 12 per cent of the missing survived as prisoners-of-war and a large portion of these were wounded. Barely 1 per cent evaded capture and returned. See Martin Middlebrook, *The Nuremberg Raid* (London: Penguin Books, 1986), p. 57.

109. Rexford-Welch, op. cit., Vol. II, pp. 84–5.

110. Office of the Air Surgeon, 'Report On Survey of Aircrew Personnel in the Eighth, Ninth, Twelfth, and Fifteenth Air Forces', April 1944, 141.28B, AFHRA.

111. Office of the Air Surgeon, 'Analysis of the Duties of Aircrew Personnel, Descriptions of Aircrew Performances from Theaters of Combat', 5 May 1943, 141.28D-10-19, AFHRA.

112. Ibid. See also 'The Selection, Classification and Initial Training of Air Crew', 31 March 1944, AIR 15/53.

113. Douglas D. Bond, *The Love and Fear of Flying* (New York: International Universities Press, 1952), p. 39.

114. This passage unmistakenly relates to S. L. A. Marshall's famous, if controversial, analysis of ratio of fire, battlefield participation, and combat effectiveness of infantrymen. George Doerch (359th Fighter Group) to author, 9 March 1989. See also Marshall, pp. 50–63.

115. Urban L. Drew (361st Fighter Group) to author, 6 Feb. 1989.

116. Contemporary data for one typical fighter group showed that one-quarter of the pilots accounted for 70 per cent of the kills. See Douglas D. Bond, 'A Study of Successful Airmen and with Particular Respect to Their Motivations for Combat Flying and Resistance to Combat Stress', 27 Jan. 1945, 520.7411–1, AFHRA.

117. The above data are compiled from 'Final Report of Assessed Fighter Claims Against Enemy Aircraft, Aug. 1942–April 1945', published Sept. 1945, AFHRA.

118. Veteran memoirs often comment on the absence of the enemy during many of the missions they flew. Many fighter pilots completed tours without ever actually engaging directly in combat. Between April and September 1944, Allied air forces flew more than 300,000 sorties. During the same period the Germans managed only 65,000. Other factors aside, with far more Allied aircraft in the air on any given day it is no surprise it was occasionally hard to find the enemy. See Eighth Air Force, 'Statistical Summary of Eighth Air Force Operations: European Theater, 17 Aug. 1942–8 May 1945, 520.308–1, AFHRA and *USSBS,* Statistical Appendix.

119. B-17 crews scored slightly better than did those in B-24s in bombing accuracy and, measured against average number of missions before loss, lasted longer in combat. See USSBS Report No. 3, 'Bombing Accuracy USAAF Heavy and Medium Bombers, European Theater of Operations, 3 November 1945'. For a monthly summary of bombing accuracy see James Hoseason, *The 1,000 Day Battle* (Lowestoft, Suffolk: Gillingham Publications, 1979), p. 142.

120. This would make the target 'circle' more than 75 square miles. A full copy of the Butt report can be found in Webster and Frankland, op. cit., Vol. IV, Appendix 13.

121. See Middlebrook, *War Diaries*, p. 481 and Operational Research Section, Bomber Command, 'Final Plots of Night Photographs, 15–16 March 1944, AIR 24/269.

122. See Craven and Cate, op. cit., Vol. III, pp. 792–808; Overy, op. cit., pp. 262–4; and

USSBS, Vol. 1, 'The Effects of Strategic Bombing on German Morale', p. 7 and 'Overall Report (Europe)', p. 37.
123. Harris to Portal, 26 Jan. 1943, AIR 20/2860.
124. Very much the theme of Michael S. Sherry's *The Rise of American Air Power* (New Haven: Yale University Press, 1987).

3

Combat Stress, Emotional Breakdown and their Treatment in the Allied Air Forces

THE UNIQUE characteristics of air combat placed extraordinary strains on Allied airmen during the strategic bombing offensive against Germany. Like soldiers throughout the centuries, the young aviators who flew with the Eighth Air Force and Bomber Command were required to adapt to the startlingly new experiences of combat. As we have seen, the environment was often overwhelmingly demanding and life-threatening, the physical challenges often seemed intolerable and the pressure to perform relentless. For many, the only tangible reward was survival; yet the all-too-apparent statistics frequently showed this to be mathematically unlikely.

In these kinds of circumstances, it is little wonder that men were rendered vulnerable to the physical and mental symptoms of stress. In many ways, and for many men, just staying in combat meant fighting and winning a personal battle, the full extent of which became all too clear soon after their arrival in a combat flying squadron.[1] To begin with, they suddenly became aware of the devastating violence of air war. Even those more or less toughened by having seen aircraft losses during training, were shocked at the unremitting carnage of combat, both in the air and on the ground. Similarly, the frequency and randomness of death and casualties severely tested their confidence. Most airmen considered themselves part of a highly select élite group, yet the large numbers of killed, wounded and missing argued that training and mastery of complex flying skills did not necessarily ensure success or survival. Finally, they quickly became aware of their own shortcomings. While perhaps few might have been able to put it in words, there seemed to be a widespread recognition that personality – doctors might say pre-existing psychological factors – rendered some men more susceptible to combat breakdown. Among others, timid men, excessively nervous types and those who were overtly self-centred, had difficulty meeting the demands of this personal battle.

Many of these same men lacked the ability to identify with a group, and thereby lost any hope of winning the struggle to understand and control their fears.

This personal struggle will become the focus of this chapter. To understand it more completely it is worthwhile beginning with an investigation of the causes of combat stress as they were understood at the time. Such a review will highlight some of the similarities and differences in the stresses endured by British aviators, operating mostly at night, and their day-flying American counterparts. Thereafter, we shall consider the results of stress, especially as they led to aircrew emotional breakdown. Without getting too involved in medical terminology, it is none the less important to review the principal manifestations of excessive strain.

A subsequent section will summarize the statistical evidence. The numbers of neuropsychiatric casualties and the rate at which they occurred reveal a great deal, not just about the nature of combat, but also about the quality of leadership and the efficacy of medical care. It is worth emphasizing beforehand, however, that at no time did the number of emotional casualties ever seriously jeopardize the operational capability of either air force.[2]

The final sections of the chapter deal with the treatment of emotional casualties. This area – largely the responsibility of the leadership and medical support personnel – was affected by the dissimilar philosophies of the two services. Ultimately, prevention and treatment made much of the difference between success and failure in the individual struggles waged by each airman.

COMBAT STRESS: ITS CAUSES

It is no surprise that much of what we know about the emotional stresses imposed by Second World War air combat comes from medical officers and psychiatrists of the period. Combat and its effect on combatants were topics of considerable medical and official interest from the very start of the war. The Royal Air Force's view of combat stress is covered in detail in a lengthy series of reports generated for the Flying Personnel Research Committee (FPRC) between 1942 and 1945.[3]

In 1942 Air Commodore Symonds and Wing Commander Williams wrote one of the earliest reports on psychological disorders in aircrew. Their investigation supported a view, largely accepted by the RAF's medical establishment, which held that two of the most potent causes of stress in aircrew were fatigue and fear.[4] These will be considered separately.

In the broadest terms, both British and American airmen were subjected to comparable kinds of physical fatigue. Flying had long been known to place unusually severe demands on the human body, but the prolonged nature of the strategic air offensive subjected airmen to a new magnitude of strain.[5] Moreover, rapid advances in aviation technology did more than just improve the performance of combat aircraft; they placed a heavy burden on aircrew stamina. Lengthy exposure to higher altitudes challenged airmen, for example, and brought life-threatening problems resulting from lower pressures and a lack of oxygen. The frequent application of multiple 'G' forces, with their potential for rapidly inducing unconsciousness, reduced human abilities and menaced safety. Similarly, large numbers were affected by the extremely low temperatures at combat altitudes. Ill-fitting and bulky flight clothing only partially protected them from the rigours of open windows and sub-zero temperatures. Electrical suits often malfunctioned and even burned their wearers. Sometimes a combination of the environment, lack of knowledge or simple inattention led to dangers, as in this American example:

I knew nothing at all about breaking the ice out of my oxygen mask. After [I] almost passed out because of lack of oxygen, a crew member detected my plight . . . He showed me how to squeeze the ice crystals out of the hole.[6]

Not only was the frostbite casualty rate for both the Eighth Air Force and Bomber Command enormous, but also men simply could not function efficiently in the icy cold.[7]

During the course of their missions many flyers suffered problems with vision, hearing, balance and perception as a result of trying to operate in a mostly inhospitable and always unforgiving environment. It was not unusual for airmen to spend hours in cramped, spartan and dimly lit cockpits or turrets with very little chance for movement. Blood pooling occurred, boredom was not unusual and, subjected often to the insidious effects of carbon monoxide, some aircrew even fell asleep or lapsed into unconsciousness.[8] Human engineering was in its infancy, so even the placement and operation of flight controls, weapons, or instruments often contributed to general fatigue.[9]

The result of this physical discomfort was frequently disaster, as a split-second of inattention, confusion or momentary lack of co-ordination could lead to the aircraft's loss, either by shoot-down or by accident. The effects of routine physical ailments could be magnified in the air, and, given the high cost of losing aircraft, it is no surprise that the physical care of flyers became the number one duty of air force medical officers.[10]

Having noted these impediments to wellbeing, it is nevertheless important to understand that the physical stresses of flying normally remained well within limits for the vast majority of aviators.[11] They were, after all, a fairly select group of young and healthy men. Occasional bouts of illness were to be expected, and compared with that of ground combat troops, the physical impact of flying was not considered to be so debilitating. Moreover, air stations in England were generally safe, and offered at least some measure of physical comforts along with the opportunity to relax and rest between missions.[12] The most significant impact of this physical strain was the additional burden it imposed on the emotions, principally fear, endured by aviators. Symonds and Williams were careful to note the impact of physical fatigue on airmen, especially as it added to their levels of anxiety.

Flying is normally accompanied by some apprehension, even in the most seasoned aviators. Quite apart from enemy action, operational conditions in Bomber Command were enough to increase any man's fears. Night flying, with its attendant difficulties regarding visibility and depth perception, caused understandable levels of anxiety. Men are sometimes less afraid of what they can see, so darkness brought special fears of the unknown. Just as often, however, a bright moon combined with the right cloud conditions illuminated the sky and made RAF bombers stand out like beacons. This, too, could seem terrifying to men whose survival depended greatly on stealth. Similarly, bad weather, which came so frequently, reduced visibility and did not allow crews to see the results of their raids.

There were a myriad other elements which contributed to an airman's level of anxiety. Even without hard data, it was widely accepted, for example, that married men, and men with sweethearts, showed more unease than bachelors – if only because they were worried about what might happen to their spouses if they were killed or went missing.[13] Domestic factors, including financial difficulties, pregnancy, illness, and divorce, added to a man's concerns.[14] There was a corresponding reluctance to allow families to live near stations, where their influence might alarm airmen and distract them from the task at hand.[15]

Men became anxious almost from the moment they were briefed about a particular raid. Some describe the tense and quiet atmosphere in the briefing room, while others recall the groans of men as distant operational targets were revealed. Even the hours spent in preparation for missions and waiting for the signal to begin brought incredible strains and apprehensions to the surface. Nothing, it would seem from the evidence, resulted in more tension than the sudden or last-minute cancellation of a flight. And even when the mission was 'on', some veterans report no let-up in the burdens. Night-time take-offs in Bomber Command's heavily laden aircraft could be harrowing in the extreme.[16]

Once actually on the operation itself the requirements of performing one's duties kept virtually all crewmen occupied. But the length of missions contributed to a general state of anxiety, especially if unusual amounts of time were spent over enemy territory. Naturally, the intensity of enemy defences also added to the worry. In this regard, each airman had his own list of specific fears. To some, flak was the most worrisome, while others were more concerned with the threat of enemy night-fighters.[17] Being 'coned' by German searchlights was frequently mentioned as causing an extraordinarily frightening and helpless feeling. One Bomber Command veteran later recalled it felt like 'being naked in broad daylight in Piccadilly Circus with everybody shooting at you'.[18]

Even the portions of the mission which took place after bombing the target were no less stressful. Long hours separated crews from the safety of England. Anxious moments were occasioned by the continuing possibility of interception, the unforgiving necessity of monitoring aircraft systems – especially if battle damage had occurred – and the ever-present danger of bad weather upon return. Crews were not truly safe from the moment of take-off until after engine shutdown.

There is evidence, too, that the alternating nature of air war increased the strain on an airman's personality. Both British and American veterans often recall the unreality of returning to a peaceful England after spending an agonizing few hours over Germany in the most horrific of circumstances. Many of them would be able to spend a few hours of relative comfort, and a few might steal some precious time with family, wives or sweethearts. Afterwards they would find themselves right back up in the air facing the same daunting odds as on the previous mission. The toll on the human psyche for such an 'on again, off again', war was immeasurable.

Life on the squadron was seldom far from fantasy. We might, at eight, be in a chair beside a fire, but at ten, in an empty world above a floor of cloud. Or at eight, walking in Barnetby with a girl whose nearness denied all possibility of sudden death at twelve.[19]

Although psychiatrists said at the time that some airmen's fears were irrational, these anxieties contributed no less to the burden to be overcome. This opinion was shared by many medical officers on various bomber and fighter command stations. Among them, Squadron Leader David Stafford-Clark was perhaps the most prominent.

Squadron Leader David Stafford-Clark spent more than four-and-a-half years in Bomber Command at Horsham St. Faith and Waterbeach stations. Feeling very strongly about the role of medical officers treating aircrew stress and morale, he not only observed more than 4,000 aircrew members but also went along on 15 combat operations himself.[20]

Stafford-Clark's observations of Bomber Command crewmen convinced him that the principal cause of anxiety was a flyer's instinctive fear of death, maiming, burning or capture. These were possibilities many had seen over and over again. It was, therefore, an airman's emotional reaction to anxiety that produced symptoms. In short, he was reacting to a conflict between his desire to do his duty, and thereby maintain self-respect, and his instinct for self-preservation.[21]

Like their British colleagues, American medical officers also produced detailed reports on the topic of combat stress. Eighth Air Force doctors were not slow to react to the problems faced by aircrew flying B-17s, B-24s and fighter aircraft. Pioneering work was done by Drs Douglas Bond, Donald W. Hastings, Roy Grinker, John Spiegel, David G. Wright and Bernard C. Glueck.[22] A commendable amount of co-ordination would take place between the Americans and their British counterparts. Even so, there would be some differences relating to how combat stress was viewed by the executive and identified by doctors.

Hastings, Wright and Glueck worked together to produce a summary of data collected during the initial 12 months of the Eighth Air Force's operations. The first work of its kind to be published, the report was submitted to senior authorities in Washington and covered the Eighth's critical period of growth and development between July 1942 and July 1943.[23] But it did not include comprehensive data on the fighter component of the command because during that period fighters were not particularly active.[24]

Like the British, the three American doctors recognized that flying duty imposed special physical strains on aviators which contributed to the overall stress on their personalities. In the American view there were certain mechanisms which 'defended' a man from excessive stress. Among these were his sense of patriotism, his understanding of why he was fighting, his pride in his unit, the quality of his leaders and his ability to identify with his comrades.[25] Against that was the overwhelming sense of fear engendered by the visible impact of physical harm or death.

According to one American view it was not just death or personal injury that caused fear. Airmen in both air forces were also clearly afraid for their friends. Seeing them going down in a flaming aircraft was bad enough; but having on occasion to deal with wounded and dying men on board one's own aircraft could push men to the limit of their endurance.[26] Some psychiatrists postulated that traumatic events might be endured for some time without an additive effect; but when incidents took place involving close friends the situation was different:

The experience of one pilot illustrates this point remarkably well. On his tenth mission the plane in front of him exploded, and what he took for a piece of debris flew back toward him. It turned out to be the body of one of the gunners, which hit directly in the number two propeller. The body was splattered over the windscreen and froze there. In order to see, it was necessary for the pilot to borrow a knife from the engineer and scrape the windscreen. He had a momentary twinge of nausea, but the incident meant little to him. As he did not know the man, the horrifying spectacle was at a psychological distance. It was two missions later, when his plane and crew suffered severe damage and he became intimately involved in the trauma, that the first incident was revived with its full traumatic meaning.[27]

Similarly, dealing with the human remains of aircraft accidents, especially those which had occurred in near proximity to home airfields, brought a special sense of anxiety.[28] In addition to all of this, to a greater or lesser degree, there might be fear of flying itself. For higher ranking men, more important was the fear of making a mistake or the fear of failure in front of others.[29]

As with British aviators, Americans often suffered their worst fears even before a mission began. It is not difficult to imagine the heart-stopping anticipation which went with the break of dawn at an Eighth Air Force station.

The worst part was being awakened for briefing, sullenly eating the breakfast, going to briefing, and awaiting the moment when the blue curtain was pulled back, revealing our target and the route to it. When it was France or the Lowlands, instant relief occurred. When the target was deep in Germany, utter terror. I will never forget how I felt on the morning of 17 August 1943 when the curtain was drawn and we saw the long, long red line to Schweinfurt.[30]

According to the data collected by Hastings, Wright and Glueck, the greatest tension was occasioned between briefing times and actual take-off. Various veterans recall cold sweats, pounding hearts, or 'butter-flies' as before a big sporting event. Nausea and vomiting were not uncommon.[31]

Although it is likely that take-offs were slightly less stressful for Americans – especially because the vast majority were in daylight – the rendezvous and formation procedures were extraordinarily demanding. The frequent occurrence of overcast weather along with the rudimentary state of electronic equipment combined to make this portion of any mission terribly dangerous and correspondingly frightening.[32] Tragically, mid-air collisions were all too common.[33]

Once en route to Nazi targets, American airmen faced virtually all the same rigours as did their Bomber Command counterparts. The challenges of navigation, formation flying and tending equipment kept them busy, but long hours of tedium could be punctuated by minutes of complete terror when combat started. Inside the large American bomber forma-tions there was great concern over German fighters and flak. It was frequently easier to observe the two in daylight and, to a very real extent, see the effect they both had on friendly aircraft. American doctors believed this played a significant role in the overall level of aircrew stress.

In simple terms, for some it was easier to be afraid when subjected to the repeated spectacle of seeing one's comrades shot down.[34] Moreover, these losses often occurred within sight of hundreds of American aircrew in other aircraft. The combat history of the 91st Bomb Group gives one graphic example from the Schweinfurt raid:

From 23,000 feet in the vicinity of the target, 12 B-17s were seen going down or exploding in mid-air. In almost every case an engine was afire and finally the whole airplane was burning. Thirty-six 'chutes were observed.[35]

On a previous raid to the same target, similar losses produced this recollection:

I have a graphic memory of those funeral pyres, those tall columns of smoke which were the last resting places of our '17s. The poor bastards! Subconsciously you felt, 'There but for the grace of God go I'. You could only live from one moment to the next.[36]

Of course British airmen were also subjected to the unhappy experience of seeing numerous aircraft shot down, often in brilliant explosions.[37] But the spacing and distance of Bomber Command's night-time bomber stream more frequently reduced the number of observers to these tragedies and may have mitigated an aircrew's worst fears.

Another factor added to the stress of daylight strategic bombing and distinguished it from night-time attack. Because American formation integrity was so vital for success and survival, it was generally forbidden to assist a threatened comrade. In fact, in some units, breaking formation integrity was a court martial offence.[38] For bombers this meant flying straight and level while making the attempt to fly in a tight defensive grouping. This certainly improved the defensive firepower of the formations and granted them the necessary bombing accuracy, but it extracted a significant toll on the emotional well-being of crewmen. Many aircrew recall that 'sitting and taking it' from flak and fighters was the worst possible stress and fear-inducer.[39] Formation leaders and pilots enjoyed only very limited ability to avoid flak and were obviously restricted in manoeuvring against fighters.[40] Gunners, on the other hand, might occupy themselves by shooting at the Germans, but could only watch flak as it arced toward their aircraft. Bomber pilots more often feared fighters, while their gunners feared flak. If there was an identifiable tendency, it was to fear things more that one felt helpless to act against.[41]

This partly explains the fact that fighter pilots often tended to show less anxiety than did their bomber aircrew counterparts. Fighter pilots were more in a position to 'control their own destinies' in any given situation. Moreover, many preferred the solitude of single-seat flying and the concentrated activity which that required took their minds off their fears.[42] Additionally, apart from personality or skill factors, they generally carried much less of a burden in the sense of having others depending directly on them.[43] Despite survival rates which, at various times, were actually less than that of bomber aircrew, fighter pilots evinced fewer emotional problems.[44] In sum, by virtue of being quasi-independent combatants, fighter pilots apparently had less to be anxious about.[45]

THE MANIFESTATIONS OF STRESS

It is clear that stress, primarily in the form of fatigue and fear, took a measurable emotional toll on Allied airmen of the Combined Bomber Offensive. Anxiety was accepted as the normal result of stress but, in the case of some Allied aircrew, the abnormal stresses of flying and combat led to excessive anxiety. This, in turn, had the potential to cause genuine symptoms of emotional disorder as some men were unable to adapt efficiently to the demands placed on their personalities.

Even at the time, defining the exact nature of these disorders was less important than correctly identifying some of their visible signals and treating them. In other words, physical symptoms were afforded more weight than the emotions themselves.[46] In general terms, and depending on which contemporary medical authority was consulted, the symptoms of aircrew emotional disorder were categorized in several ways.[47]

First, there were symptoms which openly demonstrated the effects of emotional tension. These might include changes in appearance, speech, or behaviour. Among the more discernible were weight loss, aggressiveness, irritability, insomnia, excessive use of alcohol, startled reactions and even hypersexuality.[48] With the abundant evidence of such behaviour all around them, even medical officers without formal training in psychiatry were not slow to recognize such signs.

No one who saw the mask of age which mantled the faces of these young men after a period of continued standing punctuated by inevitable false alarms, is likely to forget it. Their pallor, the hollows in their cheeks and beneath their eyes, and the utter fatigue with which they lolled listlessly in chairs about their mess, were eloquent of the exhaustion and frustration which they felt.[49]

Moreover, it did not take a doctor to tell aircrews that they were feeling the effects of excessive anxiety. Tempers flared, crews bickered, and there were disruptive incidents in the barracks and messes.[50] During sleep, nightmares were common, many of these having to do with aircraft on fire, exploding or spinning, with men unable to get out. To many men these vivid recollections of combat seemed inescapable.

Sometimes they had immediate consequences. About mid-tour, a co-pilot in a top bunk, in the middle of the night began yelling 'Fire, fire – Bail out', which he did and broke his leg when he hit the floor. The routine procedure was for your neighbours to wake you up and talk until you got it out of your mind, then try to get back to sleep. Sometimes that required getting up and going for a walk.[51]

A second general category of distress might reflect deeper and more severe problems. At this level some aircrew suffered a serious loss of keen-ness for flying duties, mental confusion, erratic behaviour, melancholic states, guilt or subsequent depression. An airman might be especially vulnerable to this if he had been a witness to or unwitting participant in the death of close friends. Loss of efficiency was an inevitable result. A few aircrew in both air forces showed evidence of this state from time to time. Dr Stafford-Clark documented a Bomber Command case which can be considered one of this type:

A Flying Officer Navigator, single, aged 28 . . . consulted me after completing 16 operational sorties because he felt he could no longer continue to fly. He was on the verge of tears throughout the entire interview and broke down twice. He said that he hated flying and that he had always hated it from the first time he ever went into the air . . . Despite this enormous handicap he was considered to be one of the best navigators in the squadron; a remarkable testimony to the determination with which he tackled his disability . . . His mood during consultation was one of utter dejection; he could neither smile nor laugh and he was acutely miserable at his final inability to overcome his mounting dread of flying, by day or night, operational or non-operational. Physically he was perfectly normal . . . His 16 trips did not constitute a full operational tour but his persistence in the face of innate fear of flying which had never left him deserved and received the sympathetic appreciation of the executive.[52]

In addition to all these signs, it was not unusual by any means, for men to show other physical reactions to severe anxiety. Air-sickness, headaches, backaches and various stomach ailments were not uncommon.[53] Sick-call rates were known to increase with higher casualties, but this did not necessarily mean that men were faking illnesses.[54] In fact, despite their worsening states of health during their tours, aircrew were actually less inclined to report themselves sick.[55] Most wanted to get through the missions and be done with their tours. Moreover, doctors knew that actual physical pain could be associated with fear.[56]

Finally, when the physical symptoms of anxiety got bad enough, doctors could categorize them as 'hysteria' or 'conversion reactions'. Airmen subjected to sustained or particularly harrowing experiences might respond with shakes, tremors, muscular rigidity or some other visible – yet apparently non-organic – physical phenomena. There were even dramatic cases of paralysis, blindness and catatonia, seemingly without any concrete cause. Thankfully, these conditions were comparatively rare.[57]

It is important to note that none of the responses to excessive stress were considered mutually exclusive. Aircrew subjected to a terrific level of strain during their tours might show symptoms from more than one category of disorder. For many men, periods of intense activity inevitably accentuated the symptoms resulting from fatigue and fear. On the other hand, rest and relaxation just as often brought a corresponding reduction in the strains. According to most of the evidence collected at the time, virtually all flyers suffered some of the effects of fatigue and fear.[58] But a review of actual emotional casualty statistics in both Bomber Command and the Eighth Air Force confirms that the overwhelming majority of men won the battle to stay in combat, even if faced with setbacks from time to time.

EMOTIONAL CASUALTIES: THE STATISTICS

For purposes of understanding the impact of anxiety on aircrew, and before summarizing the statistical evidence, it is important to distinguish between aircrew emotional casualties – those men temporarily or permanently removed from duty – and men who were grounded for what was considered their personal failure to face the rigours of combat. Men who fell into the latter category were known by a variety of terms, but very frequently were labelled by the pejorative 'LMF', or 'Lack of Moral Fibre'. Subsequent chapters will cover that topic in more detail. In the interest of clarity, however, this section deals purely with the men who, to varying degrees, suffered neuropsychiatric disorders and were treated as casualties of war.

It is fair to say that there were a large number of emotional casualties in the US Army during the Second World War. The total number of admissions for neuropsychiatric problems was 929,000, a rate equivalent to 44 men per 1,000 who served. Just over 486,000 of these men were permanently separated as a result.[59] Looked at another way, out of every seven American army casualties, one died, five were wounded, and one was a psychiatric case.

The alarming scale of these numbers was apparent even at the earliest stages of American involvement in the European war. During the North African campaign, for example, some American infantry units in combat were suffering an emotional casualty rate that approached 250 per 1,000 men. Significantly, treatment at the time was only returning five per cent of these casualties to duty. In 1943 the admission rate represented almost 6.76 per cent of the total strength of the US Army and, for units on the continent between June and November 1944, 26 per cent of divisional combat strength.[60] Such a situation could not be tolerated for long and, as a result, major efforts were initiated to understand the problem and improve the rate of successful treatment.

The Eighth Air Force was part of the US Army and therefore contributed to these overall totals, but it would appear that the rate of removal for aircrew emotional casualties – at 42.7 per 1,000 between 1943 and 1944 for example – was slightly less than the ground army's rate. Moreover, only about 40 per cent of affected aircrew were taken off flight status permanently for these difficulties. During the period specified, this represents a loss of only one-tenth of one per cent per month.[61]

Specifying an absolute total number of Eighth Air Force casualties between 1942 and 1945 is somewhat problematical. Evidence is fragmentary and, as will be explained subsequently, varying terminology prevented accurate record-keeping. A spring 1944 report stated that four per cent of all aircrews entering heavy bombardment units were removed from flying status, at least temporarily, before the end of their tours. Given that somewhat more than 100,000 American airmen served in the Eighth Air Force during the course of its bombing offensive, this would indicate that at least 4,000 were treated as emotional casualties at one point or another.[62] Moreover, this total roughly corresponds to the result which can be calculated from the 42.7 per thousand figure previously cited.

Dr Douglas Bond, assigned to the Eighth Air Force's Central Medical Establishment, used a mathematical correlation factor of one permanent emotional casualty for every two bombers lost in combat during the campaign.[63] Altogether the Eighth lost about 4,200 bombers missing in action, which would indicate a total of about 2,100 permanent neuropsychiatric casualties. This number corresponds with existing records.

It is important, however, to differentiate between permanent casualties and temporary casualties. Under criteria established at the time, a man removed from flying for 15 days or more was considered a 'permanent' emotional casualty. Once grounded for 15 days, such men generally stayed out of combat from two to six months and were effectively lost to their crews and units. Men treated for less than 15 days, often much less, more frequently continued combat flying.

These distinctions are important to reconfirm the overall picture. It is known, for example, that 1,716 US airmen were examined by senior doctors and psychiatrists at the Eighth Air Force's medical headquarters. One-quarter were considered to have physical disabilities, while three-quarters, or 1,230 men, showed symptoms of emotional disorder and were permanently grounded. These men, estimated to represent only 30 per cent of the total neuropsychiatric casualties, were classified and dealt with under the changing provisions of American regulations.[64] However, their number supports an overall emotional casualty total ranging between 4,000 and 5,000.

Final evidence for this total figure comes from a May 1945 report to the Eighth Air Force's chief surgeon. The report cites a total of 2,102 permanent emotional casualties, once again citing the 15-day criteria.[65] Adding this total to a figure of 3,067 'temporary' removals validates a figure just over 5,000 for the entire period of operations.[66] It is difficult to be more precise.

A number of details about these emotional casualties can be gleaned from various reports. Officers tended to suffer at a rate which was about 25 per cent lower than enlisted men. Psychiatrists considered this to be a result of their more rigorous selection criteria and their generally higher levels of education and training. American statistics also tended to show that crewmen who had less to do throughout the missions tended to suffer a higher emotional breakdown rate than those who were constantly busy. Crew position was also a factor.

As an example, one might expect that the rather exposed ball-turret gunners would have the most difficulty coping with the stresses of combat. This was not so. The most vulnerable position was that of the radio-gunner, a position on American bombers which was not only isolated and confining, but offered a very limited field of view for its occupant.[67] It would appear that being able to see what was going on in combat was as important as the freedom to participate actively. Bombardiers, navigators and bomber pilots, in that order, were less susceptible to accumulations of anxiety.[68]

Another report makes it clear that fighter pilots were the least vulnerable of all. Data on this group are somewhat sparse, but one report indicates only 106 permanent removals (under the 15-day criteria) for the entire period of Eighth Air Force operations. It should be borne in mind, however, that this figure, which corresponds to one permanent emotional casualty for every 17.5 fighter planes lost, ignores the much larger number of men who might have been temporarily grounded. And while the number appears strikingly low, especially when compared with bomber aircrews, when fighter pilots are compared with their real equivalent, bomber pilot aircraft commanders, the rates are roughly the same.[69]

Turning to British statistics, we find similar sorts of problems in determining the exact number of emotional casualties suffered by airmen in Bomber Command. The collection of data was uneven during the earliest years of the war and depended, to a very real extent, on the nomenclature and diagnoses used by different observers. It does appear, however, that the incidence of neuropsychiatric disorder was at least two per cent of flying personnel during the first year of Bomber Command's operations.[70]

There was to be a significant increase in this rate as the intensity of operations rose. By 1942, emotional casualties were reportedly running at five per cent of strength,[71] but even this number does not tell the whole story. According to a FPRC report, the five per cent figure included only airmen who were sufficiently impaired to require hospitalization or permanent grounding. In short, the figure did not include cases seen as out-patients or temporarily taken off flying. The total number of disorders among aircrew may therefore have been higher still.[72] Approximately 125,000 British aircrew served in Bomber Command between 1939 and 1945.[73] Accepting a five per cent baseline, this would confirm that something like 6,250 airmen suffered, at one time or another, symptoms associated with emotional disorder.

Other figures shed some light on the situation. Symonds and Williams recorded the total number of neuropsychiatric cases seen by the RAF's central medical establishment. They found about 3,000 cases of 'nervous breakdown' annually and estimated that just over one-third of the total, that is about about 1,000 per year, had come from Bomber Command.[74] To this figure must be added the large number of men who, as with the Americans, were treated locally and never seen by specialists. It might therefore be reasonably expected that Symonds and Williams's numbers generally correspond with the five per cent calculation. Thus, six years of Bomber Command's war would have produced around 6,000 emotional casualties.

Recalling, too, that Dr Bond's investigations revealed a strong connection between aircraft losses and emotional casualties, Bomber Command's 10,321 crashed and missing bombers tend to support a minimum number of at least 5,000. Although Bond's data were based on his observations of Americans, British statistics tended to support his views.[75] Professor Cyril Burt, a university psychologist, independently produced a study for the Air Ministry which also confirmed a high correlation between flying stress and casualties.[76] It might therefore be safely concluded that Bomber Command's total for emotional casualties fell somewhere between 5,000 and 6,500, with an indeterminate number of men never being recorded by senior psychiatrists or neuro-surgeons.

Thus, the numbers of emotional casualties for Bomber Command and the US Eighth Air Force were roughly on the same scale. Interestingly, however, investigations of British aircrew suffering breakdown showed occasional variations between the two crew forces. British doctors found, for example, that air gunners made up the majority of cases. This corresponds generally with American findings. However, in Bomber Command, pilots ranked closely behind gunners in incidence of emotional disorder . Wireless operators and air gunners contributed one-quarter, with the balance split between other crew positions.[77]

Why this should be slightly different from American findings is difficult to explain. After initial indications that commissioned and non-commissioned pilots were faring about the same, there was evidence that sergeants 'had not lasted the pace as well as officers'.[78] Dr Stafford-Clark, while sympathetic to non-commissioned flying crews, noted the difficulties which occasionally arose as a result of training and education.[79] It was widely accepted that 'imaginative' men – apparently those smart enough to recognize the dangers which faced them – were more susceptible to strain. Perhaps most important, after 1942 British bombers flew without second pilots. This had the effect of placing an additional burden on men who faced an already high-pressure situation. In the end, British doctors concluded that the relatively higher breakdown rate for pilots was due to the special stress to which they had been subjected. The most important of these factors was doubtless the psychological strain imposed by being solely responsible for the lives and welfare of others.[80]

British evidence also revealed that nearly 40 per cent of emotional breakdowns were occurring in crews which had not reached operational status, and a surprising eight per cent had not flown at all. It is likely that the period between the fifth and 14th operations in a tour were the most stressful. By that time the excitement and novelty of combat flying had worn off and crews became increasingly aware of their vulnerability. For many men, full recognition brought resignation to death and possibly a lowering of stress. But disorder levels increased slightly towards the end of tours as men who had survived that long began to 'sweat out their survival'.[81]

Based on a hypothetical RAF index of 1.0 created to predict the incidence of emotional disorder, bomber crewmen laboured against a 2.27 factor. An August 1943 report indicated that the incidence of neurosis in Bomber Command was four times that of the entire Royal Air Force.[82] In sum, it would appear that the rate of psychological disorder related directly to the amount of hazard undertaken.

TREATMENT OF EMOTIONAL CASUALTIES IN BOMBER COMMAND

No area better serves to illuminate the similarities and differences between Bomber Command and the Eighth Air Force than does the actual identification and treatment of emotional casualties. Both air forces were guided by medical and institutional philosophies whose origins preceded the events of 1939–45. Additionally, individual personalities played important roles in the practical efforts made to modify and adapt medical technique to fit the demands of combat operations. The results of these factors can be discerned by the dissimilar approaches taken by British and American authorities on the subject.

It is no oversimplification to suggest that the prevailing philosophy in Britain during the Second World War was that soldiers or airmen who broke in battle were innately weak or cowardly. Military authorities, especially those traditionalists who believed that courage was a function of background and breeding, were especially inclined to accept the characterization. Men of strength and character were judged immune from emotional disorder.[83]

Events of the First World War should have shown the rigidity of this view. To a few officials it had became clear that 'good' men might also suffer from the effects of stress. Although possibly a function of character, a man's reservoirs of courage – the ability to adapt to fear – were limited, could be used up, and were only replenishable by rest. Lord Moran later summarized it this way:

How is courage spent in war? Courage is will-power, whereof no man has an unlimited stock; and when in war it is used up, he is finished. A man's courage is his capital and he is always spending.[84]

As explained in an earlier chapter, a small number of distinguished British medical officers laboured to change even this simplistic view. Among others, Gillespie, Symonds, Williams and Reid argued that if enough stress was added to a man's predisposition, no matter how 'good' he was, emotional breakdown would result.[85]

Despite their pseudo-mathematical formulation, the two 'integers' of breakdown were subjects of wide interpretation. It is clear, for example, that in terms of predicting aircrew emotional disorders, British medical men placed more emphasis on predisposition than they did on stress.[86] This helps explain their great insistence that psychiatric interview play a prominent part in the selection and classification of aircrew. Moreover, intense scrutiny of men who had actually suffered emotional breakdown seemed to confirm the accuracy of the model.[87] Predisposition was most often considered the predominant factor; so much so that some medical men seemed comfortable with the traditional view that the 'correct' sort of men could be selected for combat operations.

Those cases with a bad psychological history, either familial or personal, should be eliminated from flying duties. Experience has shown that it is a waste of time to endeavour to patch them up or give them a rest, because they invariably break down again at a later stage.[88]

It went without saying that the correct sort of men were the kind who would put up a fierce struggle in the battle against fatigue and anxiety. Reflecting another view widely held by the executive, some British doctors believed that the identification, treatment or disposal of emotional casualties had to be swift and clearcut, because, they held that neurosis was an 'infectious disease'.[89]

This philosophy had an impact at the lowest medical levels, where squadron and station medical officers tended aircrew on a daily basis. Charged principally with maintaining the physical health of airmen, the young doctors – the majority with no background in psychiatry – were nevertheless forced to become the first line of defence against emotional breakdown. Generally ill-equipped by training, their major weapons in the struggle were their willingness to get to know their aircrew, their ability to understand their problems, and their skill in recognizing difficulties when they arose. This made a close relationship mandatory and, like the authority of leaders, rested on competence and credibility.[90] Moreover, the job was made doubly difficult by the natural reluctance of some aircrew to share their problems openly.[91] Some commanders openly scorned the opinions of specialists and showed their feelings by calling psychiatrists 'trick cyclists'.

Medical officers were admonished not to go around 'suggesting to people that they are suffering from a mental disorder', but rather to maintain a close, informal contact with aircrews.[92] Once identified, those suitable airmen suffering from symptoms of stress could, in the words of an expert committee on the work of psychiatrists, 'be put right on the spot'.[93] Prompt diagnosis was to be followed by reassurance and encouragement. Otherwise, the doctors were told that afflicted men were to be transferred quickly.

The intensity of operations all too frequently demanded a maximum effort. It follows that there was considerable pressure on medical officers to sustain their flyers in combat and make as many available to fly as possible. To do so, doctors needed to get to know the men personally, and even fly with them.[94] In the latter case, the risks were obvious, but if medical officers were going to be effective, they had to overcome aviators' general reluctance to share their problems. This, in turn, led to stress on medical officers because many felt a direct sense of guilt for those whom they had 'patched up' and returned to combat flying, and who were subsequently lost.[95]

Treatment for airmen in distress on Bomber Command stations varied from place to place and from doctor to doctor, but was generally not complicated. Preventive treatment took place as early as aircrew debriefs after missions. Met with hot tea, cigarettes and doughnuts, crews were encouraged to relax, smoke and talk through their experiences. In addition to the normal military value of such post-mission debriefings, these sessions and the inevitable discussions over bacon and egg breakfasts allowed men to ventilate some of their strong emotional reactions to combat.[96]

Despite the impediments, it was usually not very difficult to spot those airmen headed for difficulty.

Attention was drawn to an individual most often by a combination of factors, eg, remarks by friends that his general behaviour was changing in some way; fellow crew members were becoming concerned about his ability to do his job properly; he was reporting to the Medical Officer rather frequently with slight or obscure symptoms; it was noted that he was responsible for his plane's aborting missions for reasons that ground crew were later unable to confirm.[97]

However identified – either by doctor, commander, or self-reported – patients were usually taken off flight duties for a short period, given rest, warmth, sedatives, food and drink. British methods emphasized the value of sleep, so treatment manuals recommended giving men drugs like sodium barbatol. Medical training films explained that textbook limits should be ignored and that 'whacking big doses' might be required to allow a man to rest.[98]

For a large number of cases, treatment of this kind was effective. Sleep and time off allowed the men to recover from the worst memories of combat. Irrational fears and horrifying images frequently subsided and flyers had a chance to reflect on their identification with the group. Occasionally, men were granted a day or two off. Aircrew were sent to psychiatric centres only when their problems were too severe to respond to local treatment.[99] Additionally, however, some medical officers doubted the value of sending stress cases to neuropsychiatric specialists. There were fears that specialists far removed from operational pressures would not be in a position to evaluate properly a man who would not, or could not, fly.[100]

It is likely, therefore, that men who were locally treated – especially those grounded only for a day or two – would never have been listed as emotional casualties, despite actually being so in the strictest sense. This situation is what accounts for much of the previously noted mathematical uncertainty of overall casualty figures. It is possible that as many as two-thirds of all men suffering from temporary or less severe emotional disorder were successfully treated locally. This speaks for the professionalism and commitment of junior medical officers on the station. But it also reconfirms the courage and endurance of aircrews.[101]

Treatment at the major neuropsychiatric centres was more intensive despite the fact that the RAF's complement of specialists was never large.[102] The pressures of wartime did not permit extensive periods of time for psychotherapy nor especially for the complexities of psychoanalysis. The simple goal was to return as many of the men as possible to flying duty. Accordingly, treatment was usually administered in a three-stage process and, like that done locally, initially emphasized sleep therapy, lots of food, rest and relaxation. Afterwards, men were encouraged to talk out their fears with sympathetic psychiatric specialists. The final stages of treatment featured organized activities to give the men something to do, and then retraining to restore their confidence and make them feel once again part of the team.

Given time, a significant percentage of men could be returned to their squadrons. As ever, statistics varied, but in general, about one-third of all emotional casualties were eventually returned to combat flying duty.[103] Many even managed to finish their tours. An additional five per cent was returned to limited flying duty, but about 60 per cent were permanently grounded.

TREATMENT IN THE EIGHTH AIR FORCE

Turning now to the American philosophy regarding neuropsychiatric casualties, we find much to compare with the British approach. Based on the experiences of the First World War, the largest majority of American military and medical authorities accepted, apparently with little question, the model which suggested that predisposition and stress could lead to emotional breakdown.[104] So strong was this conviction that the United States Army instituted a massive psychiatric screening programme for recruits. Using a combination of examination and interview, doctors hoped to exclude the weaker elements of the population from military service. Unlike in Britain, there was the medical manpower and resources to carry out the programme. As we have seen, between 1940 and 1945 more than 15 million men were examined. Almost one million of these were rejected on purely neuropsychiatric grounds.[105]

This scale of early rejections led many to believe that only those strong enough to endure the hardships of combat were being admitted. Accordingly, Americans went to war with a great deal of faith that the system was working. So confident were psychiatrists and military authorities that insufficient preparations were made to deal with the numbers which actually occurred.[106] The first shock came, as noted, in North Africa where as much as one-third of non-fatal casualties were psychiatric. This was true in Sicily during the early stages of the Italian campaign as well. At one point, upwards of 10,000 men per month were being treated and discharged from the army as a result.[107] Significant, too, was the fact that inadequate facilities and treatment meant that only a tiny percentage of these casualties were recovering.

If these statistics startled the military medical community, further evidence to undermine pre-war suppositions was coming from the Eighth Air Force during 1942. Aircrew had, for a considerable period, been pre-selected for their intelligence and stamina. Tested and trained for lengthy periods of time, they were widely assumed to be among the fittest combatants, both physically and emotionally. But, as we have seen, from the earliest missions they too suffered emotional casualties. Moreover, the rates of breakdown, while arguably slightly lower than elsewhere, nevertheless seriously called into question the idea that pre-selection was the most important criteria. In short, by 1943, American military authorities and medical experts increasingly recognized that emotional breakdown could happen to anybody, not just 'the weak' and predisposed.[108]

This recognition carried at least three adjuncts. First, from a practical point of view, it shifted much of the emphasis away from predisposition and more towards stress. In other words, the intensity of stress applied, and the length of time it was endured, was more often considered the important factor in any emotional breakdown. Second, because by implication even the best men might eventually suffer the effects of combat stress, the stigma of emotional breakdown was largely removed. It followed that showing some of the effects of stress or becoming an outright emotional casualty was something to be expected and dealt with. Both were legitimate products of combat.[109] Finally, Americans were often less likely to believe that emotional disorder should be considered infectious. Although contentious and certainly not a universally held view, this was nevertheless vastly different from that common to British military and medical authorities.[110]

As a result of this philosophical view, the US Army – and the Army Air Forces – adopted a generally more understanding policy with regard to the entire question than did the British. American soldiers and airmen were encouraged to view fear as perfectly natural. Helped to recognize their own panic symptoms, they were told to direct them in a positive way. Training films patiently explained that 'everybody going into battle is always afraid'. Effective soldiers and airmen had merely to learn to get into 'condition red' at the right time. 'Fear', intoned one dramatization, 'was a fighting man's friend.'[111]

Even the terms military and medical authorities preferred to use for emotional disorder was a strong indicator of the reluctance to stigmatize men suffering from its effects. The American army intentionally used the terms 'combat fatigue', or 'combat exhaustion' to describe what the British collectively called psychoneurosis. The US Army Air Force's parallel terms were 'operational fatigue' or 'operational exhaustion'.[112]

Of the two, operational fatigue was considered less severe, because the term partly connoted the physical strain on aircrew. Operational exhaustion, on the other hand, came closer to describing cases which had progressed to the more severe levels of emotional disorder. By using these more understandable descriptors, and thereby avoiding easily misunderstood medical terms, it was hoped that men would be less inclined to see themselves as 'crazy'.[113] Moreover, commanders, many of whom admittedly remained sceptical of permissive medical diagnosis, might be more convinced that the occurrence of emotional casualties was the natural product of war itself. In sum, the appellation given to the state of these men was intended to indicate that they were sick, that they were recoverable, and that they were certainly not shirkers.

This attitude had an impact at the lowest operational levels of the Eighth Air Force. American flight surgeons in the squadrons, like their British counterparts, were charged with caring for the physical and mental health of their aircrews. Their simple and practical goal was to keep men in combat for as long as possible and remove them only when they gave an indication of breakdown.[114] Forewarned that all men were susceptible to the rigours of stress, flight surgeons needed to get to know aircrew personally; it was important to detect early signs of irritability, depression or personality changes.[115] For their part, men were not generally afraid to admit a certain amount of anxiety. In this regard, terms like 'flak happy' or 'Focke-Wulf jitters' were used openly, without shame, to explain everyday mistakes.[116]

From a practical standpoint American flight surgeons spent much of their time on prevention. By catching men before they got to debilitating stages of operational fatigue, it was possible to mitigate its worst impacts and prevent it from progressing to full-blown operational exhaustion. Personal contact between doctors and aircrew on the flight line, at briefings, interrogations and informally at clubs gave airmen the opportunity to discuss their problems.[117] Doctors were most often in the position of confidant or observer. When crewmen were identified as beginning to suffer the effects of prolonged exposure to combat, doctors could recommend they be granted a pass, furlough, or be grounded for a couple of days of rest.

To support the doctors' efforts, beginning in 1942 the Eighth Air Force successfully instituted a programme involving the use of English manor houses and hotels as rest homes. Despite being jokingly referred to as 'flak farms', these facilities, which eventually totalled 15 in number, were remarkably successful in providing an atmosphere of ease and freedom. They were designed as a place where operationally fatigued officers and men could get completely away from the war, participate in a variety of leisurely activities, and enjoy the company of hostesses of 'strong moral character'.[118] In an effort to divert aircrews' minds completely from combat operations, there were no military duties and the use of uniforms and rank were discouraged. The average stay was between six and eight days.

Expansion of the rest home programme never quite caught up with demand. Even so, a huge number of men – almost 13,000 in the first two years – recuperated in these facilities. In some fighter and bomber groups, men were sent as a matter of routine halfway through their tours. In other units, doctors sent men who showed visible signs of fatigue or after some particularly harrowing experience. Ultimately, about one in four men with 15 or more combat missions visited a rest home. One signal of this programme's success was that more than 90 per cent of men who had gone expressed great satisfaction with their stay.[119]

Despite signs of great success in dealing with operational fatigue, doctors were inevitably forced to deal with an unfortunate number of more severe cases. As in Bomber Command, most of these, which, if we accept the American definition, might be considered operational exhaustion, were treated locally or sent to a nearby general field hospital.[120] American procedures also underscored the importance of talking through problems, reassurance, relaxation, rest and food in the recovery. However, largely as a result of the North African campaign experiences of Drs Grinker and Spiegel, American flight surgeons more often emphasized techniques called 'narcotherapy' and the 'pentathol interview'.

In layman's terms narcotherapy encompassed general procedures which allowed disturbed airmen to 'sleep off' their problems. Drugs and sedation had long been used in civilian psychiatric practice and their use was recommended, even by doctors with scant training. Large doses of

1 Dr David Stafford-Clark, a medical officer in Bomber Command who did pioneering work on aircrew stress and LMF (author's collection)

2 Maurice L. Wells, rejected as a pilot for 'nervousness', was trained as a B-17 gunner and later piloted USAF combat aircraft in two subsequent wars (author's collection)

3 C. H. Chandler, Stirling flight engineer, recalled crew discussions on aborting damaged aircraft under the onus of LMF (author's collection)

4 Edgar Spridgeon, who won his American wings as part of the Arnold Scheme for training RAF aircrew in the United States

5 Thomas L. Hair (top row, second from right), waist gunner in the 385th Bomb Group, recalls men struggling to control their fears (author's collection)

6 William M. Thorns (bottom row, second from left), 96th Bomb Group, like thousands of other American airmen doubted he would survive (author's collection)

7 General Curtis E. LeMay, Commander of a Bomb Group and later of an Air Division in the Eighth Air Force (USAF Academy)

8 Squadron Leader S. A. Booker, Halifax navigator, whose experiences convinced him that a successful crew was like a family (author's collection)

9 W. T. MacFarlane (third from right) described vividly the haphazard but successful British crewing procedure (author's collection)

10 S. N. Freestone (far right), accused of an unnecessary abort, courageously proved his decision was correct (author's collection)

11 Theodore R. Milton, who retired as a four-star general, was the tough and successful commander of the 384th Bomb Group (USAF Academy)

12 Geoff Parnell, Stirling crew member, recalled being asked by the examining board the extraordinary question, 'Can you ride a horse?' (author's collection)

13 Urban L. Drew, American fighter ace of the 361st Fighter Group, was told to examine bombers leaving formations for evidence of damage (author's collection)

14 Colonel Hub Zemke, CO of the famous American 56th Fighter Group, was an advocate of aggressive leadership (USAF Academy)

15 Flight Lieutenant D. H. Hawkins, DFC, who like most airmen had great respect for the RAF's ground staff

16 Lieutenant W. F. Miller, pilot, whose bomber squadron lost 10 of 12 B-17s in a single German fighter attack

17 John C. Ford, tail gunner, who, like thousands of others, visited comrades in an Eighth Air Force rest home (author's collection)

18 Maintenance crews struggled to ensure battle-damaged aircraft could still be flown (USAF Academy)

19 Nose-art frequently displayed a healthy regard for the opposite sex (USAF Academy)

20 B-17s flying in formation over Germany. The vistas could be grand (USAF
Academy)

21 Bombing accuracy was the measure of combat effectiveness (Don Stull)

22 Accidents over Britain were frequent. Such non-combat losses were a blow to morale (USAF Academy)

23 Taxi accidents often occurred when airfields were shrouded in fog (USAF Academy)

24 Colonel Shilling in his P-47 (56th Fighter Group), preparing for take-off (USAF Academy)

25 Refreshments boosted morale after stressful missions (USAF Academy)

26 Intelligence debriefing sessions were a fact of life (USAF Academy)

27 General LeMay appraising crews after the raid on Regensburg, 17 August 1943 (USAF Academy)

28 Awards and decorations were very important to morale (USAF Academy)

29 Flak vests offered some protection from shrapnel (USAF Academy)

30 Wounded men were brought back from almost every mission (USAF Academy)

31 92nd Bomb Group pickles over target (Don Stull)

32 Ambulances on an Eighth Air Force airfield waiting for the bombers' return (USAF Academy)

33 Strafing at low altitude was extraordinarily demanding and dangerous (USAF Academy)

34 Eighth Air Force bases were scratched out of the East Anglian soil (USAF Academy)

35 A B-17 bomber and its crew

36 A Lancaster bomber and its crew

sleep-inducing drugs – sodium amytal being typical – were administered to 'interrupt a man's constant preoccupation with the combat situation'.[121] Men could be made to sleep from 48 to 72 hours usually without negative effect.[122] This seemed particularly helpful if the man had witnessed or gone through some particularly harrowing event. At some stations it became standard practice to give heavy barbituate sedatives to entire crews who had come through difficult missions.[123] It was expected that the long period of rest, supplemented by food and a later visit to a rest home, would allow men to return to flying duty.[124]

The pentathol interview – which might also be considered a type of narcotherapy – was a more proactive technique. Using what crews called 'truth serum', some doctors drugged patients into semi-consciousness, then attempted to talk them through their worst experiences. By reliving experiences which were at the root of emotional disorder, and by being helped to 'abreact' or release tension, men might face squarely and overcome their worst fears.

To some extent, medical literature and training films made both these procedures look easy. In the case of the pentathol interview, the fact that it allowed a flight surgeon to take an active and vigorous role in healing disturbed aircrew doubtless increased its appeal.[125] No figures exist relating to the number of times narcotherapy was employed but, according to the official history, it was 'used rather extensively in the field'.[126]

The results of the treatment are, however, easier to determine. The original enthusiasm for narcotherapy was tempered by data in 1944 which showed that only about 12 per cent of airmen subjected to the technique were actually returning to combat flying.[127] In a large study which followed the cases of 200 airmen, only 73 of this group returned to combat flying after treatment. Worse, of these, 37 performed poorly. Further studies confirmed that narcosis procedures were not sufficiently effective to support widespread use. Even attempts to centralize treatment under specialists failed to produce return to flying rates much above 13 per cent.[128]

Because facilities and time were constrained in the European theatre, it followed that a large number of men suffering from operational exhaustion were transferred back to the United States. While as many as 80 per cent of men there showed eventual improvement, only a few ever returned to combat. The majority – about 60 per cent – took non-combat flying jobs in transport or training commands.[129]

SOME INTERIM CONCLUSIONS

By way of concluding this chapter on the subject of combat stress, breakdown, and its treatment, it is interesting to consider a letter written in spring 1945 by Air Commodore Sir Charles Symonds, who, although a neurologist by training, shared duties as a senior consultant in neuro-psychiatry. His opinions encapsulate much of the prevailing institutional view of the RAF and draw comparisons with those of the US Army Air Forces.

Symonds's correspondence was prompted by a report he saw which detailed American treatment efforts both in the theatre of war and at reception centres in the United States. Writing to his superior, Air Marshal Sir Harold Whittingham, Director General of the Medical Service, Symonds summarized his views regarding American philosophy and medical procedure. He considered American efforts a control experiment against which Britain's might be measured. On that basis he was convinced, in his words, that 'the American introduction of the term operational fatigue was the main cause of trouble they got into'. Unaware, or unwilling to admit that the RAF's problems, whatever the definition, were on a scale roughly comparable to those of the USAAF, he was persuaded that by using terms like 'neurosis' to describe the same symptoms, the RAF had effectively minimized the number of casualties.[130]

Symonds criticized American openness, especially any policy which told airmen or patients that their condition of nervous tension was natural and to be expected. In his view, men unfit for flying with no organic basis suffered simply from neurosis. More important, use of that term helped prevent the condition, because aircrew considered the label a confession of weakness and would work harder to avoid it. It was considered vital not to give men any 'easy way out of combat'. By implication, neurosis was a contamination to be controlled before it spread. These and other widely-shared convictions would find further expression in the RAF's procedures for disposal of the special category of emotional casualty called LMF. As we shall see, the same was true for the Eighth Air Force and its institutional beliefs.

None of this suggests that there was any right or wrong approach to the subject of stress, its results, identification and treatment. During the Combined Bomber Offensive American and British doctors laboured diligently to prevent and then care for the worst of the problems which confronted them. If examining their efforts makes it appear that they were not successful, it is worth repeating that the numbers of emotional casualties never jeopardized the conduct of the air war.

Returning for a moment to the daily struggle waged by each airman against fatigue and fear, it is clear also that flyers in Bomber Command and those in the Eighth Air Force were assisted in different ways, by different philosophies, and by different organizations. Yet both faced similar levels of physical and mental hardship and responded with equal levels of courage and endurance. In the end, regardless of what medical experts or command authorities argued, for many men success in the struggle came down to finding the strength and fortitude from deep inside and from those around.

NOTES

1. When recalling this struggle airmen frequently used terms like 'fighting to control one's fears'. Psychiatrists identified one fundamental source of this conflict as the clash between a man's concept of duty and his impulse for self-preservation. See Roy R. Grinker and John P. Spiegel, *Men Under Stress* (London: J. and A. Churchill, Ltd., 1945), p. 36; David Stafford-Clark, MD, 'An Investigation into the Reactions of Bomber Aircrew to the Stresses of Operational Flying: With Results and Conclusions', (PhD thesis University of London, 1945), Stafford-Clark MSS, p. 7, IWM (hereafter cited as Stafford-Clark MSS); Interview with General Theodore R. Milton, USAF (retd), USAF Academy, 28 Oct. 1991.
2. A point emphatically supported by reports prepared after the end of hostilities. See Eighth Air Force, 'Statistical Survey of the Emotional Casualties of the Eighth Air Force Aircrews', 25 May 1945, 520.7421 1944–1945, AFHRA; and Symonds and Williams, 'Occurrence of neurosis in RAF aircrew in 1943 and 1944' FPRC 412(i) and 'The occurrence of neurosis in Royal Air Force (air crews), 1944–1945, FPRC 412(l), AIR 2/6252.
3. The largest number of these reports is maintained at the Public Record Office in AIR 2/6252. After the war they were edited and compiled into one publication. See Charles P. Symonds and Denis J. Williams, *Psychological Disorders in Flying Personnel of the Royal Air Force 1939–1945* (London: HMSO, 1947) and Dr Denis Williams to author, 10 March 1989.
4. Symonds and Williams, 'Investigation into Psychological Disorders in Flying Personnel, Section 2, Review of Reports', FPRC 412(d), April 1942, AIR 2/6252.
5. Grinker and Spiegel, op. cit., p. 29.
6. Similar sorts of incidents occurred in Bomber Command where clothing and equipment caused continuing difficulties. See Roger A. Freeman, *The British Airmen* (London: Arms and Armour Press, 1989), pp. 85–6 and Brice E. Robison (306th Bomb Group) to author, 28 Sept. 1989.
7. The three major occupational disorders of flying were low pressure problems (often called 'the bends'), frost-bite, and lack of oxygen (anoxia). These accounted for 12,200 permanent removals from flying in the Eighth Air Force. See Link and Coleman, op. cit., p. 679.
8. A Lancaster pilot vividly described 'the long grey hours before dawn . . . when each man was drained to capacity and the gunners had been staring into the darkness watching for the ever-lurking fighters'. L. J. Hay to author, 31 July 1989.
9. Craven and Cate, op. cit., Vol. VII, pp. 424–8.
10. Rexford-Welch, Vol. II, op. cit., pp. 43–5.
11. Stafford-Clark MSS, p. 7.
12. Rexford-Welch, op. cit., pp. 23–9 and Samuel A. Stouffer, Arthur A. Lumsdaine, Marion Harper Lumsdaine, Robin M. Williams, Jr., M. Brewster Smith, Irving L. Janis, Shirley A. Star and Leonard S. Cottrell, Jr., *Studies in Social Psychology in World War Two*, Volume II: *The American Soldier: Combat and its Aftermath* (Princeton: Princeton University Press, 1949), p. 352.
13. Tempest, op. cit., pp. 45–7.
14. Reflecting the views of some veterans, one wrote 'the UK has not got a very good reputation for looking after the dependants of those killed in the service of their country'. S. N. Freestone (Stirling pilot) to author, 20 March 1990.
15. Some station commanders felt that all British aircrews should be required to live on station and that families should be kept a minimum of 30 miles away. Symonds and Williams, 'Personal investigation of psychological disorder in flying personnel of Bomber Command', FPRC 412(f), Oct. 1942, AIR 2/6252.
16. An excellent memoir's title alludes to the continuing presence of anxiety on board each aircraft. The normal complement of bombers was seven men. See Miles Tripp, *The Eighth Passenger* (London: Heinemann, 1969), p. 37.

17. Statistical data demonstrated that bomber losses varied with defences encountered en route, defences at the target, weather, aircraft performance, and crew experience. It appeared that German fighters accounted for most of Bomber Command's losses. Even so, flak was much feared. See Air Ministry, *Operational Research*, pp. 60–73.

18. Various letters to the author comment on the sudden intensity of searchlight illumination. Other veterans wrote about their fears of fire, ditching or capture: C. H. Chandler (Stirling flight engineer) to author, 28 March 1990, Group Captain H. R. Hall, (Halifax navigator) to author, 19 July 1989, and B. D. Davis, (Halifax pilot) to author 6 April, 1990.

19. Don Charlwood, *No Moon Tonight* (Australia: Angus and Robertson, 1956; Goodall Publications, 1990), p.77 and Verrier, op. cit., pp. 201–3.

20. David Stafford-Clark, MD, 'An Hour of Breath', *Bulletin of the Royal College of Psychiatrists* 11 (July 1987), pp. 218–23.

21. David Stafford-Clark, MD, 'Morale and Flying Experience: Results of a Wartime Study', *Journal of Mental Science* (Jan. 1949), p. 22.

22. Hastings, Wright and Glueck collaborated to produce the monograph called *Psychiatric Experiences of the Eighth Air Force: First Year of Combat* published by the Josiah Macy, Jr., Foundation in 1944. Major Wright also collected a number of Flight-Surgeon articles and included them in a 1945 report entitled 'Observations on Combat Disturbances in Combat Flying Personnel'. According to a leading military psychiatrist, 'this remarkable document stands alone in the annals of flight medicine'. See David R. Jones, MD, 'The Macy Reports: Combat Fatigue in World War II Fliers', *Aviation, Space, and Environmental Medicine* (Aug. 1987), p. 810.

23. Eighth Air Force, 'Report of Medical Activities, Eighth Air Force', 520.7411–10 1943–1944, AFHRA.

24. In great measure this was due to the lack of a long-range escort fighter. See Hastings, *et al.*, op. cit., pp. 1–3.

25. Ibid.

26. Diary of William M. Thorns (96th Bomb Group), 17 May 1943 entry, copy in the author's possession.

27. Bond, *Love and Fear*, pp. 100–1.

28. Symonds and Williams, *Psychological Disorders*, p. 50.

29. A source of immense concern to squadron and group commanders, whose mistakes would endanger the lives of the men they led. See Major General James M. Stewart, USAFR (retd), Thames Television Interview No. 002889/02/01–02, IWM, and Grinker and Spiegel, pp. 33–4.

30. William G. Ryan (306th Bomb Group) to author, 11 Oct. 1989.

31. Interview with General Theodore R. Milton (384th Bomb Group), USAF Academy, 28 Oct. 1991.

32. Bert Stiles, who, like almost everybody, had his own techniques for dealing with the tension before a mission, decided that anybody who could make rendezvous easier, 'deserved to win the Legion of Merit'. Bert Stiles, *Serenade to the Big Bird* (London: Lindsay Drummond Limited, 1947), pp. 62–3.

33. John J. Cochrane and John M. Rogan, 'Experiences in the American Eighth Air Force bombing offensive', Thames Television interview No. 002821/02/01–02, IWM.

34. Robert Nichols, a civilian assigned by the Air Ministry to observe and document the experiences of Bomber Command personnel, had the opportunity to compare the reactions of American and British airmen. His notes support the view that psychological release was more difficult after daylight raids. See Robert Nichols, 'US Air Force Psychiatrists and RAF Psychiatrists', Memorandum 28 Nov. 1942, AIR 20/3085.

35. '91st Bombardment Group', 14 Oct. 1943, Record Group 18, National Archives.

36. Edwin D. Frost (381st Bomb Group), quoted in Middlebrook, *Schweinfurt,* p. 251.

37. One Group Captain recalled seeing no less than five British bombers shot down on one mission, each characterized by 'a small red fire, growing steadily into a larger red ball' before plummeting to earth. See Sawyer, op. cit., p. 83.

38. General LeMay also directed that a following Group never, under any circumstances, abandon its lead Group, even if the lead Group was off course or heading into trouble. See General Curtis E. LeMay, USAF (retd), 'Strategic Airpower: Destroying the Enemy's War Resources', *Aerospace Historian* 27 (Spring 1980), pp. 9–10.

39. Among other letters, John A. Tellefsen (96th Bomb Group) to author, 19 June 1990.

40. It is noteworthy in this connection to consider the difference for Bomber Command's air-crew. Experiments conducted in 1942 showed that the chances of an aircraft being hit by flak, whether or not it was taking evasive action, were roughly even. But the widely employed 'corkscrew' manoeuvre, even if only slightly more effective against fighters, gave crews something to 'do' during situations of high stress. See Air Ministry, *Operational Research*, pp. 64–5.

41. This does not, however, exclude the strong mutual fears of fire, ditching, wounding and capture. See John K. Bember (385th Bomb Group) to author, 24 Feb. 1989. For an excellent discussion on the impact of inactivity on stress and fear see Stouffer, *et al.*, pp. 408–9.

42. Psychiatrists reported that combat offered them an 'emotional outlet'. See Captain James Goodfriend, 'Temporary Duty in the ETO', 8 March 1945, 248.4212–17, AFHRA.

43. Stouffer, *et al.*, pp. 405, 409.

44. Data collected in the summer of 1944 showed that only 432 out of every 1,000 fighter pilots were surviving a 300 hour tour. By that point, 589 out of every 1,000 bomber aircrew were making it through. See Headquarters, European Theater of Operations, 'Survey of Fighter Pilots in the Eighth Air Force, A Comparison with Heavy Bomber Pilots', 7 Aug. 1944, 141.28 July–Aug. 1944, AFHRA.

45. Evidence relating to the levels of anxiety may be extrapolated from aircrew surveys. Seventy per cent of fighter pilots expressed a willingness to undertake another tour of operations after completing their first one. Only one in four bomber pilots was willing to do the same. Ibid.

46. This was doubtless the result of the fact that the huge majority of men were being cared for by physicians with little or no training in psychiatry. See Bond, p. 150.

47. Some psychiatrists believed emotional disorders came on in stages. An airman's initial 'enthusiasm and eagerness' gave way to weariness. Transient fears turned to permanent apprehensions. See Grinker and Spiegel, op. cit., p. 54.

48. In some barracks it was not unknown for the men to put out the lights with a burst of a 'tommy gun' or to attempt to shoot their initials in the wall with a pistol. Several men reported they had seduced women, in quantity, not for sexual satisfaction but for the sake of subduing and conquering their defences. See Office of the Air Surgeon, 'Report of Psychiatric Study of Successful Air Crews', 11 Oct. 1943, 141.28J 1943, AFHRA.

49. Stafford-Clark, 'Morale', p. 12.

50. Tripp, op cit., pp. 72, 79.

51. Walter F. Hughes, 'A Bomber Pilot in WWII', Photo-copied manuscript, nd, p. 71, 2nd Air Division Memorial Room, Norwich Central Library.

52. Stafford-Clark MSS, p. 53.

53. Symptoms which may be called 'psychosomatic disturbances'. See Colonel William S. Mullins, editor-in-chief, *Neuropsychiatry in World War II*, 2 vols. (Washington: Government Printing Office, 1973) Vol 2: *Overseas Theaters*, edited by Colonel Albert J. Glass, pp. 888–9.

54. Eighth Air Force, 'Effects of Repeated Daily Operations on Combat Crews', 9 Oct. 1943, 519.7411–1, AFHRA. See also Hastings, *et al.*, p. 60.

55. Stouffer et al., pp. 381–2 and Headquarters, European Theater of Operations, 'Effects on Combat Personnel of Number and Frequency of Missions Flown', 6 July 1944, 527.701 Jan. 1943–Oct. 1944, AFHRA.

56. Chest and stomach pain being common. See John Dollard, *Fear in Battle* (Washington: The Infantry Journal, 1944), p.8.

57. See Grinker and Spiegel, op cit., pp. 103–4; Symonds and Williams, FPRC 412(f) and 412(k), AIR 2/6252; Glass, p. 887; and Richard A. Gabriel, *Military Psychiatry* (New York: Greenwood Press, 1986), p. 43.

58. Grinker and Spiegel, op cit., p. 53.

59. US Army Medical Department, *Medical Statistics in World War II* (Washington: Government Printing Office, 1975), p. 43.

60. Martin van Creveld, *Fighting Power: German and U.S. Army Performance 1939–1945* (London: Arms and Armour Press, 1983), p. 95.

61. Eighth Air Force, 'Venereal Disease and Anxiety Removal Rates, Eighth Air Force', June 1943 – June 1944, 519.7401–1, AFHRA.

62. Office of the Air Surgeon, 'Report on Survey of Aircrew Personnel in the Eighth, Ninth,

Twelfth, and Fifteenth Air Forces', April 1944, 141.28B, AFHRA.

63. Bond, *Love and Fear*, pp. 126–7.

64. Because most aircrew physical and emotional problems were dealt with on a unit level, the Central Medical Establishment saw only a percentage of overall cases. See Eighth Air Force, 'The Reclassification of Personal Failures in the Eighth Air Force', 16 Oct. 1944, 520.742–4, AFHRA.

65. Eighth Air Force, 'Statistical Survey of the Emotional Casualties of the Eighth Air Force Aircrews', 25 May 1945, 520.7421 1944–1945, AFHRA.

66. The figure of 3,067 'temporary' removals is cited by Link and Coleman in the official history of the medical services. Against a total of 5,000 emotional casualties are about 46,000 killed and missing-in-action. See Link and Coleman, op. cit., p. 679, and Roger A. Freeman to author, 29 Oct. 1991.

67. The radio operator's compartment in a B-17 had only a small window on either side of the fuselage. The gun position opened upward with a similarly restricted field of view. See Edward Jablonski, *Flying Fortress* (Garden City: Doubleday and Company, 1965), pp. 323–7.

68. Grinker and Spiegel, p. 208.

69. 1:20 for bomber first pilots. Eighth Air Force, 'Statistical Survey of the Emotional Casualties of the Eighth Air Force Aircrews', 25 May 1945, 520.7421 1944–1945, AFHRA.

70. The RAF total of permanently invalided rose from 973 in 1940 to 1482 the following year. See AIR 2/5998.

71. There were doubtless variations from Group to Group, but even the aircrews in OTUs and instructors in Training Command were reported to have a four per cent incidence of neurosis. See Symonds to Whittingham, 27 April 1945, AIR 20/10727.

72. Symonds and Williams, FPRC 412(d), AIR 2/6252.

73. Air Marshal Sir Arthur T. Harris, *Bomber Offensive* (London: Collins, 1947), p. 267.

74. Symonds and Williams, *Psychological Disorders*, pp. i–ii.

75. Squadron Leader D. D. Reid, 'Neurosis on Active Service: Experience among aircrew on a Bomber Station', April 1943, in Major-General Sir Henry L. Tidy (ed.), *Inter-Allied Conferences on War Medicine 1942–1945* (London: Staples Press, 1947), p. 231.

76. See Professor Cyril Burt, 'The Value of Correlational Methods for Investigating the Causes of Flying Stress and for Predicting its outcome', Sept. 1944, AIR 20/10727.

77. Symonds and Williams, 'Statistical survey of the occurrence of psychological disorder in flying personnel in six months (3 Feb. to 3 Aug., 1942)' FPRC 412(g), AIR 2/6252.

78. Symonds and Williams, FPRC 412(k), Air 2/6252.

79. Stafford-Clark, 'Morale', pp. 16–17.

80. See Wing Commander Kenneth G. Bergin, *Aviation Medicine: its Theory and Application* (Baltimore: The Williams and Wilkins Company, 1949), p. 362 and Symonds and Williams, FPRC 412(g), AIR 2/6252.

81. Stafford-Clark MSS, pp. 11–12.

82. Symonds and Williams, *Psychological Disorders*, p. 170.

83. There were concurrent fears that because of medical explanations, 'the path out of danger had been made too easy'. See Richardson, op. cit., p. 63.

84. Moran, op. cit., p. xvi.

85. Symonds and Williams, 'Clinical and Statistical Study of Neurosis Precipitated by Flying Duties', FPRC 547, Aug. 1943, AIR 2/6252.

86. Professor Burt argued in 1944, 'Whether a particular man will break down depends primarily upon the kind of man he is, and not upon the degree of stress to which he is submitted'. Wing Commander D. D. Reid wrote that predisposed men should be removed from flying duty. Attempts to salvage them were 'useless and dangerous'. See 'The Influence of Psychological Disorder on Efficiency in Operational Flying', FPRC 508, Sept. 1942, AIR 20/10727.

87. Recall the 1943 investigation which showed that three-quarters of 2,200 cases of emotional breakdown were strongly predisposed. See Symonds and Williams, 'Clinical and Statistical Study of Neurosis Precipitated by Flying Duties', FPRC 547, Aug. 1943, AIR 2/6252.

88. Bergin, op. cit., p. 364.

89. Reid, 'Neurosis', p. 232.

90. '. . . the diagnosis and management of significant stress in aircrew were complex matters that called for an unlimited exercise of insight, imagination, and experience'. Professor J.

K. Russell, MD, (Bomber Command MO) to author, 26 March 1992.

91. 'The boys stay away from MOs. They know they are being watched'. Memo Robert Nicholls, 1 Sept. 1942, AIR 20/3085.
92. Rexford-Welch, op. cit., Vol. II, p. 70 and AIR 2/5998.
93. Meeting 17 Sept. 1942, AIR 2/5998.
94. At least one doctor won his pilot's brevet and flew 98 operations in Bomber Command. Among others, Stafford-Clark also flew regularly. See Dr Roland Winfield, *The Sky Belongs to Them* (Abingdon: Prunell Book Services, 1976), p. 141.
95. Stafford-Clark MSS, pp. 83–5.
96. Memo Robert Nicholls, 28 Nov. 1942, AIR 20/3085.
97. Russell to author, 26 March 1992.
98. Film No. 1167, 'Psychiatry'.
99. Squadron Leader Stafford-Clark believed that men 'who had it in them to complete tours' would recover locally within 48 hours. Stafford-Clark, 'Morale', p. 32.
100. Rexford-Welch, op. cit., Vol. II, p. 132.
101. Symonds and Williams, FPRC 412(i), Sept. 1944, AIR 2/6252.
102. Twenty of the 37 specialists were at the 11 centres designated to diagnose and treat neuro-psychiatric patients. See meeting minutes of the Expert Committee on the work of Psychologists-Psychiatrists in the Services, 11 Feb. 1943, AIR 2/5998.
103. Early disappointing results, as at RAF Hospital Matlock where only 25 per cent recovered in 1942, gradually improved as doctors gained more experience. In general terms, however, the longer the men had been in combat before breaking down, the better their chances of full recovery. See Symonds and Williams, FPRC 421(d), AIR 2/6252.
104. The relatively large number of emotional casualties in the First World War had made General John J. Pershing a strong advocate of screening recruits. See Lee Kennett, *G.I.: The American Soldier in World War Two* (New York: Charles Scribner's Sons, 1987), p. 28.
105. Despite the overall numbers, not every single soldier was seen by a psychiatrist. And even when they were examined, the interviews were often only minutes long. See Eli Ginzberg, *The Ineffective Soldier* 3 Vols.(New York, 1950), Vol. 2, pp. 26–7, 34–5.
106. Gabriel, *Heroes*, p. 117.
107. Facts not hidden from the American public. See 'The Psychiatric Toll of Warfare', *Fortune*, Dec. 1943, pp. 141–8.
108. Gabriel, *Heroes*, p. 118.
109. In a detailed study of 150 American bomber aircrew who had finished their tours, 100 per cent reported experiencing subjective tension in relation to combat. Significantly, 95 per cent developed definite symptoms of emotional disorder. This further supported the view that 'all men had their limits'. Among other things revealed by the survey were that 39 per cent of the men suffered from insomnia, 71 per cent reported irritability, 37 per cent were depressed, and almost half reported an increased alcoholic intake. See Office of the Air Surgeon, 'Study of 150 Successful Airmen', Oct. 1943, 141.28J, AFHRA.
110. Towards the end of the war Bond cited a special experiment which mixed 550 'healthy' flyers with 110 identified as 'emotionally disabled'. Over a nine-month period only six of the 550 were subsequently relieved for showing stress. In fact, the most important finding was that the healthy men had a harmful effect on the sick by talking too much about their combat experiences. See Eighth Air Force, 'Disposition of Combat Crews Suffering from Emotional Disorders', March 1945, 520.7411–2, AFHRA.
111. 'Introduction to Combat Fatigue', Training Film No. 1402, 1944, USAF Motion Media Records Center, Norton AFB, California. Copy in author's possession.
112. Terminology was a continuing problem in the Eighth Air Force. These two labels were in wide use and reflected notions which were formalized at the end of the war. See Eighth Air Force, 'Memorandum No. 25–2, Medical Reports and Records', 12 April 1945, 520.7411–3, AFHRA.
113. It was considered especially important that an airman should not see any reference to psychiatric problems on his medical records or transfer papers.
114. Grinker and Spiegel, op. cit., p. 167.
115. US Army Air Forces, *Outline of Neuropsychiatry in Aviation Medicine* (Randolph Field, Texas: USAAF, nd).
116. Confirmed by scores of letters to the author. See also Hastings *et al.*, p. 7.
117. In a decision which was particularly popular with aircrews, flight surgeons were authorized

to allow shots of 'medicinal whisky' at combat debriefings. Crews were watched closely for problems which might have arisen as a result, but apparently the innovation went over quite well and had its intended effect on improving morale. See Link and Coleman, op. cit. p. 664.

118. Staffs made equipment available for golf, baseball, football, tennis, archery, skeet, boating and bicycling. There were dances and motion pictures several times weekly. See Eighth Air Force, 'The Use of Rest Homes in the Eighth Air Force for the Two Year Period November 1942–44', 11 Dec. 1944, 520.747.1, AFHRA.
119. Headquarters, European Theater of Operations, 'Research Findings and Recommendations', 11 July 1944, Box 91, Spaatz MSS, Library of Congress.
120. Jack McKittrick, MD, 'Flight Surgeon', cited in Hawkins, *B-17s*, pp. 260–1.
121. Hastings, *et al.*, p. 73.
122. Evidence does exist, however, that sodium amytal poisoning, and even deaths, occurred from treatment.
123. Captain James Goodfriend, 'Temporary Duty in the ETO', 8 March 1945, 248.4212–17, AFHRA.
124. Insulin was sometimes administered to stimulate appetite. It was not unknown for some patients to respond by eating 12½ pounds of food per day and gaining half a pound daily in body weight. See 'Combat Exhaustion', Army Training Film No. 1197, 1944, USAF Motion Media Records Center, Norton AFB, California. Copy in author's possession.
125. Bond, *Love and Fear*, pp. 110–11.
126. Glass, op. cit., p. 868.
127. Original projections optimistically projected a 70 per cent return rate. See Bond, *Love and Fear*, p. 111.
128. More complex psychotherapeutic measures carried out at specially selected rest homes in 1944 returned only nine men out of 100. A unit for prolonged narcosis and treatment at the 5th General Hospital, under Dr Glueck, treated patients for between four and six weeks. At best, not more than 13 per cent returned to efficient combat duty. See Eighth Air Force, 'Value of Rest Home in Anxiety Reactions Occurring in Flying Personnel', nd, 520.7421, 1943–1945 Vol. II, AFHRA and Glass, op. cit., pp. 866–7.
129. Craven and Cate, op. cit., Vol. VII, p. 420.
130. Symonds to Whittingham, 27 April 1945, AIR 20/10727.

4

Attitudes and Morale in the Eighth Air Force

THE CONCEPT of military morale is difficult to define with exactness. Even so, its importance to the success of military operations has been clearly recognized for centuries. Scores of experts have explored the subject with varying degrees of insight while numerous explanations of morale have been put forward. For modern warfare Clausewitz's nineteenth-century magnum opus *On War* still provides a reasonable definition of morale by assigning to it the virtues of bravery, adaptability, stamina and enthusiasm. Together these qualities constitute 'military spirit'. When military spirit is lacking, according to the Prussian, 'the results will fall short of the efforts expended'.[1]

Clausewitz's thoughts are very much in line with the definition accepted by the US Army Air Forces during the Second World War. Cautioning that the term was 'abused and misunderstood', air force historians nevertheless recorded that aircrew morale

denotes an attitude of mind which, when favourable, leads to the willing performance of duty under all conditions, good or bad, and which when unfavourable, leads to the unwilling or poor performance, even perhaps to non-performance, of duty under the same good or bad conditions.[2]

Craven and Cate's definition is a necessary starting point to assess the morale of the Eighth Air Force during the Combined Bomber Offensive. Its key element, and one which was fully understood during the war, was that good morale led to completed missions. Because so often the overall success of air war was measured by operations completed, enemy aircraft shot down or bombs dropped, so too it was felt that morale might be gauged in a numerical way. This statistical approach to the question is characteristic not just of the air force but also, arguably, of the entire American way of war.[3]

In many ways, however, the whole exercise is an attempt to measure something that resists quantification. The truth is, no simple yardstick of 'good' or 'bad' morale exists today; nor did it during the conflict. Despite an air war which had elements of continuity and similarity, separate units and thousands of individual airmen each fought very personal battles. Disparate training experiences, different leadership styles, and a myriad of individual combat circumstances made morale a very personal experience.[4] Veterans today talk frequently about having fought and won a very private struggle before ever setting foot in an aircraft or flying a combat mission.

These reflections notwithstanding, during the war frequent attempts were made to gauge the spirit of fighting men. In fact, the record shows a considerable effort in this regard. Statistical analyses, surveys and questionnaires were commonly used to investigate and document the attitudes and morale of American airmen.[5] Fortunately, these polls still exist, preserved in various archival repositories.[6] Alongside these statistical data, are various letters and memoranda which indicate the concerns of the Eighth Air Force's commanders. It is worth noting that, at the time, the US Army's leadership linked morale with the rate of venereal disease. Arguably this dubious connection between a low rate of social infection and high willingness for battle, particularly in air force units, has never been demonstrated. Even so, the venereal disease statistics were meticulously recorded and invariably to be found under the general topic of morale.[7]

Fortunately, other evidence exists in the form of combat histories. These were largely the work of unit historians; typically young officers or junior enlisted personnel. Not surprisingly, these records are notoriously uneven in quality. Some of those assigned the duty of recording their squadron or group's combat participation, and by doing so giving insight into the unit's morale, regarded the task as an onerous burden. While most could write coherently, few provided any rich detail. Many apparently wrote the minimum necessary to rid themselves of the daily task, while others were anxious to avoid recording anything which might be seen as unfavourable. Despite this, there are occasional comments from which an overall impression can be discerned.[8]

These older sources are reinforced by the scores of more recent memoirs and reflections of veterans which have found their way to print. Much of what we are to know about the nature of morale in the Eighth Air Force must be gleaned from diaries, memoirs or first-hand accounts of various famous careers or important missions. But it must be kept in mind that many of these vivid, often gripping, recollections of 'how it was', have been filtered through the passage of almost 50 years. While scores of pilots, navigators, bombardiers and gunners have not been reluctant to record their impressions of what they were fortunate enough to live through, many of these reminiscences gloss over sensitive subjects or ignore them completely. In sum, Craven and Cate's post-war admonition to handle the evidence on morale with unusual care is well taken and still valid.[9]

For purposes of this chapter it will be useful to examine the subject in two major parts. The first, which might be called, 'Why they Fought', will encompass several sub-topics. These include the reasons men volunteered for aircrew duty, a survey of their backgrounds and nature, their motivation to combat, and finally, their views of the enemy.

The second part of the chapter focuses on elements of morale which were defined largely by the intensity of combat. In this regard it is important to understand the relationship between attrition, morale and tour length. Also, the number of aborted sorties gave real clues to the overall status of aircrew attitudes during the Combined Bomber Offensive. Finally, the highly sensitive subject of aircraft flying to neutral countries deserves comment.

By considering these major topics individually we can more accurately appraise the morale of the Eighth Air Force some 50 years on. In doing so we can move significantly beyond generalization to explain the origins and evolution of aircrew fighting spirit during the Combined Bomber Offensive.

WHY THEY FOUGHT

The airmen who eventually found themselves engaged in combat over occupied Europe and Germany as part of the Eighth Air Force joined the service for a variety of reasons. The US Army Air Corps – later Army Air Forces – had been expanding steadily since 1938. In the following six-year period, for example, it grew from 20,196 to more than two million men. At its peak in May 1945, the AAF had some 388,295 commissioned officers alone. But at no time during this remarkable expansion did the service suffer from a truly serious lack of volunteers. In fact, even as early as the autumn of 1943, the real problem was how to stem the vast numbers of recruits and deal with a huge backlog of men awaiting flying and technical training.[10] Among other things, these statistics underscore the patriotism and enthusiasm which was such a visible part of America's wartime airmen.

Veterans write nostalgically and unashamedly of their fervour, especially in the days just after the US entry.

You have to understand how it was. The war was a total thing. It was everyone's first priority. It was a time of great patriotism. Even before Pearl Harbor, people were going to Canada to get into the war . . .'[11]

In the frenzy of nationalism which swept the country after the Japanese attack, recruiting stations were swamped. Even so, it is clear that not everyone who jammed into the offices was similarly motivated. One typical volunteer, who was later to be an Eighth Air Force B-17 bombardier, wrote,

Facing the sure prospect of being drafted for military service I started 'shopping around' to enlist for some activity or speciality that was appealing to me – flying was a strong attraction.[12]

A similar attraction to aviation was to excite the interest of countless thousands of other young Americans. Despite the small size of the air forces in the years preceding the war, the United States had become an aviation-minded nation. Moreover, the military aviator held a special attraction and glamour to the public. Young men of the time were thrilled by stories of courageous airmen of the First World War, most had seen barn-stormers at state fairs, and almost all knew of the exploits of Billy Mitchell or Charles Lindbergh.[13] So when war came so dramatically in 1941, it is little surprise that there was a deluge of volunteers for flying duty.

From a very early age I became obsessed with being a pilot. It was my only ambition in life and since I didn't have the money to reach this goal on my own the Army seemed the next best way.[14]

It is comparatively easy to understand why flying seemed so attractive to so many. According to wartime psychiatrists, aircraft afforded very special gratifications to those motivated to fly.[15] Flyers enjoyed a special sense of power by controlling modern aircraft. In other words, dominating a powerful machine could be emotionally satisfying. Also, the visual and kinesthetic sensations could seem almost intoxicating.

The rest was wonder, a joy compounded of exhilaration, a limitless sense of freedom and reach to the very limits of the sky. How many pilots have shared this sensation which defies adequate description! The instant of knowing that the skies truly are yours in which to fly and soar, to glide and swoop, is truly a moment of sweetness incomparable to any other.[16]

Moreover, these feelings were not restricted to pilots. Virtually all air-crew members took a special pride in their ability to master a difficult and very often dangerous environment.[17] In simple terms, flying could be challenging, glamorous and fun.

The Army Air Force did an excellent job selling and maintaining this impression even during the war. Distinctive uniforms, badges and insignia easily distinguished airmen from their ground counterparts. Dramatic and vivid recruiting posters furthered the élite image of aviators and emphasized the exciting appeal of technology. Unreservedly patriotic songs blared from every radio and included lines like 'we live in fame or go down in flame' and 'he wears a pair of silver wings'. These were enough to steer thousands of high school boys and college students towards the recruiting stations.[18]

Combat flying was to be an exclusively young male preserve in the American forces and in the Eighth Air Force. Often the men selected for flying duties were mere teenagers growing to young adulthood.[19] It was not difficult for scientists to identify the general characteristics of the most successful volunteers. They were young, vigorous and healthy. More than half of them might be considered 'extroverts', but, as might be expected, many of these young men were terribly immature from an emotional standpoint. There were corresponding fears that they came from a generation which had enjoyed too easy a lifestyle and that they lacked acceptable standards of conduct. As it turns out, few had led independent lives before volunteering. Rather than truly representing the 'cream of the crop', they were actually closer to a cross-section of society.[20] Many probably had strong narcissistic components in their personalities. This was manifested in their powerful sense of invulnerability and was nourished by a system that told them how important and valuable they were.[21]

However strong the psychological support provided by this élitism, it mainly served aircrews during their training days. The realities of combat quickly dispelled most of their more glamorous and inaccurate notions, as well as many of the more general satisfactions of flying.[22] The truth is their motivations to combat had less to do with patriotism and glorified self-image than it did to their unwillingness to let down their buddies and their desire to get on with their jobs.[23]

As the intensity of operations increased, the hope of merely surviving was also a key. Summarizing the views of many, one senior bomber group commander cited peer pressure, self-esteem, cohesiveness and teamwork as the fundamental underpinnings of aircrew morale.[24] Of these elements it was principally the spirit of teamwork that allowed these men to participate daily in combat operations. This was true whether they flew in single-seat fighters or in multi-place bomber aircraft.[25] The cohesive unit not only set standards for behaviour but also rewarded good performance with acceptance and security.[26]

For most airmen this teamwork was manifested in their intense loyalty to each other and to their units. All other military factors were subordinated to the need to feel a part of a unit – strong and mutually supportive. The greater the threat from the enemy, the greater the need to grow together.[27] Flyers were intensely proud of their personal combat records and especially those of their outfits. Occasionally this gave rise to an inaccurate impression that they were more concerned about how a particular group was doing in relation to another than how the war was going overall.[28]

It is not difficult to find evidence of the strongest emotional bonds shared by the fighting airmen of the Eighth Air Force. Intense and lasting friendships between bomber aircrew members, fighter leaders and their wingmen, or flyers and non-flyers were common.[29] The formality of traditional military structure signalled by rank or position was frequently blurred by these relationships. In this regard the American system was probably less rigid than the British. US heavy bombers typically had a crew of four officers and six enlisted men. This basic team was rightfully characterized as a 'miniature army', but in many ways acted more like a band of brothers.[30] While there were almost always separate facilities for messing, billeting and entertainment, much informal socializing went on between the ranks.[31]

So, miniature army or not, bomber flight crews often had an element of cohesive family in them, complete with pilots as the father figure. Pilots not only bore the major burden of decision-making, but also were clearly responsible for the physical safety of crew members. One moment of indecision, lack of attention or problem with co-ordination and all could perish. There were constant reminders regarding the responsibilities of leadership:

You are the combat crew commander. In the air you are the leader, encouraging and directing your men. On the ground you are a training officer, disciplinarian and general advisor. You will catch hell in the air if your ball turret man can't operate a ball turret satisfactorily, and you will catch hell on the ground if your tail gunner gets the awful-awful in Piccadilly.[32]

Not surprisingly, these aircraft commanders were usually older than their crews, if only by a couple of years. Many, by virtue of two years of college education, seemed mature, responsible and worldly-wise. Few crew members, either in the air or on the ground, questioned a pilot's authority. An astonishing number of veterans still speak in reverent tones about their pilots, using terms like 'outstanding flyer', 'calm under stress', 'absolutely fearless', 'stern but effective disciplinarian', or 'best damn pilot in the Group'.[33]

Despite these generalizations, care must be taken to avoid the assumption that thousands of highly-stressed young men flew happily together without the slightest anger, strife, or problems. There were plenty of personality conflicts among airmen, especially if one or more crew members were seen as incompetent.[34] Sometimes these spilled over into the air and affected the cohesiveness of the entire bomber flight crew. In the case of fighters, these conflicts might develop between leader and wingman. Bert Stiles, a young co-pilot in the 91st Bomb Group, vividly recounted his problems with his bomber aircraft commander. Recalling getting along with the man on the ground, Stiles wrote:

But in the air I hated him. I couldn't fly to suit him. He couldn't fly to suit me. I never said anything, except cuss him out in my oxygen mask. I couldn't say anything. He could fly better.[35]

Most veterans recall at least an occasional crew with visible signs of personality conflicts. So aircrew personnel changes in the Eighth Air

Force were common. The goal had almost always been integral crews; that is, the ten men beginning and ending their tours together. But the almost infinite demands of operations, the unpredictable nature of individual aircrew health and the continuing requirement for leave and furlough, made it extraordinarily difficult to keep crews together from start to finish. In situations similar to the one faced by Stiles, voluntary changes sometimes were necessary. In the face of these variables it is surprising that any number of crews at all managed to stay together, but many did.

The necessity for fighter pilot cohesion and teamwork was likewise recognized, encouraged and rewarded. Several 'teams' even received wide recognition by the media. Among them Captains Don S. Gentile and John T. Godfrey of the 4th Fighter Group were arguably the most famous duo. These two clearly enjoyed some special connection which led to more than 36 aerial victories between them.[36] But fighter pilots were certainly not immune to personality conflicts. With life itself depending on the trust and mutual confidence of two men, it is little wonder that few were reluctant to dismiss those they felt had let them down. Finally, some aces did not completely accept the notion that they should be inseparable pairs in the first instance.

I found that most wingmen were more of a burden than a help in actual combat situations . . . wingmen, for the most part, were the new pilots, with little combat experience, and to expect them to 'cover your ass' was asking a lot.[37]

Despite the widespread recognition, both now and during the war, that this spirit of cohesion was vital to survival and morale, there were, of course, scores of other interrelated factors which kept men motivated. Dr Douglas D. Bond, a major contributor in the field of neuropsychiatry during the war, focused attention on another incentive for combat. Probing deeply into personalities, he postulated that aviators' motivation had much to do with an excessive love of their aircraft – he called it libidinization – and a concurrent aggressiveness stirred by fears of homosexuality.[38] Men whose childhood passion for flying had been manifested and satisfied by reading adventure novels and building aircraft models grew frequently into airmen who were most at peace with themselves in the air. Bond pointed out that outsiders sometimes considered those who were visibly in love with their aircraft and flying as slightly crazy. Even other flyers not so deeply affected frequently admired those who were, despite not knowing the cause. At least some of those 'afflicted' with this passion were aware that aircraft and flying had become an inseparable part of themselves. Significantly, the channelling of their most powerful emotions into the activity allowed them more resistance to the stresses of combat.[39] Furthermore, according to Bond, these same men reacted with aggression when faced with the impulses stimulated by a cloistered and virtually all male environment.[40]

There is much evidence to support Bond. Clearly, many airmen were passionately attached to their aircraft and were vocal about it. In diaries and memoirs aircraft are frequently referred to as living things – complete with personalities and even 'souls'. The positive attributes of particular models were extolled and their technical shortcomings minimized. Unavoidably, men compared the virtues and capabilities of various types and typically ended up defending their own. Those who flew Boeing B-17s, for example, frequently felt sorry for men consigned to Consolidated B-24s, which were viewed as less robust and more difficult to fly.[41] When asked, 89 per cent of P-51 Mustang pilots claimed to prefer their aircraft over any other, while a similar percentage of P-47 Thunderbolt pilots thought theirs superior. Ninety-two per cent of Flying Fortress crews thought they had the best plane, compared with 76 per cent of Liberator crews. In short, with individual exceptions, most airmen resolutely rated their aircraft the best for each particular type of mission.[42]

There were other visible symbols of this aggression and passion everywhere. Most bomber and fighter aircraft carried personalized messages or names, with the vast majority being feminine. Flight crew jackets often carried graphic pictures or decorative schemes with a mildly anti-social or more violent motif. Bond saw these signals as another sign of the strong connection between the uncertainties of male psyche and the need to demonstrate potency and strength.[43]

All this notwithstanding, it is impossible to rule out the fact that many thousands went to war as wide-eyed innocents. Very likely a huge majority of Americans were perfectly amenable to training, authority and discipline, but even among these many there was a strong element of youthful adventure. One must only consider the vulgarity of aircrew day-to-day language, the lurid names and often lewd artwork on their aircraft to recognize how important it was to test and prove manhood.[44]

Bond's analysis is further supported by the frank assertions of successful aviators, especially fighter pilots. The connection between sex, flying, competition and fighting was never very far below the surface. One ace jokingly but accurately recalls being inspired by war stories which favourably compared air combat to being in bed with a blonde.[45] A passage in a recent memoir probably summarizes the views held by many fighter pilots of the time and is worth reproducing almost in its entirety.

We were fighter pilots, flying the damnedest, fastest, most lethal airplanes anyone ever dreamed up, the forward line in defence of the entire free world . . . We weren't like other people, at least not in our own minds. We were bolder, braver, smarter, more spirited . . . better. Our eyesight was keener, our reflexes quicker. We were risk-takers who worked hard and played hard. We were confident, self-reliant, able to stand on our own and proud of it.

Most of all we were motivated, aggressive. Only the fittest and most competitive survived the training, and then the deadly winnowing out imposed by
our last and best teacher, the German Air Force . . . I enjoyed combat, which
is not quite the same thing as saying that I enjoyed killing. Combat was
exciting, addictive, a test of our mettle and manhood – a crucible in which
men became a cut above the ordinary.[46]

Such attitudes were not unknown on Eighth Air Force bomber airfields
as well, and were apparently frequently expressed, if perhaps with a little
less swagger. From the executive viewpoint, all airmen were known for
their 'independent' outlooks, most often reflected in casual attitudes
towards ground discipline, the wearing of uniforms, saluting or other
minor military regulations. This rebellion, while certainly not universal,
nevertheless represented an unconscious aggressive attitude towards
whatever restrictions were placed on them.[47] The aggression need not be
expressed or vented in a negative way. There were plenty of activities on
an air station – sports being typical and least harmful – which allowed
some relief. Even so, wild parties, drunken brawls, and fierce unit
rivalries were not uncommon. Overindulgence in alcohol was a favourite
stress reliever.[48] Ultimately, the target of most of this pent-up aggression
would be the Germans, and even the most frustrated or aggressive flyers
knew that teamwork would best see them survive the challenges of
combat.

VIEW OF THE ENEMY

Much of what America's young Eighth Air Force airmen believed about
their enemies was inaccurate and largely the result of the mass media,
popular literature and Hollywood. Just as they had few concrete notions
about the truth of combat flying, so too there were many illusions about
the nature of the foe. In an attempt to explain what the war was all about,
Why We Fight Director Frank Capra cleverly used German and Italian
film to show the tyranny and terrorism of both regimes.[49] So effective was
the result that the Army's Chief of Staff, General George Marshall,
directed that every American serviceman should see the 50-minute
movies. Allied propaganda frequently produced an image of a pitiless
Nazi automaton who rained indiscriminate destruction on cities, or would
machine-gun helpless Allied airmen in their parachutes.[50] Hitler's Reich
was rightly depicted as monstrously evil but the truth was that the
Luftwaffe's airmen fought very much like their opponents. Despite
occasional depredations, air combat over Europe largely conformed to the
rules of civilized warfare as then understood.[51]

Few would dispute that German aviators felt all the same pressures and
stayed in combat for most of the same reasons Americans and British airmen did. But, as in almost any war, it was felt important to depict the

enemy in bloodthirsty, cowardly and hateful terms. This was seen as rein-
forcing patriotism and having a beneficial effect on fighting spirit.[52] Even
so, evidence indicates that American airmen never quite accepted the
official line. Germans were more frequently seen as first-rate and
courageous opponents whose equipment often inspired as much envy as
healthy respect.[53] One contemporary report compared American attitudes
towards their enemy as one of 'intense rivalry', very much like a view of an
opposing college football team just before a big game.[54] In this regard, it is
no accident that Americans stationed in England quickly adopted much of
the language of the Royal Air Force, and usually referred to the Germans
with the relatively mild sobriquet of Jerries or Krauts.[55] While it is going
too far to suggest that the air war was fought with chivalry, it certainly had
elements which were clearly different from the callous brutality evident in
other theatres.[56]

The Eighth Air Force's high regard for the Luftwaffe's capabilities was
prudent, but could occasionally lead to problems. These problems were
more significant when they caused uncertainties about US combat skills
or equipment capabilities. American aviators were too quick, for example,
to identify any yellow-nosed German fighter as one of 'Goering's
Abbeville Boys', and assign to it undeserved élite fighting qualities. About
the same time there were related concerns, largely unjustified, that the
massive P-47 Thunderbolt would not compare favourably with the
smaller German fighters.[57]

None of this suggests that any significant number of airmen had
fundamental reservations about what they were doing. The goals of the
war were clear enough. Despite the fact that official patriotism and
intellectual attitudes about the enemy were not the most important factors
in keeping spirits up, they nevertheless underpinned those that were more
significant.

One manifestation of this in the Eighth Air Force was the aircrews'
commitment to the value of daylight precision bombing. Surveys taken at
various times during the Combined Bombing Offensive show consistent,
and strong aircrew support for the campaign. A sizeable majority of airmen believed their units were playing a critical part in winning the war.
This was true whether they were officers or enlisted men. Less than one
in four felt their efforts unimportant. When speaking of their latest raids,
over half said they did serious damage to important targets. Moreover,
this estimate of damage was a substantial factor in their motivation to
combat. There was a direct correlation between those men who claimed
effective damage to targets and those who believed in the overall value of
daylight strategic bombing. In fact, this group, by an overwhelming
margin, was convinced that strategic bombing would play an important, if
not the most important, part in winning the war.[58]

Interestingly, the surveys taken during the war reveal something else with regard to the Eighth Air Force's view of the enemy. Perhaps not surprisingly, a number of Americans in Britain were listening to German radio during the war. The practice was frowned upon officially, but continued throughout the Combined Bomber Offensive. There were corresponding concerns that the morale of crewmen would be affected or that their attitudes towards the Germans would be somehow softened. Anonymous surveys of 3,000 officers and men just before D-Day revealed that one-quarter were tuning in more than three times a week, with at least 15 per cent listening every day. Without saying why the men listened, the survey showed that only two in ten admitted to believing anything they heard. Additionally, 38 per cent of those questioned believed there was very little truth in the broadcasts. The data collected came to the encouraging conclusion that listening to German radio had no adverse effect on attitudes toward combat flying or toward the value of strategic bombing.[59]

Some recent scholarship might give the impression that American airmen found themselves fighting a wholly impersonal war, engaged with a faceless enemy from a great distance away.[60] While many narratives comment on this sense of remoteness, the evidence which makes the opposite case is far more compelling. Contrary to the notion that airmen were mere technicians, 'not concerned with killing and . . . hardly aware of an enemy', the truth is that many had come face-to-face with death and destruction. Countless hundreds, even thousands, saw combat of terrible intensity, and, despite the mind-numbing technical aspects of flying, nevertheless took the time to contemplate the effects of their weapons on other human beings.

Bomber aircrew, especially those directly concerned with flying or dropping bombs, even had occasional reservations about what they were doing. Some, like Stiles, admitted they had no hatred for Germans and thought the idea of inflicting civilian casualties repugnant. The cynicism born of this repugnance is a feature of one B-17 navigator's recollections:

Our losses, including those of the main and diversionary forces, amounted to twenty planes, two hundred men, roughly ten per cent. Nevertheless, our superiors were pleased with us because we had dropped 422 tons of bombs and, according to the reconnaissance photos, only 333.4 tons had been wasted on homes, streets, public parks, zoos, department stores and air-raid shelters. This passed for precision.[61]

If gunners on bombers expressed fewer reservations, perhaps it was because they were more involved in hair-raising, face-to-face encounters with German fighters. As reel after reel of captured German gun-camera film makes graphically clear, most of these confrontations were neither as 'remote' nor 'antiseptic' as some might conclude.[62] In fact, whether attacking from the front or from directly astern, the Germans often came well within 100 yards before delivering their deadliest blows. Scores of

American veterans can even recall seeing individual Luftwaffe pilots moving about in their cockpits as they flashed by.

Similarly, fighter pilots sometimes saw the Germans very close-up. Trained to get to minimum range before shooting, those who were fortunate enough to secure an advantage in a dogfight frequently saw the terrible impact of cannon and machine-gun fire on vulnerable aircraft and fragile human bodies.

The tracers race upward and find him. The bullets chew at the wing root, the cockpit, the engine, making bright little flashes. I hose the Messerschmitt down the way you'd hose down a campfire, methodically, from one end to the other, not wanting to make a mistake here . . . My momentum carries me to him. I throttle back to ease my plane alongside, just off his right wing. Have I killed him? I do not particularly want to fight this man again. I am coming up even with the cockpit, and although I figure the less I know about him the better, I find myself looking in spite of myself . . . and then he falls away suddenly . . .

This narrative concludes with the veteran asking himself whether or not he felt any permanent guilt for what he had done. After struggling with remorse briefly, he concluded, 'Not then, and not now'.[63]

Others shared the fascination for combat but appeared untroubled by any remorseful emotions at all:

I had no idea why the German people were stuck with Hitler and the Nazis and could not care less. History was not one of my strong subjects. But when the time came, I would hammer those Germans any chance I got. Them or me. Even a 'D' history student from Hamlin High knew that it was always better to be the hammer than the nail.[64]

This kind of passage makes it impossible to exclude the supposition that many aviators took some measure of pleasure or delight in the destruction of the enemy.[65] The spectacle of exploding or crashing German aircraft or the destructive effects of incendiary and high-explosive bombs doubtless stirred many,[66] but psychiatrists during the time found that true hatred of the enemy motivated only a few. and almost none of the most successful.[67]

One of the reasons for this was that anger generated over casualties and the death of comrades generally faded away. Whatever vindictiveness or moral blunting existed was not the result of heavy losses but rather the by-product of enemy atrocities. As these were comparatively rare in the air, the issues behind the war and thoughts of revenge were less important to airmen than the struggle for day-to-day survival.[68]

Undeniably, some airmen of the Eighth Air Force had only fleeting impressions of the Germans. Missions might be hours long with the chance encounter with the enemy lasting only seconds. Some American aviators may never have actually come in contact at all. A great many others had many missions where they felt as if they were engaged with the

Germans almost from take-off until their wheels touched down on landing. Moreover, even if during the course of a normal mission the actual time engaged with the enemy seemed relatively short, the frequency and intensity of these encounters, not to mention the results, certainly left a huge impression on American airmen. A summary of casualties between January and June 1944 showed that in just six months returning aircraft brought back 1,175 dead and 4,689 wounded airmen. These grim statistics dispel the notion that Eighth Air Force airmen could have been 'distanced from the war and the enemy's threat' as has been suggested.[69]

It is no accident that long hours were devoted to mission planning and preparation for the terrifying moments of combat. German training, tactics and equipment were diligently investigated and studied. This would not only help increase the accuracy of American bombers and improve the efficacy of American fighters, but also simultaneously reduce German defensive effectiveness. The fundamental goal was to lower the Eighth Air Force's attrition rate because attrition was linked to morale.

ATTRITION, MORALE AND TOUR LENGTH

Central to the beliefs of America's air strategists during the Second World War was the notion that 'the bomber would always get through', and that daylight precision-bombing could therefore be conducted with acceptable loss rates.[70] Unfortunately for Eighth Air Force aircrews, however, the American air war plan, originally called AWPD-1, failed to define 'acceptable' in any real sense. Optimistic and naïve projections about bombers being able to strike long-range targets and defend themselves without escort crumbled under the realities of combat.[71] By December 1942, for example, Eighth Air Force bombers were suffering a 5.8 per cent loss rate as a percentage of total effective sorties. During 1943 the overall attrition rate increased, even reaching 9.2 per cent during the month of October.[72] On the second mission to Schweinfurt, 60 aircraft, or fully 20 per cent of the attacking force, were lost.[73] This brought the average to more than five per cent for the entire year.

The impact of this scale of attrition could be calculated with mathematical precision. If 1,000 men began operations in the face of a five per cent attrition rate, only 277 could be expected to remain available for duty after 25 missions. Increasing the number of missions to 30 reduced the number of survivors to 215 while 35 missions allowed only 165.[74] Calculations like these were done from the beginning of the campaign, prompting early recognition that heavy bombardment missions over Europe were 'the most hazardous military operations which have been conducted over a sustained period'.[75]

Studies by the Eighth Air Force's chief flight surgeon, Brigadier

General Malcolm Grow, in January and February 1944 reconfirmed the hazardous nature of operations while linking loss rates explicitly to experience levels and morale. During the period covered by the reports just over one man in four was surviving a 25-mission tour. Crew members arriving incrementally as replacements affected the unit's overall experience level by lowering it. They also probably had an adverse impact on unit cohesion, at least initially. At the end of the 25th mission the effect might be particularly dramatic as more than a quarter of the unit – the survivors – had to be replaced all at once.[76] Moreover, while few crewmen may have been statistical experts, it did not take a mathematical genius to consider the long odds against survival. The visual impact of empty bunks and the constant influx of new faces were stark reminders of bleak prospects. Reflecting a view mutually held by medical authorities and the executive, Grow wrote that 'morale of crews is primarily influenced by their having a reasonable chance of survival'.[77]

It is evident that the Eighth Air Force's commanders understood the link between morale and attrition rate early in the campaign. Further support came from Dr Bond, who convincingly demonstrated a correlation between the number of emotional casualties and the number of aircraft lost. Emotional casualties had long been thought of as a signal of morale. Bond discovered between May 1943 and May 1944 that there was one emotional casualty for every two aircraft lost. In other words, as attrition increased, the number of permanent groundings for battle fatigue increased at about half the same rate.[78] Almost all Eighth Air Force units experienced periods where unrelenting demands for operations, poor weather and German opposition led to high attrition rates. This, combined with a large turnover of new crews or poor bombing results, contributed to increasing strain on already fatigued airmen. Many veterans frankly recall these difficult periods.[79]

It is important not to carry Bond's correlation between attrition and morale too far. Some of the bomber groups in the Eighth Air Force seeing the most intense combat and subjected to the highest attrition managed to sustain their fighting spirit.[80] Nevertheless, those in charge saw the necessity of using some method to ameliorate the effects of aircrew casualties and aircraft losses. The best way seemed to be to establish a set length of time for which men had to stay in combat.

From the beginning there was constant pressure to fix these tours of duty, as it was recognized that men could be used up like any expendable. It was easily recognized that heavy casualties had a depressing effect on morale. As early as December 1942 American airmen were experiencing visible signs of fatigue and were asking for a 'yardstick' of performance. In a letter to General Hap Arnold, Major General Spaatz stressed that the crews were still full of fight but that some operational limit was needed.[81] After initially opposing the suggestion and expressing some uncertainty regarding the actual criteria, Arnold eventually directed his theatre commanders to determine the policy for their areas individually.

Brigadier General Ira Eaker, the commander of the bomber component in the Eighth Air Force, felt strongly that for a man to stay and fight he needed at least an even chance of survival. He had accepted this position after some early discussions with Sir Arthur Harris. As with his British counterpart, Eaker's real problem was to balance his crews' chances of survival with operational needs. In 1942 he was under great pressure to get the daylight bombing campaign under way. A long tour length might increase the number of crews available, at least for a time, but would also have an adverse effect on their willingness and capability to sustain combat. Conversely, too short a tour length would restrict the manpower available by sending many men home early and put too great a strain on the facilities training their replacements. Additionally, research showed that once a crew had made it past the first five missions, the chances for survival increased.[82]

Disregarding some of the grimmer statistical evidence of the British experience, Eaker optimistically accepted the prediction of a two- or 2.5 per cent attrition rate for bombers and three per cent for fighters – based on 10–12 missions per month respectively.[83] Combining all the factors, Eaker's staff officers and others in Washington worked backward through the mathematics and deemed a minimum tour of 25 missions for bomber crews sufficient. Fighter pilot tours were initially set at 150 hours. Although the maximums were set at 30 missions and 200 hours respectively, until later in the war the upper limits were ignored. Even with the lower requirement,

It is quite evident . . . that a combat crew must be very good or very lucky to complete an operational tour by the above yardstick. We cannot expect them to do more efficiently.[84]

General Spaatz, Eaker's commander, went along with the policy. He continued to do so when he assumed overall command of US Strategic Air Forces, Europe.[85]

From the aircrew point of view there were problems with such a mathematical approach to their survival. First, of course, was the fact that attrition rates never quite matched the model and, for much of the campaign, much less than 50 per cent would actually come through. Second, pure mathematics ignores the nature of the casualties, which sometimes seemed more important than the actual numbers. In units that had been in combat a long time, the loss of new crews sometimes had almost no effect while the death of close friends or key leaders could be devastating. Some losses could be treated quite casually, even coldly, as if part of the daily routine.[86] But others, especially if sustained over a long period or linked to a perceived lack of success against the enemy, had a terrifically depressing effect.[87] Third, no simple actuarial accounting could compensate for the vagaries of individual missions.

Relatively easy, short-range missions to France might suffer few casualties, while deep penetrations to Germany inevitably suffered crippling losses, at least until long-range escort fighters became available. During each one month period from May to October 1943, for example, almost a full third of all available crewmen were lost. These 6,300 killed and missing represented a 200 per cent turnover in personnel, and even aircraft that returned safely very often brought back cargoes of wounded and dying airmen.[88] Finally, by setting limits on the flying tour, the authorities unwittingly created a contractual arrangement between flyers and the air force.[89] Some men, perhaps understandably, saw the completion of their tours as fulfilling all their responsibility to the war effort. When General Jimmy Doolittle officially increased the minimum tour to 30 missions in the spring of 1944, there was a predictable drop in unit morale, and he was the subject of bitter feelings by many, especially bomber crew members, who felt their 'contracts' had been unfairly broken.[90] Worse, perhaps, USAAF headquarters in Washington eventually recommended the abolishment of tour lengths altogether, substituting 'positive evidence of combat fatigue' as the requirement for relief from combat flying duties. The Eighth Air Force circumvented this remarkably short-sighted proposal and, in practice, tour lengths based on missions remained the norm.[91] Even so, at various periods, a very few men, characterized decades later as 'barrack-room accountants', spent much of their time calculating odds of survival and disturbed those among the vast majority who were rightly concerned with just doing their jobs.[92]

ABORTED SORTIES

During all phases of the Eighth Air Force's operations the daily number of sorties was monitored very carefully. As was inevitable in any campaign on this scale, especially one involving the repetitive employment of hundreds of complex aircraft and thousands of demanding missions, there were aircraft and aircrews which, for one reason or another, failed to complete their assigned tasks. Between 1942 and 1945 the Eighth Air Force flew more than 300,000 bomber sorties alone. A similarly huge number of fighter operations were scheduled. Inevitably some aircraft had to turn back. 'Abortives', as these missions were called, obviously affected overall effectiveness by reducing the available offensive or defensive firepower of the formations and, in the case of bombers, decreasing the amount of bombs on target. A major portion of a Bombardment or Fighter Group's overall efficiency rating rested on the number of completed sorties it could manage. Naturally, there were other measures – number of enemy aircraft shot down or bomb damage assessments – but these could never be as accurately quantified. So, sortie counting became an easy yardstick of success. Not surprisingly, then, considerable effort was expended investigating aborts.

In the Eighth Air Force there was a statistical control unit whose responsibility it was to summarize mission data and make periodic reports to the Eighth's commanders. The information was quite detailed and included abort statistics. It is interesting to examine the report of this unit for a one-month period to consider its implications. In January 1944, for example, a total of 6,770 heavy bombers took off on operational missions over enemy and enemy-occupied territory. According to the data, 4,745 or 70 per cent completed their missions and 2,025 or 30 per cent failed. By any measure, 30 per cent is a large figure, but slightly more than half of these aircraft (1,241) turned back because of weather-related problems. Another 446 returned for mechanical reasons, primarily problems with engines or superchargers. A further seven per cent of aborts were due to miscellaneous equipment failure, with oxygen systems, turrets and electrics the prime offenders.[93]

It is no surprise that weather and various mechanical problems would cause the bulk of aborts. Great Britain was certainly not known for the predictable quality of its flying weather and the unsophisticated flight instruments of the day did not encourage pushing the limits.[94] The worst months for weather aborts were January to April, with the toll averaging almost 20 per cent of all bomber sorties.[95] Moreover, the long bouts of cold, wet weather along with inadequate hangar facilities further contributed to a maintenance nightmare for mechanics and ground-crews, and this does not include the immense difficulty of repairing battle-damaged aircraft. Even so, tremendous efforts were made during the campaign to improve the quality of engineering support.[96] Still, besides more accurate forecasting, little could be done about the weather.

Mechanical defects and bad weather did not furnish all the reasons for abortives, however. The record also shows 109 aircraft returning during the month for 'personal failures'. Without giving individual details, the information was supplied to Eighth Air Force's senior commanders and flight surgeons. This five per cent of sorties attracted considerable interest because everyone at the time, from commanding general to tail-gunner, knew it was a reflection not just of the physical health of a unit but also of its morale.

A unit's reputation rested on many factors, but clearly the number of aborts was one of them. According to more than one commander, poor groups showed evidence not only of sloppy ground discipline and weak formation flying, but a high number of aborts as well.[97] Frequently, too, there was a correlation between the number of aborts on a particular mission and the target selected for that day. The further away or more difficult the target, the higher the number of aborts. Such facts did not escape the attention of the leadership. At various times several groups had higher than average return rates.[98]

Given the importance of sustaining morale, part of the concern for aborts came as result of uncertainties regarding their actual cause. The overwhelming majority of 'personal failures' probably came as a result of physiological problems – air sickness, anoxia or pressure altitude disorders being the most common. But as might be expected under the circumstances, some crews got the reputation for aborting unnecessarily and faced terrific pressure to explain why. One Group Commander even established a policy of making aborting aircraft, those without safety or flight problems, circle the airfield until all others from the mission had successfully landed.[99]

To a very real extent all crew members were interdependent, but sometimes the decisions made solely by the pilot carried the rest along, willingly or not. There were rare occasions when pilots decided to abort – sometimes two or three missions in a row – where evidence of mechanical failure could not be easily found. Inevitably there were confrontations or even accusations of cowardice, although it is rare to read about such matters now.[100] Because virtually all crews were anxious to complete their mission requirements in the shortest possible time, an aircraft commander seen to be lacking fortitude could cause tremendous interpersonnel problems.[101] Moreover, it was not unknown to have additional missions assigned for aborts unsatisfactorily explained.

Aborts for this kind of personal failure were not always the domain of pilots, however. Other crew members were also in a position to ensure some vital piece of equipment would not function properly and guarantee an abort. Whoever's idea such actions were, there were some whose sense of duty prevented their going along with sabotage or subterfuge.

As I prepared my turret, the co-pilot, a total stranger to me, walked up and astounded me with the following proposition: 'You know we're going to Munich and it's liable to be a bad one and neither you or I want to fly with this pilot. For instance, when you get into the ball you might just accidentally smash the gun sight or break off the intercom wires with your foot. In that case we'd have to turn around and come back'. I replied that I had been doing my job for some time, was extremely careful and was damn sure that no such damage would ever take place. He turned and indignantly walked off.[102]

It seems clear that there was some basis for concern on the part of local commanders, but the weight of statistical evidence on mission aborts supports the conclusion that, although occasionally there were suspicious returns, in the clear majority of cases aborts were justified. At the very senior level, the Eighth Air Force's leadership seemed to share this view, and strongly supported the aircrews when questions regarding aborts and morale arose.

AIRCRAFT LANDING IN NEUTRAL TERRITORY

Command-level support for aircrews was very evident when the subject of Eighth Air Force aircraft landing in neutral countries came up. Starting about the time the bomber formations began to make deeper penetrations into Germany, and continuing throughout the campaign, a number of damaged aircraft landed in Switzerland and Sweden.[103] By the summer of 1944 there were about 100 aircraft in each country.[104] About the same time official fears arose that some American airmen were intentionally trying to escape combat operations by diverting perfectly flyable aircraft from their assigned missions.[105] These concerns had largely come as a result of a letter written by William W. Corcoran, an American consulate officer in Goeteborg, Sweden. Corcoran, a retired Army officer, was, like many diplomats in Sweden at the time, also employed as an intelligence collector. On the basis of his interviews with downed American flyers he came to several startling conclusions.

Among other things, Corcoran wrote that interned American flyers expressed opposition to further flying, seemed cynical or apathetic in outlook, and 'may be compared to chauffeurs who have completed their work and abandoned their cars'. They distrusted and expressed hatred for General Doolittle who was seen as being unsympathetic and sending them towards certain doom. More damning still was Corcoran's allegation that flying to Switzerland or Sweden as a means of getting out of the war with impunity was 'openly discussed among bomber crews in Great Britain'.[106]

Corcoran's letter, forwarded to the US Embassy in Stockholm, drew an immediate response from the Air Attaché there, who indignantly discounted the report on the basis of the small number of interviewees. Despite this, the letter was forwarded to London along with an endorsement from the senior US officer in Sweden, Colonel Charles E. Rayens. Rayens, noting the superb treatment afforded the internees, added, 'there seems to be substance to Mr Corcoran's observations'.[107]

In London, General Spaatz, by then the overall commander of both the Eighth and the Fifteenth Air Forces, secretly directed that an investigation be conducted. Acting on the advice of one of his deputies, his plan was to send at least three men, two from operations and one from intelligence, to Sweden to look into the matter.[108] This quick investigation produced a report which tended to support the innocence of the aircrews.

Unfortunately, the rumours of intentional diversions had found their way to Washington. General Arnold cabled Spaatz on 27 July that an 'appreciable' number of aircraft seemed to be escaping without evidence of battle damage. Moreover, such landings were 'intentional evasions of further combat service'. Deeply concerned over the issue, Arnold wanted a complete investigation, while simultaneously mandating aggressive action to offset any increase in the numbers.[109] Within days he ordered an intelligence officer to conduct a clandestine survey in the European theatre. This officer's assignment was to determine the veracity of the allegations about aircrew feelings by mingling with combat crewmen of all ranks.[110]

Spaatz's response to Arnold's message was swift and angry. Already armed with the information collected from Sweden, he cabled Arnold only two days later. The preliminary report had shown that virtually all the aircraft in the country had suffered some life-threatening battle damage. Shot-up engines, control difficulties, badly wounded crewmen or lack of fuel had forced the overwhelming majority of diversions.[111] This was independently confirmed by neutral officials.[112] Going on to cite the combat statistics of a six-month period beginning in January 1944, Spaatz's rebuttal noted that the Eighth Air Force had sent 51,457 sorties aloft. Of these, 2,128 were shot-down and 15,346 returned battle-damaged. In view of the large number of damaged and shot-down aircraft, Spaatz indicated less than half of one per cent landed either in Switzerland or Sweden.[113]

It is worth noting, too, that after the war, only 71 of the 166 aircraft that had been flown to Switzerland were considered reparable. An average of 200 hours of labour per aircraft was necessary to make them flyable.[114] Moreover, post-war interviews with some internees, especially those repatriated from Switzerland, show that conditions were often quite spartan.[115] At least one report indicated that the major problem was actually trying to prevent American airmen from escaping their internment.[116] Rumours relating to 'vows of silence' mandatorily taken by former internees were fallacious. As a matter of routine, *all* escaped prisoners-of-war, evadees or repatriated internees signed forms which admonished them not to reveal details of their captivity or mechanism of escape. Such information might have furnished useful intelligence to the Germans, put many people in the underground networks at considerable risk, and would clearly have jeopardized future escapes, evasions or releases. In short, signing the forms had nothing to do with keeping men silent about their treatment.[117]

Spaatz's response became even more emphatic when it called attention to the fact that most American attacks had been made against the strongest and most heavily defended targets, and 'never had the Eighth or Fifteenth Air Forces been turned back from their mission by enemy action'. Summarizing his and General Eaker's opinions on the entire situation, Spaatz wrote

.After observing the combat crews of the American Air Forces in Europe in over two years we resent the implications by a non-military interrogator that any of these crews are cowards, are low in morale or lack the will to fight. Such is base slander against the most courageous group of fighting men in this war. There may have been isolated individuals, but certainly these cases have been rare indeed and are not representative of the morale and fighting spirit of our airmen.[118]

General Spaatz's comments are a fitting way to conclude this chapter's look at morale and attitudes in the Eighth Air Force. By any measure, statistical or otherwise, the fortitude of thousands of young Americans left little to be desired. Drawn into a war they did not ask for, excited by the thrill of flying, yet ultimately held together by their grim determination to survive while not letting their buddies down, these young men certainly fulfilled Clausewitz's virtues of bravery, adaptability, stamina and enthusiasm.[119] Moreover, even if the achievements of strategic bombing were not quite what the pre-war airpower advocates had anticipated, this was certainly not the result of human efforts expended. All things considered, the morale of the Eighth Air Force was undeniably high.

NOTES

1. Clausewitz, *On War*, pp. 188–9.
2. Craven and Cate, op. cit., Vol. VII, p. 431.
3. Barry D. Watts, *The Foundations of US Air Doctrine* (Maxwell AFB: Air University Press, 1984), pp. 17–23.
4. Office of the Air Surgeon, 'Report on Survey of Aircrew Personnel in the Eighth, Ninth, Twelfth, and Fifteenth Air Forces, Office of the Air Surgeon, April 1944', 141.28B, AFHRA.
5. More than 500,000 Army and Army Air Force personnel eventually filled out questionnaires, 'on everything from the taste of C rations to psychological breakdown in combat'. Geoffrey Perret, *There's a War to be Won* (New York: Random House, 1991), p. 464.
6. The best collection is at AFHRA at Maxwell Air Force Base, Alabama. After the war the surveys, which numbered over 200, were used by social scientists to summarize the feelings of servicemen. See Stouffer *et al.*, *passim.*
7. One cannot exclude the possibility that some men intentionally exposed themselves to disease to avoid combat duty, and hence reflected poor morale. But at least part of the executive's interest in the VD rate must have had to do with the fact that it was included on commanding officers' efficiency reports. A high rate reduced available manpower and could adversely affect a commander's chances for promotion. Perret, op. cit., p. 471.
8. Eighth Air Force combat reports and unit histories are to be found both at AFHRA and at the National Archives, Suitland, Maryland facility.
9. Craven and Cate, op. cit., Vol. VII, p. 432.
10. A situation explained in detail in Craven and Cate, op. cit., Vol. VI, pp. 516–21.
11. Colonel Clarence E. 'Bud' Anderson, *To Fly and Fight* (New York: Bantam Books, 1991), p. 50.
12. John K. Bember (385th Bomb Group) to author, 24 Feb. 1989.
13. Arnold and Eaker, *Flying Game*, p. 105.
14. Carter Hart (385th Bomb Group) to author, 18 Feb. 1989.
15. Grinker and Spiegel, op. cit., p. 5.
16. Johnson, op. cit., p. 29.
17. Stouffer also says many airmen got satisfaction from thinking about the potential for post-war careers. Stouffer *et al.*, Vol. II, p. 351–2.
18. One of the songs even moved to the top of the popular music charts in 1942. See Bruce D. Callander, 'They Wanted Wings', *Air Force Magazine* (Jan. 1991) p. 82.
19. Even in the theatre of war, more than 40 per cent of fighter pilots and one-quarter of

bomber pilots were 22 years old and younger. See US Strategic Air Forces Europe, 'Combat Crews Attitudes', July 1942, Spaatz MSS, Box 91, Library of Congress, Washington, DC.

20. Young black Americans were only reluctantly admitted as flying cadets in 1941. They performed with distinction in segregated units like the famous 99th Fighter Squadron (later 332nd Fighter Group) of the 15th Air Force. On aviator traits see Grinker and Spiegel, op. cit., pp. 7–9. A detailed examination of these traits can also be found in Office of the Air Surgeon, 'Report of Psychiatric Study of Successful Air Crews', 11 Oct. 1943, 141.28J 1943, AFHRA.

21. See Stouffer *et al.*, Vol. II, p. 342 and David R. Jones, MD, 'US Air Force Combat Psychiatry', USAF School of Aerospace Medicine, Brooks AFB, Texas, 1986, p. 7.

22. A fact made clear by scores of letters to the author. See also Stouffer *et al.*, Vol. II, pp. 332–3.

23. In this regard airmen were little different from their ground counterparts. See Richard A. Gabriel, *Military Psychiatry* (New York: Greenwoood Press, 1986), pp. 44–5 and J. Glenn Gray, *The Warriors: Reflections on Men in Battle* (New York: Harcourt, Brace and Company, 1959), p. 40 and Stouffer *et al.*, Vol. II, p. 108.

24. Interview with General Theodore R. Milton, former commander 384th Bomb Group, USAF Academy, 12 Oct. 1991.

25. Office of the Air Surgeon, 'Analysis of the Duties of Aircrew Personnel, Description of Aircrew Performances from Theaters of Combat', 5 May 1943, 141.28D–10–19 1943, AFHRA.

26. 'The camaraderie and pride in shared accomplishments', according to Richard P. Woodson (96th Bomb Group) to author, July 3, 1991.

27. S. L. A. Marshal suggested, 'Man is a gregarious animal. He wants company. In his greatest danger his herd instinct drives him toward his fellows'. See Marshall, p. 141 and Gregory Belenky, *Contemporary Studies in Combat Psychiatry* (New York: Greenwood Press, 1987), p. 120.

28. The sometimes not-so-friendly rivalry between the 56th and 4th Fighter Groups for the highest total of combat victories is noteworthy. James A. Goodson, *Tumult in the Clouds* (London: William Kimber, 1983), pp. 82–3. See also Bond, *Love and Fear*, pp. 38–9.

29. Veteran support for combat unit associations and their reunions is notable. Fifty years after the war, the 8th Air Force Historical Society's convention still attracts more than 500 veterans annually. An average of six Bomb Group reunions take place in Britain every year. James W. Hill, editor, *8th Air Force News* 91 (Jan. 1991), p. 7.

30. See USAAF, *Flight Operating Instructions For Army Model B-17F* (Patterson Field, Ohio: USAAF, 1944), p. 13. and D. A. Lande, *From Somewhere in England* (United Kingdom: Airlife Publishing Ltd., 1991), pp. 60–61.

31. Grinker and Spiegel, op. cit., p. 22.

32. Major General Curtis E. LeMay, 'Combat Crew Handbook', Eighth Air Force, 3rd Bombardment Division, nd, Box B4, LeMay MSS, Library of Congress.

33. Among other descriptive letters are Robert Bowen (351st Bomb Group) to author, 14 June 1989; Thomas L. Hair (385th Bomb Group) to author 25 Feb. 1989; and Harold W. Bowman (401st Bomb Group) to author 10 July 1989.

34. Brig. Gen. Donald A. Gaylord (351st Bomb Group) to author, 11 July 1989. Some interesting anecdotes can be found in Freeman's *American Airmen*, pp. 99–101.

35. Stiles, a 23-year-old veteran of bombers and fighters, contributed evocative stories to prominent US magazines like the *Saturday Evening Post*. Decorated with the Distinguished Flying Cross and having completed 35 missions in B-17s, he was killed in action while on an escort mission in P-51s during 1944. His short book, published just after the war, provides some of the very best insights into the spirit and attitudes of American combat flyers. See Stiles, op. cit., p. 49.

36. Raymond F. Toliver and Trevor J. Constable, *Fighter Aces of the USA* (Fallbrook: Aero Publisher, Inc.,1979), pp. 133–4.

37. Letter Urban L. Drew (361st Fighter Group) to author, 9 April 1989.

38. Douglas D. Bond, 'A Study of Successful Airmen with Particular Respect to their Motivations for Combat Flying and Resistance to Combat Stress', 27 Jan. 1945, 520.7411–1, AFHRA.

39. Ibid. See also Johnson, op. cit., p. 29.

40. Bond, *Love and Fear*, p. 38.
41. Roger A. Freeman, 'The Consolidated B-24J Liberator', *Aircraft in Profile*, Vol. 1 (Garden City: Doubleday and Company, 1969), p. 224.
42. Exceptions being the admission by Mustang pilots that their aircraft was too vulnerable during ground attack and the general lack of enthusiasm for the P-38 Lightning. See Headquarters, European Theater of Operations, 'What Fighter Pilots Say About Types of Planes', 141.28 July – August 1944, AFHRA and 'Combat Crew Attitudes', 11 July 1944, Spaatz MSS, Box 91, Library of Congress.
43. A view supported by Stouffer. See Stouffer *et al.*, Vol. II, pp. 131–2.
44. Gray, a veteran, noted wryly that the vulgar expression for sexual intercourse was used as adjective, adverb, verb, noun, and in any other form possible, however ridiculous or inappropriate. Psychiatrists considered the continuous use of obscenity 'clearly an act of aggression and represents a regression to a childhood method of expressing anger and accomplishing revenge'. The development of aircraft nose art is a fascinating study in itself. But regarding its psychological implications James W. Hill, a veteran, said, 'I think one has to stretch pretty far to make anything more of it than that we were just a bunch of horny guys'. See Gray, op. cit., p. 61; Office of the Air Surgeon, 'Report of Psychiatric Study of Successful Air Crews', 11 Oct. 1943, 141.28J 1943, AFHRA; and Jeffrey L. Ethell and Clarence Simonson, *The History of Aircraft Nose Art* (London: Motorbooks International, 1991).
45. Letter George A. Doerch (359th Fighter Group) to author, 9 March 1989.
46. Anderson, op. cit., pp. 140–1.
47. Office of the Air Surgeon, 'Report of Psychiatric Study of Successful Air Crews', 11 Oct. 1943, 141.28J 1943, AFHRA.
48. Bond, *Love and Fear*, p. 38.
49. Roger Manvell, *Films and the Second World War* (New York: A. S. Barnes and Company, 1974), pp. 167–76.
50. See David H. Culbert, 'Hollywood goes to War', Banquet Address, Tenth Military History Symposium, USAF Academy, October 1982 and Perret, pp. 473–4.
51. On the separate issue of the morality of strategic bombing, I accept the position of James L. Stokesbury when he wrote, 'That particular question could be indulged only after the passions of the war had cooled'. James L. Stokesbury, *A Short History of World War II* (New York: William Morrow, 1980), p.287.
52. John M. Blum, 'United Against: American Culture and Society During World War II', *The Harmon Memorial Lectures in Military History 1959–1987* (Washington, DC: Office of Air Force History, 1988), pp. 577–81.
53. Even a censored wartime memoir by a famous fighter pilot admitted the Germans fought well, were crafty, and had courage. See Gentile, op. cit., p. 11 and Kennett, *G.I.: The American Soldier in World War II*, p.156.
54. Office of the Air Surgeon, 'Report on Survey of Aircrew Personnel in the Eighth, Ninth, Twelve, and Fifteenth Air Forces', April 1944, 141.28B, AFHRA, p. 60.
55. Glossaries of British terms were available for those who needed help. USAAF, 'A Short Guide to Great Britain', 1944. AFHRA.
56. This ranged from the implicit agreement by both sides to avoid shooting parachuting airmen to the generally acceptable treatment of Allied aircrew in Luftwaffe prisoner of war camps. See Galland, op. cit., p. 120 and Arthur A. Durand, *Stalag Luft III* (Baton Rouge: Louisiana State University Press, 1988), pp.357–63.
57. Johnson, op. cit., pp. 101–2. For the truth about the often repeated myth of the Abbeville Boys see Donald L. Caldwell, *JG 26: Top Guns of the Luftwaffe* (New York: Orion Books, 1991), pp. xxi–xxii and Martin Middlebrook, *The Schweinfurt–Regensburg Mission* (London: Penguin Books, 1985), p. 91.
58. This was one reason the most effective units made an effort to disseminate bomb damage assessments to aircrews as quickly as possible. Data from Headquarters, European Theatre of Operations, 'Survey of Combat Crews in Heavy Bombardment Groups in ETO, June 1944', Box 18, Spaatz MSS, Library of Congress.
59. Perhaps, like one navigator, a few of the men occasionally liked to hear Wagner. See Elmer Bendiner, *The Fall of the Fortresses* (London: Pan Books, 1982) p. 144 and Headquarters, European Theatre of Operations, 'Survey of Combat Crews in Heavy Bombardment Groups in ETO', June 1944, Box 18, Spaatz MSS, Library of Congress.

60. Sherry, op. cit., pp. 208–12.
61. Elmer Bendiner, op. cit., p. 95.
62. The largest collection of these films is maintained by the Department of Film, Imperial War Museum, London.
63. Anderson, op. cit., p. 10.
64. Yeager, op. cit., p. 16.
65. Gray would agree that the possibility existed. Gray, op. cit., pp. 28–9.
66. Yeager, who characterized himself as a confident hunter, recalled the sight of a disintegrating enemy aircraft as 'pleasing and beautiful'. Yeager, op. cit., p. 67.
67. Douglas D. Bond, 'A Study of Successful Airmen with Particular Respect to their Motivation for Combat Flying and Resistance to Combat Stress', 27 Jan. 1945, 520.7411–1, AFHRA.
68. Stouffer *et al.*, Vol. II, pp. 162–7.
69. In the same period more than 17,671 went missing-in-action. See Office of the Air Surgeon, 'Memorandum for War Department Special Staff, Battle Casualty Data', 5 June 1946, 519.741–1, 1943–1945, AFHRA.
70. Watt, op. cit., p. 18.
71. General LeMay argued that everybody knew fighter escorts were going to be necessary; it was just that no suitable aircraft were initially available. Richard H. Kohn and Joseph P. Harahan, editors, *Strategic Air Warfare: An Interview with Generals Curtis E. LeMay, Leon W. Johnson, David A. Burchinal, and Jack J. Catton* (Washington: Office of Air Force History, 1988), p. 22.
72. Eighth Air Force, 'Statistical Summary of Eighth Air Force Operations, European Theater, 17 August 1942 – 8 May 1945', 520.308–1, AFHRA.
73. Roger A. Freeman, *Mighty Eighth War Diary* (London: Jane's, 1981), p. 126.
74. Reported to General Spaatz in a confidential and hand-carried report. See Eighth Air Force, 'Memorandum on Tour of Duty in Heavy Bombardment', 519.7411–1, AFHRA.
75. Ibid.
76. Eighth Air Force, 'Level of Experience and Replacement Requirements – Heavy Bomber Combat Crews', 2 Feb. 1944, 519.7411–1, AFHRA.
77. Eighth Air Force, 'Psychological Aspects of extending the Operational Tour in Heavy Bombardment', 31 Jan. 1944, 519.7411–1, AFHRA.
78. With better than a 0.7 coefficient of correlation, Bond considered this statistic an accurate 'index of morale'. See Eighth Air Force, 'Statistical Survey of the Emotional Casualties of the Eighth Air Force Aircrews', 25 May 1945, 520.7421 1944–1945, AFHRA.
79. The problems of the 384th Bombardment Group are summarized in the memoirs of one of its commanders. The 91st Bombardment Group, which suffered the highest losses of any Eighth Air Force unit, also came through a period of poor morale. See Dale O. Smith, *Screaming Eagle: the Memoirs of a B-17 Group Commander* (New York: Dell, 1990), pp. 64–5 and General Theodore Ross Milton, Oral Interview, 9 July 1982, 239.0512–1339, AFHRA.
80. Notable among these was the 100th Bombardment Group, called 'The Bloody Hundredth'. Two days after losing 15 aircraft, or almost 50 per cent of the entire unit, on a March 1944 raid to Berlin, the 100th put up another 15 for the same target. See Jablonski, op. cit., pp. 208–9.
81. He accurately noted that the British had long before learned the necessity of establishing tour lengths. Spaatz to Arnold, Box 9, Spaatz MSS, Library of Congress.
82. In bombers a 5.4 per cent loss rate during the first five missions typically fell to 1.2 per cent during the last five. In short, experience seemed to pay dividends. Eighth Air Force, 'Length of Operational Tour in Heavy Bombardment', Undated report, 519.7411–1 1944–1946, AFHRA.
83. This was another clear signal that Americans were very confident – at least early on – that heavily-armed B-17s and B-24s could do the job with loss rates measureably lower than the British. General Ira C. Eaker, USAF (retd), Thames Television Recorded Interview, No. 002820/03/01,02,03. IWM.
84. Eaker to Stratemyer, 2 Jan. 1943, 168.491, AFHRA. See also Eighth Air Force, 'Memorandum 75–1', 21 Oct. 1943, 519.2171–1 1942 – 1945, AFHRA.
85. The complete details regarding the establishment of tour lengths is interesting but not vital to this discussion. By the spring of 1943, 25 missions was the universal standard in Eighth

Air Force. What it is more important to understand is the connection between tour length, attrition, and morale. See Craven and Cate, op. cit., Vol. I, p. 627; David R. Mets, *Master of Airpower: General Carl A. Spaatz* (Novato, CA: Presidio Press, 1988), pp. 184–6; and Spaatz to Arnold, Spaatz MSS, Box 9, Library of Congress.

86. The non-personal effects of men missing in action were 'fair game' to be divided among survivors. There were always various customs and rituals associated with casualties. See Freeman, *American Airmen*, p.26 and Lande, op. cit., pp. 61–2.

87. Particularly harrowing incidents like the spectacle of losses on the Schweinfurt raids could also be a factor. Martin Goldman, 'Morale in the Army Air Force in World War II', USAF Historical Study No. 78, 1953, Air University Library, Maxwell AFB, Alabama. (Mimeographed).

88. Eighth Air Force, 'Statistical Summary of Eighth Air Force Operations, European Theater, 17 August 1942 – 8 May 1945', 520.308–1, AFHRA.

89. A July 1944 survey revealed that only 10 per cent of bomber pilots who were completing their tours were willing to do another. Seventy-five per cent would have refused if given the option. The fighter pilot figures were 29 and 29 per cent respectively with a further 42 per cent undecided. 'Survey of Fighter Pilots in the Eighth Air Force: A Comparison with Heavy Bomber Pilots', July 1944, Box 91, Spaatz MSS, Library of Congress.

90. Some argued that every man lost between missions 26 and 30 was an 'unnecessary tragedy'. Others claimed, 'we do 25 for ourselves, and 5 for Jimmy!' See James H. Doolittle, *I Could Never Be So Lucky Again* (New York: Bantam Books, 1991), pp. 386–8; Sherry, op. cit., p. 217; Stouffer *et al.*, Vol. II, p. 384; and 'Research Findings and Recommendations', 11 July 1944, Box 91, Spaatz MSS, Library of Congress.

91. Evidence uncovered recently indicates that some units independently gave crews double credit for certain missions. Criteria for such a policy was never formally established and almost certainly never received official sanction. See Dr Kenneth P. Werrell, 'A Case for a 'New' Unit History', *Air Power History* 39 (Spring 1992), p. 37.

92. Second Lieut. Joseph Baggs, cited by Middlebrook, remembers a navigator who was a college mathematics professor using a slide-rule to calculate the odds of survival. 'The odds were so phenomenal that he threw the ruler away and said there was no chance'. See Middlebrook, *Schweinfurt*, p. 62. For comments on 'barrack room accountants' see interview with General Theodore R. Milton, USAF, (retd) (Commander, 384th Bomb Group). US Air Force Academy, 28 Oct. 1991.

93. Eighth Air Force, 'Abortives – January, 1944', Eighth Air Force, 11 Feb. 1944, 519.7411–1 1944 –1946, AFHRA.

94. 'Two kinds of weather plagued us in the ETO, both over England and the Continent – lousy and worse'. General Curtis E. LeMay, 'Strategic Airpower: Destroying the Enemy's War Resources', *Aerospace Historian* No. 27, Spring 1980, p. 11.

95. *USSBS*, Weather Factors, Table IX.

96. LeMay, 'Strategic Airpower', p. 11.

97. Changes of command for reasons of poor performance against these criteria were common. Colonel Frank Armstrong's reputation as the 'fireman' of the Eighth Air Force came as a result of his employment in this capacity. His strong leadership of the 97th and 306th Bomb Groups was later fictionalized by veteran authors Beirne Lay and Sy Bartlett for the book and movie, *Twelve O'Clock High*. Brent L. Gravatt and Francis H. Ayers, Jr., 'The Fireman: Twelve O'Clock High Revisited', *Aerospace Historian* 35 (Sept. 1988), pp. 204–8.

98. Middlebrook, *Schweinfurt*, p. 63.

99. Milton interview, 28 Oct. 1991.

100. Dale O. Smith covers an incident in some detail. See 'Lieutenant Jacob's Example', Smith, op. cit., pp. 80–90.

101. After unwillingly participating in three unexplained aborts, Bendiner became suspicious that his pilot 'was joining that band of determined survivors'. Bendiner, op. cit., p. 103.

102. John F. Kirkpatrick cited in Freeman, *American Airman*, p. 100.

103. 166 USAAF aircraft entered Switzerland by the end of hostilities. Sixty-eight B-17s and 59 B-24s landed in Sweden. See Roy J. Thomas, *Haven, Heaven and Hell* (Monroe, Wisconsin: privately published, 1991) and Len Morgan, *Crackup* (NY Arco Publishing Company, Inc., 1969), p. 33.

104. Spaatz to Arnold, 30 July 1944, Box 18, Spaatz MSS, Library of Congress.

105. Rumours among airmen had existed for some time. There were stories circulating in

American prisoner-of-war camps, for example, that some crews had 'packed their luggage' before taking off on missions. Although generally discounted and frequently related as a joke, the underlying notions troubled some. One fighter ace, from the 361st Fighter Group, recalls being briefed to watch for bombers leaving formations and to note their condition. He feared such instructions could be taken to mean that American fighter planes were to shoot-down those deliberately trying to evade combat. How such determinations were to be made was unclear and absolutely no other evidence exists that such drastic action was seriously contemplated or ever took place. Interview with General Albert P. Clark (senior American POW in Stalag Luft III), USAF Academy, 30 Oct. 1991 and Urban L. Drew (361st Fighter Group) to author, 6 Feb. 1989.

106. These charges were apparently made after speaking to only three American aircrew members in Sweden. Corcoran to Rayens, 23 May 1944, Box 91, Spaatz MSS, Library of Congress.

107. Rayens to London Military Attaché, 8 June 1944, Box 91, Spaatz MSS, Library of Congress.

108. 'Carrier Sheet Headquarters USSTAF, Subject – Air Force Morale', Box 91, Spaatz MSS, Library of Congress.

109. Arnold to Spaatz and Eaker, 27 July 1944, 622.1621–2, AFHRA.

110. Arnold to Lieut. Col. James W. Wilson, 14 Aug. 1944, Box 18, Spaatz MSS, Library of Congress.

111. Facts supported by another exhaustive report in January 1945. See US Strategic Air Forces Europe, 'Forced Landings in Neutral Countries', 22 July 1944, 519.8021–3, AFHRA and 'Engineering and Supply in Sweden', 519.8021–2, AFHRA.

112. Craven and Cate, op. cit., Vol. III, p. 307.

113. Eaker said one-quarter of 1 per cent. Eaker to Major General David Grant, 7 Aug. 1944, Box 26, Eaker MSS, Library of Congress.

114. Robert A. Long (President, Swiss Internees Association) to author, 30 July 1989.

115. Swiss records on internment camps at Wauwillermoos and Hunenburg are closed until 1995. A 1989 British television documentary, 'Whispers in the Air', covered the subject of Allied aircraft in neutral countries. It began with a review of unsubstantiated allegations, similar to those made during the war. Eventually, however, it came to calmer conclusions with regard to numbers and causes of diversions.

116. Craven and Cate, op. cit., Vol. III, p. 307.

117. US Army, Adjutant General's Office, Directive 383.6, 31 July 1944. Copy in author's possession.

118. Spaatz to Arnold, 29 July 1944, 622.161–2, AFHRA.

119. It is interesting to note that even as Arnold was pressing for an investigation he wrote to Spaatz, 'I do not blame you for rising to the defence of your crews. So far as I am concerned you have no need to defend them. Their achievements have written and are writing glorious pages in the history of air warfare'. Arnold to Spaatz, 14 Aug. 1944, Box 91, Spaatz MSS, Library of Congress.

5

Aircrew Morale in
Bomber Command

NO HISTORIAN should ever seriously question the gallantry of the Royal Air Force's Bomber Command aircrews during the Combined Bomber Offensive. In addition to its earlier efforts, between 1942 and 1945 Bomber Command flew more than 300,000 operational sorties. During that period about 8,000 aircraft were lost and a further 1,500 written off for battle damage. The human toll was just as high. In six years of conflict almost 56,000, or about half of the 125,000 aircrew who served in the command, were killed, 8,400 injured, and a further 11,000 were missing or held as prisoners until the war's end.[1] The impact of these statistics is even more graphic when considered in a slightly different way. Out of any 100 airmen who joined an operational training unit, 51 would be killed on combat operations, 12 more would be killed or injured in non-operational accidents, and 12 would become prisoners-of-war. Only 24 of the original 100 would come away unscathed.[2]

In the light of these figures and considering the ferocity of the opposition, the scale of British and Commonwealth aircrew achievement in overcoming fear and adversity almost defies description. No other group of Western Allied combatants, except for their American daylight-bombing counterparts, suffered the same huge casualties, nor faced the mathematical certainty of their own deaths so routinely and so unflinchingly. Most often historians ask how it was that young men taken from virtually all rungs of society, with varying levels of training and education, could bring themselves, night after night, to clamber aboard cold, often underpowered, and all too vulnerable aircraft, and set off for Germany, knowing that fewer and fewer would return each time.

It might have been, as recent histories have intimated, that these men were roughly comparable with the unfortunate British infantry of the Somme in 1916. According to some accounts, airmen faced German flak, searchlights, and *Schräge Musik* in the same way their fathers had braved the Kaiser's machine-guns.[3] Presumably, they flew blindly and without protest to their doom while holding little hope for success or victory. One

of the many problems with this kind of analysis is that it does not satisfactorily explain what it was that sustained aircrew morale as they faced,
in their own words, the almost inevitable 'chop' or 'going for a Burton?'[4]

The explanation, at least in part, can be found in an examination of
their attitudes at the time. Unfortunately for those interested, no in-depth
sociologiçal studies of British soldiers or airmen during the Second World
War exist.[5] The multitude of data which was collected on American
servicemen, and eventually published after the war, finds no equivalent in
the British service. Part of this is explained by the peculiarly American
inclination to use the scientific method to measure, quantify or analyse
almost everything, even morale, in war. A further reason is probably that
the British could spare neither the time nor resources on an in-depth
collection of human factors data. What effort was expended in this regard
– especially as it concerned collecting and analysing statistics from air
raids, seemed rightly focused on operational research efforts designed to
improve man's interaction with the machinery and weapons of war. In
this way, it was hoped, combat effectiveness might be improved and
casualties come down.[6]

Despite the fact that it is not possible to draw on any single, easy source
regarding Bomber Command's morale, one can still make some sensible
and perfectly supportable statements regarding the state of its combat
spirit during the war. Enough documentation exists in the Public Record
Office, Air Historical Branch and in various libraries to build a reasonably
accurate picture. Furthermore, published materials in the form of
memoirs are plentiful. Finally, private letters from veterans provide rich
sources, as do oral reflections.

What seems abundantly clear from all this evidence is that British airmen of Bomber Command sustained themselves in much the same way as
did their Allied counterparts and German foes. While patriotism, love of
country, 'desire to do their bit', or even love of flying may have helped
bring them into the Royal Air Force, it was for a variety of complex – and
sometimes not so complex – reasons that they stayed to face air combat.
These reasons ranged from self-esteem, supported and sustained by
group cohesion, to simple day-to-day survival. Like the airmen of all
nations, they were concerned about pay, privilege, rank and prestige to
some extent. But ultimately, their morale, much like that of American airmen, depended to a great degree on the quality of their equipment, the
length of time they were kept in combat, the results they attained and the
rate of attrition. A measurable signal of morale was the abort rate. All
of these issues will receive attention in the chapter that follows, as we
continue our look at human factors in Bomber Command.

DOING THEIR BIT

Commenting on Bomber Command aircrews, one 20-year-old book indicated that the collective personality of the crews was hard to describe.[7] While it may be going too far to suggest that they represented 'the cream of young manhood of the British Empire', by the time they had completed all their training, they had been tested and culled to a greater extent than many of the men who found themselves in other services. Even if no distinguishable or mutually shared personality existed, many of the men were quite similar in their motivations.

These men had joined for most of the same reasons as those in the US Eighth Air Force. Thousands were doubtless excited by the physical and emotional appeals of flying, just as many others probably felt a strong sense of obligation to contribute in some way to the war effort. Britain had been at war since 1939, and it is impossible to exclude the very real desire for revenge for cities and families bombed or friends and brothers killed.[8] The country's wartime build-up doubtless received impetus in the surge of determination which came as result of the Blitz. At the time, a flying career was seen by many young men as the best way to 'get back at the Hun'.

From necessity, the Royal Air Force almost doubled its total of 97,000 personnel in the first year of the war. Always relying on volunteers for aircrew, the service used a scheme of deferring young men after their initial enlistment and testing, in order to create a pool of available man-power. By mid-1943, during peak periods of intense air operations and losses, there was often as much as a one year waiting period for flying training positions – another clear indicator of the attraction of aircrew service.[9]

For similar reasons there was a steady flow of volunteers from Commonwealth nations, helped along by the Empire Air Training Scheme. In fact, one out of every four aircrew was from the Dominions.[10] An Australian with Bomber Command wrote after the war that his nation, which in the 1940s still reflected a predominantly British cultural mixture, not only recognized the evils of Nazism, but felt strong bonds with the threatened 'homeland'. A corresponding feeling of unity was to pervade the Commonwealth during the war years and explains much of the participation.[11] Also writing after the war, a medical officer who had served on a Bomber Command base, summarized the views of all those, British and Commonwealth, that he tended:

It is a poor type of fellow who will not fight to the utmost of his capacity for his country. Each man must fight in the way best adapted to himself, and there is a particular lure of the skies which has an uncanny pull on many people . . . The choice of the Air Arm is very often fortuitous.[12]

During the period of their most frequent operations Bomber Command aircrews fell broadly into two categories. At the top, there were a number of pre-war regulars, short-service officers, and RAF reservists who usually served at the more senior positions. Steadily reduced by attrition during the early years of the war, by 1942 and 1943 these men directed the second category, which was generally a much younger group of volunteers. It was to fall to these more inexperienced men, mostly in their early 20s, but frequently 18 or 19 years old, to fight the bulk of Bomber Command's battles. They served in every aircraft position, from air gunner to pilot, and alongside ground support people as well. And because Bomber Command depended solely upon volunteers to wage its war in the air, it was necessary to sustain and enhance both the image and the benefits afforded them.

Many veterans still recall the special pride which went along with wearing the aircrew brevet. This was not just a badge signifying graduation from a difficult training course, but a symbol of hard-earned status and continued qualification.[13] In military society, where visible signs of rank and prestige carried clearly defined weight, being seen as aircrew brought great emotional satisfaction.[14] Inside the air force, there were sometimes not so subtle distinctions between those who served in the air and those who worked on the ground. This same factor extended even to differences between the various aircrew trades. More openly expressed were class distinctions between officer and NCO.[15]

Clearly, countless thousands probably saw the winning of an aircrew position – and its simultaneous promotion to at least non-commissioned officer status – as an important statement regarding their social standing outside the Royal Air Force. Working-class families must have taken particular pride in the success and accomplishments of thousands of elementary school boys who worked side by side with their public school counterparts. That rank and prestige were important to non-commissioned aircrew seems unarguable.[16] Moreover, if they survived their first tour, the status of a commission beckoned. The rewards for successful service with the Royal Air Force and Bomber Command to men like this seemed real enough.[17] The RAF had always had a gentlemanly air of glamour and panache which appealed to young males.[18] Returning on pass or leave could be especially rewarding:

At home with friends and family one could not help basking just a little when they all realized that you had been in the front line. It gave one the sense that you had done your bit, that you had not been found wanting and no matter how modest one might be, the esteem was flattering.[19]

There was even a term which simultaneously connoted the image and envy generated by airmen; they were 'the Brylcreem Boys'. While it may have been that beyond the recruiting stations there were few illusions about the grim survival statistics, for some the opportunity to fly and eventually earn a commission must have outweighed dark thoughts about one's own mortality.[20] Youth brings with it peculiar notions about invulnerability in the face of extreme danger. To say that aircrew volunteers, especially early on, were enthusiastic, eager and hopelessly naïve is no exaggeration. Despite the steady human toll taken during training – always immensely dangerous – the full risks of flying were rarely understood until actual operations commenced.[21]

GROUP COHESION AND MORALE

Carrying on centuries of British military tradition in their own ways, the Royal Air Force, especially Bomber Command, clearly understood the relationship between primary group cohesion and morale.[22] It may be more than just a coincidence that the designers of the principal British bombers – aircraft such as the Wellington, Halifax, Stirling, and Lancaster – all generally grouped the main elements of their crews together in a small compartment.[23] Unlike the members of an American bomber crew, who were dispersed from one end of the aircraft to the other, RAF airmen could more easily watch each other in action and take a measure of support and comfort.

There is similarly little doubt that each bomber's crew considered itself, in many ways, a separate and individual unit. No other military relationship, whether one involving superiors or dealing with subordinates, carried as much weight nor was quite as critical to a man's eventual survival. The very nature of the battle waged by these crews had the effect of increasing their tendency to grow together. Bomber Command airmen flew the vast majority of their missions individually, without formation, at night, and largely out of sight of other aircraft. Many hours could be flown without seeing another aircraft. There was no single moment from take-off to landing during which they could truly relax or take their security for granted. Even the knowledge that one was part of several hundred bombers in a stream thousands of feet thick and stretching scores of miles ahead or behind did little to alleviate the solitary and disturbing nature of an aircrew's war. In such a situation the interdependence of Bomber Command aircrew became essential.

In view of this, it is amazing that the well-known procedure used for 'crewing-up' worked as well as it did. Certainly, no amount of investigation can satisfactorily explain why, when hundreds of young men, very frequently total strangers, were herded into open hangars and told to 'sort themselves out into crews', they managed to do it so successfully. The huge majority of veterans who recall the method seem unable to explain why it seemed effective. Probably tried first as an expedient way to reduce time and paperwork, eventually it became – with individual exceptions –

almost a standard procedure. Nevertheless, however it worked, it was never more than an extraordinarily haphazard way to bring pilots, navigators, bomb-aimers and gunners together. Flight engineers were usually assigned to crews at a later date during conversion training.

During these noisy hangar sessions, men could be drawn to each other for innumerable reasons. Age or physical appearance sometimes brought them together, as did similarity in smoking or drinking habits. Even proximity in the hangar might be the reason. Boisterous, extrovert types almost inevitably crewed-up faster, leaving the quiet, reclusive types often on the same crews. The results of the approach have been likened to the nervous preliminaries to a 'marriage' by more than one participant. After some small talk, or jokes, someone had to ask the important question along the lines of 'would you be my pilot' or 'would you be my navigator?' [24] As often as not, bomber crews ended up with a mixture of backgrounds or nationalities – Scots, Irish, New Zealanders, Canadian, English. Luck and serendipity must account for much of what transpired.

Bomber Command mythology has it that the results produced crews remarkable for their spontaneous cohesiveness. While it is true that an astonishing number of these crews – even the majority – fused together in a very short time and, as a result of their shared experiences, maintain bonds unbroken even by the passage of fifty years, it is also true that many crews turned out to be ill-matched. Various incompatibilities or inadequacies became apparent only after the first few flights together. One veteran accurately recalled his early OTU missions by writing: 'We were not a crew, we were a 'plane load of bewildered individuals'.[25] This factor may go a long way to explaining the horrific accident rate at training units. Some classes lost as much as 25 per cent of their strength in three or four months.[26]

Moreover, for some men, crewing-up was an ordeal of fretting, loneliness, chain-smoking and rejection. Results could be less than satisfactory:

I don't quite know now why we weren't cohesive . . . Nevertheless, for my part I didn't like the cocky bomb-aimer who thought he knew everything, and I didn't like the Welsh gunner who was clearly disinterested (*sic*). Who wants a disinterested (*sic*) tail gunner? The wireless operator and navigator hung together, being married men. The pilot and bomb-aimer stayed together because the bomb-aimer tended to take charge and the pilot was a quiet chap. That left we two gunners as mates, a situation in which I wasn't very happy.[27]

It is impossible to know, even in rough estimate, how many times crews might have fallen into this category. When asked, veterans today do recall personality conflicts which occasionally led to crew break-ups. There were even crews which developed something of a bad reputation. Occasionally, flight or squadron commanders intervened. However, most conflicts were probably resolved quickly, good-naturedly, and with humour.

On most crews, it would appear that the triangular relationship between pilot, navigator and bomb-aimer was vitally important to team cohesion, but there can be little doubt that the key position for all crews was that of the pilot or captain. Especially because British bombers typically did not carry second-pilots after 1942 – except on occasional missions like those selected to initiate new men – other aircrew were solely dependent on the skills of the 'skipper'. Those aircrew who had not been trained actually to manipulate the controls of a large bomber aircraft, or any aircraft for that matter, tended to regard pilots with a degree of respect, sometimes bordering on awe. This feeling probably came as a result of the inability of some to understand the mysteries of flight itself. And while science and education might have explained the simple truths about aerodynamics, pilots practised a language of their own to maintain the aura.

For these and other reasons, British veterans, like Americans, have a tendency to recall their pilots most favourably. A real sense of achievement which came as a result of hard training, shared experiences and mutual danger usually bonded all the members of an aircrew to the pilot and to each other as well.

The personality of the pilot was undoubtedly the key factor as to what made a crew special, and thus survivors. Happy crews – those who stuck together as chums – had a happy family relationship, seemed to have a sense of purpose, and enjoyed their achievement. Being a successful bomber crew gave a tremendous sense of purpose and pride, especially off the station.[28]

Even crews that admitted to being scruffy, casual, and clamorous on the ground, defended themselves with memories of airborne alertness, discipline and cohesion.[29] A prominent and most successful squadron commander was convinced that good captains of strong personality set the tone for their crews, both on and off duty. When captains remained calm during stress, it had a salutary effect on others.[30] This argues convincingly that stronger personalities had the effect of shaping the crews' ethos. Moreover, such a thing is typical for small group dynamics.[31] Everybody else went along because non-conformity in such a small group at best might lead to ostracism, at worst to the death of all in an aircraft accident.[32]

Despite the obvious importance of the pilot, he was not always the 'leader' of the crew. In some instances, navigators or bomb-aimers – especially on crews skippered by non-commissioned officers – served as aircraft commander. Guidance on this subject was contradictory and the situation occasionally became awkward and affected morale as a result of the RAF's commissioning policies.

AIRCREW COMMISSIONING POLICY

To some extent, the Air Ministry's position with regard to who was in charge of bomber aircraft was a reflection of its views on commissioning. Even as the requirements for manpower expanded, the Royal Air Force maintained the philosophical mind-set of a very small, élite service manned by regulars. Notwithstanding the expanding criteria for aircrew selection, the fundamental benchmarks for commissioning during the pre-war years had been leadership or 'displaying officer-like qualities'. These, in turn, once again reflected requirements for character, intelligence and ability to set a good example – in short, the public school ethos. This underlying philosophy continued during the war, despite various attempts to open the ranks and increase the number of officers.

The real problem had to do with navigators, bomb-aimers and especially pilots. In May 1942, the Canadians, who by then were supplying an ever increasing percentage of the RAF's personnel, argued at a training conference in Ottawa that,

Rank commensurate with duties should be granted to all aircrew personnel, there being no justification for the commissioning of certain individuals whilst others are required to perform exactly the same duties but in NCO rank. The responsibility resting upon the individual in aircrew capacity is sufficient justification for commissioned status. NCO rank is not compatible with the heavy responsibilities imposed in commanding large and expensive aircraft.[33]

There were a number of issues related to the policy, not the least of which seemed fairness. The Canadian position, much like that of the Americans, was that inequalities in pay, allowances and messing, arising from differences in rank among airmen doing similar jobs, had a damaging effect on morale. Cohesion and teamwork were similarly undermined as crews of various ranks were unable to socialize freely. Moreover, it was argued, automatic commissioning of pilots, navigators and bomb-aimers, upon their graduation, would not only increase enlistments but improve the quality of enlistees.[34]

It is clear from various documents that the Air Ministry was unpersuaded by these arguments. Nevertheless, when confronted with the inability of normal commissioning sources to supply the necessary officers, the Royal Air Force did begin commissioning some of its airmen at the end of their initial flying training. Assessment was supposed to be based principally on four factors: peer ratings, instructor assessment, ground-school performance, and flying skills. Such a procedure brought its own problems, however.

Fairness was again the major issue. Authorized to commission as many as one-third of any graduating class of airmen, Flying Training

Command often fell well short of the goal.[35] Moreover, while the criteria for commissioning might have been clear on paper, the long-held institutional biases proved difficult to overcome. As a result, the commissioning lists sometimes seemed unjust to scores of trainees.

Prior to completing the course at Cranfield we had to attend an interview for officer selection. We had been told at the commencement of our training that the granting of commissions depended entirely on our individual efficiency during training. Of the 43 pilots who finally completed their training, only 11 were granted commissions as Pilot Officers. It was noted that all of these had been educated at public schools. We others were given the rank of Flight Sergeant.[36]

Bitterness and anger were not uncommon and morale suffered to some extent. Also, there were men, especially from the thousands trained in the Empire Training or Arnold schemes, who felt they would not have won commissions had they not been on courses in North America.[37] It is interesting to consider the comments from a wartime letter of an American volunteer for Bomber Command. This Sergeant Pilot completed his first tour and won the Distinguished Flying Cross before transferring to the Eighth Air Force. Although his views may reflect a superficial understanding of British culture, they nevertheless reveal some of the frustrations of RAF aircrew:

Unlike the US Army Air Corps, commissioned rank is not conferred on all. Ordinarily they are granted only to those with the Old Schoool tie and/or those who play rugger. Seriously, the situation is just that. Someday I'll try to explain how such a system works, practically, in this great stronghold of democracy.[38]

One of the major and far-reaching results of commissioning only a percentage of flying training graduates was to produce a mixed crew force. It was not unusual by any means to have a sergeant pilot flying an aircraft crewed by an officer bomb-aimer or navigator. In fact, 65 per cent of Bomber Command's aircraft were flown by these sergeant pilots and, of course, complete non-commissioned officer aircrews were just as common.

Early in his tenure as Commander-in-Chief of Bomber Command, Air Marshal Harris recognized that problems were arising as a result of the situation, especially with regard to mixed crews. In his view, the pilot was most properly the 'captain' of the aircraft. In at least some cases, crews with sergeant pilots and officer aircrew members faced real problems with regard to who was in charge. In the air, it was usually obvious that a pilot's authority and decision-making had to be respected, but even this was not an absolute.[39] There was also the question of leadership once the aircraft was on the ground.[40] Harris used these uncertainties to argue for the authority to commission those men displaying leadership, reliability and initiative.[41]

Harris's fundamental concern was for aircrew discipline and morale, which, at various times, he was very worried about. Yet he was also convinced that Flying Training Command was not in as good a position to make commissioning determinations as was Bomber Command. Better, he thought, to wait until graduation from the Operational Training Units to commission candidates than prematurely after initial flight training. Finally, Harris's personal views reflected at least superficial support for the skills and fortitude of his airmen:

In any case, I regard all pilot and navigator aircrew personnel who have successfully passed their training as *ipso facto* suitable for commissioning, unless there is something abnormal in their personality or other trait in their character which would make this withholding a commissioned rank inappropriate.[42]

One also gets the distinct impression that, by ensuring the pilot, navigator and bomb-aimers were commissioned, Harris hoped to avoid the spectre of all-NCO aircrews making decisions by majority vote.[43] Despite his frequently outspoken support for his airmen, like others in the executive he had private fears that some men were not up to the task.[44] Sergeant pilots, who, in at least rare cases, seemed unable to develop their powers of authority, were immediately suspect.[45] Similarly, it was common knowledge, especially in main force squadrons, that not all crews manifested the same determination towards reaching and bombing their targets. Harris and others were aware of various 'dodges', which included things like cruising up and down the North Sea and dumping bombs in the water. Even if the rate of these incidents was always exaggerated, because some degree of intra-crew collusion seemed necessary, NCO aircrews were doubtless deemed more liable to the affliction.[46]

Harris's campaign to commission more of Bomber Command's airmen was not as successful as he would have liked. Inside the Command itself there were those who felt they did not have the time to select and interview suitable candidates for commissioning.[47] In practice, non-commissioned pilots, bomb-aimers and navigators who survived their first tours were usually promoted anyway, even if often subjected to exasperating paperwork and bureaucratic delays.[48] This reduced concerns about fairness, as mere survival had a way of demonstrating a man's 'fitness' for officer rank. It is worth noting too, that at one point in the élite No 8 Group of pathfinders, Group Captain (later Air Vice-Marshal) D. C. T. Bennett had only three pilots without commissions.[49] So if there was a bright side to the entire situation, it was that the hope of eventually wearing officer's insignia gave many of the men something to look forward to.

TOUR LENGTH AND MORALE

It was not long after Bomber Command's eager volunteers joined operational squadrons that the daunting odds against their survival became apparent. Hardened to some extent by the steady toll taken during training, the airmen were nevertheless frequently shocked when confronted by the visible evidence of combat casualties. Britain's experiences in the First World War, particularly on the Western Front, had taught the armed forces the value of front-line rotation. If men were going to be able to sustain themselves during night after night of arduous and extraordinarily dangerous flying, some sort of rotation policy was necessary. A recent history of the RAF rightly characterizes tour length as 'a sheet anchor of morale in Bomber Command', which made 'the unbelievable endurable'.[50]

It did not take the actual commencement of operations to make this fact evident. Initially, however, the Air Ministry was reluctant to specify formal periods of time required for rotation. The Air Member for Personnel, writing as early as February 1940, argued that it would be wrong 'to let it be generally understood that we expect flying crews to display symptoms of war strain after any specified period'.[51] His real concern was that men would begin to regard their service in finite terms. In other words, by establishing tour lengths, the Air Ministry feared it would formalize a contractual arrangement with airmen and thereby limit their military obligation. This philosophy and the corresponding general reluctance to offer aircrews a 'contract' explains much of the resulting confusion on the issue. One finds that a whole series of policy letters and meetings were conducted between 1941 and February 1943 to clarify the subject of tour lengths.

The earliest Air Ministry rules established 200 hours of operational flying as 'datum line'. Aircrew who finished their flying period were to be used in operational training units or flight training schools for six months. After this interval, second tours were authorized, but Sir Richard Peirse, who was Commander-in-Chief of Bomber Command before Harris, made it clear that his organization had thought more in terms of number of operations. Thirty sorties were deemed sufficient for tour completion, with the actual flying hours not to exceed 200.[52]

The uncertainty on the subject at the Air Ministry – the record of which can be followed in various documents – was not subsequently a real factor in Bomber Command.[53] Certainly by 1942 there was little question in the minds of Bomber Command's aircrews, who universally considered 30 missions as their goal – 45 if pathfinder – followed by a six-month break and another tour.[54]

Not unexpectedly, there was considerable support for these limits at the

operational level. When surveyed by senior medical officers, 40 of 43
squadron commanders expressed their strong preference for defining tour
lengths. They argued that the men needed a reference point to measure
achievement. Limiting tours offered a way to maintain efficiency and
handle the substandard. Moreover, crews would know the degree of
effort required of them. Finally, the limits gave the crews a goal, something to look forward to without the alternative of being killed or going
missing.[55]

It must be noted that after he took command Harris was no keen
admirer of the 30 operations limit:

I am most unwilling to do anything to foster the idea that our crews are under
some description of Trade Union contract to carry out a certain number of
carefully defined operational missions, after which they are free, at any rate
for a fixed period, to take no more part in the war.

Having expressed his true convictions, Harris none the less allowed that
the 30-mission requirement would stand:

I do not deprecate our existing arrangements in that regard, but I most
emphatically denounce the exaggerated solicitude and attitude now displayed.
It can but have, and is having, the most deplorable effects on morale.[56]

Harris's qualified support for limits on the first tour underscores the view
that such restrictions were designed in great measure simply to secure a
man's unimpaired return for a second set of operations.[57] Summarizing his
opinions, Harris ended by arguing that ultimately it was up to a crew's
squadron commander to certify completed tours on the basis of whether
or not they had 'done their best'.[58]

ATTRITION RATE

By the time Harris wrote his letter regarding aircrew attempting 'their
best', it should have been clear to all concerned that they had been doing
so despite daunting odds. Bomber Command flew just over 35,000 sorties
in 1942, the huge majority at night. During this same period 1,716 aircraft
crashed or went missing from operations, constituting a loss rate of
approximately 4.89 per cent.[59] There were months during the year,
particularly in the winter, when the rate dipped slightly, but also there
were individual missions – such as the 24/25 August raid on Frankfurt –
where losses were significantly higher.[60] Moreover, certain aircraft always
seemed to take a disproportionate share of the losses. Stirlings and
Halifaxes, in particular, suffered from lack of armament and were underpowered.[61] Units flying the latter aircraft, especially squadrons in No. 4
Group, sustained terrific losses until the aircraft was withdrawn and
replaced. Stirlings were also eventually suspended from operations, but in
both cases the action took place too late to save many. During one savage

month later in the war, No. 434 Squadron sustained a horrific 24.2 per cent loss rate.[62]

It is true enough that casualties were always expected, but loss rates anywhere above three per cent had a devastating impact on aircrew survival statistics. A secret memorandum circulated in the Air Ministry showed that aircrew on heavy bombers had only a 44 per cent chance of surviving their first tours. Exclusive of the very considerable risks during the six-month 'break' at an OTU, the percentage of those who might be expected to finish a second tour in combat fell to only 19.5. In short, only one in five airmen was expected to come through the entire ordeal from start to finish.[63]

By the early months of 1943, the numbers told an even grimmer story. By that point, only about 17 per cent of men could be expected to finish 30 operations safely, and an incredibly small 2.5 per cent would survive two tours.[64] Bombers were being shot down at such a rate that the life expectancy of a new aircraft on an airfield was only about 40 hours of flying time.

In light of the facts, it is small wonder that Sir Charles Portal felt compelled to write to the Air Member for Training,

I am extremely anxious that statistical information relating to the 'chances of survival' of aircrews in certain types of operational employment should be confined to the smallest number of people . . . the information can be so easily distorted and is then so dangerous to morale that all possible steps must be taken to safeguard it.[65]

The subject was so sensitive that correspondence was handled outside normal channels. Discussions about survival statistics, especially at the squadron level, were forbidden. There were fears that airmen who spent their time calculating the odds would 'crack-up' or damage squadron discipline.[66]

The Royal Air Force's senior leadership had every reason to be guarded about the topic. Clearly the scale of casualties could not be hidden and the continuing losses had a profound impact on the aircrews. Losses almost always had an impact by lowering a squadron's experience level and thereby reducing efficiency. But, as the Americans were soon to learn too, attrition was inextricably linked to morale.[67] Among historians there is some agreement that morale became a particularly serious factor twice during Bomber Command's campaign. These two periods – the late summer and autumn of 1942 and the winter of 1943-44 – correspond to intervals of terrible attrition. They also correspond to major efforts over the Ruhr and Berlin.[68]

In the face of such odds, aircrew eagerness to get on with the job was tempered by the daily reminders that the task they faced sometimes seemed almost insurmountable. During various periods of particularly intense operations, losses caused a dizzying turnover in personnel.

NCO aircrew shared huts holding around 16, and each hut billeted parts of 4 or 5 crews. My crew was the only crew to complete its operational flying out of the two huts I was billeted in. In both squadrons I saw these huts completely changed more than once as crews went missing. Most beds were replaced by new crews several times.[69]

In these circumstances, if the bombing campaign was to be continued it was necessary to have an almost continuous flow of new aircrew to make up for losses. Many people in the same squadron hardly knew each other. Most airmen seemed inclined to stick to their own crews in any case, but it was best not to get too well acquainted with other crews.[70] The inevitability of death hung over friendships and hampered closer relationship among many in a squadron. New crews and the inexperienced were considered especially vulnerable – so much so, that there were occasions when their loss was noted quite casually:

. . . and on the following day a little tragedy was posted on the squadron notice boards. Under the heading 'new arrivals' seven names were listed, and directly below, under the heading 'missing in action', were the same seven names.[71]

In general terms, casualties from among the most experienced men seemed more significant, if only because it would cause the less seasoned to wonder what chance they might have.[72] The stoicism shown by many crews was not to be mistaken for lack of emotion. More often than not, there was considerable sadness among aircrews at empty beds in huts or empty tables at the mess, especially if the losses seemed disproportionate to the results. Good news about how the war was going had a salutary effect on morale. Moreover, this effect was magnified when the contribution to eventual victory appeared to come as a result of Bomber Command's efforts.[73]

In some squadrons the matter of casualties was handled better than in others. There were certainly variations in the casualty rate from unit to unit and from month to month, but, for the most part, crews seemed to accept the fact of missing comrades and went on with their duties.[74] For many men there was the psychological defence mechanism symbolized by the saying, 'it will not happen to me'.[75] Additionally, however, aircrews rarely knew the real fate of others less fortunate, and could always assume they had bailed out and were sitting out the balance of the war in a comfortable prisoner-of-war camp.[76]

'BOOMERANGS'

During periods when aircrew morale was put to its severest tests, another signal of its overall condition received attention. From time to time concern grew among Bomber Command's executive that higher than average abort rates pointed to an impending breakdown in morale, either in specific units or in the command as a whole.[77]

Naturally, mission aborts were an integral part of aircraft operations such as those undertaken by Bomber Command. It was recognized at the time that rates always varied and depended on scores of interrelated factors; among these were aircraft type, weather, and the quality of maintenance. Unit leadership and the experience of aircrews were obviously critical, as well. While no absolute numerical standard was established, it became clear that these 'boomerangs' – also sometimes called early returns – increased dramatically under some circumstances.

Reports of higher than average return rates – which hovered around 7 per cent at the time – occurred in No. 4 Group in the autumn of 1943. As noted earlier, this unit, made up of squadrons flying Halifaxes, sustained very significant losses during the spring and summer of the previous year. In fact, at one point, it had been withdrawn from operations for three or four weeks to rest and train the crews.[78] By October 1943, 14 per cent of the group's aircraft were returning without having dropped their bombs on target – this coming on top of casualties approaching ten per cent. These jolting statistics prompted the commander to order an investigation from his operational research section. A resulting interim report, dated 13 December 1943, showed an average abort rate of just above ten per cent, with rates going down slightly during the summer months.

The group's final report was more complete. It rightly pointed out that some aircraft, popularly called 'hangar queens', had poor maintenance records and inflicted more than their share of breakdowns on perfectly willing airmen.[79] Individual aircrew also came under the report's scrutiny. Eighty-one crews aborted once in a two-month period. A further 25 aborted twice and 17 three times. More alarmingly, perhaps, ten crews aborted five or more times. This last statistic led to the report's conclusion which alleviated little of the executive's concerns:

From an aircrew point of view early returns due to defects are unavoidable and the crew should receive consideration rather than otherwise. Only about one third of early returns fall in this class and it might be worthwhile to allow such a trip to count as one-half sortie if the defect was genuine and beyond the aircrew's control. On the other hand, the avoidable type of early return requires very close investigation on the part of the Station and Squadron Commanders.[80]

Station and Squadron Commanders took their duties of investigating early returns very seriously. Crews knew that when they landed there would be a very careful examination of the causes. Virtually every crew also understood, at least in broad outline, the Royal Air Force's policy regarding 'Lack of Moral Fibre', or LMF. Even if they could not explain the details, airmen were aware that unsatisfactory explanations for aborts might leave them facing accusations of cowardice. Occasionally there were confrontations and rancour, particularly if the specifics of mechanical failure could not be duplicated on the ground.[81] Face-offs with commanders must have been almost as stressful as the missions themselves. One pilot remembered the results of aborting a Stirling with supercharger trouble. The aircraft was leaving a blazing trail of sparks across the sky.

To continue to the Ruhr at about 8,000 feet would have been very hazardous . . . the operation was aborted and upon returning to base I was very thoroughly debriefed. The aircraft was test flown the next day and the symptoms could not be reproduced. Two nights later I was off to Düsseldorf in the same aircraft. A complete repetition of the symptoms occurred. This time the debrief upon my return took on a most serious complexion. The line of questioning, after yet another test flight of the aircraft showing no malfunction, was followed by an interview with the unit Medical Officer and the Commanding Officer. I stuck to my decision as right and to clear myself suggested that I go on the next offensive operation in another aircraft . . . thus I was granted my 'last chance' to prove myself.[82]

Fortunately for this veteran and his crew, he was able to fly the following mission without incident. Significantly, perhaps, the young pilot who took the original aircraft on its very next mission failed to return. It is difficult to avoid the conclusion that, at least in some cases, aircrews continued flying aircraft that properly should have been aborted. The fear of being branded LMF forced many to go on.[83]

Rare was the aircrew, however, who did not abort at least once during their tour. Despite powerful urges to get on with the job and finish the operations, many men would take an understandable measure of comfort from aborting – if only temporarily. Conflicting emotions often led to discussions inside aircraft during flight as the nature of the airborne problem was investigated and options weighed. Occasionally, there were votes, with simple majority ruling whether to continue or to return early.[84] Sometimes powerful premonitions of disaster were assuaged by returning. In what must have been isolated cases, crews who felt their chances of survival had been unfairly reduced took action in their own hands. Weariness and anger were powerful motivators.

Sometimes called 'fringe merchants' by unsympathetic commanders, there were always a few crews that deliberately managed things to increase their chances of coming back alive.[85] Among many of the techniques recorded by veterans were dropping bombs in the North Sea to lighten loads, 'cooking' log-books to falsify mission routes and releasing bombs early over target. Occasionally mechanical failure was intentionally induced.[86]

On the very troubling question of intentionally avoiding combat one further topic is of interest. The British were aware of rumours regarding some American bomber aircrew escaping to neutral countries.[87] Bomber Command's problem in this regard was also very small. Post-war documentation shows that only 13 British aircraft crashed-landed in Switzerland, only one of them reasonably intact. Sweden, which was generally much closer to flight routes, reported 64 British aircraft. Among a few damaged Bomber Command Mosquitos were 20 wrecked Lancasters and 13 destroyed bombers of other types. The numbers certainly support historian John Terraine's comment that the evidence 'seems flatly to contradict any suggestion of deliberately seeking to take refuge in a neutral country'.[88]

No part of any discussion on early returns would indicate that the problem was rampant across Bomber Command. In fact, what seems clear from the weight of evidence is that abort rates were highest in units which suffered from rigid leadership and poor equipment.[89] To his great credit, Harris complained constantly about the inadequacies of certain aircraft, most especially the Short Stirling and Handley-Page Halifax, and characteristically minced few words.[90] Despite this, equipment remained a nagging problem and, combined with periods of long missions, high losses and poor bombing results, seemed to lead inevitably to higher than average early returns. Moreover, men wanted to believe what they were doing was important to the overall war effort, and in some measure they wanted to see the immediate results of their daily sacrifices.[91] Bomber Command's recognition of the true causes, however tardy, brought improvements in each area.[92] Although this certainly helped the situation, the principal reason attrition fell and morale improved after the middle of 1944 was because of the huge toll taken on the German night-fighter force and its early warning system.

SUMMARY

It is worthwhile at this juncture to reconsider some of the main points of the discussion regarding attitudes and morale in Bomber Command. Very much like their American counterparts, the young men who volunteered for flying duty with the RAF did so for a variety of reasons. Even without any in-depth sociological data on national differences or human behaviour to prove the point, it nevertheless seems apparent that Britain's airmen went to war with more stoicism and less of the visible emotion so characteristic of Americans. Both were determined to get the job done and generally expressed support for the value of strategic bombing. Many Britons and Commonwealth men were just as motivated by the glamour and thrill of flying as Americans. But, while rank and prestige lured scores of Americans to the Air Corps, it is evident that Britain's society of the 1920s, 1930s and 1940s had a special impact on the motivations of its airmen.

The Royal Air Force never shed all of its pre-war philosophy during the conflict. In fact, for most of the war, there were almost two air forces

– a small, élite group of reservists, and regulars who supervised a great mass of citizen volunteers. The repercussions of this schism could be felt not only in the policies which guided commissioning, but also in the way discipline was administered. Despite the incredible skill and fortitude demonstrated by the overwhelming majority of airmen, there always seemed to be an undercurrent of doubt in the Air Ministry and even occasionally at the command level regarding the morale and discipline of flyers, especially NCOs.

British airmen of Bomber Command, like the Americans in the Eighth Air Force, faced a daily routine that pointed to the inevitability of combat death. Their response, which was to cling together, overcome their fears and to go on, is a tribute to man's ability to survive almost any hardship. These were not cold, hardened men, but rather youngsters forced to endure terrific and unrelenting stress. When the more visible measures of their morale – whether losses or abort rate – tended to rise, it had more to do with poor equipment or poor leadership than it did with any failure of the internal motivations discussed in this chapter. If there was any significant difference between the morale of American airmen and the British and Commonwealth men of Bomber Command, it was that Americans might generally, and with some justification, express more confidence in their aircraft.

All of this seems demonstrable by the evidence, but no analysis of morale can be complete without discussing the role of leadership. Without a doubt, its impact is almost impossible to overestimate. During the war it was understood that sustaining war-fighting spirit was any commander's principal duty. Assisted by a large medical establishment, the Royal Air Force and Bomber Command executive laboured to keep the men motivated, fit and ready to fly. The next chapter will directly compare their efforts and those of the American Eighth Air Force.

NOTES

1. For the best statistical summary see Webster and Frankland, op. cit., Vol. IV, Annexes and Appendices, pp. 429–57.
2. Figures from Webster and Frankland and Charles Messenger, *Bomber Harris and the Strategic Bombing Offensive, 1939–1945* (London: Arms and Armour Press, 1984), p. 191.
3. See Dyson, op. cit., p. 21 and John Terraine, *The Right of the Line* (London: Hodder and Stoughton, 1985), pp. 520–2.
4. Killed or Missing in Action.
5. Robin Higham, editor, *A Guide to the Sources of British Military History* (Berkeley: University of California Press, 1971), p. 345.
6. Air Ministry, *Operational Research*, pp. xvii, 43–4.
7. Verrier, op. cit., p. 70.
8. Typical is one veteran, whose parents' house was destroyed by German bombing. He wrote: 'If a strong lad is not moved by his mother sitting on the steps of her damaged home

and weeping then he is half dead already.' S. N. Freestone (Wellington pilot) to author, 20 March 1990.

9. Air Historical Branch, *Flying Training*, pp. 64–5.
10. By January 1945, 46 per cent of Bomber Command's pilots were from Canada, Australia, or New Zealand, with more than half of these from Canada. See Terraine, note 18, p. 765.
11. Charlwood, op. cit., p. 10.
12. Tempest, op. cit., p. 32.
13. Sir Archibald Sinclair to W. Denis Kendall, MP, 11 April 1941, AIR 2/8271.
14. Dr Stafford-Clark, when speaking of veteran aircrew, indicated they enjoyed the adoration of the public but, 'their reaction to the popular conception of the RAF was one of amused contempt'. Stafford-Clark MSS.
15. Confirmed by, among many others, Tripp, op. cit., p. 17.
16. Clear from scores of published memoirs and letters to the author. From among others see David Hodgson, *Letters from a Bomber Pilot* (London: Thames Methuen, 1985), pp. 76–7.
17. The possibility that a number of men joined strictly to avoid less desirable duties in other services cannot be excluded and seemed perfectly legitimate. This was certainly true for the US Army Air Forces. But the length of RAF training periods and the possibility of dodging combat operations altogether may have led a very tiny fraction of men to join with no intention of ultimately serving. How many will never be known. Interestingly, the statistics on LMF indicate a high proportion of men so accused came from the group which feigned enthusiasm. See Squadron Leader D. D. Reid, 'The Influence of Psychological Disorder on Efficiency in Operational Flying', FPRC 508, Sept. 1942, AIR 20/10727.
18. By the mid-1930s the RAF had convinced the public that it was an élite force. This élitism was born of romantic and chivalrous notions about air combat. Michael Paris, 'The Rise of the Airmen: The Origins of Air Force Elitism', paper presented at the Military History Research Seminar, King's College, London, 22 Oct., 1991.
19. Freestone to author, 20 March 1990.
20. For a good discussion on aircrew volunteers see Freeman, *British Airmen*, pp. 4–8 and Longmate, op. cit., pp. 174–6.
21. Eight thousand aircrew died in accidents; almost one in seven of Bomber Command's losses came in training. See Martin Middlebrook, *The Nuremberg Raid* (London: Penguin Books, 1986), p. 52 and Stafford-Clark MSS, p. 83.
22. This was an indirect result of the country's experience with the regimental system which has been called, 'the most significant of Britain's military institutions'. John Keegan, 'Regimental Ideology', in Geoffrey Best and Andrew Wheatcroft (eds), *War Economy and the Military Mind* (London: Croom Helm, Rowman & Littlefield, 1976), p. 16. See also Richardson, pp. 14–22.
23. Usually seated close together were the pilot, flight-engineer, navigator, bomb-aimer, and wireless operator. Tail-gunners and mid-upper gunners were in isolated crew positions. See William Green, *Famous Bombers of the Second World War*, 2 vols. (New York: Doubleday and Company, 1960).
24. Among others, W. T. MacFarlane (Halifax pilot) to author, 20 July 1989, Geoffrey R. Whitten (Halifax navigator) to author, 30 May 1990, and Tripp, op. cit., p. 9.
25. Charlwood, op. cit., p. 26.
26. The RAF lost 5,327 officers and men killed in training between 1939 and 1945. A further 3,113 were injured. If, as one historian has suggested, the crewing-up procedure was 'natural selection', this was an appalling price to pay for it. See Max Hastings, op. cit., p. 167.
27. Stirling veteran to author, 15 April 1990.
28. S. A. Booker (Halifax navigator) to author, 20 June 1990.
29. Air Vice-Marshal D. J. Furner (retd) to author, 9 April 1990.
30. The late Group Captain Sir Leonard Cheshire, VC, RAF, to author 14 March 1989.
31. Richardson, op. cit., p. 10.
32. G. Dyer, *War* (London: The Bodley Head, 1985), p. 106.
33. Air Historical Branch, *Manning Plans and Policy* (AHB Monograph/II/116/14), Appendix 18. Also quoted in Terraine, op. cit., p. 464.
34. Responding to manpower concerns, between 1941 and 1942 the USAAF trained about 2,000 enlisted pilots. Institutional support for doing so was half-hearted at best and these pilots were often socially segregated and subjected to hostility. The programme was phased out and

most of its graduates were commissioned by the time they went overseas. Bruce D. Callander, 'Enlisted Pilots', *Air Force Magazine,* June 1989, p. 100. See also Terraine, op. cit., p. 464.

35. Message to Commander, No. 92 Group, 18 Feb. 1943, AIR 14/1008.
36. Before the rank of Flight Sergeant was instituted, many thousands were made Sergeant Pilots. Edgar L. Spridgeon (Instructor Pilot) to author, 9 March 1992 and George Irving, quoted in Freeman, *British Airmen*, p. 35.
37. H. F. S. Mitchell (Lancaster navigator) to author, 30 April 1990.
38. Robert S. Raymond, *A Yank in Bomber Command* (New York: Hippocrene Books, 1977), p. 52.
39. Various letters to the author make it clear that there were some strong personal conflicts on the issue.
40. As late as July 1942 the King's Regulations and Air Council Instructions precluded non-pilots from being 'captains' of aircrew. Faced with mixed crews and the prospect of sergeants 'commanding' officers, the instructions were amended to put the officer – whatever his air-crew position – in charge. From a practical point of view this was next to impossible to enforce. See Air Ministry Letter, 1 July 1942, AIR 20/3053.
41. Harris to Undersecretary of State for Air, 23 Oct. 1942, AIR 14/1008.
42. Harris to commanders, Nos. 1,3,4,5,6, and 8 Group, 6 Feb. 1943, AIR 14/1008.
43. An allegation made directly by Cochrane to Harris in a letter of 19 Sept. 1942. On a preced-ing attack on Essen, No. 3 Group had dispatched 72 aircraft as a part of a raiding force of 369. Only two of the 19 bombers which aborted did so for 'justifiable reasons'. According to Cochrane the problem was with NCO skippers. AIR 14/3544.
44. Views expressed at various times by Portal, Joubert, and the Air Council Committee on Morale and Discipline. See 'Morale and Discipline in the Royal Air Force'. AIR 20/3082.
45. Given that Air Marshal Portal had written that good discipline started with 'a clearly defined and thoroughly understood chain of command', the strains which resulted from mixed air-crews and questions about who was in charge of an aircraft should have come as no surprise. See Portal to Babington, 3 Dec., 1942, AIR 20/3082.
46. The more elaborate the scheme to abort, the more complicated the cover story and more likely the entire crew's participation. Log books and charts were routinely checked after missions. Longmate wrote regarding early returners that, 'though British films tended to show the officers as being superior to the other ranks in courage as well as accent, the skippers responsible were just as often commissioned as not'. Geoffrey R. Whitten (Halifax navigator) to author, 30 May 1990 and Longmate, op. cit., p. 184.
47. Cochrane to Harris, 15 Feb. 1943, AIR 14/1008
48. From January to February 1943, 95 men had been recommended for commission in No. 6 Group. By 11 February only eight promotions had come through. It also cannot be excluded that some NCO aircrew were offered commissions and declined. See AIR 14/1008.
49. Air Vice-Marshal D. C. T. Bennett, *Pathfinder* (London: Frederick Miller, 1958; London: Goodall Publications Ltd, 1988), p. 169 and AIR 14/1008.
50. Terraine, op. cit., p. 527.
51. AIR 2/8038.
52. Peirse to Air Ministry, 13 Jan. 1941, AIR 2/8038.
53. Terraine's analysis is more than adequate, except that he does not explain the reason for at least part of the confusion; namely, the senior leadership's deep-seated philosophical opposi-tion to giving men a limit on their combat service. Another factor must simply have been the lack of communication between the flying commands and the Air Ministry. See Terraine, op. cit., pp. 522–7, AIR 2/8038, and AIR 2/8039.
54. Saundby to Group Commanders, 20 Aug. 1942, AIR 2/8039.
55. Symonds and Williams, *Psychological Disorders*, p. 38.
56. Harris to Air Ministry, 2 Feb. 1943, AIR 2/8039.
57. See also Symonds and Williams, *Psychological Disorders*, p. 40.
58. In general, proof was a satisfactory night photograph. Otherwise it was left to the squadron commander. AIR 2/8039.
59. By way of comparison it is interesting to look at the American Eighth Air Force's losses for the same period. Just beginning their operations, the Americans lost only 42 aircraft between August and December. These numbers make it dramatically clear that the weight of the strategic bombing offensive was being borne by Bomber Command's aircrews at

the time. Roger Freeman, *The US Strategic Bomber* (London: Macdonald and Jane's, 1975), p. 156.

60. Two-hundred and twenty-six aircraft were launched against Frankfurt. Six Lancasters, 5 Wellingtons, 4 Stirlings, and 1 Halifax were lost – 7.1 per cent of the force. See Middlebrook, *Diaries*, p. 302.

61. Philip J. R. Moyes, 'The Handley Page Halifax', *Aircraft in Profile* Vol. 1, edited by Martin C. Windrow (New York: Doubleday & Company, 1969), p. 126.

62. Middlebrook, *Diaries*, p. 447.

63. Air Member for Personnel, 16 Nov. 1942, AIR 20/2859.

64. According to a spring 1943 table in AIR 20/2860.

65. Portal to AMT, 24 Dec. 1942, AIR 20/2860.

66. Dyson later wrote of 'the whole weight of Air Force tradition and authority' discouraging conversations on odds. Similarly, he noted the stringent precautions taken regarding survival statistics documents. Dyson, op. cit., pp. 22–3.

67. A good short discussion of the relationship is in Webster and Frankland, Vol. IV, p. 446.

68. Among several descriptive letters was one that cited the 'gloom and weariness among the crews' who sometimes had the feeling that they were not accomplishing their objectives despite their efforts. R. B. Vennard (Halifax flight engineer) to author 12 Aug. 1990.

69. Leonard J. S. O'Hanlon (Halifax gunner) to author, 25 Feb. 1990.

70. Middlebrook, *Berlin*, p. 318.

71. Tripp, op. cit., p. 101.

72. Symonds and Williams, *Psychological Disorders*, p. 49.

73. George Mead (Lancaster bomb-aimer) to author, 27 April 1990.

74. 'Their attitude to losses and the death of friends was particularly striking; it was one of supreme realism. . .'. Dr David Stafford-Clark, 'Morale and Flying Experience: Results of a Wartime Study', *Journal of Mental Science*, (Jan. 1949), p. 15.

75. Although crews knew that in all likelihood they would be killed, wounded, or go missing, they 'did not all accept their own deaths'. Interview with Dr David Stafford-Clark, 19 Jan. 1992, Brighton. Echoed by Tripp, op. cit., pp. 180–1.

76. Among other letters to the author, S. A. Booker (Halifax navigator), 20 June 1990.

77. High abort rates were evident for some aircraft during the Nuremberg raid and on various raids to Berlin. See Middlebrook, *Nuremberg*, p. 119, and *Berlin*, p. 37.

78. Webster and Frankland, Vol. IV, p. 445.

79. Twenty-nine of 140 aircraft aborted two or more times. Seven aircraft were aborted by their crews five or more times in two months. It is not difficult to imagine what men must have thought when assigned to these hard-luck machines. See 'Investigations into causes of Abortive Sorties', AIR 14/1886.

80. 'Investigations into causes of Abortive Sorties', AIR 14/1886.

81. Max Hastings cites an incident regarding 'magneto drop', which was one of the more difficult mechanical problems to duplicate. The pilot in his anecdote was accused of LMF and dismissed. Hastings, op. cit., p. 190.

82. Freestone to author 20 March 1990.

83. The deterrent effect of LMF policy will be discussed more fully in a subsequent chapter. See also Middlebrook, *Nuremberg*, pp. 117–19 and Longmate, op. cit., pp. 187–8.

84. Among other veterans who remembers discussions is C. H. Chandler (Stirling flight engineer). Letter to author, 1 July 1990.

85. Air Vice-Marshal D. C. T. Bennett used the term in the official history. See also Bennett, op. cit., p. 174.

86. It should be noted that many crews practised unconventional, if perfectly legitimate, techniques to improve their chances. Some skippers, unconvinced of the value of flexible gunnery, ordered machine-gun ammunition thrown overboard on outbound legs to lighten the load and raise maximum allowable ceilings. On mechanical failure, information from Geoff Parnell (Stirling gunner) to author, 15 April 1990.

87. Max Hastings's uncited comment regarding desertion being openly discussed at USAAF bomber stations is at best a gross exaggeration. His similarly unsupported allegation that many Americans, 'did not feel the personal commitment to the war that was possible for Englishmen' is undemonstrated and, worse, insulting to the memory of the 100,000 airmen who saw combat with the Eighth Air Force and their 19,876 dead comrades. See Hastings, op. cit., p. 253.

88. Terraine cited Swiss and Swedish documents held by the Air Historical Branch. Terraine, op. cit., pp. 535–6.
89. The impact of equipment is difficult to overestimate. So poor were the relative performances of the Halifax II and the Stirling compared with that of the Lancaster that many crews regarded their assignment to those two aircraft as a virtual death sentence. Tragically for many, the Operational Research Section at Bomber Command often operated against bureaucratic inertia in improving safety equipment. See Green, *Famous Bombers*, Vol 1., p. 134; Vol. 2., pp. 43–4, 90 and Dyson, op. cit., pp. 25–30.
90. He wrote that the manager of Short was an 'incompetent drunk' and recommended that 'Handley-Page and his gang be kicked out, lock, stock, and barrel'. Harris to Sinclair 30 Dec. 1942, AIR 14/3512.
91. Verrier noted accurately that 'a good blaze' on the target raised morale. Verrier, op. cit., p. 203.
92. Harris, who after the war insisted that morale had not been a factor, allowed that the entire question hinged on aircrews' sense of accomplishment. Men became disappointed if they could not see the results of what they were doing; they needed to know their sacrifices were important. Air Marshal Sir Arthur Harris, Thames Television recorded interview, No. 002893/03/01,02,03. Imperial War Museum.

6

Sustaining Morale:
The Impact of Leadership

JUST AS NO absolute definition of morale exists, so too is it difficult to cite any all-encompassing list of the characteristics of good air force leadership. No single successful style or pattern existed during the Second World War's Combined Bomber Offensive, nor was any completely finite set of attributes ever established. The variations of style were almost as infinite as the background, character and training of the thousands of individual men who led others in the air war. This is not to say, however, that airmen of both Bomber Command and the Eighth Air Force did not understand the importance of leadership to morale. They certainly did. While there seemed little doubt even at the time that love of flying, peer pressure, group cohesion, desire to see things through, attrition and tour length, among other things, played major roles in sustaining an airman's psychological motivation, it was leadership that provided much of the day-to-day external support for staying in combat.[1]

Leadership was rightly characterized as the 'keystone' upon which any fighting unit was built, and this recognition led to the almost universal acceptance of dicta such as the following:

Send a good leader to a squadron of low morale and in a short space of time he will build it up; put a bad leader into a squadron with high morale and, given time, the standard will deteriorate.

It is my conviction that good group commanders insure good units and that poor group commanders cannot possibly have good units.[2]

Our understanding of the human dimension in the Combined Bomber Offensive would therefore be incomplete without considering the importance and impact of leadership. In this regard it is especially useful to attempt – despite the difficulty – to summarize a composite list of characteristics which contemporary sources indicated were particularly important to effective leadership of air combat units during the Second World War. By doing so it will also be possible to compare American and British styles. Much of what were taken at the time for dissimilar patterns was more the result of different air combat environments. Some, too, was doubtless the result of philosophy or national characteristics, and a couple of examples will highlight the similarities and differences. But rather than simply reviewing characteristics and well-known cases which come to mind in any history of the Combined Bomber Offensive, it will also be important to consider the specifics of where and how leadership most affected the lives of airmen. In addition to the major activity of actual combat flying, these areas fall broadly into the 'health and welfare' category and include leaders' policies relating to aircrew comradeship, rest, recreation, training and decorations. They deserve attention.

THE CHARACTERISTICS OF EFFECTIVE AIR LEADERSHIP

Airmen in Bomber Command and the Eighth Air Force were never reluctant to comment on the quality of the men appointed to send them into battle. In general terms their thoughts regarding leadership, both at the time and now, indicate that they best followed men who showed courage, competence and compassion.[3] The optimum may have been to have unit commanders with equally dynamic portions of all three characteristics, but as long as no single quality was totally lacking, for the most part, airmen were prepared to get on with their missions.

Courage was an obvious prerequisite for leadership because, as we have seen, very few airmen of the time were excited by or responded to flamboyant rhetoric or patriotic exhortation.[4] Nor was there any absolute requirement for reckless heroism or histrionics. Rather, leaders who displayed steady, unflappable demeanour were more often admired.[5] It is no surprise that British and American aircrews looked to the courage of their leaders for example.

Showing courage typically extended from making difficult decisions affecting personnel to participating in the toughest missions. In this regard, leaders who failed to fly regularly risked almost instant loss of credibility and social ostracism. Inevitably, some commanders, particularly those who felt they had already 'done their bit', decided not to go on further operations. A very few, often openly derided by others who were risking their lives daily, chose only easy missions or 'milk runs'.[6] When airborne, leaders who openly displayed fear or panic had a predictable impact on the morale of their units.[7] Not surprisingly, units with commanders like this usually had higher than average early return rates.

The majority of commanders, however, and especially the most successful, saw flying missions as an indivisible and necessary part of their job.[8] The youngest Air Vice-Marshal in the history of the Royal Air Force felt very strongly about the issue:

I always made a point of flying with a different crew each night, leaving the captain concerned at home. I was thus able to check up on the efficiency of each crew, and at the same time to give them what I could in the way of instruction in navigation and how best to do their work.[9]

Similar sentiments were expressed by one of the Eighth Air Force's most famous combat commanders during a wartime interview:

How can any commanding officer send his people into combat when he knows nothing about it? So I started out leading all missions personally. Not only did I feel that I ought to lead the people fighting under me, but I had to find out things . . . You have to get in there and fight to find out what it's all about.[10]

Occasionally, too, a strong, even impulsive act of leadership could have an electrifying effect on a unit. A Bomber Command medical officer recalls an incident on a station where morale was at a low ebb:

One night, shortly after his arrival, when the squadron had been briefed for an extremely dangerous target, in bad weather, a telephone message was received from the outlying dispersal point, where an aircraft was standing, to the effect that a pilot felt unwell and could not take off. Whether the cause was organic or functional was a matter of opinion: what was clear was that the success of the operation would be interfered with if one aircraft failed to take off with the others. Without hesitation, with no preparation in the way of a meal, adequate briefing for the target, suitable clothing, or any other desirable preliminaries, the new squadron commander, without comment, handed over his duties to a subordinate, got straight into the aircraft, and was airborne within a few minutes. He completed a successful sortie under difficult conditions, and was extremely exhausted on return, having had no food for many hours. The effect, however, on the morale of that squadron was dramatic.[11]

In many ways, such memorable signals of leadership and courage were easier to spot in the Eighth Air Force than they were in Bomber Command. The more solitary nature of Bomber Command's war was a contributing factor, but also the fact that American operations took place in daylight cannot be ignored. In Bomber Command's air war, there were doubtless thousands of individual acts of bravery that went unwitnessed and unrecorded except on board individual aircraft maintaining radio silence. When these nocturnal raiders were shot down, as they so often were, their stories of leadership and heroism often went with them.

In contrast, the large American daylight formations meant that many more airmen might actually hear and see individual acts of bravery and heroism in the Eighth Air Force's bomber squadrons.[12] The courage which comes as a result of leadership by example was similarly more apparent. There were countless incidents of highly visible burning and damaged aircraft continuing to lead bomb runs or navigate formations to safety.[13] A number of well-deserved awards for gallantry in the Eighth Air Force must have been made because there were hundreds of eyes watching lead aircraft as events unfolded.[14]

Just as aircrew expected their leaders to display the courage to lead by example, they also expected these commanders to be competent. Flying a Second World War four-engine bomber or single-seat fighter was very much a technical skill which routinely required mental agility as well as a modicum of physical strength and co-ordination. Moreover, both types of aircraft frequently demanded quick motor-reactions and split-second decision-making, especially in combat. In the case of bombers, communication skills were critically important, because co-ordinating the activities of a crew was paramount to success. And, for Americans, the complex requirements of managing multi-aircraft formations called for formidable talent. Commanders who displayed weak flying skills themselves often had difficulty leading units made up of men whose lives depended on these abilities.

Junior airmen were never slow to identify or criticize poor commanders, inevitably using terms like 'weak sisters' or something worse to describe them.[15] One veteran bombardier of the 384th Bomb Group noted that the practice of sending high-ranking but poorly prepared officers on bombing missions had its risks:

No criticism would be fair if such a leader were qualified and experienced, but in the cases to which I refer these attributes were conspicuous by their absence. On a recent raid over Germany, it was found upon arrival over the target that cloud cover made location of the objective next to impossible. By direction of inexperienced leadership we remained over the target for about 30 minutes trying to locate same. As a direct result, 96 [sic] of our aircraft were later forced to ditch in the channel because of fuel exhaustion . . . The type of leadership in his case was at least partially responsible for such a catastrophe in that his judgement in remaining over the target area so long made such a situation possible.[16]

Another airman was even more direct in venting his frustration and anger at those not performing adequately:

It has been a source of concern among combat crews that too often the rank leading the formation are not qualified . . . We had a similar experience with our Squadron CO. Before he was named CO he had flown a great deal in the States, and in the wing position and as element leader on two or three missions, but as for being a seasoned combat pilot, he was green and inexperienced. After his promotion, in flying position on the Group leader, he would jockey the throttle back and forth. The other pilots trying to follow him were exhausted after a long mission and the formation became loose and vulnerable to attack. He was very set in the ideas that he had formed in the States and wouldn't adjust them to combat conditions. His inexperience and attitude made him unfit for duty as Squadron CO.[17]

Finally, a veteran wryly recalls another incident involving a Group Commander and the procedure for dealing with incompetents:

His fifth trip I was on. We formed under 7,000 ft. clouds, headed toward Germany at the same altitude. The damn fool was going to take us over the coast at that altitude. At the last minute, the lead pilot convinced him of his folly so we turned around, found a hole, climbed and went on in; by now the 400 odd ships in the formation were scattered all over the sky. But we went on in 37 minutes late, without fighter cover, the target already bombed by other divisions. They gave him the DFC and sent him home.[18]

Small wonder, then, that British and American units which enjoyed the most success, and managed to sustain their morale despite terrific losses, enjoyed commanders with laudable leadership and flying skills. In some cases, the reputation of these aviators became widespread. A few were probably 'natural pilots' with God-given advantages in hand-eye co-ordination. The majority, however, practised and honed their skills with long training flights, hours of technical study and mind-numbing repetition.[19] The best among them recognized that the success of the mission, their own lives and the lives of their airmen depended on their meticulous attention to detail. Airmen could be especially appreciative of a leader whose competence led to the destruction of targets with minimum risk:

I noticed that the squadron commander that . . . sort of ended up bringing the squadron back all in one piece . . . he was always a pretty popular fellow.[20]

A widely accepted aphorism of the time, and one which contained a considerable amount of truth, was that units took on the personality of their commanders.[21] Units with the best records had skilled and disciplined commanders. Sloppy, indifferent or lax commanders often led units to disaster in the sky.[22]

Displaying the correct blend of practical leadership characteristics demonstrated what was universally known as 'guts'. At the operational and tactical level of air combat, courage, skill and tenacity often outweighed pure intellectual abilities.

I really don't recall any mental genius running around as commanders of fighter groups in the Eighth Air Force. Neither can I say that there were any dullards among the ranks. A few silently dropped from the pack for not possessing the degree of emotional attitude needed to participate in the combat environment. Most of us who became group commanders were only junior captains in 1942. With rapid, temporary promotion and delegation of responsibilities, we took over. Rightly or wrongly those units that were led and acted aggressively ultimately resolved their problems and came out on top.[23]

This does not suggest for a moment that men could act recklessly or without thinking. In fact, especially with regard to their concerns for the morale of their men, leaders had to act with deliberate understanding and compassion.

The ability of any leader to inspire confidence in the personnel of his unit was dependent, to some extent, on circumstances and his own personality, but those leaders who took a genuine interest in the welfare of all personnel – both flyers and non-flyers – were generally rewarded with better performance all around. As in any military situation or circumstance involving marshalling the efforts of large numbers of people and divergent personalities, one of the keys of effective leadership was to demonstrate fairness and firmness without appearing harsh or arbitrary. Squadron commanders, group and station commanders not only often dealt with the daily pressures of combat flying but also faced the less dramatic but no less necessary duties of ground administration and disciplinary chores.

In very real ways these officers inescapably represented the rigid institutional authority of their air forces.[24] But, because many were combat leaders as well, they wielded more informal power as a part of an élite social group of fighting men. This partially highlights the importance of their personalities. For all its negative pressures, combat usually fostered a close sense of group identity and unit solidarity. Because so many of the combatants, especially in the Eighth Air Force, were officers, the sense of shared hardship broke down many barriers and improved relations.[25] In short, a competent, humane officer might still maintain a command presence but nevertheless be regarded as 'one of us' by enlisted men.

Examples of this kind of leader are not hard to find. In Bomber Command, at least three names were routinely mentioned as approachable, inspirational commanders; these were Leonard Cheshire, Mickey Martin and Guy Gibson. In addition to being a superb pilot and tactician, Cheshire made it a point to know the name of every man in his unit. Given the steady turnover of people in any squadron of Bomber Command, this was no mean feat.[26] Gibson was similarly admired as the gallant leader of No. 617 Squadron, and Mickey Martin justifiably enjoyed his reputation as an extraordinary aviator. These men rightly earned the accolades of a grateful nation, but it is important to remember that there were very many others, less well known to the public perhaps, but no less imbued with effective leadership attributes.[27]

The Eighth Air Force also had men who exercised admirable leadership. The hand-picked commanders of the original four 'pioneer' bomb groups – Frank Armstrong, Curtis LeMay, James Wallace and Stanley Wray – all had distinguished careers. From among the scores who subsequently achieved notable success were Archie Old, Maurice Preston, Budd Peaslee, Theodore Milton, Harold Bowman and Dale Smith. Also, fighter pilot leaders like Donald Blakeslee, Hub Zemke, Dave Shilling and Claiborne Kinnard not only led superb groups, but all became aces themselves.[28]

As successful as these men were, in some measure they took their example from a more senior level. In Bomber Command the Group COs were often necessarily removed from the action. Even so, there seems little doubt that a couple of the Groups fared better than others owing to superior leadership. Number 5 group's commander, Sir Ralph Cochrane, assembled a stellar group of squadron commanders. Donald Bennett – who was apparently anything but likeable – similarly commanded great respect from his aircrews and built the Pathfinders into an élite force. Finally, Air Marshal Harris, while also not generally considered a warm or approachable man, nevertheless, in the main, received immense respect from his aircrews.[29] Perhaps it was his very remoteness and single-minded approach that inspired confidence and gave them the impression that everything he did was to their advantage. Ultimately, it may have been his ability to hit responsive chords with his rhetoric and the gift of sending 'Churchillian signals'.[30]

On the American side, both General Eaker and General Doolittle got on well with their men, despite occasional grumbles about tour length. Unlike their British counterpart, both were seen frequently at bomber stations where they often ate and socialized with aircrew. Eaker was a taciturn man with a simple and easy-going manner. Doolittle, for his part, especially liked to mix with aviators. This may be partly explained by his background as a stunt and racing pilot, but he clearly made calculated efforts to fire up his men.

Doolittle impressed all of us. He had a great combination of flamboyance and common sense, which we all liked. He would come into your airfield, buzz the tower, do a Chandelle, land and jump out – possibly he had not shaved in a day or two. We all thought that he was a tremendously effective commander.[31]

Occasionally, however, Doolittle got more than he bargained for when he visited units. His recent memoirs recall a March 1944 trip to check the long-suffering 100th Bomb Group:

On a visit to another unit that had been having bad luck and many losses, Tooey Spaatz and I went to the officers' club to try to buck them up a little. When we were about to leave, one of the young pilots, having imbibed a little too much, approached us and said, 'I know why you're here. You think our morale is shot because we've been taking it on the nose. Well, I can tell you our morale is all right. There's only one thing that hurts our morale – that's when generals come around to see what's the matter with it'.[32]

SITUATIONAL LEADERSHIP AND NATIONAL DIFFERENCES

Even if the evidence supports the contention that courage, competence, and compassion were characteristics common to effective leadership in both the Eighth Air Force and Bomber Command, we must still allow that certain situations arose which demanded exceptional patterns of direction. The unrelenting demands of operations and the almost infinite combination of circumstances thrust hundreds and hundreds of relatively young airmen into leadership roles during the war. Some failed. Those who were not killed were frequently replaced. Whatever the result of their tenure, some unit commanders left powerful impressions on the people who served under them.

There were occasions when the effectiveness of particular combat units was called into question and commanders were specially selected for their ability to save the situation. One famous incident occurred in the 306th Bomb Group in January 1943. Measured against the criteria established at the time, this unit had been performing poorly for several weeks.[33] Its losses had been high, the abort rate had increased, and the number of aircraft prepared on any given mission was too frequently lower than other groups.[34] Moreover, there were indications that military discipline was lax and that the previous commander of the 306th had over-identified with the problems of his men.[35] It was clear the 306th was in need of a change.

General Eaker sent Brigadier General Frank A. Armstrong to Thurleigh to command this 'hard-luck' unit.[36] Successfully employing a technique which has been studied and pondered by subsequent generations of US Air Force officers, Armstrong correctly identified the real problem, assessed the maturity of his followers, and modified his leadership to fit the task.[37] By nature an intelligent and personable man, Armstrong intentionally toughened his approach to re-motivate the unit to action. Fundamentally, the skills required were already in place. What was necessary had more to do with restoring the confidence of the unit than retraining it. Armstrong's replacement of key personnel, constant cajoling, and enforcement of a return to the basics of military decorum eventually paid off. The 306th Bomb Group's formation flying got tighter, bombing accuracy improved, and casualties came down.[38] Six weeks after his arrival, Armstrong was moved to another unit.

Similar and no less critical incidents took place in Bomber Command, perhaps with a little less lasting drama. The historian and journalist Max Hastings has written convincingly about the problems in the spring of 1943 in No. 76 Squadron.[39] These were effectively dealt with by Group Captain Cheshire. Cheshire's efforts and subsequent comments on the subject reveal an enormously compassionate man struggling to balance the conflicting demands of operations with the welfare of his men.[40] But Cheshire's squadron was not alone. The staggering casualties suffered from time to time by No. 4 Group prompted occasional visits by its commander to squadrons.[41] In sum, Bomber Command's leadership responded in ways similar to the Eighth Air Force's when special circumstances warranted it.

Another striking example of the importance of situational leadership relates to the frequently different rhetoric and styles employed at bomber and fighter stations. There was considerable evidence at the time suggesting that the temperament of successful bomber aircrew was different from that of fighter pilots.[42] Squadron and group commanders were not reluctant to encourage their airmen in ways which were designed to appeal to these differing characteristics.

In successful fighter units in the Eighth Air Force, for example, there was a tendency to lead from the front. To some extent this was the result of the nature of air combat, but also partly sprang from the aggressiveness of young fighter pilot leaders and their followers. Few would dispute the words of the squadron commander who ended the war with 28 victories:

Only through professional flying and training can one become a combat leader. Professional leadership is only an ultimate step of professional airmanship, coupled with aggressiveness, judgement, keen eyesight, and understanding the capabilities of your wingman, element leader, flight leader, and the makeup of the entire team.[43]

Significantly, ten of the Eighth Air Force's top 25 aces served as squadron or group commanders. Despite an average age of only 26 years, they clearly demonstrated the competence to lead and to fight. Moreover, by war's end, nine of the ten had been shot down, captured or killed in action. No statistic could more convincingly establish their willingness to put themselves at risk to inspire others.

As a part of this style, American daytime fighter pilots were most often told that they were the best trained, best equipped and best led men in the theatre. While outright recklessness in the air was to be avoided, they were nevertheless admonished to be as aggressive as possible, and constantly seek the enemy. In short, one of the major goals of leadership was to inculcate the idea of absolute superiority over the enemy.[44] In other words, these men were encouraged to believe it was important that they live to fight so the enemy might be killed. Significantly, these ideas were given even further emphasis when General Doolittle published an order largely freeing the Eighth Air Force's fighters from close escort duties.[45] Early in January 1944, fighter pilots were given formal permission to carry out what had been their true inclinations all along – finding and destroying German fighters.[46]

The contrast on bomber bases could not have been more stark. Unlike their fighter pilot counterparts, bomber crewmen were less frequently told that they were superior, or that their own aggressiveness would ensure success. Rather, commanders often used messages more designed to take their aviators' minds off their gnawing fears. In fact, many bomber unit commanders spoke to crewmen in terms similar to the following:

Is anyone scared? If not, there is something wrong with you. I'll give you a little clue how to fight this war – *make believe you're dead already* [author's emphasis]; the rest comes easy.[47]

To what extent bomber crewmen took exhortations like this to heart may never be known. While the goal must have been to help men over some of the daily stresses, the likely effect of leadership in this instance was to engender a fatalistic attitude on the part of many crewmen.[48] Similar approaches were common in Bomber Command at various times. They led to melancholy scenes like the one observed by Dr Stafford-Clark:

Flying Officer: 'What do you think you're going to do after the war, Eddie?'

Squadron Leader, gazing thoughtfully into the bottom of his glass: 'Oh, I don't know. I don't really think I shall last as long as that'.

According to Stafford-Clark, this was said quietly, matter-of-factly and sincerely by a sound, intelligent man of calm and cheerful disposition.[49]

Although Bomber Command and Eighth Air Force data are understandably sparse on the subject of national character as they related to command – and there are always dangers in generalizing – one can still discern some variations in leadership styles based on cultural and educational factors. Britain of the 1940s was still very much a society where socio-economic class counted for much.[50] Despite the fact that very many officers in the RAF and Bomber Command were not necessarily public school trained, much of the philosophy of the upper classes permeated the service.[51] From this group a pattern of leadership could sometimes be seen which reflected a gentle civility and occasionally a paternal attitude towards NCOs and enlisted men.[52] Faltering airmen were admonished 'not to let our side down', or 'let's get on with it, chaps', in the same manner as a cricket or rugby team might be encouraged. Understatement, restraint and humility were virtues of leadership. Bragging or showing emotion was eschewed. It was especially important not to admit weakness and 'maintaining a stiff upper lip' was more than a wartime cliché.[53] In this pattern, courage and leadership were inseparable from the character of a man.[54]

While such behaviour was certainly not universal, it nevertheless contrasts with what was widely accepted as a brasher, more vocal and exuberant American style.[55] The huge majority of American officers were not regulars. Only a few had come from West Point. Most had had at least some college education, but the gulf between them and those they commanded was not as wide as was the case with some of the British. The result was a large group of enthusiastic amateurs collectively directing a rapidly expanding Eighth Air Force filled with men very much like themselves. These thousands of young officers and scores of squadron commanders could not simply rely on military tradition or trite exhortations to motivate their men. American airmen were generally well trained, but frequently seemed to demand more explanation and encouragement. No less willing, they simply wanted to know what they were doing, and why.[56]

Similarly, combat flyers were particularly sensitive to pledges made by higher headquarters.

Few things disturb the American soldier more than to feel that his superiors have made him a promise which they have not kept . . . Furthermore, even when no promises were intended men often believe that promises have been made. Sometimes such 'promises' are spread by rumour. It is, therefore, highly important to recognize and take counter-measures against these 'latrine rumours'.[57]

On those occasions when American airmen were not satisfied, they tended to let their leaders know. Although he was in the army, the officer's comments which follow were probably echoed by many British observers at Eighth Air Force stations.

Americans seem to spend just as much time on spit and polish as we do, but their standard of results in this direction is lower. Perhaps this is an expression of their constant determination to resent being ordered about. Englishmen, of all ranks, take orders with far less question. The ignominies of KP (fatigues to us) are much less keenly felt . . . Americans look on the Army more as a nine-to-six job. Their loyalty is more akin to the pride of a business-man employed by a first-rate firm, whereas the British soldier's loyalty is based on the feeling that we mustn't let the old place down, plus personal attachment to officers, which I think Americans are too independent to develop to the same extent unless their officer is an acknowledged hero . . .[58]

It is important not to carry this analysis too far. Despite much that was different about the leadership in the two air forces, both managed to allow for the eccentricities of the other.[59] Occasionally, too, the earliest meetings of British and American aviators could produce amusing results:

Out popped a very strange gentleman from this aircraft that I noticed had American markings, but I still did not know what the aircraft was. I had a vague idea but I was not sure. This strange gentleman came round who was wearing a sort of baseball cap like all my Canadians were. He came towards me and stopped about 10 to 15 yards away, put his hand inside his bomber jacket and brought out a monster hand-held cannon which he pointed in my direction. It was the sort of weapon that you saw John Wayne wielding so well and twisting around his finger, but I did not like the idea of this thing which I was looking straight down the barrel of.
'Hi Bud', he called, 'do you speak English?'
'Well', I said, 'there is some considerable doubt about that; I am a Scots-man'.[60]

It should be noted, too, that Bomber Command's distinctly inter-national character gave it a diversity and special strength of its own. In the end, contrasting leadership styles which came as a result of national characteristics probably furthered the partnership between the British and Americans, as each could learn from the other.

LEADERSHIP AND ITS ROLE IN HEALTH AND WELFARE

The impact of leadership was felt not just in the air, but also on the ground. If it was axiomatic that 'every man had his breaking point', both the Eighth Air Force and Bomber Command recognized that this limit could be extended by close attention to the qualities of life their airmen endured when not flying. It is useful to review a few of these, especially ones much in the control of unit commanders.

Among the most important were the facilities and services available to airmen. Where and how men lived either prepared them well for combat or reduced their capability and will. The food they ate was also important. Moreover, the social life on and around an air station was a factor which established much of a unit's spirit and cohesiveness. Finally, like soldiers of any army, airmen demanded recognition for their work. Like the other factors, promotions and decorations were a clear responsibility of the leadership.

With regard to the facilities generally available at air bases, Bomber Command fared slightly better than did the Eighth Air Force. More than a few of Bomber Command's stations had been constructed before the war and therefore enjoyed more permanence.[61] Buildings were larger and more comfortable. Cold and damp weather, so often recalled by Nissen-hut veterans of the European air war, was not so debilitating in the pre-war brick barracks. Local facilities, including pubs and cinemas, were often closer and therefore more accessible.[62]

To be accurate, however, the huge majority of Bomber Command stations and Eighth Air Force bases were scratched from the empty and flat fields of Lincolnshire and East Anglia respectively. Construction was hurried, at best, and airmen were often required to tramp around muddy avenues and live in draughty open bay huts with single inefficient stoves for warming.[63] While there was considerable variation from base to base, American airmen consistently expressed a low rate of satisfaction with various support facilities. Occasionally, the numbers of airmen – up to 3,000 in a bomb group – would overwhelm the small communities nearest the airfields. Local pubs were tremendously popular, but much social activity necessarily took place on stations. Shower and laundry facilities were often cited by the men as terribly inadequate.[64]

Leaders needed to be concerned with these arrangements, largely because they affected aircrews' ability to relax and rest. After coming home from tough missions crews found it difficult to unwind in noisy, dirty, damp or cold environments. At various times in the Eighth Air Force, more than half of combat crews reported getting less than seven hours of sleep in any 24-hour period. Worse, during the spring and summer of 1944 one in five bomber pilots claimed to be getting less than six hours a day.[65] Moreover, as the number of missions increased, there was a corresponding rise in the numbers of men reporting difficulty with sleeping and physical problems. In so far as Bomber Command was concerned, there was plenty of medical evidence to indicate that the 'sleep during the day, fly at night' schedule of British aviators similarly reduced their ability to rest and, as a result, hampered efficiency and threatened safety. In short, tired airmen put themselves at considerably more risk than those that were fit and rested, and the executive knew it.[66]

It is certainly true, compared to much of the service in the army or navy, that life on an air station during the Second World War, British or American, was infinitely more accommodating. Occasional German air-raids could be tolerated because the opportunity for a hot meal and warm bed, not to mention the chance for female companionship, helped compensate for the extraordinary dangers of combat flying.[67] To many outsiders it appeared that airmen led a pampered life and that they enjoyed rank, pay and privileges far out of proportion to their comrades in other services.[68] In fact, airmen themselves frequently looked down on those who were consigned to non-flying or support positions. There were eight to ten of these for every flyer in the air forces.

It is impossible to gauge to what extent such opinions were shared, other than to say the attitude was widespread. American aircrew veterans often recall referring to support personnel as 'dirt-crunchers', 'gravel-agitators', or 'ground-pounders'. British aircrew seem to have preferred the terms 'wingless wonders' or 'penguins' when speaking of non-flyers. Difficulties between the two groups were most often caused by misunderstandings and assertions that one or the other was securing unfair advantage in a difficult situation. Airmen, who were daily risking their lives in the air, doubtless envied men who enjoyed the security of ground duty. Protecting prerogatives was important and the smallest slight could cause unnecessary friction.[69] Intellect nevertheless weighed against the worst of these adolescent outbursts and, deep down, virtually all veterans fundamentally understood the importance of ground support people.

Ground technical staff were, in my experience, to a man, superb in their dedication, bearing always the burden of knowing that if their servicing was defective, aircrews lives were at risk. The conditions were not good – working often with numbed fingers on a bitterly cold Lincolnshire winter's day with perhaps only a tin hut for shelter from the elements.[70]

Even if used in mild jest, and not by everyone, these humorous nicknames are nonetheless clues to the existence of a clearly defined social hierarchy, at the top of which stood the pilots.[71]

There were complex subdivisions within this hierarchy. Day fighter pilots thought themselves in many ways superior to night fighter pilots, just as the reverse was true. Fighter pilots in general looked down on bomber pilots, who mirrored this feeling and, in turn, felt sorry for transport pilots and instructors.[72] Visible distinctions were even noted in dress. British fighter pilots, for example, had the unspoken, but scrupulously observed habit of leaving their top tunic button undone. American and British bomber pilots worked just as hard to develop and preserve peaked caps with '50-mission' crushes. For a time Americans were encouraged to wear a blue rectangular patch under their wings to signify their combat status. Commanders at the operational level often overlooked many of these youthful affectations, and even the senior leadership seemed occasionally tolerant.[73]

In bombers, pilots of whatever rank obviously enjoyed the status of being the principal controller of the aircraft. Below them, in both the Eighth Air Force and Bomber Command, came the navigators. Navigator status rested, in part, on the demanding mathematical requirements of their duties. In the vernacular of the time, 'it took some brains to be a good navigator'. But also, quite simply, their status was enhanced by their ability to tell pilots where to fly the aircraft. Next stood the bombardiers, who similarly shared a technical profession and on whom, ultimately, the success of a bombing mission relied. At a lower strata were the radio operators and gunners, whose jobs were clearly no less essential to overall success or survival, but who were often considered less well trained and educated.

In some measure, the role of an effective commander in the entire social structure of an air station was to serve as a lubricant between the various groups. His awareness of affairs, his willingness to smooth communications and his ability to settle differences were essential to the growth of unity and spirit.

Through him in this capacity (and also because of their segregation on the station), the various occupational groups were made conscious of their being part of one whole unit.[74]

It followed that good commanders went to considerable lengths to improve the quality of life for all personnel at their bases. On both British and American stations airmen and ground crew could generally enjoy clubs, canteens, libraries, sports facilities and occasional variety shows. There was considerable tolerance for the use of alcohol.[75] In addition to the inevitable – if officially discouraged – card games and gambling activities at all the bases, there were innumerable tours, dances and special events.[76] In some places great attention was devoted to these activities and the entertainment became quite elaborate.[77] If it helped take men's minds off the possibility of death, even for only a few hours, it was helpful.

Getting men away from the spectre of their own deaths was also one of the reasons for frequent leaves and passes. Within the general constraints of higher headquarters, commanders had the leeway to grant furloughs and time off to their men. In the Eighth Air Force crewmen were usually granted 24 or 48-hour passes after every one or two weeks in action. Bomber Command typically granted seven days' leave every six weeks. In special circumstances – during long periods of bad weather or after a particularly harrowing incident – men might be let off more often.[78] As always with military service, extended periods of inactivity, no less than those characterized by overwork, tended to gnaw away at men's spirits and increase the number of disciplinary problems.[79]

Interestingly, one of the things which caused much of the strain with aircrew morale was the inability of commanders to signal or give advance notice of stand-downs.[80] This came partly as a natural result of the difficulty in predicting weather. Some, too, arose from operational demands. As a result, airmen all too frequently were briefed and prepared for missions, sat for long hours in aircraft, only to be told that the mission was scrubbed. One bomber veteran recalled:

The worst aspect was the waiting periods before action. For example, we would have a target – stand down – we would have a target – stand down. This, in some cases, could go on for a week and I found it rather nerve-shredding and almost a relief when we finally took off on an op.[81]

Few things, according to veterans and medical authorities of both nations, caused more anxiety, stress or anger.[82] There were similar lapses when granting simple passes or leaves.[83]

These sometimes unavoidable incidents occasionally contributed to a feeling that commanders and higher headquarters did not truly understand the problems of crewmen.[84] A fairly typical phenomenon was for Allied aircrew in a squadron to blame the next higher echelon for their problems. Those at group or wing headquarters, in turn, accused higher headquarters at Pinetree or High Wycombe of a lack of empathy. American surveys confirmed the point, while simultaneously demonstrating that men with the strongest willingness for combat shared the conviction that commanders were sympathetic and that their needs were being cared for. The best commanders communicated this feeling by actually spending time at the airfields and not in London. There was evidence that some group leaders did much better in this regard than others.[85]

Another area where this was evident was recognition and decorations. Here there were discernible philosophical differences between Bomber Command and the Eighth Air Force.

In general terms, the Americans did everything they could to encourage and reward aircrew. Recognition took many forms. Commanders, especially at the most senior level, sometimes actively sought favourable publicity in newspapers and magazines. Newsreel footage was shot, journalists were allowed on missions and special documentaries prepared. Probably also motivated by a desire to demonstrate the efficacy of airpower, these commanders nevertheless understood how important it was for their men to believe what they were doing was significant. Moreover, even inaccurate publicity was appreciated by airmen as long as it was laudatory in tone.[86] Other more typical types of recognition included unit citations, letters of commendation, streamers for unit flags and individual medals.

The American policy regarding decorations reflected a deliberate attempt to increase the number of medals and decrease the amount of time it took to confirm the award. The US Army's Chief of Staff, General George Marshall, was convinced that the system used during the First World War was inadequate and, more important, that the number of awards had been far too small. Fully aware of the impact of medals on the morale of American fighting men, he was determined to correct this, even if it meant that the proliferation of medals might result in criticisms about their 'value'.[87]

General Marshall's intentions were confirmed and re-emphasized in an early Eighth Air Force commanders' meeting. Aside from detailing the requirements for various awards, the resulting declaration directed commanders to be 'extremely prompt' in sending recommendations.[88] The American system had long emphasized meritorious conduct as opposed simply to bravery as the basis of a medal. In the event, the intensity of combat soon led to a significant number of awards. Moreover, given the rate at which casualties were being sustained, it was only natural that men wanted to receive awards while they were alive and around to enjoy them.[89]

Between 1942 and 1945 the Eighth Air Force awarded just over 500,000 medals. The majority – around 441,000 – were Air Medals, a decoration typically awarded for completing five or six individual bomber sorties.[90]

The standard citation for such an award read:

For meritorious achievement while participating in heavy bombardment missions in the air offensive against the enemy over Continental Europe. The courage, coolness, and skill displayed by this enlisted man upon those occasions reflect great credit upon himself and the Armed Forces of the United States.[91]

More often than not, several names would appear under the narrative. Occasionally the large numbers of these awards made for ceremonies with 50 or more slightly jaded recipients.[92]

Next in terms of numbers of awards was the Distinguished Flying Cross. Some 45,000 examples of this medal were received. By direction it was given to any pilot or gunner who shot down an enemy aircraft. Bomber aircrew also often received them for episodes during particularly arduous missions and for tour completion. Fighter pilots typically received them for completing 100 missions. Common too was the Purple Heart; it was awarded to men who had been wounded as a result of enemy action.

Not surprisingly, the Americans were more discriminating with medals for valour. In the Eighth Air Force there were just 14 Medals of Honor, which was the equivalent of the Victoria Cross, and only 220 Distinguished Service Crosses. Finally, US airmen in Britain won only 864 of the 73,651 Silver Stars received during the Second World War.[93]

Generally speaking the American policy paid great dividends in respect of morale. Such minor problems that arose from time to time usually came from disgruntled members of other American air forces who considered the Eighth to be getting an unfair share of awards. Additionally, there were always individual units or commanders who seemed too arbitrary or indiscriminate with awards. Finally, men in support units occasionally felt their efforts were not being adequately recognized because the higher decorations inevitably went to flyers.[94]

Bomber Command's policy on the issue of recognition and medals likewise reflected a philosophy which not only originated at the senior levels of the service but was also a hold-over from the attitudes of the First World War. During that conflict British leaders steadfastly resisted the temptation to over-glamorize airmen by encouraging publicity about aces.[95] Despite great pressure to do so, the RAF never substantially increased the number of combat flying awards and only reluctantly acquiesced to the public demand for heroes. Given what was going on in the trenches, it was most important to demonstrate the idea that all the services were equally important.

Bomber Command inherited this philosophy. As a result, compared with the practice in the Eighth Air Force, Bomber Command's awarding of decorations was downright miserly. The RAF had no equivalent to the American Air Medal, although officers who completed a complete tour of 30 operations were routinely awarded the Distinguished Flying Cross. It could also be granted for some immediate act of bravery, but its use at the end of a tour prompted some to call it a 'survival gong'.[96] Only 20,354 were awarded throughout the RAF along with 1,592 bars. Enlisted men would usually receive the Distinguished Flying Medal for the same feat and hence suffered somewhat from rank discrimination. Just over 6,600 aircrew received the DFM. At the upper ends of the scale were the Air Force Cross and Distinguished Service Order – the latter awarded in recognition of meritorious service before the enemy to officers or warrant officers – and, at the very top, the Victoria Cross. Only 23 of the latter were awarded to Bomber Command airmen, and most of these posthumously.[97]

Although the RAF succeeded in keeping down 'award inflation', this does not suggest that British airmen were any less interested than their American counterparts in receiving medals. In fact, on a personal level the reactions were very much the same. Awards were highly prized. Even so, it should be noted that there was little evidence to indicate – anyone apart from the tiniest fraction of men – would intentionally risk their own or others' lives just to 'win' a medal. Rather, men in danger every day or night quite understandably needed the encouragement and recognition offered by ribbons, which was quite a different thing. Scores of British commanders accepted this and worked to increase the number of awards and reduce inequities based on rank.[98]

Occasionally the relative paucity of British awards would seem all the more apparent when British airmen met Americans in a social setting. By comparison, American uniforms carried far more ribbons. Good-natured jibes and humour were most often the result, but many British veterans harboured not so secret thoughts that Americans were unjustifiably over-decorated.[99] For their part, Americans felt sorry for the British and were amused by the British custom of appending names with scores of incomprehensible initials.

LEADERSHIP RECONSIDERED

We thus come to the end of our analysis of successful leadership, having examined some of the ways it affected and supported the more personal motivations of combat airmen. It is clear that combat leaders in the Eighth Air Force and Bomber Command faced particular pressures caused not only by the scale of the military task which confronted them, but also by its uniqueness. As the directors of an innovative and massive strategic air campaign these young airmen operated to a great extent on uncharted ground. Yet, as we have seen, they employed styles of leadership consistent not only with the characteristics of their men, but also with their national and military traditions.

The most successful of these commanders led by example. They displayed a courage and coolness which gave confidence to their men. Moreover, in a highly technical environment, they showed a laudable proficiency in the same tasks they asked their men to carry out. In combat flying, a successful leader's credibility was linked inextricably to his competency.

Similarly, to be most successful, these same leaders had to encourage their followers. Within the boundaries of individual personality, they had to pass along their concerns for the health and safety of those they commanded. Some could give pep talks, or joke, or even 'become one of the boys'. More than a few might display an informal or friendly attitude. Others, similarly successful, might seem more reserved but no less inspirational. The key was to encourage and give confidence to the men who were flying daylight and night missions over Germany.

In this regard, adaptability was also vital to success. Leaders at every level in both air forces were forced occasionally to modify or change their styles depending on the situation. Sometimes this meant replacing popular leaders or taking an approach which seemed unnecessarily harsh, but the stakes were unbelievably high, and the penalties for errors, especially in terms of men's lives, were severe.

As might be expected, there were unique cultural and philosophical traits intrinsic to the two air forces. Among other things, these occasionally led to discernibly different leadership styles and dissimilar approaches to awards and decorations. In the main, each service managed its personnel issues with a minimum of disruption, maintained a reasonable standard of effectiveness and thereby undergirded morale.

In sum, both at senior and junior level, the record of British and American leaders was good. Conspicuous failures simply did not last long. The contribution of leadership to morale in the Eighth Air Force and Bomber Command was a major one and contributed much to sustaining their combined campaign.

NOTES

1. Scores of contemporary documents and reports, both British and American, identify leadership as the primary factor in keeping men flying and fighting. Among others see, Office of the Air Surgeon, 'Report on Survey of Aircrew Personnel in the Eighth, Ninth, Twelfth, and Fifteenth Air Forces', April 1944, 141.28B, AFHRA and 'Note by IG II on Discipline and the Fighting Spirit in the RAF' 14 May 1943, AIR 20/3082.

2. The first comment comes from one of Bomber Command's medical officers. The second is General Ira Eaker's. See Bergin, op. cit., p. 376; and Eaker to Major General H. I. Edwards, 27 Nov. 1943, 520.161-1, AFHRA.

3. The use of the term compassion does not necessarily suggest pity. Rather, true compassion reflected an understanding of the stresses of combat and demonstrated a consistency in thought process and action. For further opinions on the traits see 'Analysis of the Duties of Aircrew Personnel, Descriptions of Aircrew Performances from Theaters of Combat', 5 May 1943, 141.28D-10-19, AFHRA; 'Combat Crew Returnees' 1944–1945, 142.053, AFHRA; Ira C. Eaker, 'The Military Professional', *Air University Review* Vol. XXVI, No. 2, (Jan.–Feb., 1976): 2–12; Group Captain Leonard Cheshire to author, 16 Feb. 1989; and Martin Goldman, *Morale in The Army Air Force in World War II*, USAF Historical Study No. 78, 1953.

4. The usual term which was invoked for talk of a flag-waving variety was 'bullshit', which conveyed the combat veteran's scornful and tough-minded point of view. Stouffer *et al.*, Vol. II, p. 150.

5. 'It was very noticeable that a good captain who clearly knew his job, remained calm no matter what was happening outside, to the extent of never letting the least sign of strain show in his voice and who knew how to keep in touch with each member of the crew without talking unnecessarily, made all the difference to the individual members of that crew'. Group Captain Leonard Cheshire to author 16 Feb. 1989.

6. The Bomber Command epithet for COs who flew only the easy missions to France was 'François'. Max Hastings, op. cit., p. 257.

7. A confidential report by one B-17 pilot cites an instance over Wilhemshaven when, facing heavy flak, a frightened Lieutenant Colonel in the lead ship kept shouting, 'drop your bombs, drop your bombs, and everyone dropped them in the water'. See Office of the Air Surgeon, 'Combat Crew Returnees', 141.053L-1, 16 May 1944, AFHRA.

8. So eager were the Eighth Air Force's senior commanders to fly that General Eaker was compelled to issue a memorandum which spelled out the rules and restrictions. Dewitt S. Copp, *Forged In Fire* (Garden City: Doubleday & Company, 1982), p. 286.

9. Bennett, op. cit., p. 106.
10. General Curtis E. LeMay cited in M. Coffey, op. cit., p. 94.
11. Bergin, op. cit., p. 377.
12. Air Vice-Marshal Charles Symonds, the RAF's chief neurologist, suggested on this basis that 25 daylight missions in the Eighth Air Force were more stressful than 30 in Bomber Command. AIR 20/10727.
13. Among others see incidents described in Ian Hawkins, *The Münster Raid* (Blue Ridge Summit, PA: Tab/Aero Books, 1984), p. 31 and SQ-Bomb-349-HI, SQ-Bomb-350-HI, SQ-Bomb-351-HI, Oct. 1943 and March 1944, AFHRA.
14. One of the most dramatic episodes took place during the largest air strike operation of the war on 24 Dec., 1944. Leading the 3rd Bomb Division was Brigadier General Frederick W. Castle, who was posthumously awarded the Medal of Honor. Freeman, *War Diary*, pp. 403–4.
15. This frequently used term of derision relates to Dr Bond's views on sex-typing and aircrew motivation, while indicating how combat was seen as a challenge. Proving oneself and not being branded by social censure was important for leaders. See Bond, *Love and Fear*, pp. 38, 146, and Stouffer *et al.*, Vol. II, p. 131.
16. Combat records show that 64 aircraft were actually lost due to all causes on raid No. 298, 11 April 1944. But the sentiment expressed is no less valid. See Office of the Air Surgeon, 'Combat Crew Returnees' 11 April 1944, 142.053L-1, AFHRA.
17. 97th Bomb Group pilot, cited in 'Combat Crew Returnees', 17142.053L-1, 9 May 1944, AFHRA.
18. Walter F. Hughes, 'A Bomber Pilot in WWII', Photocopied Manuscript, nd, p. 73, 2nd Air Division Memorial Room, Norwich Central Library.
19. Among the very best known, Group Captain Cheshire and his commitment to practice and study became legendary in Bomber Command. He called his habit 'hibernation'. Another leading airman, Guy Gibson of dam-busting fame, was similarly inclined. See Group Captain Leonard Cheshire, *Bomber Pilot* (London: Hutchinson and Company, 1942), p. 101; Guy Gibson, *Enemy Coast Ahead* (London: Michael Joseph, 1946; London: Goodall Publications, 1986), pp. 250–66 and Longmate, op. cit., pp. 246–55.
20. Major General James M. Stewart, USAFR (retd), Thames Television Interview, No. 002889/02/01–02, IWM.
21. See Thomas L. Lentz, 'Combat Leadership: 56th Fighter Group 1943–1944', (MA thesis, University of Alabama, 1986), p. 39 and General Theodore R. Milton, oral interview 9 July 1982, 239.0512–1339, AFHRA.
22. Milton interview, 28 Oct., 1991. The British version of this was, 'sloppy on the ground, sloppy in the air'.
23. Colonel Hubert Zemke, USAF (retd), 56th Fighter Group, to author 29 Jan. 1992.
24. 'The unit was the CO, in himself. He was the substitute for the total group, 'the station', and was the only cohering influence. He was the king in a monarchic state'. T. E. Paterson, *Morale in War and Work* (London: Max Parrish, 1955), p. 84.
25. Stouffer *et al.*, Vol. II, pp. 118–19.
26. During periods of the most intense operations, both British and American crews calculated the odds of their survival at roughly 11 missions. Even those who managed, however miraculously, to finish their first tours did so usually within five to seven months of their arrival on station. Harris to Portal, 26 Jan. 1943, AIR 20/2860.
27. Other names frequently mentioned are Jimmy Marks, Fraser Barron, Johnny Fauquier, and E. Rodley. Hamish Mahaddie, *Hamish: The Story of a Pathfinder* (London: Ian Allan, 1989), pp. 63–8.
28. These men commanded the three top-scoring Eighth Air Force fighter groups. Their units destroyed a combined total of 2,876 German aircraft. Their personal scores accounted for 60 of this total. See Freeman, *Mighty Eighth*, pp. 274–81; Toliver and Constable, op. cit., pp. 370–89; Lentz, op. cit., p. 54; and USAF Historical Study No. 133, 1969, Air University Library, Maxwell AFB, Alabama.
29. Air Commodore John Searby, *The Bomber Battle for Berlin* (Shrewsbury: Airlife Publishing, 1991), pp. 80–1.
30. Save for the issue of LMF, no subject seems to be as sensitive among veterans as are their feelings towards Harris. During the war it is likely that many saw him ambivalently. Some regarded him as a cold, remote and remorseless figure. This would explain the continued use

of the chilling nickname, 'Butcher'. But a significant number gave him their total confidence and fondly called him 'Bert'. The passage of almost 50 years has softened the opinions of many and makes it difficult to be more precise. It is clear from recent events, however, that Harris' memory symbolizes much of the struggle, sacrifice and frustration of all aircrew in Bomber Command. Cheshire to author, 16 Feb. 1989; Bomber Command Association Newsletter, No. 19, Feb. 1992; and Group Captain Hamish Mahaddie, Thames Television Interview, No. 002897/03/01–03, Imperial War Museum.

31. Milton interview, 2 July 1982.
32. Doolittle, op. cit., pp. 391–2.
33. The official history notes that the winter of 1942–43 was a particularly tough one for what was then the VIII Bomber Command. Replacements were slow in arriving, the weather was bad and, despite great expectations, no missions had been flown over Germany up to that point. Craven and Cate, op. cit., Vol. II, pp. 235, 270, and 306.
34. On a 30 December 1942 mission to Lorient, 17 of the 18 306th B-17s had turned back before the start point. Between October 1942 and August 1943, the 367th Squadron of this group sustained the heaviest losses in the entire command. See 306th War Diary, 30 Dec. 1942, AFHRA; William C. Van Norman, Dwain A. Esper, and Arthur P. Bove, 'History of the 306th Bombardment Group (H)', nd, Statistical Report, GP-306-HI (Bomb), March 1942–June 1945, AFHRA; and Freeman, *War Diary*, p. 31, 248.
35. After making the observations on an unscheduled visit, Eaker later cited these as important causes. Russell A. Strong, *First Over Germany* (Winston-Salem: Hunter Publishing Co., 1982), p. 62.
36. Armstrong, a clear favourite of Eaker's, had already been given credit for salvaging the misfortunes of the 97th Bomb Group. See Gravatt and Ayers, op. cit., pp. 204–8.
37. See Kenneth H. Blanchard, 'Situational Leadership Revisited', in *Concepts for Air Force Leadership* (Maxwell AFB Alabama: Air University Press, 1983), pp. 4-23 to 4-28; and Charles E. Gries, 'Situational Leadership: The Key to More Effective Leadership in the USAF', Air War College Student Research Paper, April 1981, Air University, Maxwell AFB.
38. Van Norman, Esper, and Bove, 'Statistical Report', GP-306-HI (Bomb), AFHRA.
39. Max Hastings, op. cit., pp. 258–62.
40. Revie, op. cit., pp. 247–9; Cheshire to author, 16 Feb. 1989 and 14 March 1989; and 'I don't think I was ever really frightened; Group Captain Leonard Cheshire talks to Ray Connolly', *The Times*, 21 July 1990.
41. Middlebrook, *Nuremberg*, p. 38.
42. A more detailed discussion of these characteristics will be found in Chapter Two under the topic of air combat effectiveness. See Office of the Air Surgeon, 'Analysis of the Duties of Aircrew Personnel, Descriptions of Aircrew Performances from Theaters of Combat', 5 May 1943, 141.28D-10-19, AFHRA.
43. Colonel Francis S. Gabreski, USAF (retd), cited in Lentz, op. cit., p. 40.
44. Colonel Hub Zemke, USAF (retd), Commander, 56th Fighter Group, 'Leadership', Lecture to the Tennessee National Guard Commanders' Conference, 20 Oct. 1989. Copy in author's possession.
45. Doolittle's decision was partly based on seeing a sign at VIII Fighter Command headquarters which said, 'The first duty of the Eighth Air Force fighters is to bring back the bombers alive'. He had it changed to read, 'The first duty of the Eighth Air Force fighters is to destroy German fighters'. He later called it the most important decision he had made during the war, but bomber commanders were understandably less enthusiastic. Doolittle, op. cit., pp. 380–81.
46. Eighth Air Force, 'Minutes of the Eighth Air Force Commander's Meeting', 21 Jan. 1944, 520.141–1, AFHRA.
47. Colonel Maurice Preston, Commander, 379th Bomb Group, quoted in Middlebrook, *Schweinfurt*, p. 61. Other veterans remember similar speeches in their bomber units. Beirne Lay and Sly Bartlett accurately included a version of it in their script for the Hollywood movie, *Twelve O'Clock High*.
48. A fact made clear in scores of letters to the author from British and American bomber veterans. Typical was, 'I never in my fondest dream thought I was going to make it, in fact I've mentioned to my wife and five children many times, that every day I've lived since 1943, has been a day of grace'. Bill Thorns (96th Bomb Group) to author, 26 Aug. 1990; A Bomber

Command veteran wrote, 'But they were hard times; there was no future; you lived for the day or the night and you rejoiced that you were still there to drink with your buddies'. Air Vice Marshal D. J. Furner, RAF (retd) to author 24 Feb. 1990.

49. Stafford-Clark MSS, p. 15.

50. Professor Stephen Haseler, 'Britannia rules – but she's enslaved to class', *The Times* 22 Dec. 1991.

51. A fact independently supported by the wartime letters of Robert S. Raymond, an American volunteer in Bomber Command, who could claim a reasonably unprejudiced viewpoint. Raymond, op. cit., pp. 27–8, 52–3. See also Richard A. Preston, 'Perspectives in the History of Military Education and Professionalism', *The Harmon Memorial Lectures in Military History 1959–1987* (Washington, DC: Office of Air Force History, 1988), pp. 289–90.

52. 'The good leader must know how to combine the strong right arm of the father with the protective understanding approach of the mother.' Richardson, op. cit., p. 88.

53. The desirability of these traits was reinforced by popular British films. Carol Reed's 1944 production *The Way Ahead*, called 'one of the finest of all Second World War films', tells the story of British draftees trained and moulded into a homogeneous unit by officers who fit the pattern. See Carol Reed, director, *The Way Ahead*, 91 minutes, Film Department, IWM; and Manvell, op. cit., p. 72.

54. Moran, p. 194.

55. A British pamphlet called *Meet the Americans* explained that GIs 'delight in tall tales, wordy battle full of cross-talk, wisecracks, and jeering remarks which are meant to sound (but not meant to be) fantastically offensive'. Quoted in Lande, op. cit., p. 80.

56. Interestingly enough, this was a characteristic also noted about American soldiers in some detail by Baron von Steuben at Valley Forge in 1777. Christopher Ward, *War of the Revolution*, Vol. 1 (New York: Macmillan, 1952), p. 554.

57. Headquarters, European Theatre of Operations, 'Research Findings and Recommendations', 11 July 1944, Box 91, Spaatz MSS, Library of Congress.

58. Anthony Cotterell, British Army, cited by Kennett, p. 125.

59. Doolittle was struck by the coolness and formality of his first meeting with Harris. He later wrote: 'The British, probably since the Middle Ages, have been suspicious of outsiders until they prove themselves loyal to the Crown.' Some of Harris's reserve was the result of his close friendship with Eaker, whom Doolittle abruptly replaced. See Doolittle, op. cit., p. 378 and Terraine, op. cit., pp. 471–2.

60. Interview with Group Captain T. G. Mahaddie, RAF (retd), 27 June 1989, RAF Club, London, and Mahaddie, *Hamish*, p. 81.

61. About one-third of Bomber Command's 54 stations had been built before the war. Popular with aircrews, these airfields were sometimes called 'gin palaces'. See Middlebrook, *Nuremberg*, p. 34.

62. Rexford-Welch, op. cit., Vol. 1, pp. 22–6.

63. For a good description of aircrew life on bases and in Nissen huts see Lande, op. cit., pp. 93–4 and 'The Liberator Men of "Old Buc"', Typewritten manuscript, nd, 2nd Air Division Memorial Room, Norwich Central Library. Dale Smith graphically recalls his battles with morale and the environment at the 384th Bomb Group's station he derisively called 'Grafton Under*mud*'. See Smith, op. cit., pp. 72–5. British airmen called the aircraft dispersal point Lakenheath 'Forsakenheath'. See Freeman, *British Airmen*, p. 102.

64. 'Research Findings and Recommendations, 11 July 1944', Box 91, Spaatz MSS, Library of Congress.

65. 'Survey of Fighter Pilots in the Eighth Air Force: A Comparison with Bomber Pilots', July 1944, Box 91, Spaatz MSS, Library of Congress.

66. Symonds and Williams, *Psychological Disorders*, pp. 43–8.

67. Peter B. Gunn, *RAF Great Massingham: A Norfolk Airfield at War 1940–1945* (King's Lynn: Watts & Rowe, 1990), p. 78; Lande, op. cit., pp. 89–92; Freeman, *British Airmen*, pp. 59–60.

68. Various sources document the occasional difficulties inside RAF non-commissioned officer messes. Pre-war regulars sometimes resented the 'instant' rank and privileges granted flyers. See Max Hastings, op. cit., pp. 254–6; L. Y. Easby (Lancaster wireless operator) to author, 9 Nov. 1990; and the Lawson Memorandum, Air Historical Branch.

69. In Bomber Command there were occasional hard feelings over 'perks' that aircrew enjoyed like milk on the table and eggs – a great scarcity in wartime Britain – before and after

operations. Similarly, American and British aircrews would become livid, if, after a cancelled operation, they discovered the best food at the chow hall had been eaten by non-flyers. Squadron Leader S. A. Booker, RAF (retd) to author, 20 June 1990; and Gordon M. Maddock (306th Bomb Group) to author, 15 Dec. 1989.

70. Ft/Lt D. H. Hawkins, RAF (retd), to author 19 March 1990.

71. See Paterson, op. cit., pp. 59–63.

72. Underlying these superficial rivalries – which were sometimes signalled by pub altercations – was the notion that one group or the other was not contributing enough. Up to 1942, for example, Fighter Command had received much of the publicity for carrying on the war. Afterwards it seemed to many that Bomber Command bore the burden. Aircrew in both forces knew little about each other's job. Similar feelings existed in the Eighth Air Force, especially until the introduction of long-range fighter escort aircraft like the P-51. See Ronald H. Bailey, *The Air War in Europe*, Time-Life Series World War II (New York: Time-Life, 1979), p. 29 and Gibson, op. cit., pp. 114–17.

73. 'Many of the scruffy and unshaven merely do it to preserve their "warrior" appearance.' Air Marshal Sir Edgar Ludlow-Hewitt, RAF Inspector General, to Air Vice Marshal D. Coyler, Assistant Chief of the Air Staff for Personnel, 4 June 1944, AIR 20/4583.

74. Paterson, op. cit., p. 84.

75. Americans needed no prompting to adopt many of the rowdier traditions of RAF messes. Guy Gibson's frank recollections of his pilots' binges prompted Sir Arthur Harris, writing years later, to remind readers of the intolerable strain of operations. Gibson, op. cit., pp. vii, 77–8.

76. One American veteran ruefully noted the daily gambling where, ' A pound is $4.03 but since it's a single piece of paper, it's treated the same as a dollar bill, especially in a crap game. Consequently small fortunes change hands overnight'. William Y. Ligon to parents, 5 Sept. 1944, 'Bill's Letters', 2nd Air Division Memorial Room, Norwich Central Library.

77. Craven and Cate, op. cit., Vol. VII, pp. 470–471 and Mahaddie, *Hamish*, pp. 99–101.

78. Based on the recommendations of flight surgeons and medical officers. See Link and Coleman, op. cit., p. 662.

79. See Craven and Cate, op. cit., Vol. VII, pp. 453–5 and Symonds and Williams, *Psychological Disorders*, p. 45.

80. In 1944 nearly half of American men surveyed said they usually received no notice and a third said they 'practically never' got notice. Rightly or wrongly, most felt they should have been told so that they could best use their time off. See 'Research Findings and Recommendations', 11 July 1944, Box 91, Spaatz MSS, Library of Congress.

81. R. B. Vennard (Halifax flight engineer) to author, 20 Aug. 1990.

82. See Rexford-Welch, op. cit., Vol. II, p. 125; Stafford-Clark MSS, p. 21; and Bond, *Love and Fear*, p. 87.

83. Fewer than one-third of bomber aircrew had more than a few days notice. Interestingly, two-thirds of American fighter pilots claimed to know a week or more beforehand. Rather than signalling better leadership in fighter units, it more likely came as a result of an excess in the number of pilots. 'Survey of Fighter Pilots in the Eighth Air Force: A Comparison with Heavy Bomber Pilots', July 1944, Box 91, Combat Crew Attitudes, Spaatz MSS, Library of Congress.

84. Assigned to investigate the experiences of bomber crews, the poet Robert Nichols wrote: 'Unlike the old days, orders need explanation; the boys aren't nitwits.' Memorandum, Robert Nichols to Sir Charles Medhurst, 1 Sept. 1942, AIR 20/3085.

85. See 'Survey of Fighter Pilots in the Eighth Air Force', op. cit., and comments by Colonel Hub Zemke, USAF (retd) to author 9 April 1992.

86. Goldman, op. cit., pp. 23–49.

87. van Creveld, p. 111.

88. Meeting of Commanders, 24 Aug. 1942, Box 9, 'June–August 1942', Spaatz MSS, Library of Congress.

89. Stouffer points out that airmen were 14 times more likely to receive a medal or decoration than their infantry counterparts. Stouffer, *et al.* Vol. II, p. 344; see also Goldman, pp. 23–50.

90. 'Combat crewman who complete a normal operational tour of 35 missions will be awarded the Air Medal with five Oak Leaf Clusters'. 'A Handbook for New Arrivals', 388th Bombardment Group (Heavy), Knettishall, England, 15 Feb. 1945. Fighter pilots were

supposed to receive an Air Medal at the end of each tenth mission. Colonel Hub Zemke, USAF (retd) to author, 9 April 1992.

91. General Orders No. 707, 27 Sept. 1944, 'Bill's Letters', 2nd Air Division Memorial Room, Norwich Library.

92. Stiles noted cynically during the ritual that it was the first time he had stood at attention since arriving in Great Britain. His name, at the end of a mimeographed citation, was only barely discernible and, 'the exceptional gallantry part was pretty thin'. Stiles, op. cit., pp. 63–4.

93. For details on the types of medals and numbers see Freeman, *Mighty Eighth*, p. 267 and *War Department, Decorations and Awards* (Washington, DC: US Government Printing Office, 1947).

94. The American attitude towards decorations is best summarized by humorist Bill Mauldin, himself a veteran, who wrote, 'Civilians may think it's a little juvenile to worry about ribbons, but a civilian has a house and a bankroll to show what he's done for the past four years'. See also Goldman, pp. 23–52.

95. Lee Kennett, *The First Air War* (New York: The Free Press, 1991), pp. 154–7.

96. Middlebrook, *Nuremberg*, p. 54.

97. It is important to remember that Bomber Command had been at war three years longer than the Eighth Air Force. Even so, the US rate of award per 1,000 battle deaths was three times that of the British. See P. E. Abbott and J. M. A. Tamplin, *British Gallantry Awards* (London: Nimrod Dix & Company, 1981), pp. 91–131, 283–96 and A. A. Nofi, 'For Your Information', *Strategy and Tactics* 90 (Jan.–Feb., 1982), p. 20.

98. Historian Richard Holmes, quoting Martin Lindsay, wrote, 'The monstrously inadequate distribution of awards to other ranks was a flaw in the British system, and they regretted that there had not been enough awards available for the brave men they led'. Richard Holmes, *Acts of War* (New York: The Free Press, 1985), p. 355.

99. One joke frequently heard in pubs was that Americans got ribbons for 'eating Brussels sprouts'. Juliet Gardiner, *Over There: The GIs in Wartime Britain* (London: Collins & Brown, 1992), pp. 61, 76.

7

Moral Fibre and the American Experience

THE FIRST Eighth Air Force heavy bomber attack over Europe occurred on 17 August 1942. On that day 12 B-17Es from the 97th Bomb Group attacked Rouen. They not only dropped 18 tons of bombs with commendable accuracy but all returned to base, with only two aircraft suffering superficial damage. One hundred and eleven combat airmen safely made the trip. By the time the war ended, 31 of these veteran aviators would be listed as missing in action or killed.[1] Their survival rate was slightly better than the huge number of airmen who followed.

During the peak period of American daylight raids over Germany, the Eighth Air Force had some 31,000 combat flying personnel. At any one time about 22,000 of these were in heavy bombers with the balance divided between fighters and medium attack aircraft.[2] During the entire period of the Eighth Air Force's operations, well over 100,000 American airmen saw combat. About 60,000 successfully completed their tours; roughly 26,000 were killed. Another 20,000 spent time as prisoners-of-war. After the war, General Doolittle reported only 1,230 aircrew permanently removed from flying due to emotional disturbances.[3] More surprising, perhaps, is the even smaller number of men classified with 'Lack of Moral Fibre'. Based on a statistical analysis of various documents, it would appear that less than 700 men were so classified between 1942 and 1945 in the Eighth Air Force.[4]

Given the tremendous attention the subject received, both by medical and administrative authorities, these figures tell a remarkable story of bravery and endurance. In the face of horrific odds, just four per cent of Eighth Air Force airmen were removed from combat for emotional reasons, and only about one-quarter of that permanently. Even more significant, despite an overall casualty rate approaching 50 per cent, fewer than one per cent of flyers were grounded for alleged cowardice.[5] This chapter traces the development of American policy towards this controversial subject. Beginning with a review of medical and administrative terms, it summarizes various policy letters and regulations, examines the statistical evidence, looks at some typical cases and their disposition, reviews aircrew reactions and comments on the efficacy of the American efforts.

LACK OF MORAL FIBRE AND ITS TERMINOLOGY

There is no better way to begin an analysis of the American attitude towards Lack of Moral Fibre than by discussing its evolving administrative and medical definitions. Almost immediately, a pattern of change emerges. Throughout the course of the Combined Bomber Offensive a huge variety of terms were used to describe a condition which was later most frequently referred to as LMF. One authority recalled more than 60 different expressions in use during 1944. At the time the 97th Bomb Group carried out the Rouen raid, however, General Ira Eaker's Eighth Bomber Command had no firm definition of policies for those airmen who might be identified as emotional casualties. Despite the Royal Air Force's already considerable experience with the subject and what Air Marshal H. E. Whittingham described as a 'very close' relationship between the two countries' medical authorities, American commanders did not address themselves formally to the question until almost a month after the first raid.[6]

On 16 September, General Carl Spaatz, the US Army Air Forces theatre commander, wrote to General Eaker and his subordinates asking for their comments on a proposed policy for the disposition of combat personnel 'unsuited for operational flying for reasons other than physical disability'. This Policy Letter 200.9x.373 was the earliest US administrative attempt to define LMF. Officially adopted on 29 October 1942, it established the term 'Temperamental Unsuitability' for those airmen who might deliberately avoid operational duty by subterfuge, feigned illness or outright refusal. It left the diagnosis of such behaviour to the individual bomb group commanders, who were to use their squadron commanders, unit flight surgeons and flight commanders to assist them. Moreover, the letter made a clear distinction between those men accused of temperamental unsuitability and others who merely displayed 'inaptitude' for their operational duties (poor formation flying being the most typical difficulty). Still other men identified with neurosis, which at this stage of the war was called 'flying fatigue', were defined as treatable, unlike those categorized as truly insane.[7]

It is not difficult to determine what prompted Spaatz's communications. Although the overall scale of the Eighth Air Force's early efforts was small, it was not long before emotional casualties began to occur. In the first eight months of operation there were 35 cases.[8] Moreover, at least 16 of these could be classified as temperamentally unsuitable. At that point few American aviators were considered to have completed enough sorties to be genuinely affected by flying fatigue. Flight surgeons in the rapidly expanding American bomb groups had begun to deal with the situation, but ran into almost immediate difficulties.[9]

A major problem was to differentiate between those men displaying inaptitude and those with temperamental unsuitability. On the surface it might appear easy. Men who had difficulty with their aviation or combat skills were likely to be identified by those flying with them inside the aircraft or within the formation. But how were flight surgeons to tell the difference between the merely inefficient and those who were deliberately seeking to avoid combat? Medical bulletins were forthcoming which further elaborated on the subject.

A winter 1942 bulletin, for example, reminded squadron flight surgeons that those men with temperamental unsuitability were cases where no medical diagnosis of illness was possible. No action was to be taken by medical officers to ground or otherwise dispose of offenders, except for the routine medical examinations conducted to determine if there were accompanying physical or mental illness. Men so accused were to be dealt with by the administrative authorities.[10] Despite this clear attempt to remove the unit medical officer from disposal responsibility, it clearly left him as the focal point of its definition and identification. His determination on the medical examination was obviously the pivotal factor. If he said the man's condition was medical, the flyer was treated as if suffering from flying fatigue. If, on the other hand, the flight surgeon found no underlying medical condition, he was supposed to turn the man over to the executive for administrative disposal.

For scores of medical men these early attempts to define or clarify terminology were unsatisfactory. Many, especially those with even rudimentary academic backgrounds in the science of human behaviour, knew the real cause of temperamental unsuitability; namely anxiety reaction, which truthfully can become a kind of neurosis or mental disorder. As a result, some doctors felt all unsuitability for combat flying, whether temperamental or otherwise, was caused by some degree of neurosis and hence should have been labelled appropriately.[11] In the opinion of others, whether the neurosis was considered debilitating or cause for grounding was more the responsibility of the executive. They felt their job as flight surgeons was merely to report the condition. A January 1943 examination summarizing the psychiatric activities of the Eighth Air Force tended to confirm this.

The report was based on observations carried out during the first five months of Eighth Air Force operations. It clearly shows the evolving nature of American policy regarding the definition of LMF by introducing yet another term, 'Primary Flying Fatigue'. Discarding temperamental unsuitability and much of the previous analysis, the new expression was applied to psychoneurotic breakdowns which occurred early in operational flying. It also was expanded to include people who quit even before their first mission. Interestingly, it compared primary flying fatigue to the ordinary mental disorders of civilian life. Further, it declared that those subject to it would ordinarily suffer the same fate in a peacetime environment. Combat flying or the anticipation of combat flying merely 'served as the precipitating mechanism'.[12] Significantly, the report indicated that prognosis for aviators with primary flying fatigue was poor and stated that few cases were ever returned successfully to combat. Despite the psychological origins of the problem, the paper concluded that ultimate disposal of these kinds of men was best left to the executive. Technically speaking, the airman might still be capable of flying. This was true despite the possibility of a variety of external symptoms and regardless of the safety risks to those around him. His inability or reluctance to do so was not considered to be caused by severe trauma, since preliminary research indicated most of these men failed either before their first missions or very early into their tours.

Subsequent documents show the Americans increasingly less reluctant to use terms which came close tó the RAF's Lack of Moral Fibre. The Eighth Air Force's Chief Consultant in Psychiatry, Major Donald W. Hastings, along with his colleagues, submitted a report to the Air Surgeon in Washington which clarified much of the previous terminology.[13] Citing the Royal Air Force's example, Hastings defined those men suffering early breakdown as 'Psychological Failures', and came near to the British understanding of the term. There were other medical authorities, however, who disliked what was implied by LMF. Lieutenant Colonel Roy R. Grinker and Major J. P. Spiegel were noteworthy for their contribution to the subject. Writing in *Men Under Stress*, a wartime publication which reviewed the incidence of combat neurosis, they asserted,

Lack of moral fibre comes closest to describing the reaction. Yet 'moral fibre' is not a good term, since it implies a philosophical or ethical value in an attitude which for most soldiers is based simply on identification with a group. Whether the group is right, whether its aims and purposes are ethical, whether giving one's devotion to it show 'moral fibre', must be left to history to decide.[14]

Such sentiments aside, by the middle of 1943 the term LMF was in wide use alongside operational fatigue and operational exhaustion. The term found expression with both Eighth Air Force doctors and commanders. While it did not prevent the occasional use of other terms such as 'lack of intestinal fortitude', 'fear reaction', or 'functional symptoms due to combat flying', LMF nevertheless was clearly meant to categorize some of those who could not carry on.

It was not until the early months of 1944 that two air force doctors, D. G. Wright and Douglas Bond, attempted to clarify a confusing situation.[15] Like scores of other flight surgeons, they found the term LMF distasteful. Beyond that, they believed the fundamental problem was with terminology which mixed diagnosis with disposition. As a result, they recommended the universal use of the general term 'anxiety reaction' to describe the condition which arises from stress. Further, they stipulated that flight surgeons estimate the man's predisposition to breakdown and the amount of stress to which he had been subjected before making any final determination of his overall condition. However, the general provisions of their instructions on the subject were not adopted until just before the war's end.[16]

Clearly there were many, many terms used for the condition pejoratively known as Lack of Moral Fibre. Despite the variation in description, the significance of its general meaning seemed clear enough to many at the time. It described a condition of character brought on by the stresses of combat. But to many, LMF was synonymous with cowardice, because it quickly implied a man had failed to do his duty. He had given up in the face of the enemy under insufficient stress; in other words, he had not tried his utmost to do his part. Despite the frequency of accompanying physical symptoms, he was considered medically fit for flying, in part, so he could not escape the punishment many felt he deserved. Thus, one could argue that the plethora of terms for Lack of Moral Fibre ultimately may not have totally obscured the general meaning of the term. Yet the variations in terminology used to describe the condition contributed to an environment which made its identification, treatment and disposal somewhat more difficult. This becomes even more demonstrable when American Air Force policy is examined.

LMF POLICY IN THE EIGHTH AIR FORCE

Just as the terminology associated with the subject changed, so too did Eighth Air Force administrative and medical disposal policy. The official American response to LMF was characterized by several trends. In the beginning, command authorities were convinced that the problem should receive quick attention at the lowest possible organizational level.[17] Anxious to give subordinate commanders a maximum amount of flexibility, Headquarters Eighth Air Force anticipated intervening in special cases only. As will be shown, this policy was gradually modified during the war. Local commanders slowly gave up their responsibilities on the subject, not altogether unwillingly. Second, and of significant importance, were the policy differences for officers and enlisted men. In general terms, much of what was written in the form of regulations, policy letters and memoranda was directed for the identification and disposal of officers suspected of LMF. While technically still falling under the provisions of the guidance, enlisted men were most often dealt with by local authorities throughout the Combined Bomber Offensive.

Third, the American effort was hampered by overlapping responsibility and frequent disagreements between commanders and their medical personnel. While the arrangements seemed to work well enough in operation, deep philosophical differences between the two groups, not to mention inside the groups themselves, hampered a more efficient response to the problem.[18] Fourth, and despite their other differences, administrative and medical authorities made allowances for men who had been subjected to unusually harrowing circumstances. Every airman was expected to do his share in the face of obvious difficulties. But those who had the misfortune to be in extreme circumstances were frequently excused for their failures. Finally, the lack of a centralized organization with the authority to classify and dispose of men identified with psychological problems caused inequities both in their identification and treatment, not to mention delays in the entire process. There were attendant morale problems as well.[19]

The earliest problems arose in 1942, when the sole Eighth Air Force guidance was provided by the Policy Letter 200.9x373. As previously stated, this letter placed the primary responsibility for the identification of men who were unsuitable for combat on the squadron commander. Assisted by his unit flight surgeon, he was supposed to prepare a report for a Group Flying Evaluation Board (FEB) mostly made up of flying officers. In the report he was ordered to state whether or not he desired the man's continued service in his unit.[20] For their part, many squadron flight surgeons removed men from flying duty once they saw what they considered any incapacitating anxiety. Sometimes this was in the absence of physical symptoms and, according to at least one authority, often done to prevent prejudicial administrative action.[21] The FEB was supposed to make a recommendation to a Central Medical Board (CMB) which, in turn, determined the man's suitability for further flying. Composed of aviation medical specialists, the CMB was located at Station No. 101 Pinetree, near Headquarters, Eighth Air Force. Ordinarily, it made one of three possible determinations.

The first finding might be that the man was fit for non-operational flying. This might include training or transport duties. If the squadron commander had written that he desired the man for further duty, the man was returned to his station immediately. If, on the other hand, the squadron commander declined his continued services, that same man could be reassigned to another unit, or even returned to the United States. The third eventuality occurred if the man was found unfit for flying. In this event, and depending also on the squadron commander's recommendation, he would either be sent back to his unit for ground duty or transferred to another.[22]

This rather lenient policy caused problems with aircrew morale almost immediately. There were cases of officers and airmen who, having been identified as 'temperamentally unsuitable', found themselves back in the same unit, serving in jobs clearly not as hazardous as those shared by their former crewmembers. Worse, because most new arrivals in the Eighth Air Force's expansion period went to flying billets, the shortage of ground staff sometimes resulted in rapid promotion for these grounded airmen.[23] It was not long before combat flyers began grumbling about this situation, particularly as the increasing tempo of operations brought more casualties. Subsequent sortie rates caused an increase in the numbers of these grounded airmen, so hard feelings against them, and against the flight surgeons who had let them escape combat, grew more pronounced.[24] Subsequent changes in policy which were designed to alleviate these early problems were only partially successful and, more often than not, merely magnified some of the philosophical differences between command authorities and medical personnel.

Conforming to the wishes of Headquarters, Eighth Air Force, the Office of the Chief Flight Surgeon issued guidance which stipulated that airmen suffering from primary flight fatigue (LMF *c.* late 1942) were not to be reclassified or grounded due to medical reasons.[25] Had they been so classified, Flying Evaluation Boards, which were usually made up of flying officers, would normally use the medical diagnosis 'unfit for flying, medical' to absolve them of cowardice, malingering or subterfuge. It was only by intentionally ignoring their physical or mental condition, and by not grounding the man, that flight surgeons could signal their real opinion to the boards. So, during late 1942 and well into 1943, flight surgeons were in the curious position of certifying people as capable of flying who they knew clearly were not. By doing so, they could ensure the man would eventually be dealt with by the executive and get whatever punishment he might deserve.[26]

The irony of this situation was partly the fault of the administrative authorities, most of whom were pilots themselves. Many aviators were understandably reluctant to stigmatize a fellow flyer, except in the most blatant cases. Few were prepared to label a man with any term related to psychoneurosis and thereby ascribe a condition which was incompletely understood. At the same time, there was no great hurry to remove aviator's flying badges, particularly since badges were regarded as training diplomas rather than symbols of continuing qualification.[27] Anxious not to appear too harsh, and seeking a humane resolution to the problem, some Flying Evaluation Boards focused on the results of the medical examination as a way out of their responsibilities.[28] Compounding the problem were individual commanders who could be quite arbitrary in their responses to the problem. There were significant variations in the treatment a man could receive depending on his unit.

Flight surgeons were also responsible for some of the variations in treatment of the overall problem, however. Few possessed a modern background in the sciences of psychiatry or psychology.[29] Many, taken almost directly from their civilian practices, received only cursory training in aviation medicine.[30] As problems with aircrew emotional disorders developed, they tried to balance the requirements of their medical oath with their relationship to their commanding officer. Some probably went too far in their desire to maintain a good working environment and let command pressure influence their medical diagnosis. Others, interested in staying on the good side of aircrews and in an honest attempt to help those afflicted were perhaps too lenient.[31] They received a continuing stream of guidance but many disagreed with much of what was suggested. No single theory regarding the identification, causes and treatment of those airmen regarded as lacking moral fibre, was ever universally accepted. Professional disagreements were common.[32]

As explained, Hastings, Wright and Glueck made one of the earliest wartime attempts to define medically those aviators best relegated to the category. Their studies indicated that aviators most likely to fail in combat either did so before the first mission or by mission number five.[33] They subdivided this group into two kinds of airmen; those with overwhelming fear reactions, and those who developed visible physical symptoms as a result of their fears. It was clear, according to these doctors, that men so affected succumbed to their fears in the absence of real stress.[34] Those who did so were not remarkably predisposed to fail by anything in their backgrounds. Moreover, no adequate selection criteria could be established to identify them before entry into training.[35] It was a puzzling problem which put an immense burden on the unit flight surgeons.

Grinker and Spiegel's view of LMF was slightly different. Stating the commonly held American view that no one was immune to the effects of combat stress, they indicated that all its symptoms could be regarded as neurotic manifestations. Like Hastings and company, they allowed that men who failed exhibited severe symptoms despite minimum stress. In other words, the LMF types had given up in the face of the enemy without, in many cases, having even flown a mission or been in combat.[36] They had a weak sense of duty and weak group loyalty. Fortunately, they also rarely occurred. Significantly, Grinker and Spiegel felt that aviators suffering from LMF (or psychological failure, as they called it), were a result of misclassification. They should not have been allowed in the air force in the first place. Reflecting the predominant British view, Grinker and Spiegel believed adequate testing before training selection could help prevent the problem.[37]

Douglas D. Bond, Chief of the Psychiatry Section, Eighth Air Force Central Medical Establishment, weighed in with yet another analysis. He concluded that airmen broke down in combat as a result of anxiety reaction. Their breakdowns could be accompanied by physical symptoms or some external display of attitude, such as outright refusal to fly.

Unwilling to connect diagnosis with disposition, and consistent in his criticism of Eighth Air Force policy for doing so, Dr Bond argued that diagnosis of such cases should be based on several related factors.[38] First, the man's previous psychological history should be taken into account. Next, the flight surgeon needed to consider the amount of stress the man had been subjected to and the changes it effected. Finally, it was important to estimate the man's potential for response to treatment. In Bond's view, the ultimate disposition of the man depended less on the doctor's diagnosis than on the aviator's character, prognosis, unit needs and possible effect on squadron morale.[39]

Bond's concern with a lack of a centralized authority for the identification and disposition of LMF cases was never adequately answered. Nevertheless, by June 1943, Headquarters Eighth Air Force had replaced Policy Letter 200.9x373. The new memorandum, numbered 75-2, enhanced the power of the Central Medical Board. While superficially leaving the primary responsibility of identification to the squadron commanders and flight surgeons, its *de facto* effect was to transfer the decision on a man's diagnosis and disposition up to the next highest level. It did this by effectively removing the Group Flying Evaluation Boards from the diagnostic chain.[40]

Few squadron or group commanders were prepared to disagree with the findings of the Central Medical Board. By the provisions of Memorandum 75-2, a central medical finding of 'operational exhaustion', protected the man from administrative punishment. If, however, the CMB found the man physically fit for flying (the diagnostic equivalent to LMF) he was returned to his Bomb Group to face the FEB. No longer advisory in nature, and therefore to a very real extent relieved of responsibility for categorizing fellow aviators, the FEB was administratively empowered to remove the man from flight duty (ironically enough, probably what he wanted in the first place).[41] Memorandum 75-2 further mandated several actions in this event. Officers faced immediate demotion, particularly if they held temporary wartime rank above their permanent grades. All eventually faced reclassification proceedings under Army Regulation 605-230. Reclassification was a euphemism for loss of commission, reassignment or separation from the service.[42]

After June 1943, men charged with LMF were not legally reassigned to other duties, particularly if doing so would bring them into contact with combat aviators. Further, action on their cases was to be taken swiftly. In principle, Memorandum 75-2 also allowed commanders, at their discretion, to hold officers and men for court martial under the Articles of War. In fact, there were no courts martial for any officers or airmen relating to LMF at any time in the Eighth Air Force's first year of operations.[43] By the autumn of 1943, however, there were occasional court procedures at stations like Horsham, Thorpe Abbots and Grafton Underwood.

Documentary evidence is fragmentary, but it is clear that by that time both officers and enlisted men were being charged with violations of the Articles of War for refusing to fly. A junior officer in the 95th Bomb Wing, for example, was found guilty of the 75th Article, 'misbehaving before the enemy', for refusing to fly his unit's mission to Saarlautern on 4 October. Interestingly, his severe sentence – to forfeit all pay, to be dismissed and to be confined at hard labour – was ultimately disapproved by General Doolittle.[44] Even so, he doubtless was quickly removed from his station. Another interesting case belonged to an enlisted man of the 384th Bomb Group. This unit had suffered significant casualties during the tough missions to Schweinfurt and had recently acquired a new commander, Colonel Dale O. Smith. Colonel Smith was quick to note the 384th's difficulties:

Having spent those weeks with Willie Hatcher's excellent group I found many things about the 384th that I didn't like. Discipline was poor from top to bottom. People slopped around in dishevelled uniforms of every description. No one saluted. The station was a quagmire of mud. In fact, it was referred to throughout the Eighth Air Force as Grafton Undermud. And instead of attempting to get rid of the mud, the troops seemed to use the mud as an excuse for their sloppy behaviour.[45]

Small wonder that Smith would be strict with 'shirkers' like the private found guilty of disobeying an order to fly a combat mission to Bremen on 13 December. A military court sentenced this man to forfeiture of pay, a dishonourable discharge and confinement at hard labour for two years. Unlike the officer cited earlier, his sentence was confirmed by General Doolittle.[46]

As it turns out, some of the officers subjected to reclassification under Regulation 605-230 were asked to resign voluntarily under a different regulation. This step was taken to avoid the stigma and subsequent effects of a dishonorable discharge. From the air force's point of view it probably speeded the whole procedure and had the additional benefit of avoiding an embarrassing administrative procedure.[47]

Enlisted men also fell under the provisions of Memorandum 75-2, although, because their cases had been handled routinely at a local level, the revised rules merely confirmed what had been going on since the beginning of the air campaign. Enlisted men and non-commissioned officers found to have LMF were to be reduced to the grade of private, removed from flying status, subjected to unspecified disciplinary action and assigned to basic duty.[48]

Eighth Air Force Memorandum 75-2 significantly clarified previous guidance. It was followed by still further directives, however, the most notable coming in March 1944. At that point, General James H. Doolittle, the Eighth Air Force's new commander, formally ordered medical and administrative authorities to consider the amount of stress a man had endured before making any determination regarding his character. The intensity of the combat he had seen was to be categorized as either none, mild, moderate or severe.[49] It became clear that aviators who broke down in circumstances of less than moderate combat were held far more liable for possible charges of LMF. There were individual variations, of course, but in general terms, the new guidance was a further effort to assist commanders, flight surgeons and the Central Medical Board in their determinations.[50]

Still not satisfied with the results, however, Headquarters Army Air Forces in Washington issued a consolidated version of three regulations in the autumn of 1944. The new compilation, referred to as Regulation 35-16, again highlighted the role of the CMB and had the net effect of further reducing the local commander's responsibility on the whole subject. By the new regulation, squadron commanders and their flight surgeons might make the initial identification of men suspected of LMF, but the authority to send them to the CMB was reserved to the Commanding General of the Eighth Air Force.[51]

The new regulation also more clearly established the organization of the CMB. It was to consist of five senior medical officers, either flight surgeons or aviation medical examiners. Three constituted a quorum.[52] The board's responsibilities remained essentially the same as before, except, in the event of a LMF ruling – once again by a 'qualified for flying' determination – all paperwork had to be referred back to General Doolittle's office. Only if the commanding general agreed with the board's finding was the man sent to a local FEB for ultimate disposition. Even then, an officer on General Doolittle's staff was ordered to monitor all local FEB decisions. If this officer disagreed with the results and General Doolittle concurred, the local decision could be overturned by a central Flying Evaluation Board. The regulation made it clear that the purpose of the ombudsman-like officer and central board was only to provide for uniformity of disposal.[53]

Late in December 1944 one further clarification was issued. Occasionally there were aviators, both officer and enlisted, who, despite any lack of major physical symptoms, might be identified as LMF by their unwillingness or outright verbal refusal to fly. It was not considered necessary to send such airmen to the CMB for evaluation. They could be dealt with at the local level and frequently were.[54] If local commanders and flight surgeons felt there were no physical reasons for a man's refusal, he was sent directly to the FEB for disposal. This usually meant grounding and administrative transfer procedures. Only if the unit commander and flight surgeons were unsure of the possibility of underlying medical or mental condition was the man sent forward to the CMB for further testing. At that point, the normal provisions of Army Regulation 35-16 would apply.[55]

The winter 1944 Policy Letter, numbered 35-18, was noteworthy not just for what it said about those who refused to fly, but also because it reflected the Chief of the US Army Air Forces' overall philosophy towards any type of LMF. General Arnold wanted his subordinates to be guided by several broad principles when dealing with the disposition of those so charged. These are worth listing because they remained in force for the remainder of the war and showed a clear maturation of the Army Air Force's policy:

1. Allowances were to be made for older officers, or those with 'mature judgement and extensive service'. Their waning motivation for combat flying was not to be construed as LMF.

2. Young officers, usually commissioned solely for the purpose of combat flying, ordinarily lacked utility if not qualified to do so. If found disqualified by an FEB, they were to be swiftly eliminated.

3. Officers who declined to fly were required to so state in writing.

4. FEBs were responsible for differentiating between character deficiency and simple inaptitude for flying.

5. LMF findings by FEBs were to result in immediate reclassification proceedings. No delay for appeal was officially provided or considered necessary.

6. Officers appearing before FEBs were to have full rights under the provisions of army regulations, including the right to legal counsel.

7. Officers medically disqualified for flying (and thus with no LMF) were to be reassigned to ground duties, commensurate with qualifications.

8. Particularly harrowing experiences were to be considered by medical boards for initial determination of an aviator's condition. They frequently disqualified a man medically from flying and thus saved him from an LMF ruling and administrative punishment. If so considered, these men should not be reconsidered by subsequent FEBs, if the determination was that he was qualified.

9. Non-flying officers who exhibited inability to cope with stress were to be swiftly eliminated from the service.

10. Reclassification procedures remained with Army Regulation 605-230. Officers were normally afforded the opportunity to resign under the provisions of Army Regulation 605-275.

11. Flagrant cases of refusal to fly or wilful violations of discipline were court martial offences under the 104th Article of War. Officers found guilty were to be immediately suspended from flying.

General Arnold also advised his subordinate commanders that he considered the resolution of LMF a function of command and not of medical authorities. He admonished them to inculcate a sense of moral responsibility in their flyers. Experienced combat veterans were ordered to lead frequent discussions on the subject of combat stress and the willingness of aviators to meet it. Arnold summarized his views by writing:

Commanding officers will not subject officers of their command to disproportionate degrees of stress beyond the necessity of the military situation.
Commanding officers and flight surgeons will deal considerately and tact-
fully, but firmly, with all rated flying personnel.[56]

LACK OF MORAL FIBRE: THE STATISTICAL EVIDENCE

It is very difficult to determine with certainty the exact number of
combat failures in the Eighth Air Force between 1942 and 1945. Part of
the problem is the fragmentary state of statistical evidence. But also, as
has been demonstrated, much of the confusion relates to the variable
terminology which made any kind of contemporary statistical analysis
confusing at best.[57] Various policy changes and written guidance, while
designed to bring uniformity to identification and disposal, were often not
followed to the letter. The failure need not be considered wilful mal-
feasance on the' part of command authorities, but rather the perfectly
understandable result of a military bureaucracy struggling to deal with a
problem, the causes and extent of which were only beginning to be understood.[58] Clearly, however, not all men who might be considered LMF
were treated the same way. Some escaped identification and punishment
altogether. Others, depending on the current state of the military situation, received strict treatment.[59] Only by examining the numerical evidence, such as it is, can reasonable conclusions be drawn about the overall
extent of the American problem during the Combined Bomber Offensive.

In the first year of Eighth Air Force operations, Hastings, Wright, and
Glueck reported 166 cases (69 officers and 97 enlisted men) of 'psychological failure' or LMF. The Central Medical Board considered a total
of 255 cases of emotional disturbance during the same period, but saw
only 60 of the 166 cases judged to be combat failures.[60] In other words, a
significant portion of the total problem was being handled by local
administrative action.

Before drawing hasty conclusions about the percentage of LMF from
the total of emotional casualties, it is important to remember what the first
year numbers demonstrate. First, the vast majority of enlisted men were
diagnosed and disposed of in their squadrons or bomb groups, and therefore would not be seen by the Central Medical Board. To an indeterminate extent this could also be said of some officers, especially those guilty
of outright refusal to fly. Throughout the campaign there were those who
were administratively grounded or transferred without being seen either
by the CMB or reclassification board.[61]

It is interesting to look at these first 60 aviators identified by the CMB.
Hastings and his fellow doctors interviewed them extensively. The
average age of the officers was almost 25 and the enlisted men 23. Pilots
and co-pilots accounted for most of the officer failures and all the enlisted

men were gunners. Slightly less than half the total were married. Interestingly, since only about 20 per cent of crewmembers in the entire Eighth Air Force had wives, it would appear that married men suffered a disproportionate amount of combat failures. Even more significant, was the fact that 51 of the 60 failures came in the first five missions of the operational tour.[62] This tended to confirm the Royal Air Force's experience and analysis.[63]

Table 7.1 shows the Central Medical Board cases for the entire Combined Bomber Offensive. Of 2,102 total emotional casualties which show up on the records, the CMB saw 1,716. One thousand two-hundred and thirty were permanently grounded. Table 7.2 shows the results of a follow-up study done on bomber crew emotional disorders. Its utility is hampered by its failure to extend through April 1945. Despite the record's incompleteness, it is clear that only about 30 per cent of airmen seen by the CMB for emotional disorders were ultimately classified as LMF. About one-third of these were sent directly to the reclassification board. The balance of the LMF group were turned back over to their local units for disposal and mostly transferred to the United States administratively. According to these data, there were only four courts martial in two years.[64]

Table 7.3 relates to the 14-month period between May 1943 and August 1944. During that time the CMB saw 1,198 total cases. Two-hundred and forty-nine were seen under the LMF reference. Ninety-two eventually met the reclassification board and disposal results are known for 74. These records indicate almost three-quarters of airmen charged with LMF received an other than honourable discharge. Interestingly, the board accepted very few resignations. Ninety-five per cent of officers who met this board were separated from the Army Air Forces.[65] A similar report of the same time-frame noted nearly 400 'administrative removals' (LMF) for enlisted men.[66] In any one year period after the spring of 1943 there were approximately 250 to 300 cases (mostly officers) who might be tentatively classified as combat failures before they met the Central Medical Board. Since only about 30 per cent of these were ultimately classified as LMF, some extrapolation of figures shows a combined officer and enlisted Eighth Air Force LMF rate of about 200–300 cases per year. That works out to about 20 per month.

Table 7.1

CENTRAL MEDICAL BOARD CASES
Monthly Anxiety Reactions (AR) and Physical Disability (PD)

	AR	*PD*	*Total*
1942			
August	1	1	2
September	2	0	2
October	2	3	5
November	6	2	8
December	2	3	5
1943			
January	10	3	13
February	18	7	25
March	15	4	19
April	8	6	14
May	26	9	35
June	33	10	43
July	26	7	33
August	34	17	51
September	24	12	36
October	45	12	57
November	37	28	65
December	36	26	62
1944			
January	48	29	77
February	48	28	76
March	83	40	123
April	75	16	91
May	95	19	114
June	86	27	113
July	98	31	129
August	72	21	93
September	47	22	69
October	51	20	71
November	32	22	54
December	40	15	55
1945			
January	52	19	71
February	24	9	33
March	28	8	36
April	26	10	36
	1230	486	1716

Source: Eighth Air Force, 'Statistical Survey of the Emotional Casualties of the Eighth Air Force Aircrews', 25 May 1945, 520.7421 1944-1945, AFHRA.

Table 7.2

DISPOSITION OF HEAVY BOMBER EMOTIONAL DISORDERS
August 1942–August 1944

1. Returned to US through hospital	101
2. Completed tour	86
3. Ground duty	298
4. Full flying duty	13
5. Non-operational flying	8
6. Killed in action	5
7. Missing in action	20
8. Follow-up to a replacement depot	10
9. Follow-up to a hospital	10
10. Transferred to fighter	4
11. No follow-up	25
12. Died, not in combat	4
13. Reclassification [LMF]	78
14. Returned to US Administratively [LMF]	165
15. Courts martial [LMF]	4
TOTAL	831

Source: Eighth Air Force, 'Statistical Survey of the Emotional Casualties of the Eighth Air Force', 25 May 1945, 520.7421 1944-1945, AFHRA.

Table 7.3

RECLASSIFICATION BOARD RECOMMENDATIONS
74 of 298 cases seen by the CMB
May 1943–August 1944

a. Honorable Discharge	7
b. Other than Honorable Discharge	55
c. Reassignment	3
d. Resignation Accepted	1
e. Pending or Unknown	8
TOTAL	74

Source: Eighth Air Force, 'The Reclassification of Personnel Failures in the Eighth Air Force', 16 Oct. 1944, 520.742-4, AFHRA.

LMF – THE HUMAN SIDE

While a review of terminology, policy and statistics can show how the problem of LMF was dealt with, only by examining the human side of the situation can its impact on those involved be truly understood. It is difficult to make such an examination without reflecting on the tremendous pressure endured by these aviators. Fortunately, much of the evidence of this pressure and its effect survives in a surprising number of medical and administrative case histories. Although preserved in slightly abbreviated and mostly sanitized format, they are sufficient to make several points.[67] First, despite the quantity of official guidance on the subject, the disposal of LMF cases was never completely uniform. While it is obvious that no two cases were alike, it is nevertheless clear that enough similarities existed in many situations to justify equal disposal. Yet inequities lasted until the end of the war.[68]

On a related issue, it might superficially appear that officers suffered less from the stigmatization of LMF than did their enlisted companions. In terms of overall numbers this is most certainly true. However, if one considers the consequences of combat failure, the punishment for officers was potentially much greater, especially with its concurrent loss of commission, removal of the flying badge and threat of retention in an enlisted grade.[69] Another point emphasized by the evidence is the relationship of combat experience to disposal. As demonstrated, the amount of stress a man was considered to have endured was probably the single most important factor in how his case would be viewed, both officially and by those around him. Finally, the individual histories reveal interesting details about the timing of LMF cases. For a variety of reasons it was considered important to handle potential morale problems with alacrity. In fact, there were often maddening delays.[70]

With regard to the first point, some individuals' case histories show the Central Medical Board occasionally guilty of lack of uniformity. Consider the following two summaries:

Second Lieutenant, 412 Bombardment Squadron. This 29-year-old navigator had five combat missions. He was performing satisfactorily until he was wounded in the right arm when his plane was badly damaged on the fifth mission. He was hospitalized for three weeks, developed marked tension symptoms, was unable to perform his duties on subsequent practice missions and asked to be grounded. He was found to be tense, depressed and to show evidence of weight loss. He had an excellent record, went to college for two years, held good jobs, was well motivated towards flying and did well as a navigator. The Central Medical Board qualified him in October 1943 because it was not felt that he was suffering from 'Operational Exhaustion'. He was recommended for an other than honorable discharge by the Reclassification Board.

Second Lieutenant, 527 Bombardment Squadron. This 25-year-old navigator flew only two combat missions. He complained of many symptoms which were tensional and hysterical in nature. He was also inefficient in the air, becoming nauseated and unable to hear over the interphone. This patient had some evidence of instability in his family background but had no previously outstanding neurotic trends and had a good school, work and military record. He was fairly well motivated towards flying and had an excellent record at Navigation School. The findings of the Central Medical Board in February 1944 were: '2nd Lt. G. is permanently disqualified for all duties involving flying because of psychoneurosis, anxiety type, due to fear of combat flying. It is further the opinion of the Board that this condition is of a temporary nature and will automatically disappear when the prospect of combat flying is removed.' This man was not referred to the Reclassification Board but was reassigned as a personal equipment officer, in which capacity he has done outstandingly excellent work ever since.[71]

These are two very similar individuals, both with good backgrounds and records. Yet the one who was wounded was the one eventually dismissed from the service. Obviously, other factors bore on the situation. Not only were the strict details of each case important to its final determination, but also critical was the episode's timing, the overall composition of the board, the results of the psychiatric interview, the recommendations of commanders and even the physical appearance of the aviator himself. Unofficial correspondence with the Medical Board might also help sway its decision.[72]

Inevitably, not all cases were like the previous two. Most frequently, if a man attempted to do his duty in the face of his fears he was accorded more lenient treatment. The major evidence for his efforts came in the number of missions he had flown or the amount of actual combat he had participated in. Those who broke early or without trying were almost certainly going to be dealt with strictly.

Captain, Pilot, B-17. Chief Complaint: 'Scared to death'. The officer states that he never had any particular trouble until the time came for his first combat mission. On being alerted for this mission, he states that he became scared and frightened, began to tremble, felt like running away to hide, and states that he realized the entire trouble was due to a fear of being killed . . . In 1940 he joined the RCAF as an instructor and was sent to Canada. In 1942 he transferred to the USAAF as a captain . . . He arrived in the ETO six months later as a first pilot of a B-17. He has 2,300 hours official time . . . No other family history of insanity or nervous breakdown . . . He stated that he realized this might be considered as a court martial offense, but that he could not force himself to go on a combat mission and was ready to accept any consequences . . . Fear Reaction . . . may be considered as a 'predisposed' individual. This officer was returned to his unit by the Central Medical Board as fit for full flying duties . . . the officer resigned his commission for the good of the service when he met the Theatre Reclassification Board.

Technical Sergeant, Radio gunner-engineer, B-17. Chief complaint: irregular breathing, feeling of constriction in the chest, feeling of heart beating all through him, numbness of the finger tips. Patient reported the above symptoms first to the surgeon at the Combat Crew Replacement Centre, the day before he was to be sent to a combat station, saying that he had had them off and on for about two weeks. The day after he arrived at his operational station he came to the surgeon twice, and complained so vigorously of these symptoms that he was admitted to sick quarters. Inducted February 1942. Did not choose the Air Corps . . . on flying status for seven months and has about 200 hours total flying time . . . No operational missions, no crashes, no other traumatic experiences . . . Patient describes his symptoms with a 'belle indifference', and yet with insistence on their importance. He seems to have no conception of the possibility of their relationship to situational anxiety. He spends most of the time in the hospital curled up in bed . . . No psychotic manifestations were seen . . . Functional symptoms due to combat stress (anticipation of combat). Was returned to unit by Central Medical Board as fit for full flying duties. Reduced to grade of private, removed from flying status and assigned to basic duty by the unit.[73]

Contrast their disposition with this enlisted man whose experience must certainly qualify as 'harrowing',

Technical Sergeant, tail gunner, B-17, Chief Complaint: fear of flying. On 2 October, 1942 . . . Pilot put ship in a vertical dive . . . the right wing and engines pulled off, and the plane caught fire . . . sliced off the tail section . . . The patient, in the tail section, went hurtling down end over end . . . tried to smash his way out through the glass . . . failed . . . kicked his way through the skin . . . became wedged . . . He must have been blown clear at about 1,000 feet and had time to get his parachute open . . . The plane had crashed about 100 yards away . . . The following morning he felt 'jittery' and 'ill at ease', and went out to the wreck with the Commanding Officer and the medical officer . . . saw the charred bodies of the other eight men who were in the plane . . . sleeps poorly . . . Whistling and whining noises startle him . . . has developed severe anxiety attacks on riding in planes . . . In spite of these symptoms he has flown on five operational missions since the accident . . . his plane badly hit by flak . . . went on forcing himself to fly . . . he was instructed to report to the Central Medical Board . . . does not wish to be regarded as 'yellow' or a 'quitter' but now that the thing has come to a head, he states that he never wants to get into an airplane again . . . a case of functional symptoms (anxiety state) occurring in a person of sound moral fiber and without neurotic predisposition . . . unlikely that any form of therapy can return this patient to combat flying. Central Medical Board recommend relief from all duties involving flying and assignment in grade to ground duties.[74]

As a way of summarizing this section it is worth considering the case of one officer, whose complete records throughout the process are available. This case, typical of scores of others during the Combined Bomber Offensive, illustrates the American LMF procedure in operation.

Although his actual name is recorded, for the purposes of this discussion he need be identified only as John Doe.

First Lieutenant Doe, a 25-year-old B-17 pilot with the 332nd Bomb Squadron, 94th Bomb Group, arrived with his unit in England in April 1943. An aircraft commander with about 500 flying hours in bombers, he flew his first combat mission on 13 May. On his third mission his group lost three aircraft. After one abort for allegedly defective fuel gauges, he flew again on 13 June. During this raid to Kiel his aircraft was badly damaged by shellfire and he saw several of the nine total aircraft losses suffered by the 94th. After some reflection, he decided he 'could not take it any more'. Ten minutes into his next mission he aborted a perfectly functioning aircraft. After landing he went directly to the flight surgeon and refused to fly further.[75]

The squadron flight surgeon examined Doe on 29 June. Despite finding no overt evidence of physical disorder, he put Doe in sick quarters. After consultation with the squadron commander, the flight surgeon prepared a report for a 94th Bomb Group Flying Evaluation Board. Composed exclusively of local flying officers, the group FEB removed Doe from flight status and ordered him to report to Pinetree and the Central Medical Board. The FEB's 3 July report along with the squadron commander's recommendation went with him. Doe's squadron commander had no desire for his continued service and the group commander's endorsement was even more emphatic.

Before meeting the CMB, Doe was given another complete physical, this one accompanied by a psychiatric examination. Three doctors, two of them behavioural specialists, found him healthy. Despite identifying his 'emotional instability', and noting his proneness to crying, they made no medical diagnosis. When the CMB convened on 14 July its three senior flight surgeons likewise found Doe 'qualified for all duties involving flying'. In accordance with the provisions of Memorandum 75-2 he was returned to his unit as 'temperamentally unsuited'.

Reconvened to deal with Doe's disposal, the 94th Bomb Group FEB immediately recommended he be sent to the Reclassification Board. This board, ruling sometime late in July, gave Doe one of 55 'other than honourable discharges' it meted out between May 1943 and August 1944.[76] His subsequent activities are unrecorded.

Doe's case seems pretty typical for that very small percentage of aviators in the Eighth Air Force who were unable to continue in combat. Actually identified under the provisions of the early policy letter, his disposal was in accordance with the rules of the subsequent memorandum.[77] The records of his case obviously give considerable information about the routine adjudication of LMF, but they are silent on the attitudes of his contemporaries.

For information regarding the feelings of typical combat aviators it is necessary to turn to diaries, memoirs, letters or oral history. Unfortunately, there would appear to be few direct references to LMF in these kinds of sources. One reason might be that the problem, at least in the minds of many, was not considered significant enough to comment on. Far more likely is the understandable tendency of veterans to remember the good things about their arduous service, and to minimize those things more unpleasant.[78] The memories of aviators who failed to measure up are probably not pleasing ones. Passing years soften many of the hard feelings.

Despite a general reluctance to discuss such matters, there have been veterans who have recorded their feelings. When asked if they remember any fellow aviators who gave into their fears, either by outright refusal or with functional symptoms, a majority of combat veterans agree that they do recall such cases. Most seem to remember at least one or two cases grounded for psychological reasons.[79] One B-17 waist gunner remembered his views of men asking to be relieved:

I would say that these cases were caused by an overwhelming fear of combat and death. A fear so strong that any penalties could be suffered . . . It was best to get the severe emotional problems off the crew. In some cases the pilot asked that the individual be relieved from flying status.[80]

These kinds of sentiments were shared by many. One bombardier recalled:

We had a pilot in our hut that felt he couldn't continue in this and his co-pilot took over his crew. I didn't know what happened after he left the group but it was obvious that he was a hazzard [sic] to the other people who had to fly with him and he'd likely never get them through their missions in the shape he was in.[81]

In general terms Second World War combat veterans had a compassionate attitude towards those who failed to measure up.[82] They could be especially understanding of those who had been through several combat operations and then broke down. If, however, airmen gained the impression that insufficient effort was being made, their contempt became obvious. Elmer Bendiner, a navigator on the Schweinfurt raids, described a senior officer in his unit this way:

Major Culpepper was more likely to occasion resentment because he flew combat but with a fastidious eye to the relative safety of the missions he chose for himself. His executive duties in the group always interfered with his flying if the mission was over Germany, if the escorts were insufficient, or if the group's position in the wing seemed likely to prove excessively hazardous. He became known as the 'Milk-Run Major' and his name was welcomed on the battle roster as a sure sign of an easy day.[83]

Bendiner's insight extends to the Major's inner conflicts. Aware that such men suffer very personal agonies, Bendiner concluded that those who resigned from combat 'had fierce obsessions with personal survival', and 'an overriding personal necessity to preserve their bodies intact'.[84]

Even though most aviators apparently knew someone or somebody who had broken in combat, a surprising number of veterans are unable to describe, even in rough estimate, the policies or procedure for the disposal of the afflicted. Most merely noted the man's disappearance from the Nissen hut. When asked for their impressions of the fairness of treatment they are more certain. Most believed the men were fairly treated. Quite a few recall no severe punishments whatsoever. Several note the lenient or 'humane' treatment.[85] A few, like this one, express a very different view, however:

I think they were dealt with unfairly if they refused to fly again after an extremely hard combat flight. One gunner's hair turned white overnight and I understood they broke him and had him doing manual labour (digging ditches). This could have been a way to keep more of us from following along.[86]

The top turret gunner who wrote the passage probably reflects a view shared by at least some of his companions. With enlisted people dealt with by their units, local punishment for LMF offenders might serve as a more visible deterrent, but the deterrent would have been much more effective if the policies had been more clearly enunciated. The vast majority of air-crew members recall only a few people who disappeared from their bases from time to time, having broken down as a result of stress. Since far greater numbers were leaving empty beds as a result of death in combat, true battle casualties doubtless received the greater attention. For many, combat stress was an individual battle; one that had to be waged and won on a daily basis. Concerned as they were with this day-to-day struggle for their own survival, the overwhelming majority of Eighth Air Force aviators stuck together as crews to complete their tours.

CONCLUSIONS

Several general comments can be made to summarize the American experience with Lack of Moral Fibre. First, in terms of overall numbers, the Eighth Air Force never had an unmanageable problem. Even though LMF was considered sufficiently important to receive detailed attention, overall combat effectiveness was never seriously threatened. Second, despite the general agreement which developed over operational fatigue and operational exhaustion cases, no genuine consensus ever developed regarding the identification and disposition of LMF. Disagreements between various senior executives, combat leaders and medical experts prevented a truly standardized approach. This lack of standardization caused occasional inequities in disposition or bureaucratic delays.

Attempts to remedy the situation were only partly successful. The periodic policy letters, memoranda and regulations which served to provide guidance on the problem might ultimately have led to a single philosophy, but the end of the war in Europe eventually made the point moot.

Significantly, most of the airmen who fought and died in the skies over Germany were only superficially aware of medical and administrative regulations which were designed to keep them there. Trained to trust themselves, their equipment and their leaders, few spent much time wondering what would happen to those who failed to meet the test of combat. Their letters, memoirs and reminiscences make it clear they were more concerned with their own daily performance, and that of their crew, than with the deterrent effect of incompletely understood regulations. Those that recall specific incidents almost always think that men designated LMF received fair and humane treatment.

In summary, it would appear a unique combination of circumstances made the American policy towards LMF rather more efficient and lenient than might otherwise be expected. With manpower resources far more vast than Britain's, but with far less experience dealing with the subject, the Eighth Air Force responded as best it could. Rapidly organized and directed to combat operations almost immediately, the Eighth Air Force dealt with LMF in a manner which not only reflected the fast-changing pressures of war, but also the struggles of a large combat organization to best use its personnel. That the LMF problem was not larger is more a tribute to the aircrews than to those experts appointed to care for them.

NOTES

1. Freeman, *War Diary* , pp. 9–10.
2. Office of the Air Surgeon, 'Memorandum for the War Department Special Staff, Battle Casualty Data', 5 June 1946, 519.741-1 1943–1945, AFHRA.
3. See Chapter 3 for a more complete explanation of temporary and permanent emotional casualties. A completely accurate accounting of Eighth Air Force casualties has not been presented. The Eighth Air Force's statistical branch disbanded at the end of May 1945. These numbers are from the Eighth Air Force Historical Society.
4. Bond, *Love and Fear*, p. 7; Eighth Air Force, 'The Reclassification of Personal Failures in the Eighth Air Force', 16 Oct. 1944, 520.742-4, AFHRA; and Roger A. Freeman to author, 29 Oct. 1991.
5. Eighth Air Force, 'Flight Surgeon's Care of Flyer and Statistical Report', June 1943–June 1944, 519.7440-1, AFHRA.
6. As early as February 1941, for example, the British agreed to supply the Americans with the minutes of the Flying Personnel Research Committee meetings. Letter to FPRC, 19 Feb. 1941, AIR 2/9490.
7. The terms 'operational fatigue' and 'operational exhaustion' would come into more general use slightly later. See Eighth Air Force, 'Policy Letter 200.9x373', 29 Oct. 1942, 519.2171-1 1942–1945, AFHRA.
8. Link and Coleman, op. cit., p. 672.

9. Bond, *Love and Fear*, p. 154.
10. Eighth Air Force, 'Medical Bulletin No. 27', 5 Nov. 1942, 520.741F Aug. 1942–May 1943, AFHRA.
11. Grinker and Spiegel, op. cit., p. 53.
12. Eighth Air Force, 'Psychiatry in the Eighth Air Force', 30 Jan. 1943, 520.7411-12, AFHRA.
13. Hastings, *et al.*, pp. 28–34.
14. Grinker and Spiegel, op. cit., p. 77.
15. Bond, *Love and Fear*, fn, p. 158.
16. US Army Air Forces, 'Letter 35–8', 12 April 1945, 520.7411–3 Jan. 1944–May 1945, AFHRA.
17. Spaatz to Commanding General, 8th Service Command, 16 Sept. 1942, 519.2171–1 1942–1945, AFHRA.
18. See Link and Coleman, op. cit., p. 671 and Glass, op. cit., pp. 872–3.
19. See Eighth Air Force, 'Disposition of Combat Crews Suffering from Emotional Disorders', 1 March 1945, 520.7411-2 1944, AFHRA and 'Report on Psychiatry in the 8th Air Force', 30 Jan. 1943, 520.7411-12 1943, AFHRA.
20. Eighth Air Force, 'Policy Letter 200.9x373', 29 Oct. 1942, 519.2171-1 1942–1945, AFHRA.
21. Bond, *Love and Fear*, p. 154.
22. Eighth Air Force, 'Policy Letter 200.9x373', 29 Oct. 1942, 519.2171-1 1942–1945, AFHRA.
23. See Link and Coleman, op. cit., p. 673 and Bond, *Love and Fear*, p. 154.
24. For elaboration on the difficulties facing flight surgeons see Bond, *Love and Fear*, p. 155, Grinker and Spiegel, op. cit., p. 157, and Hastings, *et al.*, pp. 65–7.
25. Eighth Air Force, 'Medical Bulletin No. 27', 5 Nov. 1942, 520.741F Aug. 1942–May 1943, AFHRA.
26. See Link and Coleman, op. cit., p. 673 and Eighth Air Force, 'Disposition of Combat Crews Suffering from Emotional Disorders', 1 March 1945, 520.7411-2 1944, AFHRA.
27. This was quite different from the Royal Air Force. Bond, *Love and Fear*, p. 170.
28. Link and Coleman, op. cit., p. 671.
29. Craven and Cate, op. cit., Vol. VII, pp. 390-1.
30. See Eighth Air Force, 'Flight Surgeon Indoctrination Course', 520.7411-12 Sept. 1943, AFHRA and Craven and Cate, Vol. VII, p. 392.
31. For a good description of the relationship see Craven and Cate, op. cit., Vol VII, pp. 366–8.
32. Eighth Air Force, 'Disposition of Combat Crews Suffering from Emotional Disorders', 1 March 1945, 520.7411-2, AFHRA.
33. Hastings, *et al.*, p. 35.
34. Ibid., p. 43.
35. Ibid., p. 39.
36. Grinker and Spiegel, op. cit., p. 53.
37. Ibid., pp. 55–6.
38. Major Douglas D. Bond to Brig. Gen. Malcom Grow, 1 March 1945, 520.7411-2 1944, AFHRA.
39. Ibid.
40. Originally issued on 25 June 1943, the memorandum was slightly revised and reissued on 23 August and 24 December of the same year. See Eighth Air Force, 'Memorandum 75-2', 24 Dec. 1943, 519.217-1 1943–1945, AFHRA.
41. Link and Coleman, op. cit., p. 673.
42. The procedures were set down in painstaking detail. US Army Air Force Regulation 605-230, 9 June 1943. An updated version dated 6 Sept. 1945 is available at the Air University Library, Maxwell Air Force Base, Alabama.
43. Hastings, *et al.*, p. 58.
44. Eighth Air Force, 'Headquarters Records', 520.7721, Jan.–April 1944, AFHRA.
45. Smith, op. cit., p. 64.
46. Maxwell AFB's files shed no further light on the circumstances of General Doolittle's decisions. See Eighth Air Force, 'Headquarters Records', 520.7721, Jan.–April, 1944, AFHRA.
47. In the words of the regulation it 'served the best interests of the service'. US Army Air Forces Regulation 35–16, p. 12.
48. Eighth Air Force, 'Memorandum 75-2', 24 Dec. 1943, 519.217-1 1943–1945, AFHRA.
49. Eighth Air Force, 'Memorandum 35-6', cited in 'The Reclassification of Personal Failures in the Eighth Air Force', 16 Oct. 1944, 520.742-4, AFHRA.

50. One unpleasant effect was to give the Central Medical Board a more punitive reputation. Glass, op. cit., p. 865.
51. See Link and Coleman, op. cit., pp. 673-4 and US Army Air Forces Regulation 35–16, 20 Oct.1944, Air University Library, Maxwell Air Force Base, Alabama.
52. Regulation 35–16, p. 8.
53. Ibid., p. 11.
54. Link and Coleman, op. cit., p. 676.
55. Ibid., p. 674.
56. General Henry H. Arnold to all Commanding Generals, 7 Dec. 1944, ' US Army Air Forces Policy Letter 35–18', 519.2171-1, AFHRA.
57. See Bond, *Love and Fear*, pp. 156–157 and Craven and Cate, op. cit., Vol. VII, p. 417.
58. Craven and Cate, op. cit., Vol. VII, p. 392.
59. Ibid., p. 417.
60. See Hastings, *et al.*, pp. 35, 50 and Eighth Air Force, 'Statistical Survey of the Emotional Casualties of the Eighth Air Force Aircrews', 25 May 1945, 520.7421 1944–1945, AFHRA.
61. Eighth Air Force, 'The Reclassification of Personal Failures in the Eighth Air Force', 16 Oct. 1944, 520.742-4, AFHRA.
62. Hastings, *et al.*, pp. 36–40.
63. Comments by Squadron Leader Denis J. Williams, 3 Nov. 1944, AIR 20/10727.
64. Eighth Air Force, 'Statistical Survey of the Emotional Casualties of the Eighth Air Force Aircrews, 25 May 1945, 520.7421 1944–1945, AFHRA.
65. Eighth Air Force','The Reclassification of Personnel Failures in the Eighth Air Force, 16 Oct. 1944, 520.742-4, AFHRA.
66. Eighth Air Force,' 'Statistical Survey of Emotional Casualties', op. cit.
67. Names and initials, which occasionally appear in US records, have been deleted in the interest of privacy.
68. A criticism levelled by almost everyone associated with the subject of emotional casualties. Glass, op. cit., pp. 872-7.
69. Bond implied the administrative punishment for enlisted men was 'relatively satisfactory', but the procedure used mostly for officers was 'debasing'. Bond, *Love and Fear*, pp. 169–71.
70. Warson to Grow, 16 Oct. 1944, 520.742-4, AFHRA.
71. Eighth Air Force, 'The Reclassification of Personnel Failures in the Eighth Air Force', 16 Oct. 1944, 520.742-4, AFHRA.
72. In addition to their mandatory inputs, unit flight surgeons could write personal letters to the CMB regarding their recommendations for disposal of cases. Alfred O. Colquitt, MD, to the Central Medical Board, 21 Feb. 1945, copy in the author's possession.
73. Hastings, *et al.*, pp. 217–40.
74. Ibid., pp. 241–51.
75. Eighth Air Force, 'Report of the Central Medical Board, 12 July 1943', 520.747B, March–July 1943, AFHRA.
76. The details are recorded in Eighth Air Force, 'Reclassification of Personnel Failures in the Eighth Air Force', 16 Oct. 1944, 520.742-4, AFHRA.
77. Eighth Air Force, 'Report of the 94th Bombardment Group', 6 July 1943, 520.747B, March–July 1943, AFHRA.
78. Clear from scores of veterans' letters in the author's possession. See also Kennett, *GI*, pp. 228–41.
79. Letters to the author from the 96th, 351st, 385th, 482nd, and 487th Bombardment Group Associations, Jan. 1989–Aug. 1991.
80. Thomas L. Hair (385th Bomb Group) to author, 25 Feb. 1989.
81. Carter Hart, Jr. (385th Bomb Group) to author, 18 Feb. 1989.
82. For a short but excellent statistical analysis of their opinions see Dollard, pp. 8–9 and 48. See also Captain James Goodfriend, 'Temporary Duty in the ETO'. 8 March 1945, 248.4212-17, AFHRA.
83. Bendiner, op. cit., p. 96.
84. Ibid., p. 97.
85. Letters to the author from the 96th, 351st, 385th, 482nd, and 487th Bombardment Group Associations, Jan. 1989–Aug. 1991.
86. David Framer (385th Bomb Group) to author, 7 March 1989.

8

Bomber Command and Lack of Moral Fibre

Morale was never a problem.
Air Marshal Sir Arthur Harris, after the war.

DESPITE Air Marshal Harris's recollection, it is clear that the issue of aircrew morale was of particular importance to Bomber Command between 1939 and 1945. Harris, and to a larger extent the entire Royal Air Force, clearly devoted considerable energy to sustaining the mental and physical capabilities of combat airmen. As with the American Eighth Air Force, one aspect of this massive organizational and medical effort dealt with an extremely sensitive subject related to the topic identified as 'Lack of Moral Fibre'.

Even today the initials LMF evoke the strongest emotions from veterans, who at once recall vivid, often painful memories. Archival records on the subject are often fragmentary, seldom consolidated, and sometimes difficult or impossible to consult. Published histories of Bomber Command frequently disagree about both the scale of the LMF problem and the impact of official policies implemented to deal with it. Considerable controversy exists on whether or not the Royal Air Force's overall treatment of LMF was too harsh or too lenient.

Fortunately, it is now possible to resolve much of the controversy. Enough detailed information is available to enable a researcher to draw up-to-date conclusions about the entire matter. Documents at the Public Record Office and at the Air Historical Branch provide much of the background necessary to sketch the picture. Further details can be obtained from combat veterans who, although sometimes reluctant to discuss sensitive issues, increasingly feel compelled to reflect critically on the more memorable events of their lives. Taken together, these sources clarify a subject recently cited by one historian as 'deeply obscured'.[1]

Several general observations will be discussed in this chapter. First, as we have seen, the Royal Air Force went to war with the realization that the problems attendant on aircrew stress would have to be faced. Almost from the beginning, executive and medical authorities were prepared to work together to find ways to address the issue. Despite their commendable efforts, professional disagreements led to as many problems as solutions. These problems, in turn, were responsible for several adjustments in policy. Second, official guidance in the form of Air Ministry orders and memoranda was mostly designed for maximum deterrent effect.

As has been shown, the RAF's combat stress philosophy was based on two fundamental beliefs. The most important – probably part of the public school ethos – was that courage was a function of character. This implied that it would be possible to identify and select the right kinds of men for aircrew training. No less significant was the strong conviction that LMF was contagious. This being considered true, many authorities felt it was necessary to anticipate and deal with the problem swiftly. The goal was to minimize LMF's impact by forcibly dissuading other aircrew from following suit. Despite occasional references to the contrary, there is considerable evidence that many men dealt with under LMF regulations were treated with harshness. Several highly placed medical and executive leaders recognized this situation, but felt it to be unavoidable. Better to misjudge the unfortunate few than allow the slow decay, and subsequent collapse, of the entire crew force. Finally, and probably most important, at no time was the problem of LMF significant enough to affect Bomber Command's combat effectiveness. Statistical analysis demonstrates quite clearly that the overwhelming majority of British and Commonwealth airmen carried on gallantly in the face of daunting odds.

LMF EARLY POLICY DEVELOPMENT

During the First World War there was a small but growing group of Royal Air Force aviation authorities who recognized the potential for psychological disorders in aircrew. Throughout the conflict, scores of individual squadron medical officers treated aircrew psychological problems of various kinds.[2] Diagnosis and treatment varied, no doubt because detailed official guidance did not exist at the time. Even if such guidance had been available, few medical officers in 1914-18 were sufficiently educated in the relatively new and sophisticated science of human behaviour to employ it properly.[3] Wartime articles on the subject frequently reflect quaint, often humorous, notions about the temperamental suitability of successful aviators.[4] Training and background notwithstanding, RAF medical efforts were successful enough. Despite psychological disorder rates as high as ten per cent in some squadrons, the majority of aircrew did their duty during the Great War.[5] This was no mean feat considering the combat casualty statistics on the Western Front at the time.

In these circumstances, it might be considered strange that administrative guidance to remove unsuitable airmen from combat did not exist. At the time such explicit directions were apparently deemed unnecessary, since squadron commanders had the authority to send pilots and observers back to Great Britain in the first instance.[6] Just how many may have been so transferred between 1914 and 1918 is not clear.

After the war a sizeable body of medical literature dealt with the general subject of neuropsychology, especially with the identification and treatment of psychiatric or mental casualties of battle. Much of the material was devoted to debunking the popular mythology concerning the use of the term 'Shell Shock'.[7] Rapid post-war technological advances in the entire field of aviation brought concurrent developments in aircrew physiological training. Moreover, even if overall numbers were still small, there were more specialists to deal with the problems peculiar to combat airmen. When the Royal Air Force went to war in 1939, therefore, there was simple and brief written guidance available to medical officers assigned to flying squadrons.

The earliest was Air Ministry Pamphlet 100, which, in its May 1939 first edition, outlined the causes of aircrew psychological problems, described their manifestations, and listed the steps medical officers should take to counter them. Squadron doctors were charged with 'keeping airmen at the highest possible pitch of efficiency'. Admonished to detect and treat airmen who might display physical symptoms of combat fatigue quickly, doctors were nevertheless cautioned against over-enthusiasm. In effect, they were warned not to put the suggestion of possible mental breakdown into the minds of their flyers.[8]

It quickly became apparent that the purely medical instructions provided by the pamphlet were going to be insufficient for the rapidly increasing scale of operations. Events of the Battle of Britain were soon to demonstrate graphically the very real connection between aircrew fatigue, morale, and combat effectiveness. The first six months of Bomber Command's war against Germany had likewise shown that aircrew involved in the strategic offensive were going to face an incredibly daunting task. Anticipating morale problems to some extent, and responding to concerns relating to medical officers' qualifications on the subject, the Chief of the Air Staff called a meeting in March 1940 to discuss the need for a policy letter dealing with operational fatigue, tour length, and 'cases of flying personnel who did not face operational risks'. Attending the meeting were the Commander-in-Chief of Bomber Command, the Air Member for Personnel and the Air Officer Commanding No. 3 Group.[9]

In April, one month after this meeting, the Air Council circulated a draft letter to the commands outlining identification procedures for those airmen 'whose conduct may cause them to forfeit the confidence of their Commanding Officer'. Under the provisions of this letter, suspect airmen fell into two distinct categories: those who were medical cases and those whose determination and reliability in the face of danger was questionable. These latter types were deemed to be 'lacking in moral fibre'.[10] The letter also authorized courts martial for flagrant cowardice.

While the language of the 22 April letter seems clear enough, it is obvious that considerable difficulty would arise in the differentiation between purely medical and non-medical cases. Doctors quickly found themselves faced with this problem with only the insufficient guidance of Air Ministry Pamphlet 100 to help them. In an attempt to improve the situation, the Director General of Medical Services issued a confidential addendum to the pamphlet during the summer of 1940. Used in conjunction with the Air Council's letter, this short publication confirmed the need to distinguish between the two types of cases. Several techniques were suggested. Significantly, however, it also cautioned against a problem which was already becoming apparent.

It has been noted that there is a tendency for medical officers to assume too readily that lack of confidence to fly or fear of flying are necessarily symptomatic of nervous illness and justify exemption from flying duty on medical grounds. Pilots, or members of aircrews are thus not infrequently taken off flying with the label 'psychoneurosis' without adequate investigation or assessment of their symptoms.[11]

In other words, it was felt that too many men were being allowed an easy way out of combat duty.

Similar sentiments were expressed in a letter to the commands dated 28 September 1940. This communication, signed by Charles Evans, Principal Assistant Secretary for Personnel, amplifies much of the previous guidance. Subsequently known as the 'Waverer Letter', it provided a definite LMF disposal policy for the first time and served as a basis for future guidance.[12] After identifying the commanding officer and his medical officer as the key personalities in dealing with the problem, the letter specified LMF disposal procedures. As before, men with evidence of true physical or nervous illnesses were to be treated initially on station, subsequently recommended for leave or, if the case was severe, admitted to a central hospital. Men whose diagnoses were unclear could be referred to neuropsychiatric specialists at the newly opened Not Yet Diagnosed Neuropsychiatric (NYDN) centres.[13] In this event the specialist was empowered to make the final determination about the true nature of the man's difficulty. In cases where no evidence of illness existed (whether diagnosed locally or by a specialist) the medical officer had the responsibility of informing the commanding officer that the individual lacked moral fibre. Subsequent action became the sole responsibility of the executive and consisted of several steps.

First, the squadron commander and station commander were to inform the Group's Air Officer Commanding who, in turn, made a personal recommendation to the Air Ministry. Complete details of the airman's operational history were required, as were the reports of the medical officers. To ensure some standard of fairness, the commanders' report was shown to the affected individual. The next step was the task of the Air Council and was delegated to a staff officer in the Director General for Personnel's office.[14] The case was carefully considered and, if the flyer was confirmed to be lacking in moral fibre, he was cashiered. For an officer, this meant his commission was terminated; an airman reverted to his basic grade or was discharged. Significantly, the provisions of the memorandum applied to men employed on non-operational duties, including those in training units. Commanders were admonished to report cases swiftly and frankly, and to make no attempt to solve their problems by posting men away on other grounds.[15]

It was not long before strenuous debates over the policy letter were taking place. Arguments over the memorandum's clarity, effectiveness and fairness continued almost without respite for the next four years, resulting in three revisions. The discussion of these problems, often very emotional, and even acrimonious, took place not only inside the Air Ministry, but also among medical officers, aircrew and command authorities. They were even taken up by the press to a limited extent.[16]

LMF POLICY: THE MEDICAL VIEW

Among those who were the most persistent in their criticism of the Air Ministry's policy letter were the RAF's chief aero-medical consultants. Burton, Symonds and Gillespie were not always in absolute agreement themselves, but nevertheless consistently objected to various aspects of the LMF letter.[17]

A new revision of S.61141/S.7 was published late in 1941. This made only minor changes to the original, and included a paragraph which partially addressed the primary objections of the neurological consultants. These experts were opposed to medical officers making *de facto* lack of moral fibre decisions. They believed the RAF's medical officers were ill-equipped, by background and training, to make such determinations. Opposed philosophically to attempts to place the onus on medical personnel, the neurologists criticized both the tone and intent of the LMF letter. Partially allowing for their objections, the 1941 version stated that medical recommendations were not to carry any implication of lack of moral fibre and would only constitute grounds for further investigation. Even this concession was not enough for the neurologists.[18]

At this point it might be useful to reconsider the opinion of at least one of Bomber Command's serving medical officers. Squadron Leader David Stafford-Clark's views accurately reflect one segment of the RAF's medical philosophy regarding LMF.[19]

As did many of his colleagues of more formal background, Stafford-

Clark regarded emotional breakdown in flyers as the result of predisposition and stress. Once again, predisposition was a man's psychological tendency to feel the effects of stress. This was considered intrinsic to his background and personality. The other factor was more external. It had to do with the wartime environment and actual combat experiences of the aviator. Stafford-Clark observed that doctors were required to determine if an airman in stress was suffering from the effects of an anxiety state or merely lacked confidence. This pivotal determination was made largely by deciding whether or not a man made any attempt to control his fears. Those who did, but whose fears were beyond their control, usually were treated as medical cases. If, however, doctors decided a man made insufficient efforts to control himself, they usually found he 'lacked confidence' and subsequently turned him over to the executive.[20]

Along these lines, Stafford-Clark divided men who showed unfavourable response to combat stress into two groups. The first group he considered to have good prospects for eventual return to duty. These were men who might be considered to have suffered temporary morale setbacks or flying fatigue. With treatment and rest they were recoverable. Stafford-Clark did not consider the second group salvageable. The second group produced those who were usually considered as LMF.

According to Stafford-Clark, genuine LMF men typically shared several characteristics. Among these characteristics were a lack of conscientiousness and an insufficient sense of responsibility to colleagues. Men in this group often displayed low self-respect and adolescent or immature attitudes. Interestingly, most knew the implications of failure. Even so, many displayed no marked remorse or distress over their unwillingness to carry on. Despite enjoying the privileged treatment accorded to aircrew, many were resistant to discipline. Ultimately they allowed their fears and sense of self-preservation to outweigh their sense of duty and obligation to their comrades.[21]

In October and later in December 1942, Air Commodore Symonds wrote lengthy memoranda to the Under Secretary of State for Air regarding this medical philosophy. He made several points relating to S.61141/S.7.C. To begin with, he believed the wording and terminology of the waverer letter were confusing. Uncomfortable with the label 'Lack of Moral Fibre', Symonds wanted to replace it with the phrase 'lack of courage'. His objection to the original term was based on its ethical connotation. He also observed that the overall title of the letter suggested a category of man not addressed in the letter itself. Readers might be persuaded that all men who were medically fit but who had forfeited the confidence of their commander were to be submitted as LMF cases. The letter's footnotes, included by way of explanation, tended to contradict this point, but were in language which was difficult to understand. Worse, under such circumstances, commanding officers had very little to guide them and faced a moral dilemma.[22] Consider the case of a 29-year-old sergeant pilot in an operational training unit, charged with forfeiting the confidence of his commander. The relevant paragraph of the report read as follows:

He is very highly strung, lacks confidence in his own ability, and is below average in air sense. It is to his credit, however, that the has tried his hardest to overcome what he realizes himself is a great handicap, and is *exceptionally keen*. (author's emphasis)[23]

In Symonds's view, this man, although unable to proceed and a burden to his unit, did not lack moral fibre. Unfortunately, the provisions of the Air Ministry's letter gave the commander little option; he must either submit the case as LMF or resort to getting rid of the man through outside channels.[24]

A close examination of the 1941 version of the letter reveals several other salient points. Obviously designed as a deterrent, the letter attempted to establish overall definitions for flyers performing inadequately under combat conditions. By categorizing these men into three groups, it gave commanders a formula to follow in dealing with the problem. The first and the third group (fit and unfit) were similar to those of the previous guidance. The second category, which was new, attempted to provide for men who, despite not being subjected to emotional stress, broke down permanently due to a nervous predisposition. Unfortunately, as in the case cited previously, the three categories made scant provision for airmen who broke down despite their best mental and physical efforts. As before, problems were to be handled swiftly and, to the extent possible, locally. The letter authorized the removal of flying badges for men in the first two categories. It also identified No. 1 RAF Depot, Uxbridge, as the place where LMF personnel were to be sent.[25]

Symonds's criticisms of the 1941 policy letter were generally supported by both his colleagues and his commander, Air Vice-Marshal H. E. Whittingham, Director General of the RAF's medical service. The Air Ministry was flexible enough to accept the need for the redrafting of the letter. Consequently, S.61141/S.7.C. was reissued on 1 June 1943. This version, although once again not going as far as the neuropsychiatric experts wanted, made things slightly easier for commanders. A portion of the redraft addressed the scope of the memorandum.

All those who wore aircrew badges were subject to its provisions. Those who might fail in training were to be disposed of in accordance with training regulations. As before, the letter specifically exempted men who had been subject to exceptional flying stress, but whose medical category was unchanged and who might be expected to return to flying duties. Significantly, it also excluded men who were on their second tours. In other words, men who had already done one complete set of operations (30 in Bomber Command), could not be categorized as LMF. Clearly, the executive was reluctant to punish second-tour airmen, many of whom had been decorated or even commissioned, even if their subsequent performance might otherwise have been questionable. Commanders were warned, however, not to publicize this particular provision. This was because Bomber Command felt it might possibly induce greater numbers of aircrew to give up after one tour.[26] The letter's language was much clearer than that of its predecessor. The 1943 version also formalized rules originally promulgated in February 1942. These granted accused men an interview with their Group's Air Officer Commanding before any reports were forwarded to the Air Ministry. This was in addition to a man's right to make a written statement in his defence.[27]

The 1943 letter reconfirmed the arrangements for disposing LMF aircrew members at the Aircrew Disposal Unit. By that time Uxbridge had proved unsatisfactory as a location. Because it also served as the major centre for the initial selection and training of airmen, there was some danger of mixing new volunteers with those removed from operations. Occasionally embarrassing situations became known. For a short period men had also been sent to the Combined Aircrew Reselection Centre at Eastchurch. This had proved unsatisfactory for the same reason. In October 1943, Squadron Leader R. I. Barker, along with two officers and five airmen, was ordered to assume command of the Aircrew Disposal Unit at Chessington.[28] He remained the CO until the end of the war, eventually moving the unit to Keresley Grange, near Coventry. Barker's organization was identified as the receiving point for all LMF cases adjudicated through proper channels.

As the central receiving point, the Aircrew Disposal Unit at Keresley Grange played an important part in the whole LMF machinery. It allowed LMF airmen to be isolated from other serving aviators. Barker apparently allowed few visitors.[29] Various rehabilitation activities were arranged for airmen before their final disposal. These activities were designed, in part, to increase the man's self-esteem, restore his confidence and renew his belief in the importance of the war effort. LMF airmen attended 'motivational' lectures, saw patriotic films, visited cultural museums, toured cathedrals, and even zoos.[30] Lawson considered Barker's efforts indispensable and wrote that he 'contributed in large measure to the smooth running of the procedure'.[31]

The June 1943 letter and the Aircrew Disposal Unit served the Royal Air Force and Bomber Command during the peak of the Allied bombing offensive. The majority of men identified during the war as LMF were judged by the terms of the letter's provisions and sent to the location it specified. This being the case, to evaluate the overall effect of the RAF's policy accurately it is necessary to consider the philosophy which guided the Air Ministry's actions.

Lord Moran's important work on the nature of courage in combat was not published until the end of the Second World War but it accurately reflected the views of many during the course of that conflict. One of Moran's more significant comments described the relationship between courage and morality this way:

I contend that fortitude in war has its roots in morality: that selection is a search for character, and that war itself is but one more test – the supreme and final test if you will – of character. Courage can be judged apart from danger only if the social significance and meaning of courage is known to us, namely that a man of character in peace becomes a man of courage in war.[32]

This passage does much to explain the underlying definition of the term 'Lack of Moral Fibre'. It does so by exposing the philosophy which permeates every version of the LMF policy letter. In effect, Moran stated that lack of moral fibre can be equated with fundamental flaws in character. Men of character will be men of courage. To be accused of lack of moral fibre is not only to be accused of cowardice; it is also to be stigmatized as lacking character.[33]

Obviously, the implications for airmen accused of LMF were indeed serious. One historian, a much decorated ex-fighter pilot, identified it as 'the most pernicious phrase' in the RAF's wartime jargon.[34] This was precisely its intention. Scores of authorities, both at the time and later, have commented on the deterrent role of the RAF's regulations. Wing Commander Lawson frankly admitted that the regulations were specifically aimed at preventing airmen of questionable morale from avoiding combat duties. In his words, 'the intention was to make chances of withdrawal without legitimate reason as near impossible as could be'.[35]

Several factors motivated this deterrent philosophy. Foremost, of course, was the widespread conviction that LMF was a transmissible disease. Lord Balfour of Inchrye, the Under-Secretary of State for Air, was one of many senior officials who were convinced that, once under way or unchecked, LMF could wreak havoc in a combat squadron.

LMF was dangerously contagious. One LMF crew member could start a rot which might spread not only through his own crew but through the whole squadron, particularly when there happened to be a lot of inexperienced crews replacing casualties.[36]

Inside Bomber Command, these feelings were even more strongly expressed. Air Marshal Harris, already fully occupied with morale problems associated with aborted sorties and the phenomenon called 'bombing creep-back', showed little sympathy for those he called 'weaklings and waverers'. Several of his letters comment on the dangers of LMF types 'contaminating' other crewmen. In the spring of 1943, Harris even suggested adding a new category of men to those identified by the waverer letter. Calling for them to be cited as 'apparently LMF', Harris meant to transfer some flyers even before their cases had been medically evaluated.[37]

The Air Ministry was similarly convinced of the dangers of unchecked LMF. Lawson later said that the memorandum's most important feature was its emphasis on speedy recognition and early punishment of waverers. The procedure, none the less, had to be somewhat elaborate in view of the seriousness of the charge. Key elements included early identification, swift removal from the unit and quick disposal. According to those responsible for enforcing LMF policy, easy withdrawal without penalty would have 'undermined the confidence and determination of others doing duty'.[38]

Another factor driving the deterrent philosophy was the determination of the executive to protect the status of those still engaged in combat operations. The unique image of aviators as brave aerial warriors was to be jealously protected and preserved throughout the war. This was absolutely necessary if sufficient quantities of willing volunteers were going to be forthcoming. As all these men were volunteers for combat flying from within a largely volunteer service, they were, by definition, men of courage. The inconsistency that they could not withdraw their agreement was glossed over.

In practical terms, extra pay and privileges were important to the prestige of airmen. So, too, much of the appeal lay with the aura surrounding the aircrew brevet. Consequently, a significant portion of this official effort dealt with the issue of aircrew badges – both their presentation and removal. Several Air Council meetings discussed this subject and a detailed policy letter resulted. In at least one sense the British were quite different from the Americans on this issue. The Royal Air Force regarded flying brevets as symbols of continuing qualification, rather than certificates of training graduation. Thus, to continue wearing a RAF aircrew badge, a man had not only to keep flying but also was required, when appropriate, to 'make an adequate contribution to the operational effort'.[39]

One final reason for the RAF's reliance on a deterrent policy bears scrutiny. As has been shown, there is plenty of evidence to suggest that aircrew morale and discipline were always a topic of concern at the Air Ministry. Beyond that, however, there are strong indications that the Air Ministry had insufficient trust in its largely non-commissioned officer aircrew force, especially those in Bomber Command. There was concern that the rapidly expanding requirements of the conflict would require men to be recruited who would not perform up to the high standards of the pre-war RAF. Commenting in a 1943 report marked 'Most Secret', Air Marshal P. B. Joubert, one of the two Inspector Generals at the time, wrote:

Broadly speaking the aircrews of the RAF though full of spirit and gallantry in the air, lack discipline and the powers of leadership, occasionally in the air, and very frequently on the ground.[40]

The huge expansion of the Royal Air Force, and Bomber Command in particular, had forced all three services to compete for traditional public school trained officer candidates. When it became clear that there was an insufficient number of these men to fill the required posts, the RAF responded by opening flying positions to those who by background and education might not otherwise have qualified.[41] In such circumstances, Joubert concluded, the fighting spirit of aircrews could suffer due to a lack of 'military qualities'. Summing up his alarming report, he asserted: 'We therefore start our military education with unpromising material'.[42]

However overstated, this kind of opinion partially explains the reluctance of the Air Ministry to commission members of RAF aircrews who routinely ranked as officers in Allied armed forces.[43] In fact, from a technical standpoint these non-commissioned officers and enlisted men performed superbly. Moreover, by any measure, their fortitude in the face of ghastly odds was more than equal to that of their supposedly social superiors.[44] Despite this, real concern for overall aircrew performance continued throughout the war. Historians have noted the crisis in aircrew confidence which came from high casualties and the meagre bombing results attained between the beginning of the war and 1942.[45]

In the personnel office of the Air Ministry, there were special fears for the morale of younger Bomber Command aircrewmen. Bomber Command's junior non-commissioned flyers often did not fit well into the traditional sergeants' mess because older, more experienced ground-trade NCOs tended to be jealous. Aviators had few, if any, station duties and this tended to exacerbate the situation. Wing Commander Lawson cited the infrequent contact between senior officers and young airmen as a factor. Moreover, he was concerned that many aviators were developing a 'spoilt child' attitude and that their preferential treatment should not be without limits.[46]

In summary, it is clear that many things contributed to the deterrent intent of the LMF letter. A combination of military philosophy, medical experience and wartime pressure made executive authorities believe that a policy which promised strong punitive action was essential if morale and discipline were to be maintained. Even more important to the success of the policy was the requirement to make its punitive nature a matter of common knowledge. All operational aircrewmen needed to be made aware, more than in just a general sense, of its provisions. Only then would it deter men from taking the easy way out of combat. A major problem, of course, was balancing the requirement for strong measures with those which called for more humanitarian considerations. Much controversy still exists about the resulting treatment Bomber Command airmen received.

No question excites more emotion than that associated with the fairness of LMF disposal policy. During the course of its major revisions, S.61141/S.7.C. gradually refined the punishment for LMF offenders. Early in the life of the memorandum some men were discharged directly into civilian employment. Progressive versions of the regulations prevented those who were found guilty of LMF from applying for high-paying jobs. Enlisted aircrew were usually remustered at the lowest RAF rank. Neither officers nor airmen were eligible for further flying appointments. Since avoiding flying was what most of them wanted anyway, the executive later decided to make offenders available to the army, or the navy, or pressed them into service in the coal mines.[47]

Courts martial were always an option under the terms of the letter and serious thought was given to their full use in Bomber Command. In an early meeting in the Air Ministry, for example, several Group Air Officers Commanding expressed the opinion that 'an occasional court martial would have a most salutary effect'.[48] The Air Member for Personnel agreed, but argued that such action should be restricted to 'cast iron cases'. More than one example of outright refusal to fly was considered for court martial, but such trials would have been fraught with problems.

A major problem was that commanders found it difficult to co-ordinate the kind of flying operation necessary to demonstrate the outright nature of a man's refusal to fly. There were understandable difficulties in holding back other aircrew members as witnesses. Many of these men went missing or were killed before they could testify.[49] Furthermore, if commanders failed to act swiftly, the normal machinery of the waverer letter took over and disposed of the accused men. In at least two documented cases, a group commander wanted grounded LMF men re-certified for flying. He planned to order them into the air again, and upon their refusal, subject them to court martial. Despite the commander's wishes, the latter never took place.[50]

The Air Ministry's obvious uncertainty on the entire question of courts martial was the major reason that the RAF sought to avoid LMF trials during the war.[51] The Air Ministry, the Air Officer Commanders in Chief, and all those responsible for implementing LMF policy were acutely aware that men so charged would have to stay too long in their units. There was always the fear that, as a result, morale would suffer. It was also possible that the RAF's reluctance to court-martial men was caused by fear of the adverse publicity such a trial would create. By 1942, there had been sporadic reports in the press of harsh treatment. One case, concerning the disposal of a certain Sergeant Hannah, was reportedly printed in the *Evening Standard* on 15 January 1943. This caused particular consternation. Subsequent reports were suppressed by calling together the editors of reputable papers and requesting them not to publish such stories. Presumably, in the spirit of wartime co-operation, the editors agreed to comply and submitted future inquiries to the Air Ministry before publication.

Members of Parliament also occasionally pressed for more details about treatment of such men. Questions from politicians were extremely sensitive, particularly since the Secretary of State for Air felt that part of the LMF policy was 'indefensible', from a popular point of view. On the whole, Lawson's replies to these periodic inquiries must have been satisfactory.[52] Whatever the reason, the Royal Air Force and Bomber Command strenuously avoided the damaging spectacle, and potential embarrassment, of trying an aircrew member on charges of cowardice in the face of the enemy – arising from lack of moral fibre – in open military court.

Turning back to the major question of overall fairness in treatment, the picture is similarly ambiguous. Two of the most recent histories of Bomber Command and the Royal Air Force openly disagree in their assessments. Max Hastings, quoting from diaries and letters, and relying heavily on interviews with combat veterans, suggests rather strongly that, on balance, Bomber Command airmen were treated poorly,

. . . in 1943 most men relieved of operational duty for medical or moral reasons were treated by the RAF with considerable harshness.[53]

Noting also the RAF's fear of contagion, Hastings cited the statements of an unnamed station commander. This officer apparently made certain that the LMF cases he adjudicated were punished by court martial and severe sentences.[54] In a more recent book, John Terraine disagrees with Hastings's analysis. Referring to the Lawson memorandum, he suggests that harsh treatment was comparatively rare. Terraine quotes the following passage as the basis for his opinion:

It must always be that a number were harshly treated and it has been our constant endeavour to reduce that to an absolute minimum and I believe this had been achieved.[55]

Terraine concludes that early posting was more important than swift punishment in dealing with the problem. In general terms, this was certainly the intention. There were, however, constant problems with getting rid of people fast enough. While easily removed from the station, accused aircrew tended to collect in disposal centres as they waited for judgement on their cases. Furthermore, there are other passages in the Lawson Memorandum which suggest that treatment was not always uniform. Commenting on the views of squadron and station commanders, for example, Lawson wrote:

Reports in general have been good, but it was very noticeable at one period that a small proportion were extremists. Some considered that drastic measures should be taken, and others have shown too much sympathy . . .[56]

Occasionally, such 'extremists' and the resulting lack of uniformity could lead to chilling treatment. In 1943 a captain of a crew who had aborted too often was disposed of in this way:

The whole squadron was formed into a square and this sergeant-pilot was brought in under guard, the verdict read, 'Cowardice in the face of the enemy', and his rank was ripped off him there, by the flight-sergeant, and he was then literally drummed out. I thought that was an awful thing. I've got to admit that I'd have sooner got killed than gone through that.[57]

Given the complexity of the situation, the almost infinite number of operational variables and the wide mix of human responses, it should come as no surprise that treatment varied from station to station. Even though they could refer to the Air Ministry's letter, commanders and medical officers still struggled to find quick answers to difficult situations. For many, one of the greatest problems was judging a man fairly who was trying his best but just could not perform satisfactorily. Even making a distinction was extremely difficult. As indicated, the LMF letter left them with little flexibility. Men like the one below suffered as a result:

A Sergeant, air gunner, aged 27, 120 hours, no operations, reported to the medical officer in a Heavy Conversion Unit, having experienced an acute fear reaction while flying. A Halifax went out of control, the patient had to abandon aircraft but at first could not open the turret. He was very afraid. He did not fly for a week; when he did so he again experienced acute fear in the air. No neurotic predisposition was discovered . . . At this point a further crash on the station occurred. The patient set out on a cross-country flight but had such acute symptoms of fear, sweating, trembling, and irrationally wanting to abandon aircraft, that the trip was abandoned after 10 minutes. The medical officer's comment was 'A good type who has made every effort to get over it. He might have been OK if he had flown sooner after the incident, but I doubt if he could make much of ops'. He was subsequently referred to the executive for disposal.

In other words, this man was tentatively classified LMF. His final disposal is unrecorded, but, like scores of other unfortunates, he clearly suffered the stigma of identification. Lawson, who wrote that he was officially responsible for interviewing all these men accused of LMF, wanted to believe that overall treatment was fair, but reluctantly acknowledged the lack of sympathy and understanding of many squadron and station commanders. Doubtless this made his job all the more difficult.[58] The question of fairness was particularly sensitive if comparisons are made between the different disposals accorded officers and NCOs. Many of the latter expressed dissatisfaction because they felt that officers received preferential treatment. Happy finally to be able to discuss their problem with Lawson, they convinced him that,

. . . many had been marched in and told they were yellow and marched out, and the requirements of the Memorandum had been carried out in a lot of cases by the NCO in charge of the orderly room.[59]

It may be impossible to determine whether or not officers and NCOs were afforded the same treatment. Even the statistical evidence is misleading. Terraine suggests that 'the dice were loaded against non-commissioned aircrews in too many ways'. He supports his position by citing Lawson's numbers. These show only about half of all officers accused of LMF were so classified; yet fully 70 per cent of accused airmen fell into the category.[60] A more complete statistical accounting of LMF will follow in a subsequent section, but certain factors need to be recalled with regard to the above figures. Lawson was aware that there was considerable concern about preferential treatment. Accordingly, he pointed out that fewer officers would have been ultimately classified as LMF for several reasons. First, only about 50 per cent of aircrew were commissioned. Since many were commissioned only late in their first tours, or afterwards, they represent the 'cream' of the crew force. The kind of men who had successfully survived one tour, and were subsequently commissioned, were usually not the kind of men who broke down. Also, a huge majority of LMF cases came before operations even started or during the man's first few missions. This contributed to the skewing of the numbers and helped create the impression that officers received more lenient treatment than NCOs.[61]

Perhaps the most qualified judges on the relative fairness of the overall treatment accorded LMF types were the veterans themselves. From squadron and station commanders at the top, all the way down to enlisted gunners, almost all had some kind of opinion on the subject. One of the most famous of Bomber Command's leaders, Group Captain Leonard Cheshire, admitted that,

I was ruthless with 'moral fibre cases', I had to be. We were airmen not psychiatrists. Of course we had concern for any individual whose internal tensions meant that he could no longer go on; but there was the worry that one really frightened man could affect others around him. There was no time to be as compassionate as I would like to have been. I was flying too, and we had to get on with the war.[62]

Clearly, Cheshire was aware of the difficult and sensitive nature of the problem. For him and other commanders, the problem was to balance kindness and understanding with the fear of 'opening the door for others'.[63] For others, especially those who felt the LMF letter was fundamentally flawed, it was better to err on the side of compassion. A few had considerable difficulty coming to terms with what they witnessed:

I never understood the treatment of LMF cases: it was something I could not understand as outlined in the Air Ministry Order, which was a very harsh document and did not give much leeway in the treatment of a chap if he felt he could not do any more. He was stigmatized, hounded, and humiliated.[64]

The Group Captain's concerns match those of the Lancaster tail-gunner which follow:

I spent three weeks at a station used for remustering aircrew, which included dealing with LMF personnel. I was and remain disgusted by the treatment of LMF charges. No sympathy was shown and they were treated like criminals. In one case I actually witnessed a pilot who had been decorated during his first tour but had lost his nerve during his second tour of operations. He was stripped of his rank and flying brevet and was a broken man.[65]

During the war there was a serious feeling that the harshness of the LMF procedure might have kept people in combat who, largely because of safety reasons, should not have been there.[66] It is not difficult to imagine the dangers to others on an aircraft of having a crewman incapable of doing his job. There is some evidence that this occurred occasionally. One veteran recalled that the humiliation and ignominy of going LMF was so great 'that some men continued to fly long after their nerves were in shreds'.[67] Since the entire LMF procedure was based on its deterrent quality it is clearly impossible to discount this possibility.

Further proof can be found in the attitude taken by combat aviators towards those of their number who broke down in combat. At first glance it would appear that the attitude of the brave towards 'cowards' might have been one of contempt. This was not generally so. More than one Bomber Command veteran believed that the attitude of the hierarchy was old-fashioned and short-sighted. Men who broke down in combat were not usually disparaged by their peers. For flyers lucky enough to complete tours the typical feeling was, 'there but for the grace of God, go I'. Successful men frequently admired those who, despite clearly facing harsh penalties, nevertheless had the strength to go to commanders and refuse to fly. Even aviators who might otherwise be critical were happy to be free of men who might endanger the rest of the crew.[68]

These feelings were not confined to crew members. More than one squadron or station commander was accused of being too sympathetic. Frequently unwilling to stigmatize men with labels, particularly ones they felt should not come under the provisions of the waverer letter, some commanders used unofficial disposal channels to let people off. The quick, quiet posting was a typical solution. Interestingly, a few commanders expressed very similar views to their subordinates when considering the cases of those openly refusing to fly. Late in the war a commander's meeting on LMF had this to say about the RAF's policy,

[it] discriminated harshly against the man who has the moral courage to say that he cannot continue in flying, while other individuals lacking the same degree of frankness, plead illness and eventually qualify for disposal under the 'W' memo.[69]

In the course of research on this subject, several letters were received which related their authors' very personal experiences with LMF. One frank recollection came from a veteran who had himself been accused. After completing his first tour as a flight engineer in heavy bombers he was posted to a training unit for what he expected to be a six-month period. A personal dispute with an officer led to a series of unpleasant duties, occasionally involving escorting detainees to disciplinary centres. During one of his absences from the station, this Stirling and Lancaster veteran was 'volunteered' for another tour in operations. Returning to the base, he refused to go along and insisted, quite rightly, that he had a further three months to go on the normal rest period. His repeated refusal to fly led to unfortunate consequences over the next ten weeks:

I saw psychiatrists, medical officers, Group Captains, boards officers, Wing Commanders in charge of flying, etc., etc. At one time when being interviewed by a particularly aggressive Wing Commander I was threatened with facing a firing squad. I am not suggesting that this was the official policy and I really thought that the man was bluffing, no doubt infuriated by my insistence that I [get] my full rest period. A threat that I did take seriously was the fact that I could be demoted, transferred to the Army, and sent to a particularly unpleasant theatre of war.

The pressure on this veteran increased when he was eventually posted to Keresley Grange. He was sustained to some extent, however, by the knowledge that the crew he had refused to join crashed during their initial training flight, and all but one were killed. The veteran's compelling narrative continued:

I was marched into a small, bleak office where at a table sat three officers. The chairman was a Squadron Leader, the other two were Flight Lieutenants. The chairman had my service documents in front of him and he told me to state my case. This was the first time that anyone had asked my side of the story. After a few moments I was marched out, then after a very short time, was marched in again. This time the Squadron Leader was on his own.

After being asked whether or not he would volunteer again when his full six months at the OTU were up – and giving an equivocal reply, the veteran was eventually remustered to a ground trade. While his punishment was not as serious as it might have been, the process he endured nevertheless was a traumatic one.[70]

In concluding this section on the overall fairness of the LMF policy it is interesting to look at the report of the RAF's Inspector General, Air Chief Marshal Sir Edgar Ludlow-Hewitt. His visits in late 1942 to the aircrew disposal centres, particularly Uxbridge, provide a good summary of some of the problems with the entire LMF procedure. Ludlow-Hewitt came to several telling conclusions. Noting problems resulting from mixing novice aircrews with those accused of LMF, he felt very strongly that the entire process could be improved by providing one disposal centre. This centre needed to have as its sole function the disposal of 'waverers'. While the interests of the service needed to be looked after, real compassion was also important. Aware of individual cases where gross injustices had occurred, Ludlow-Hewitt wrote that 'No man should suffer on account of withdrawal from aircrew through no fault, failure or weakness of his own'. Furthermore, disposal should be handled by men who were truly qualified.[71]

Ludlow-Hewitt's major complaint was that the entire LMF procedure took too long. Among other things, he blamed the documentary and record-keeping system for this 'grave injustice'. The target time for the system to operate was 30 days (from identification to disposal). According to the Inspector General, this was almost always exceeded, with some accused men suspended from four to six months before final determination. This not only wasted manpower, but also made it more likely that treatment would lack uniformity or be unfair.[72]

It should be pointed out that many of Ludlow-Hewitt's concerns received attention during the subsequent years of the war. Some of the problems were corrected, but many issues remained stubbornly unresolved.

What then does the weight of evidence seem to indicate on the issue of fairness? The senior leadership of the Royal Air Force was confident that a strong deterrent policy was necessary if aircrew morale was to be maintained. Clearly this led to harsh treatment of some aircrew. Nagging doubts about the fairness of the policy were overridden by the fear that the unchecked spread of LMF could cause a general crisis in the operational performance of aircrew. The closer an observer comes to the operational level the less these fears seem justified. It is true that combat aviators were generally aware of the penalties associated with their failure to carry on. Many had even been close enough to have had personal experience with somebody identified as LMF. Some continued to fly rather than be labelled as cowards. Yet the huge majority ignored this eventuality, and, if they thought about LMF at all, it was in the context of its 'happening to somebody else'. In overall terms, it would seem clear that the LMF policy for Bomber Command aircrews can be considered harsh. Doubtless the severity of the policy made it unpalatable to many. At the same time, however, the policy's harshness was at least partially responsible for the tiny number of total LMF cases.

LMF: THE STATISTICAL EVIDENCE

No absolutely accurate accounting of LMF has ever been presented. As with the American Eighth Air Force, any finite determination of numbers may be impossible. Early uncertainty in terminology, identification, treatment and disposal made record-keeping difficult. Moreover, various files may have been destroyed in the years after the war. Others are only now coming to light.[73] The Air Ministry's efforts to centralize the reporting and control of LMF were only partially successful. There will never be a way of counting the numbers, however small, of airmen who were dealt with locally. As shown, many were quietly posted away, transferred to other duties or even publicly humiliated. As with any military bureaucracy, rules designed to deal with sensitive problems were frequently ignored or circumvented. The continual pressure of military operations sometimes forced commanders to act contrary to the strict interpretation of regulations.

Despite this situation, it is still possible to get some idea about the extent of Bomber Command's LMF problem. This is due, in no small part, to the hard work of those responsible for treating afflicted aviators. The best statistical overview of the LMF situation is provided by the series of reports prepared by Air Vice-Marshal Symonds and Wing Commander Denis Williams. Their analytical efforts, produced for wartime use by members of the Flying Personnel Research Committee, were later compiled for publication.[74] In one of these reports, produced in 1945, they detailed the incidence of neurosis in flight crews over the preceding three years of combat operations. Their figures also cite the number of LMF cases:

Year	Neurosis	LMF
1942-43	2503	416
1943-44	2989	307
1944-45	2910	306
Totals	8402	1029

Symonds and Williams reported that approximately one-third of all cases of neurosis came from Bomber Command.[75] It follows that Bomber

Command produced at least one-third of the total LMF cases.[76] Moreover, over 30 per cent of LMF cases were disposed of by the executive without specialist consultation.[77] By working through the mathematics it is possible to arrive at what must be close approximations of the overall state of affairs. One-third of 1,029 is 343. This would represent the number of Bomber Command LMF cases diagnosed by neuropsychiatric specialists over a three-year period. Adding another 147 for those not seen by a specialist, a three-year Bomber Command LMF figure of 490 seems plausible. This works out to approximately 163 per year or 14 per month. Symonds and Williams recorded further evidence in FPRC Report No. 412(k) of March 1945. In the six-month period between February and August 1942, the doctors reported 76 Bomber Command LMF cases. Counting those not seen by a specialist, this rate closely approximated the previous figure.

There are still other figures available which can be used to check the calculation. Lawson's memorandum noted a total of 4,059 potential cases submitted during the entire war. Of these, 2,726 were eventually classified and disposed as LMF. If one-third of these were from Bomber Command, then that subtotal would be 908, or about 13 per month. Even if one-half of all cases were from Bomber Command, the Command's six-year total would indicate a rate no greater that 20 a month.[78]

The records of the Royal Air Force's disposal units are fragmentary, but not totally unhelpful. The archival history of the Disposal Wing at Brighton, in Sussex, mentions no LMF cases at all. The Air Crew Disposal Unit at Chessington mostly received genuine neuropsychiatric cases.[79] However, between November 1943 and May 1945, the Air Crew Disposal Unit at Keresley Grange received 1,142 aviators (195 officers and 947 airmen).[80] These figures similarly confirm a rate of approximately 20 per month from Bomber Command.

Lawson provided one further clue in his report. Citing statistical analysis, he suggested that slightly less than 0.4 per cent of bomber crews had been classified LMF. This figure included Bomber Command airmen actually engaged in operations and those in Operational Training Units. In 1944 the grand total for airmen employed in these capacities was almost 50,000.[81] Multiplying Lawson's percentage by the total crew force suggests a figure of 200 per year.

It seems very likely, therefore, that Bomber Command suffered an LMF rate which, at its lowest, hovered around 160 a year. Accepting a high estimation of 240, then an average of 200 per year seems reasonable by all accounts.

CONCLUSIONS

This examination of LMF in Bomber Command highlights some of the differences between the approaches taken by the British and the Americans on the subject. British LMF policy was, in many ways, far more deliberate and much less haphazard than that of the Americans. The Royal Air Force was more experienced in dealing with the problem. British medical officers had official guidance from the beginning of the war. Similarly, British commanders could refer to a single memorandum, albeit occasionally modified, to help them resolve the issue. Compared with the Americans, the RAF's policy was more deterrent-oriented. Americans, even at command level, tended to regard combat breakdowns as more psychological in origin. This was unmistakably related to their more permissive views on operational fatigue and operational exhaustion.

British executive authorities often shared the view that failure in combat originated with flaws in character. This conviction carried with it the idea that true combat volunteers could not be 'cowards', but rather that LMF represented a failure of screening. Morever, there was also considerable apprehension that LMF might be contagious. This helped increase already exaggerated concerns for the overall morale of RAF aircrews and their willingness to stay in combat. Accordingly, penalties could be very harsh indeed. For this reason, and quite unlike their American counterparts, most Bomber Command aircrews were acutely aware of the implications of 'going LMF', even if this awareness was the result of barrack room gossip. Some men even stayed in combat because of what might happen to them if they did not.

Nevertheless, any statistical analysis shows that Bomber Command was served gallantly by virtually all its members. Focusing on the issue of LMF should not imply in any way that the problem was other than very, very small, especially in the context of overall numbers. Perhaps this is what Air Marshal Harris was trying to say after all.

NOTES

1. Terraine, op. cit., p. 532.
2. Much of the pioneering work was done by Dr James Birley. See Rexford-Welch, op. cit., Vol. II, p. 137.
3. Antone E. Gajeski, 'Combat Aircrew Experiences During the Vietnam Conflict: An Exploratory Study', (MA Thesis, Air Force Institute of Technology, 1988), pp. 7–8.
4. One author noted good flyers always had the attributes of sportsmen, were resolute and alert, but lacked imagination. T. S. Rippon, 'Report on the Essential Characteristics of Successful and Unsuccessful Aviators with Special Reference to Temperament' *Aeronautics*, 9 Oct., 1918.
5. Symonds and Williams, FPRC 412(b), Jan. 1942, AIR 20/10727.

6. John McCarthy, 'Aircrew and Lack of Moral Fibre in the Second World War', *War and Society*, Sept. 1984, pp. 87–101.
7. Richardson, op. cit., pp. 62–3.
8. Air Ministry Pamphlet 100, May 1939. Copy in AIR 2/8591. See also Ch. 3.
9. Air 2/8591.
10. McCarthy suggests the term 'LMF' originated in the Department of Air Member for Personnel. See McCarthy, pp. 87–8 and AIR 20/10727.
11. Air Ministry Pamphlet 100A, AIR 2/8591.
12. S.61141/S.7.C. 28 Sept. 1940, AIR 20/10727.
13. 'Not Yet Diagnosed Neuropsychiatric Centres'. AIR 2/4019.
14. This officer, Wing Commander J. Lawson, wrote that he had dealt with all cases submitted under the Air Ministry's various memoranda. His detailed and strictly confidential post-war report is preserved at the Air Historical Branch and will be referenced in detail.
15. S.61141/S.7.C. 28 Sept. 1940, AIR 20/10727.
16. Lawson Memorandum, p. 4.
17. Part of the conflict was caused by schisms inside the medical profession. From the RAF's institutional viewpoint, psychiatry played a secondary role to neurology. Even the compound noun neuropsychiatry, 'leaves no doubt to the order of precedence'. Henry R. Rollen, *Festina Lente: A Psychiatric Odyssey* (London: *British Medical Journal*, 1990), p. 32.
18. S.61141/S.7.c.(1), 19 Sept. 1941, AIR 20/10727.
19. It should be pointed out that when Dr Stafford-Clark served as a medical officer in Bomber Command he was not formally trained in psychiatry. Much of his subsequent work in the field stemmed from his wartime experiences. Stafford-Clark MSS, *passim,* and Symonds and Williams, FPRC 412(d), April 1942, AIR 2/6252.
20. Symonds and Williams, 'Investigation of psychological disorders by the Unit Medical Officers', FPRC 412(k), Feb. 1945, AIR 2/6252.
21. Stafford-Clark MSS, pp. 19–27.
22. Symonds to Evans, 10 Dec. 1942, AIR 2/4935.
23. Symonds to Evans, 7 Oct. 1942, AIR 20/10727.
24. Ibid.
25. S.61141/S.7.c(1) 19 Sept. 1941, AIR 20/10727.
26. See Air Council meeting notes, 4 Feb. 1943, in AIR 20/2860 for the original decision and Lawson, p. 5 for Bomber Command's position.
27. See AIR 2/8591 and S.61141/S.7.c.(1), 1 June 1943, AHB.
28. Aircrew Disposal Unit, Operations Record Book. AIR 29/603.
29. Lawson Memorandum, p. 10.
30. AIR 29/603.
31. Lawson Memorandum, p. 11.
32. Moran, op. cit., pp. 159–60.
33. This relationship was understood by both the supporters and the critics of the letter. See AIR 2/4935 and Lawson Memorandum.
34. Lucas, op. cit., p. 281.
35. Lawson Memorandum, p. 1.
36. Harold Balfour, *Wings Over Westminster* (London: Hutchinson and Company, 1973), cited in Lucas, op. cit., p. 282.
37. Among others see, Harris to Air Ministry, 20 Dec., 1943, Air 2/8592 and Air Ministry meeting minutes 17 March, 1943, AIR 2/4935.
38. Lawson Memorandum, p. 1.
39. Clearly stated in S.61141/S.7.(d), 1 March 1945. See also AIR 2/8591.
40. 'Note by IG II on Discipline and the fighting spirit in the RAF', 14 May 1943. AIR 20/3082.
41. Max Hastings, op. cit., p. 254.
42. AIR 20/3082.
43. See Terraine, op. cit., pp. 464–7 for a good summary of the RAF's traditional position on the issue.
44. In this regard Harris's vociferous support for the commissioning of his NCO aircraft commanders was notable. See AIR 14/1008.
45. Webster and Frankland, op. cit., Vol. 1, pp. 256–7.
46. See Max Hastings, op. cit., pp. 254–6 and the Lawson Memorandum, pp. 5–6.
47. The various versions of S.61141/S.7.c mentioned some of these provisions. See also

McCarthy, op. cit., pp. 88–9, and Draft of Minutes, Feb. 1944, AIR 2/8271.

48. Air Ministry meeting minutes, 23 July 1941, AIR 2/8591.
49. Meeting minutes, 20 Oct. 1944, AIR 2/8592.
50. Letter, Oxland to Air Ministry, 8 June 1942, AIR 2/8591.
51. Lawson suggested there were no courts martial under the terms of the memorandum. This assertion does not agree with the recollections of several veterans. The apparent discrepancy can be explained by the nature of the charges brought against the accused. Flagrant breaches of discipline, misconduct, or cowardice were offences normally falling under the purview of the Articles of War. Courts martial would have been conducted on that basis, but the records are still unavailable. See Terraine, op. cit., p. 521.
52. See Lawson memorandum, p. 4, Middlebrook, *Nuremberg,* p. 55, McCarthy, op. cit., p. 96, and meeting minutes AIR 2/8592.
53. Max Hastings, op. cit., p. 253.
54. Ibid. Another indicator that Lawson's report of no courts martial is subject to question. For further support of Hastings's opinions about the fairness of LMF policy see Longmate, op. cit., pp. 187–8 and Middlebrook, *Nuremberg,* p. 55.
55. See Terraine, op. cit., p. 532 and Lawson Memorandum, p. 3.
56. Lawson Memorandum, p. 6.
57. Quoted in Longmate, op. cit., p. 188. Similar experiences were confirmed by Bomber Command veterans at the Uxbridge Branch Aircrew Association meeting, 19 July 1989. Also George Mead (Lancaster bomb-aimer) to author, 21 April 1990.
58. The above case cited in Symonds and Williams, FPRC 412(k), March 1945, AIR 2/6252. See also Lawson Memorandum, p. 7.
59. Lawson Memorandum, p. 7.
60. Terraine, op. cit., p. 534.
61. Lawson Memorandum, p. 5.
62. Quoted in Charles Messenger, *Bomber Harris and the Strategic Bombing Offensive, 1939–1945* (London: Arms and Armour Press, 1984), p. 206.
63. Letter to the author, 16 Feb. 1989.
64. Mahaddie, *Hamish,* p. 85.
65. Ralph T. Jones, DFC, to author, 27 Nov. 1990.
66. See Middlebrook, *Nuremberg,* p. 55. Lawson denies this, however, Lawson Memorandum, p. 2.
67. Tripp, op. cit., p. 39.
68. Various letters to the author, Bomber Command Association and The Aircrew Association, May–July 1989.
69. Meeting minutes, 20 Oct. 1944, AIR 2/8592.
70. Letter to the author, 28 March 1990.
71. Air Chief Marshal Sir Edgar Ludlow-Hewitt, 'Visits to Air Crew Disposal Centres', 26 Dec. 1942, AIR 20/2859.
72. Ibid.
73. Files of the disposal branch of the Air Member for Personnel are unavailable. Medical correspondence files on the rehabilitation centres opened in 1991. See McCarthy, p. 96 and AIR 20/9919.
74. Symonds and Williams, *passim.*
75. With one-third from Flying Training Command and the final one-third split between the other commands. See Symonds and Williams, FPRC report 412(l), AIR 2/6252. For the total Bomber Command figure see Ch. 3.
76. Lawson said 'most' of the cases classified under the memorandum came from Bomber Command. Others used the term 'majority'. It is safe to put the percentage between 33 and 50 per cent. Lawson, p. 4.
77. Symonds and Williams, FPRC report 412(i) and FPRC report 412(l), AIR 2/6252.
78. Lawson Memorandum, p. 4.
79. McCarthy, op. cit., p. 96.
80. AIR 29/603.
81. AIR 14/1803.

9

Conclusion

We meet 'neath the sounding rafter,
And the walls around are bare:
As they shout back our peals of laughter,
It seems that the dead are there.
Then stand to your glasses, steady!
We drink in our comrades' eyes:
One cup to the dead already –
Hurrah, for the next that dies!

from 'Here's To The Next Man To Die',
a song heard around Allied air bases
during the Second World War

The purpose of this study has been to investigate the human dimension of air combat during the Second World War Combined Bomber Offensive. Despite the considerable quantity of literature on many aspects of the campaign, no single source was devoted to answering questions which relate to the full experiences of combat airmen during the war. By using a comparative approach and examining the Eighth Air Force and the RAF's Bomber Command, it was possible to develop additional insights regarding what these men went through, why they fought, how effective they were, what they thought and how well they were treated. Many of the facts and personal reflections speak for themselves.

In terms of aircrew selection the Americans seemed much more systematic, even scientific, than the British. Americans relied on stanine test scores, statistics and brief psychiatric interviews to determine aircrew suitability. Even so, it seems they had more success in determining who would succeed in training rather than who would actually excel in combat.

The British, much more limited by manpower resources, seemed determined to find those best able to withstand the pressure of combat and actually succeed. But early selection methods were quick, did not include psychiatric examination and, even when the numbers of public school candidates declined, relied principally on methods which sought to identify good school-boy attributes. Later on, British selection and classification techniques were heavily weighted to measure practical skills and might even be characterized as 'survival selection'.

Despite evidence that psychiatric screening might be worthwhile, the RAF never widely employed it. It was considered too time-consuming, too costly and the necessary numbers of training specialists were not available in any case. Additionally, however, command authorities frequently doubted psychiatrists and, probably reflecting a cultural bias, often deeply mistrusted their motivations. In the main, however, both air forces succeeded in selecting high quality candidates to serve as aircrew.

When it comes to measuring the relative demands or ferocity of combat, no absolute standard exists. This is also true when gauging success. Simple tabulations of the numbers of lost aircraft or the wounded and the dead, even when they approach the horrifying totals of missions like Schweinfurt or Nuremberg, cannot really tell us anything about what it was like actually to be there. Neither can similar statistical assessments of bombing accuracy, aircraft destroyed or target destruction tell us everything important there is to know about combat effectiveness.

Yet it seems indisputable that the Anglo-Allied aerial effort ranks as one of the most intense and demanding of military history's modern campaigns. Doctrinally flawed perhaps, it nevertheless decisively influenced the course of the war. Despite the high casualties suffered by Allied airmen, the cost-versus-benefit ledger seems indisputably weighted towards strategic bombing. But it is important to note that, evaluated against the traditional criteria of the time, many of the campaign's participants, both bomber and fighter aircrew, might incorrectly be judged ineffective. The fact is, combat effectiveness rested on more than simple statistics. Cohesion, teamwork and survival were often more important human indicators of success than were victory tallies or bombing accuracy. In some measure virtually all airmen contributed to the eventual gaining of Allied air superiority, whether or not they ever dropped a bomb on target or shot down an enemy aircraft.

The Strategic Bomber Offensive's effect on its participants was profound, not just in the physical but also the mental sense. In other words, it was not simply the casualty tolls of British, Commonwealth and American airmen that made this such a unique battle, but rather the singular nature of the air combat environment. The sky itself magnified what arguably might be considered the 'normal' physical and mental stresses placed on any combatant.

Combat airmen in both air forces were motivated by a wide range of emotions. Undergirded by an understandable sense of patriotism and duty, many displayed youthful affection for flying. Specially selected, reasonably well-trained, fit, and assigned élite status, they began their missions confident that the part they were playing was an important – if not *the* most important – part in winning the war. Flyers were generally sustained by good leadership because incompetent and poor commanders usually did not last long. There were times during the campaign when morale faltered; but these generally corresponded with intense and sustained operations marked by much higher than normal casualty rates. More importantly, these spells never lasted long enough to damage the overall goals of the campaign.

As with their ground soldier counterparts, the principal reason most airmen stuck things out in combat was because of the spirit of cohesion and teamwork that permeated units and individual aircrews. If asked why they continued to face the horrific odds against survival, most would say something like 'I cannot let my buddies down'. Aviators expected courage, competence and compassion from their leaders at all levels – and generally got it.

Good leadership could not change the fundamental nature of the air war experienced by the young Allied aviators. Faced suddenly with the harsh reality of casualty statistics and empty bunks, many men, especially those who were part of bomber crews, reacted fatalistically. After initial periods of thinking 'it will never happen to me', many were forced by events to accept the apparent inevitability of their own demise. In such conditions men naturally struggled to bring a sense of order to the chaotic world of combat. Theirs was no clean, remote or antiseptic war as some historians have mistakenly described. Combat flying was often characterized by hours of tedious boredom and great physical stress, interrupted by all-too-lengthy stretches of confusion, panic, furious activity and instant death.

The major mental conflict arose from attempts to reconcile or overcome one's fundamental need for self-preservation and the relentless, and often hopeless, demands for duty. The never-ending state of anxiety which goes with such a conflict was a pitiless companion for virtually all wartime Allied airmen. As a result, there were numerous emotional casualties.

Patterns of identification and treatment varied according to the cultural and institutional beliefs of the two air forces. British neurologists and psychiatrists accepted a model which suggested that predisposition plus stress equalled breakdown. The overwhelming emphasis, however, was on predisposition, as they believed emotional casualties could be vastly reduced by selecting only the right sort of men for aviation duty.

American medical officials, while accepting the same model, became convinced around 1943 that *all* men, regardless of background and behaviour, would eventually succumb to the effects of stress. This led to a slightly more permissive attitude in the Eighth Air Force than in Bomber Command. Even the American terms 'Operational Fatigue' and 'Operational Exhaustion' consciously reflect the relative lack of stigma attached to the condition. British medical officers, and the command executive, were more committed to terms like 'neurosis' or 'neuropsychiatric disorder' to describe the same state. This was also intended to have a deterrent effect.

Scores of officials – in both air forces – regarded emotional disorders as infectious. Experiments which tended to demonstrate the fallacy of this view were either overlooked or ignored. Many of these same officials, especially in Britain, believed that courage was a function of background, breeding and character. Genuine emotional problems were regarded suspiciously and sometimes seen as an attempt to find an easy way of being excused from flying. These traditional and rigid notions were deeply ingrained and difficult for psychiatrists and others treating emotional casualties to change. Accordingly, many men who were considered to have failed to do their duty were swiftly identified, often labelled with the term 'Lack of Moral Fibre', and frequently faced harsh punishment. In the case of Bomber Command, it seems clear that the widely known deterrent nature of this policy was a result, at least in part, of some distrust of aircrew and their continued willingness to stay on operations.

Identification, treatment and disposal of men who had failed in combat was similar in the Eighth Air Force, albeit often less severe. Despite various regulations, many men were dealt with locally. Harsh treatment occurred occasionally too. But in many ways, treatment in the Eighth Air Force was less systematic than in Bomber Command, because Americans were still struggling with terminology to fit the condition.

For several reasons it is difficult to be certain about the exact number of emotional casualties in the two air forces. Some men were only temporarily removed from flying. Hundreds more, treated locally, never appear on records. By using the best documents at the US Air Force Historical Research Agency and at the Public Record Office, it appears that the numbers were roughly the same in the Eighth Air Force and in Bomber Command. Various sources confirm that both air forces suffered about 1,000 temporary and permanent emotional casualties per year. The LMF rate, which must be categorized separately, was no higher than 200 per year for each. As a proportion of the combined crew force, which, during the peak of the campaign, totalled more than 60,000, these tiny figures graphically demonstrate the physical and mental stamina of thousands of young Allied airmen.

It is impossible to imagine that the world will ever again see an aerial campaign of the size and scope of the Second World War Combined Bomber Offensive. Events during the Gulf War demonstrate that experts and pundits will nevertheless continue to argue the relative impact of air power on the conduct of war. But high-performance jet aircraft, complex electronics, computer-enhanced intelligence, and sophisticated weaponry do not fundamentally alter the essence of war in the air. Nor do they change human nature. Just like the men who crawled nightly into the

Halifaxes, Stirlings and Lancasters of Bomber Command or the young Americans who clambered into B-17s, B-24s, and a host of day-time fighters, modern airmen face daunting physical and mental challenges. Their reactions to the stresses of combat and their abilities to overcome the friction of air war are not likely to be fundamentally different from those of their Second World War predecessors. It would be a terrible mistake for future commanders and medical officers to overlook the human dimension of the Combined Bomber Offensive.

Bibliography and Notes on Method

THERE IS AN extraordinary amount of research material devoted to the Combined Bomber Offensive. Hundreds of books have appeared on this popular and fascinating subject since the end of the war. Scores more are published every year. Unit histories, campaign summaries, personal memoirs, biographies, and detailed aircraft monographs fill shelves in libraries and bookstores.

Much of the existing material is based on the easy availability of primary sources. In Great Britain, the Public Record Office, Royal Air Force Museum, Air Historical Branch, and the Imperial War Museum preserve sizeable collections of original documents relating to every phase of the RAF's night-bombing campaign. The United States Air Force maintains comparable records covering the American daylight raids over Germany at the Air Force Historical Research Agency at Maxwell Air Force Base, Alabama. Large document collections relating to the Eighth Air Force and its commanders are similarly contained in the Library of Congress and the National Archives. Many groups of personal papers are housed in Special Collections at the US Air Force Academy Library. Finally, numerous oral histories are obtainable and include audio-tapes, transcripts, and even film media.

I used material from all of these sources and added personal information which I obtained from hundreds of combat veteran volunteers. As a serving officer, I was permitted to attend meetings of various veteran associations. These included the RAF Bomber Command Association, the Aircrew Association, the Daedalians, various bomb group organizations, and the Eighth Air Force Historical Society. After scores of meetings and conversations with aviators, it became clear to me that these veterans were increasingly prepared to discuss subjects which, for many, were quite sensitive. I settled on the use of a questionnaire to reach more people, save time, and preserve a permanent written record of their reflections.

During the course of the four years of my research, more than 200 combat veterans from the RAF and US Army Air Forces responded to my detailed questions. Sometimes this led to the exchange of several letters. As a result, my correspondence files on the subjects of aircrew selection, stress, morale, combat effectiveness, and LMF grew quite large. The information I collected is often very personal and must therefore be treated with caution. Occasionally I have omitted a name when embarrassment might result. It should also be pointed out that much of what I obtained reflects distant memories of events from the 1940s. I therefore weighed its veracity and historical value carefully. Viewed together, however, it represents the first effort to compare the two air forces in regard to their different organizational and philosophical approaches to human-related combat problems. Moreover, it has been recognized as valuable enough to merit permanent preservation by Special Collections at the US Air Force Academy. All the veterans' letters cited in this book will be stored there and made available for future reference.

A. PRIMARY SOURCES

Note: Materials maintained at the Air Force Historical Research Agency (AFHRA) at Maxwell AFB, Alabama, are referenced by file number when available.

1. US Manuscript Sources

'Air Staff Post Hostilities Intelligence Requirements'. Section IV I, Vol. 2, appendix 3, AFHRA.

Anderson, Lt. Col. R. C. 'Psychiatric Training of Medical Officers in the Army Air Forces'. Record Group 112, 730, Box 1331, National Archives.

'Auswertung der Einsatz bereitsch der fliegenden Verb. vom 1 August 1943 bis November 1944'. 28 June 1949, 110.8-22, AFHRA.

AWPD-1, tab 1, 'Intelligence'. 145.82-1, 1941, AFHRA.

AWPD-2, part 4, 'Report'. 1942, Special Collections, Air University Library, Maxwell Air Force Base.

'Bombardment Aviation'. 1937–1938, 248.101-9, AFHRA.

Bond, Douglas D. 'A Study of Successful Airmen with Particular Respect to their Motivation for Combat Flying and Resistance to Combat Stress'. 27 Jan. 1945, 520.7411-1, AFHRA.

'The Development of German Aircraft Armament to War's End'. 1957, 113.107-193, AFHRA.

'The Developments of Anti-aircraft Weapons and Equipment of all types up to 1945'. 113.107-194, AFHRA.

Headquarters US Army Air Forces. Letter 35-8. 12 April 1945, 520. 7411-3, AFHRA.

Eighth Air Force. 'Abortives, Jan. 1944–Feb. 1944'. 519.7411-1, 1944–

1946, AFHRA.

——. 'Aircraft Accidents'. 1943–1944, 520.742-7, AFHRA.

——. 'An Evaluation of Defensive Measures Taken to Protect Heavy Bombers from Loss and Damage'. Nov. 1944, 520.520A, AFHRA.

——. 'Disposition of Combat Crews Suffering from Emotional Disorders'. 1 March 1945, 520.7411-2, 1944, AFHRA.

——. 'Effects of Repeated Daily Operations on Combat Crews'. 9 Oct. 1943, 519.7411-1, AFHRA.

——. 'Eighth Air Force – Wounded and Killed in Action'. 519.7411-6, Nov. 1942–Aug. 1944, AFHRA.

——. 'Flight Surgeon Indoctrination Course'. 520.7411-12, Sept.1943, AFHRA.

——. 'Flight Surgeon's Care of Flyer and Statistical Report, June 1943–June 1944'. 519.7440-1, AFHRA.

——. 'German Air Force Losses in the West'. Jan.–April 1944, 512.621 VII/133, AFHRA.

——. 'Headquarters Records'. 520.7721, Jan.–April 1944, AFHRA.

——. 'Length of Operational Tour in Heavy Bombardment'. nd, 519. 7411-1, 1944–1946, AFHRA.

——. 'Level of Experience and Replacement Requirements – Heavy Bomber Crews'. 2 Feb. 1944, 519.7411-1, AFHRA.

——. 'Location of Wounds Incurred in Action, Nov.1942–Sept. 1944, Cumulative to Date'. 519.7411-6, AFHRA.

——. 'Medical Bulletin No. 27'. 5 Nov. 1942, 520.741F, Aug. 1942–May 1943, AFHRA.

——. 'Memorandum 75-1'. 21 Oct. 1943, 519.2171-1, 1942–1945, AFHRA.

——. 'Memorandum 75-2'. 24 Dec. 1943, 519.217-1, 1943–1945, AFHRA.

——. 'Memorandum No. 25-2, Medical Reports and Records'. 12 April 1945, 520.7411-3, AFHRA.

——. 'Memorandum on Tour of Duty in Heavy Bombardment'. 519. 7411-1, AFHRA.

——. 'Minutes of the Eighth Air Force Commander's Meeting'. 21 Jan. 1944, 520.141-1, AFHRA.

——. Operational Research Section, 'Report'. 8 June 1944, AIR 14/1803.

——. 'Physical Standards for Aviators'. 520.7411-9, AFHRA.

——. 'Policy Letter 200.9x373'. 29 Oct. 1942, 519.2171-1, 1942–1945, AFHRA.

——. 'Psychiatry in the Eighth Air Force'. 30 Jan. 1943, 520.7411-12, AFHRA.

——. 'Psychological Aspects of extending the Operational Tour in Heavy Bombardment'. 31 Jan. 1944, 519.7411-1, AFHRA.

——. 'The Reclassification of Personal Failures in the Eighth Air Force'.

16 Oct. 1944, 520.742-4, AFHRA.

——. 'Report of Medical Activities, Eighth Air Force'. 520.7411-10, 1943–1944, AFHRA.

——. 'Report of the Central Medical Board'. 12 July 1943, 520.747B, March–July 1943, AFHRA.

——. 'Report of the Ninety-fourth Bombardment Group'. 6 July 1943, 520.747B, March–July 1943, AFHRA.

——. 'Report on Psychiatry in the 8th Air Force'. 30 Jan. 1943, 520.7411-12, AFHRA.

——. 'Statistical Summary of Eighth Air Force Operations, European Theater'. 17 Aug. 1942–8 May 1945, 520.308-1, AFHRA.

——. 'Statistical Survey of the Emotional Casualties of the Eighth Air Force Aircrews'. 25 May 1945, 520.7421, 1944–1945, AFHRA.

——. 'The Use of Rest Homes in the Eighth Air Force for the Two Year Period Nov. 1942 to Nov. 1944'. 11 Dec. 1944, 520.747.1, AFHRA.

——. 'Value of Rest Home in Anxiety Reactions Occurring in Flying Personnel'. nd, 520.7421, 1943–1945 Vol. II, AFHRA.

——. 'Venereal Disease and Anxiety Removal Rates, Eighth Air Force'. June 1943–June 1944, 519.7401-1, AFHRA.

——. 'Wounded and Killed in Action'. 519.7411-6, Nov. 1942–Aug. 1944, AFHRA.

Eighth Air Force and Army Air Force Evaluation Board, 'Eighth Air Force Tactical Development, August 1942–May 1945'. 1945, AFHRA.

Eighth Bomber Command. 'VIII Bomber Command Narrative of Operations'. 1943–1944, 519.332, AFHRA.

Eighth Fighter Command. 'VIII Fighter Command Narrative of Operations', 1943–1944, 168.6005-55, AFHRA.

'Final Report of Assessed Fighter Claims Against Enemy Aircraft, Aug. 1942–April 1945'. Sept. 1945, AFHRA.

Goodfriend, Captain James. 'Temporary Duty in ETO'. 8 March 1945, 248.4212-7, AFHRA.

Headquarters, European Theater of Operations. Research Branch. 'Attitudes of Fighter Pilots Toward Combat Flying'. July 1944, 141.28-21, July–Aug. 1944, AFHRA.

——. Research Branch. 'Difficulty of Missions'. June 1944, 527.701, Jan. 1943–Oct. 1944, AFHRA.

——. Research Branch. 'Effects on Combat Personnel of Number and Frequency of Missions Flown'. July 1944, 527.701, Jan. 1943–Oct. 1944, AFHRA.

——. Research Branch. 'Effects on Fighter Pilots of Number of Combat Hours Flown'. July 1944, 141.28, July–Aug. 1944, AFHRA.

——. Research Branch. 'How Fighter Pilots Feel About Assignment, Promotion, and Higher Headquarters'. July 1944, 141.28, July–Aug. 1944, AFHRA.

——. Research Branch. 'Survey of Combat Crews in Heavy Bombardment Groups in ETO'. June 1944, Box 18, Spaatz MSS, Library of Congress.

——. Research Branch. 'Survey of Fighter Pilots in Eighth Air Force: A Comparison with Heavy Bomber Pilots'. July 1944, Box 91, Spaatz MSS, Library of Congress.

——. Research Branch. 'Research Findings and Recommendations'. 11 July 1944, Box 91, Spaatz MSS, Library of Congress.

——. Research Branch. 'Research Findings and Recommendations'. 7 Aug. 1944, 141.28, July–Aug. 1944, AFHRA.

——. Research Branch. 'What Fighter Pilots Say About Their Pre-Combat Training'. Aug. 1944, 141.28, July–Aug. 1944, AFHRA.

——. Research Branch. 'What Fighter Pilots Say About Types of Planes'. Aug. 1944, 141.28, July–Aug. 1944, AFHRA.

Headquarters, US Strategic Air Forces Europe, 'Statistical Data'. 570. 677A, AFHRA.

Kuter, Captain Laurence. 'The Power and Effect of the Demolition Bomb'. 1939, 248.2208A-3, AFHRA.

Lyon, Lt. Col. Robert E., 'Trend of Losses Related to Combat Crew Experiences, Heavy Bomber Operations'. *circa* 1944, 519.7411-1 1943–1946, AFHRA.

Mashburn, Lt. Col. Neely C. and Marshall, Major Frank A. 'Aviation Medical Standards, British RAF vs. US Army Air Corps'. 141.28N, 1942, AFHRA.

Office of the Air Surgeon. 'Memorandum for the War Department Special Staff, Battle Casualty Data'. 5 June 1946, 519.741-1, 1943–1945, AFHRA.

——. 'Analysis of the Duties of Aircrew Personnel, Descriptions of Aircrew Performances from Theaters of Combat'. 5 May 1943, 141. 28D-10-19, AFHRA.

——. 'Combat Crew Returnees'. 1944–1945, 142.053, AFHRA.

——. 'Combat Crew Returnees, 97th Bomb Group Pilot'. 9 May 1944, 142.053L-1, AFHRA.

——. 'Report of Psychiatric Study of Successful Air Crews'. 11 Oct. 1943, 141.28J, 1943, AFHRA.

——. 'Report on Survey of Aircrew Personnel in the Eighth, Ninth, Twelfth, and Fifteenth Air Forces'. April 1944, 141.28B, AFHRA.

——. 'Selection and Classification of Aircrew Officers'. Feb. 1944, 141. 28F, AFHRA.

——. 'Stanines, Selection and Classification for Air Crew Duty'. 141.28-20, AFHRA.

——. 'Study of 150 Successful Airmen', Oct. 1943, 141.28J, AFHRA.

Office of the Surgeon General of the Army. 'Memorandum for the Director, Training Division'. Record Group 112, 730, Box 1328,

National Archives.

'Operational Letters'. vol. 1, 168.491, 21 July 1943, AFHRA.

'Report of the Pursuit Board'. 168.12-9, 1942, AFHRA.

US Strategic Air Forces Europe. 'Effects on Combat Personnel of Number and Frequency of Missions Flown'. 6 July 1944, 527.701 Jan. 1943–Oct. 1944, AFHRA.

——. 'Engineering and Supply in Sweden'. 519.8021-2, AFHRA.

——. 'Force Landings in Neutral Countries'. 22 July 1944, 519.8021-3, AFHRA.

——. Memorandum to Commanding General, US Strategic Air Forces Europe, 'Combat Crew Attitudes', 11 July 1944, Box 91, Spaatz MSS, Library of Congress.

2. Unit Records

GP-95-HI (Bomb), April 1943–Aug. 1945, AFHRA.

GP-303-HI (Bomb), 28 Sept. 1944, War Diary, AFHRA.

GP-389-HI (Bomb), June 1943–May 1945, AFHRA.

GP-392-HI (Bomb), Aug. 1943–June 1945, AFHRA.

SQ-Bomb-349-HI, Oct. and March 1944, AFHRA.

SQ-Bomb-350-HI, Oct. and March 1944, AFHRA.

SQ-Bomb-351-HI, Oct. and March 1944, AFHRA.

SQ-Bomb-358-HI, Sept. 1944, AFHRA.

SQ-Bomb-359-HI, Sept. 1944, AFHRA.

SQ-Bomb-360-HI, Sept. 1944, AFHRA.

SQ-Bomb-365-SU-OP-S, Aug. 1944, AFHRA.

Van Norman, William C., Esper, Dwain A., and Bove, Arthur P., 'History of the 306th Bombardment Group (H)', nd, Statistical Report, GP-306-HI (Bomb), March 1942–June 1945, AFHRA.

91st Bombardment Group, 14 Oct. 1943, Modern Military Records Division, Record Group 18, National Archives, Suitland, Maryland.

306th Bomb Group, 30 Dec. 1942, War Diary, AFHRA.

3. British Manuscript Sources

In addition to the documents listed below, the following Record Groups have been consulted at the Public Record Office, Kew:

AIR 2/4019	AIR 14/1008
AIR 2/4620	AIR 14/1803
AIR 2/4935	AIR 14/3512
AIR 2/5998	AIR 14/3544
AIR 2/6345	AIR 20/2860
AIR 2/6400	AIR 20/3085
AIR 2/8038	AIR 20/4583

AIR 2/8039   AIR 20/9919
AIR 2/8236   AIR 20/10727
AIR 2/8271   AIR 25 (Group Operations Books)
AIR 2/8591   AIR 29/603
AIR 2/8592
AIR 2/9490
Air Council. Meeting notes, 4 Feb. 1943, AIR 20/2860.
Air Ministry. Air Member for Personnel, 16 Nov. 1942, AIR 20/2859.
——. Letter. 1 July 1942, AIR 20/3053.
——. Meeting minutes. 23 July 1941, AIR 2/8591.
——. Meeting minutes. 17 Sept. 1942, AIR 2/5998.
——. Meeting minutes. 17 March 1943, AIR 2/4935.
——. Meeting minutes. 20 Oct. 1944, AIR 2/8592.
——. Meeting minutes. Feb. 1944, AIR 2/8271.
——. 'Minutes of meeting to consider training to improve morale and discipline'. 6 Jan. 1944, AIR 20/4583.
——. RAF Sub-committee on Assessment of Temperament in Connection with Aircrew Selection, 'Meeting minutes'. 5 May 1943, AIR 2/6345.
——. War Room (Statistical Section), War Room Manual of Bomber Command Ops. 1939–1945, AIR 22/203.
Aircrew Disposal Unit. 'Operations Record Book', AIR 29/603.
Burt, Professor Cyril. 'The Value of Correlational Methods for Investigating the Causes of Flying Stress and for Predicting its outcome'. Sept. 1944, AIR 20/10727.
Burton, H. L. 'Report on Gillespie's visit to the Army Initial Training Centre'. 21 April 1943, AIR 2/6400.
Expert Committee on the Work of Psychologists and Psychiatrists in the Services. Meeting minutes. 17 Sept. 1942, AIR 2/5998.
——. Meeting minutes. 11 Feb. 1943, AIR 2/5998.
'Investigations into causes of Abortive Sorties'. AIR 14/1886.
Lawson, Wing Commander J. 'Memorandum on LMF'. Air Historical Branch.
Ludlow-Hewitt, Air Chief Marshal Sir Edgar, 'Visits to Air Crew Disposal Centres'. 26 Dec. 1942, AIR 20/2859.
'Morale and Discipline in the Royal Air Force'. AIR 20/3082.
Nicholls, Robert. 'US Air Force Psychiatrists and RAF Psychiatrists'. 28 Nov. 1942, AIR 20/3085.
'Note by IG II on Discipline and the fighting spirit in the RAF'. 14 May 1943, AIR 20/3082.
'Notes for Instructors on the Recognition of Nervousness in Pilots'. June 1943, AIR 2/6252.
Operational Research Section, Bomber Command. 'Final Plots of Night Photographs'. 15–16 March 1944, AIR 24/269.

Reid, Squadron Leader D. D., Flying Personnel Research Committee. Report 508, 'The Influence of Psychological Disorder on Efficiency in Operational Flying'. Sept. 1942, AIR 20/10727.

'Report No. S.77, Casualties Among Aircrew Personnel Directly Due to Enemy Action'. 12 March 1943, AIR 14/1803.

S.61141/S.7.C. 28 Sept. 1940, AIR 20/10727.

S.61141/S.7.c.(1). 19 Sept. 1941, AIR 20/10727.

S.61141/S.7.c.(1). 1 June 1943, Air Historical Branch.

S.61141/S.7.(d). 1 March 1945, AIR 2/8591.

'The Selection, Classification and Initial Training of Air Crew'. 31 March 1944, AIR 15/53.

'Summary of Events'. No. 8 Group, 30–31 March 1944, AIR 14/450.

Symonds, Air Vice-Marshal Sir Charles P. 'Note on the predictability of breakdown by use of aircrew interview'. 21 May 1941, AIR 2/6345.

Symonds, Air Vice-Marshal Sir Charles P., and Williams, Wing Commander Denis J., Flying Personnel Research Committee. Report 412(b), 'Critical Review of the Published Literature'. Jan. 1942, AIR 20/10727.

——. Report 412(d), 'Investigations into Psychological Disorders in Flying Personnel, Review of Reports submitted to the Air Ministry since the outbreak of the war'. April 1942, AIR 2/6252.

——. Report 412(f), 'Personal investigation of psychological disorder in flying personnel of Bomber Command'. Oct. 1942, AIR 2/6252.

——. Report 412(g), 'Statistical survey of the occurrence of psychological disorder in flying personnel in six months (3rd Feb. to 3rd Aug., 1942)'. AIR 2/6252.

——. Report 412(i), 'Occurrence of Neurosis in RAF aircrew in 1943 and 1944'. Sept. 1944, AIR 2/6252.

——. Report 412(k), 'Investigation of psychological disorder in flying personnel by the Unit Medical Officers'. Feb. 1945, AIR 2/6252.

——. Report 412(l), 'The Occurrence of neurosis in Royal Air Force (air crews), 1944–1945'. AIR 2/6252.

——. Report 547, 'Clinical and Statistical Study of Neurosis Precipitated by Flying Duties'. Aug. 1943, AIR 2/6252.

Williams, Wing Commander Denis J., 'Comments'. 3 Nov. 1944, AIR 20/10727.

4. Library Manuscripts and Personal Correspondence

Arnold, General Henry H., Letter to General Carl Spaatz and Lt. General Ira Eaker. 27 July 1944, 622.1621-2, AFHRA.

——. Letter to all Commanding Generals, 7 Dec. 1944, 'US Army Air Forces Policy Letter 35-18'. 519.2171-1, AFHRA.

Boggs, Colonel Thomas R., Letter to the Chief of the Air Service. 28 Dec. 1918, AFHRA.

Bond, Major Douglas D., Letter to Brig. General Malcom Grow. 1
    March 1945, 520.7411-2 1944, AFHRA.
Cappel, Howard N. to Chief of the Air Corps, 27 May 1940, AFHRA.
Colquitt, Captain Alfred O., Letter to the Central Medical Board. 21 Feb.
    1945, copy in author's possession.
Doolittle, General James H., Letter to Commanding Generals, 1st, 2nd,
    and 3rd Bombardment Divisions. 5 Feb. 1944, 527.674, AFHRA.
Eaker, Lt. General Ira C. Personal Papers of, 1918–60. Washington, DC,
    Library of Congress.
——. Letter to Lt. General George E. Stratemeyer, 2 Jan. 1943, 168.491,
    AFHRA.
——. Letter to Major General H. I. Edwards, 27 Nov. 1943, 520.161-1,
    AFHRA.
Grant, Brig. General David N., Letter to the Commandant of the School
    of Aviation Medicine, 23 March 1942, 141.28, AFHRA.
Hansell, General Haywood S. Personal Papers of. Special Collections, Air
    Force Academy Library, US Air Force Academy, Colorado.
Hershey, General Lewis B. Personal Papers of. US Military History
    Institute, Carlisle Barracks, Pennsylvania.
LeMay, General Curtis E. Personal Papers of. Washington, DC, Library
    of Congress.
Ligon, William Y. 'Bill's Letters'. 2nd Division Memorial Room,
    Norwich Central Library.
Office of the Surgeon General of the Army. Modern Military Records,
    Record Group 112, National Archives.
Spaatz, General Carl. Personal Papers of, 1915–53. Washington, DC,
    Library of Congress.
——. Letter to General Henry H. Arnold. 29 July 1944, 622.161-2,
    AFHRA.
——. Letter to Commanding General, 8th Service Command. 16 Sept.
    1942, 519.2171 1942–1945, AFHRA.
Stafford-Clark, Dr David. Papers of. Imperial War Museum.

5. USAF Oral History Interviews

Doolittle, General James H. Interviewed by Professor Ronald Schaffer,
    24 Aug. 1979, 239.0512-1206, AFHRA.
Kepner, General William E. 15 July 1944, 524.0581, AFHRA.
Milton, General Theodore R. Interviewed for the Albert F. Simpson
    Historical Research Center, 9 July 1982, 239.0512-1339, AFHRA.
Yeager, Brig. General Charles E. Interviewed for the Albert F. Simpson
    Historical Research Center, 28 April–1 May 1980, 239.0512-1204,
    AFHRA.

6. Television Interviews, Recordings, and Films

Cochrane, John J. and Rogan, John M., Thames Television Interview, No. 002821/02/01-02, Imperial War Museum.

Eaker, General Ira C., Thames Television Interview, No. 002820/03/01,02,03, Imperial War Museum.

Harris, Air Marshal Sir Arthur T., Thames Television Interview, No. 002893/03/01,02,03, Imperial War Museum.

Mahaddie, Group Captain Hamish, Thames Television Interview, No. 002897/03/01-03, Imperial War Museum.

Meyer, General John C., Thames Television Interview, No. 002823/01, Imperial War Museum.

Reed, Carol, *The Way Ahead*, 1944. Film Department, Imperial War Museum.

Schroer, Major Werner, Thames Television Interview, No. 002950/01/01, Imperial War Museum.

Stewart, Major General James M., Thames Television Interview, No. 002889/02/01-02, Imperial War Museum.

Thomas, Wynford Vaughan and Pidsley, R., 'Raid on Berlin', BBC Broadcast, 3 Sept. 1944, Sound Recording No. 6454-8/2178, Imperial War Museum.

US Army. *Combat Exhaustion*, Training Film No. 1197, 1944, USAF Motion Media Records Center, Norton AFB, California.

——. *Field Psychiatry for the General Medical Officer*, Training Film No. 1167, USAF Motion Media Records Center, Norton AFB, California.

——. *Introduction to Combat Fatigue*, Training Film No. 1402, 1944, USAF Motion Media Records Center, Norton AFB, California.

——. *Let There be Light*, Training Film No. 5019, 1946, USAF Motion Media Records Center, Norton AFB, California.

——. *The New Lot*, Film No. 1133, nd, USAF Motion Media Records Center, Norton AFB, California.

7. US Official Documents and Studies

Arnold, General Henry H., 'Report of the Commanding General of the US Army Air Force to the Secretary of War'. 27 Feb. 1945, AFHRA.

Ayres, Leonard P., *The War With Germany: a Statistical Summary* (Washington, DC: Government Printing Office, 1919).

Craven, Wesley F. and Cate, James L., gen. eds, *The Army Air Forces in World War II*, 7 vols. (Chicago: University of Chicago Press, 1958).

Davis, Frederick B., ed., *The AAF Qualifying Examination Army Air Forces Aviation Psychology Program, Research Reports No. 6* (Washington, DC: Government Printing Office, 1947).

'Familiarization Manual for Operation of Model B-17F Bombardment Airplane' (Seattle: Boeing, 1942).

Goldman, Martin, *Morale in the Army Air Force in World War II*. USAF Historical Study No. 78. Maxwell AFB, Alabama, 1953.

Kepner, William E., 'The Long Reach: Deep Fighter Escort Tactics'. VIII Fighter Command report, 29 May 1944, AFHRA.

Link, Mae M. and Coleman, Hurbert A., *Medical Support of the AAF in World War II* (Washington, DC: Government Printing Office, 1955).

Mullins, Colonel William S., gen. ed., *Neuropsychiatry in World War II*, 2 vols. (Washington, DC: Government Printing Office, 1973).

Office of the Air Surgeon. *Stanines, Selection, and Classification for Air Crew Duty* (Washington, DC: Government Printing Office, 1946).

Schmid, Generalleutnant Josef, 'Aerial Warfare over the Reich in Defence of Vital Luftwaffe Installations and Supporting Services'. 1 April 1944–6 June 1944, 113.107-160, AFHRA.

US Air Force. 'Aerial Attack Study', by John R. Boyd. Document No. 50-10-6C, Nellis AFB, Nevada, 1960.

——. 'The Development of German Aircraft Armament at War's End'. 113.107-193, 1957, AFHRA.

US Army Adjutant General's Office. Directive 383.6, 31 July 1944.

US Army Air Forces. *Army Air Force Statistical Digest, World War II* (Washington, DC: Government Printing Office, 1945).

——. *Flight Operating Instructions For Army Model B-17F* (Patterson Field, Ohio: USAAF, 1944).

——. 'German Fighter Tactics Against Flying Fortresses'. Special Intelligence Report No. 43–17, 31 Dec. 1943. Imperial War Museum.

——. 'History of the AAF Personnel Distribution Command', 3 vols., 1945.

——. 'Letter 35-8', 12 April 1945, 520.7411-3, Jan. 1944–May 1945, AFHRA.

——. *Outline of Neuropsychiatry in Aviation Medicine*. Randolph Field, Texas: USAAF, nd.

——. 'Pilots Flight Operation Instructions for Model B-17'. Wright Patterson Field, 1944.

——. Regulation 35-16. 20 Oct. 1944.

——. Regulation 605-230. 9 June 1943.

——. 'A Handbook for New Arrivals', 388th Bombardment Group (Heavy), Knettishall, England, 15 February 1945.

US Army Medical Department. *Medical Statistics in World War II* (Washington, DC: Government Printing Office, 1975).

United States Strategic Bombing Survey, 10 vols. (Washington, DC: Government Printing Office, 1945–1949).

War Department, *Decorations and Awards* (Washington, DC: Government Printing Office, 1947).

——. *Handbook on German Military Forces*, Technical Manual TM-E 30-451. (Washington, DC: Government Printing Office, 1945).

——. 'A Short Guide to Great Britain', 1944.
——. 'Standards of Physical Examination for Flying', Army Regulation No. 40-105, 1942.
——. US Army Regulation 40-100.
——. US Army Regulation 40-110.

8. British Official Documents and Studies

Air Historical Branch. *Manning Plans and Policy*. Monograph/II/116/14.
Air Ministry. *Pamphlet 100*. May, 1939.
——. *Air Crew Training Bulletin, 1941–45*. (various issues).
——. *Flying Training*, 2 vols. (London: HMSO, 1952).
——. *Operational Research in the RAF* (London: HMSO, 1963).
Privy Council Office, *Report of an Expert Committee on the Work of Psychologists and Psychiatrists in the Services* (London: HMSO, 1947).
Rexford-Welch, Dr S. C., ed., *The Royal Air Force Medical Services*, 2 vols. (London: HMSO, 1955).
Symonds, Air Vice-Marshal Sir Charles P. and Williams, Wing Commander Denis J., *Psychological Disorders in Flying Personnel of the Royal Air Force 1939–1945* (London: HMSO, 1947).
Webster, Charles and Frankland, Noble, *The Strategic Air Offensive Against Germany*, 4 vols. (London: HMSO, 1961).

9. Books

Armstrong, H. G. and Grow, M., *Fit to Fly: A Medical Handbook for Fliers* (New York and London: D. Appleton-Century Company, 1941).
Arnold, Henry H. and Eaker, Ira C., *This Flying Game* (New York: Funk and Wagnalls Company, 1943).
Clausewitz, Carl von, *On War*. Edited by Michael Howard and Peter Paret (Princeton: Princeton University Press, 1976).
Curtiss, Glenn H. and Post, Augustus, *The Curtiss Aviation Book* (New York: Frederick A. Stokes, 1912).
DeSeversky, Alexander P., *Victory Through Air Power* (New York: Simon and Schuster, 1942).
Dollard, John, *Fear in Battle* (Washington, DC: *The Infantry Journal*, 1944).
Douhet, Giulio, *Command of the Air*. Translated by Dino Ferrari (New York: Coward-McCann, 1941; reprint edn, Washington, DC: Office of Air Force History, 1983).
Grinker, Roy R. and Spiegel, J. P., *Men Under Stress* (London: J. and A. Churchill, Ltd., 1945).
Hastings, Donald W., Wright, David G. and Glueck, Bernard C., *Psychiatric Experiences of the Eighth Air Force: First Year Of Combat*. (New York: Josiah Macy Jr. Foundation, 1944).

Marshall, S. L. A., *Men Against Fire* (New York: 1947; reprint edn., Gloucester, MA: Peter Smith, 1978).

Mitchell, William H., *Winged Defense: The Development and Possibilities of Modern Air Power* (New York: G. P. Putnam's Sons, 1925).

Moran, Lord, *The Anatomy of Courage* (London: Constable and Company, 1945; reprint edn., Garden City Park: Avery Publishing Group, 1987).

Tidy, Major General Sir Henry L., ed., *Inter-Allied Conferences on War Medicine 1942–1945* (London: Staples Press Limited, 1947)

10. Diaries and Memoirs

Anderson, Colonel Clarence E., *To Fly and Fight* (New York: Bantam Books, 1991).

Bendiner, Elmer, *The Fall of the Fortresses* (London: Pan Books, 1982).

Bennett, Air Vice-Marshal D. C. T., *Pathfinder* (London: Frederick Miller, 1958; London: Goodall Publications, Ltd., 1988).

Bond, Douglas D., *The Love and Fear of Flying* (New York: International Universities Press, 1952).

Charlwood, Don, *No Moon Tonight* (Australia: Angus and Robertson, 1956; London: Goodall Publications, 1984).

Cheshire, Group Captain Leonard, *Bomber Pilot* (London: Hutchinson, 1942).

Chisholm, Roderick, *Cover of Darkness* (London: Chatto & Windus, 1953).

Doolittle, General James H., *I Could Never Be So Lucky Again* (New York: Bantam Books, 1991).

Dyson, Freeman, *Disturbing the Universe* (New York: Harper and Row, 1979).

Gabreski, Colonel Francis S., *Gabby: A Fighter Pilot's Life* (New York: Orion Books, 1991).

Galland, Adolf, *The First and the Last* (London: Methuen, 1955).

Gentile, Don, *One Man Air Force* (New York: L. B. Fischer Publishing Corporation, 1944).

Gibson, Wing Commander Guy, *Enemy Coast Ahead* (London: Michael Joseph, 1946; London: Goodall Publications, 1986).

Goodson, James A., *Tumult in the Clouds* (London: William Kimber, 1983).

Hansell, Brig. General Haywood S., *The Air Plan that defeated Hitler* (Atlanta: Higgins-McArthur Longino and Porter, 1972).

Harris, Air Marshal Sir Arthur T., *Bomber Offensive* (London: Collins, 1947).

Hodgson, David, *Letters from a Bomber Pilot* (London: Thames Methuen, 1985).

Hughes, Walter F., 'A Bomber Pilot in WWII'. Photocopied manuscript, nd., 2nd Air Division Memorial Room, Norwich Central Library.

Johnson, Robert S., *Thunderbolt* (New York: Ballantine, 1959; New York: Bantam Books, 1990).

Knoke, Heinz, *I Flew for the Führer: The Story of a German Fighter Pilot* (New York: Holt, 1953).

Mahaddie, Group Captain Hamish, *Hamish: The Story of a Pathfinder* (Shepperton: Ian Allan, 1989).

Raymond, Robert S., *A Yank in Bomber Command* (New York: Hippocrene Books, Inc., 1977).

Richthofen, Manfred von, *Der Rote Kampfflieger* (Berlin: Ullstein, 1918).

Rollen, Henry R., *Festina Lente: A Psychiatric Odyssey* (London: British Medical Journal, 1990).

Sawyer, Tom, *Only Owls and Bloody Fools Fly at Night* (London: William Kimber, 1982; London: Goodall, 1987).

Smith, Dale O., *Screaming Eagle: the Memoirs of a B-17 Group Commander* (New York: Dell, 1990).

Speer, Albert, *Inside the Third Reich* (New York: Macmillan, 1970).

Stiles, Bert, *Serenade to the Big Bird* (London: Lindsay Drummund, 1947).

Tempest, Victor, *Near the Sun: The Impressions of a Medical Officer of Bomber Command* (Brighton: Crabtree Press, 1946).

Thorns, William M., Personal Diary. Copy in author's possession.

Tripp, Miles, *The Eighth Passenger* (London: Heinemann, 1969).

Yeager, Brig. General Charles E., *Yeager: An Autobiography* (New York: Bantam Books, 1985).

11. Articles

'The Aviation Psychological Program of the Army Air Forces', *Psychological Bulletin*, 40 (Dec. 1943), pp. 759–69.

Flanagan, Lt. Colonel J. C. and Fitts, Major P. M., 'Psychological Testing Program for the Selection and Classification of Air Crew Officers' *The Air Surgeon's Bulletin*, I (June 1944), pp. 1–5.

Ireland, G. O., 'Neuropsychiatric Ex-Serviceman and his Civil Re-establishment', *American Journal of Psychiatry*, 2 (1923).

Kindred, J. J., 'Neuropsychiatric Wards of the United States Government; their Housing and other Problems', *American Journal of Psychiatry*, 1 (1921).

Longacre, R. F., 'Personality Study', *The Journal of Aviation Medicine*, 1 (1929), pp. 33–50.

'Picture Section 1', *The New York Times*, 6 Nov. 1910.

'The Psychiatric Toll of Warfare', *Fortune*, Dec. 1943, pp. 141–9.

Rippon, T. S., 'Report on the Essential Characteristics of Successful and Unsuccessful Aviators with Special Reference to Temperament', *Aeronautics*, 9 Oct. 1918.

Rippon, T. S. and Mannell, E. G., 'Report of the Essential Characteristics of Successful and Unsuccessful Aviators', *The Lancet* (28 Sept. 1918), pp. 411–15.

Stafford-Clark, Dr David, 'Morale and Flying Experience: Results of a Wartime Study', *Journal of Mental Science* (Jan. 1949), pp. 10–50.

B. SECONDARY SOURCES

1. Books

Abbotts, P. E. and Tamplin, J. M. A., *British Gallantry Awards* (London: Nimrod Dix and Company, 1981).

Ahrenfeldt, Robert H., *Psychiatry in the British Army in the Second World War* (London: Routledge & Kegan Paul, 1958).

Air University. *Concepts for Air Force Leadership* (Maxwell AFB: Air University Press, 1983).

Bailey, Ronald H., *The Air War in Europe*. Time-Life Series World War II (New York: Time-Life, 1979).

Balfour, Harold, *Wings Over Westminster* (London: Hutchinson and Co., 1973).

Barker, Ralph, *The RAF at War*. Time-Life Series 'The Epic of Flight'. (Alexandria: Time-Life Books, 1981).

Belenky, Gregory, *Contemporary Studies in Combat Psychiatry* (New York: Greenwood Press, 1987).

Bergin, Dr Kenneth G., *Aviation Medicine: Its Theory and Application* (Baltimore: The Williams and Wilkins Company, 1949).

Best, Geoffrey and Wheatcroft, Andrew, eds, *War Economy and the Military Mind* (London: Croom Helm, Rowman, and Littlefield, 1976).

Blanchard, Kenneth H., 'Situational Leadership Revisited' in *Concepts for Air Force Leadership* (Maxwell AFB: Air University Press, 1983).

Blakebrough, Ken, *The Fireball Outfit: The 457th Bombardment Group in the Skies Over Europe* (Fallbrook, CA: Aero Publishers, Inc., 1968).

Clark, R. W., *The Rise of the Boffins* (London: Phoenix House, 1962).

Coffey, Thomas M., *Iron Eagle: The Turbulent Life of General Curtis LeMay* (New York: Crown Publishers, 1986; New York: Avon Books, 1986).

Copp, Dewitt S., *Forged in Fire* (Garden City: Doubleday & Company, 1982).

Creveld, Martin van, *Fighting Power: German and US Army Performance 1939–1945* (London: Arms and Armour Press, 1983).

Dorfler, Major Joseph F., *The Branch Point Study: Specialized Undergraduate Pilot Training* (Maxwell AFB: Air University Press, 1988).

Durand, Arthur A., *Stalag Luft III* (Baton Rouge: Louisiana State University Press, 1988).

Dyer, G., *War* (London: The Bodley Head, 1985).

Ethell, Jeffrey L. and Simonson, Clarence, *The History of Aircraft Nose Art* (London: Motorbooks International, 1991).

Franks, Norman, *Scramble to Victory* (London: William Kimber, 1987).

Freeman, Roger A., *The American Airmen in Europe* (London: Arms and Armour Press, 1991).

——. *The British Airmen* (London: Arms and Armour Press, 1989).

——. *The Mighty Eighth* (London: Jane's, 1986).

——. *The Mighty Eighth War Diary* (London: Jane's, 1981).

——. *The Mighty Eighth War Manual* (London: Arms and Armour Press, 1991).

——. *The US Strategic Bomber* (London: Macdonald and Jane's, 1975).

Fry, Garry L. and Ethell, Jeffrey L., *Escort to Berlin* (New York: Arco, 1980).

Gabriel, Richard A., *Military Psychiatry* (New York: Greenwood Press, 1986).

——. *No More Heroes: Madness and Psychiatry in War* (New York: Hill and Wang, 1987).

Gardiner, Juliet, *Over There: The GIs in Wartime Britain* (London: Collins and Brown, 1992).

Giles, Brian D., *Meteorology and World War II* (Birmingham: Royal Meteorological Society, 1987).

Ginzberg, Eli, *The Ineffective Soldier*, 3 vols. (New York: King's Crown Press, 1950).

Ginzberg, Eli, Herma, John L. and Ginsburg, Sol W., *Psychiatry and Military Manpower: A Reappraisal of the Experiences in World War II* (New York: King's Crown Press, 1953).

Gray, J. Glenn, *The Warriors: Reflections on Men in Battle* (New York: Harcourt, Brace and Company, 1959).

Griffith, Paddy, *Forward into Battle* (Novato, CA: Presidio Press, 1991).

Green, William, *Famous Bombers of the Second World War*, 2 vols. (New York: Doubleday and Company, 1960).

——. *War Planes of the Second World War*, 10 vols. (New York: Doubleday and Company, 1961).

Gunn, Peter B., *RAF Great Massingham: A Norfolk Airfield at War 1940–1945* (King's Lynn: Watts and Rowe, 1990).

Hastings, Max, *Bomber Command* (London: Michael Joseph, 1979; London: Pan Books, 1981).

Hawkins, Ian, ed. *B-17s Over Berlin: Personal Stories from the 95th Bomb Group* (Washington: Brassey's, 1990).

——. *The Münster Raid* (Blue Ridge Summit, PA: Tab/Aero Books, 1984).

Higham, Robin, ed., *A Guide to the Sources of British Military History* (Berkeley: University of California Press, 1971).

Holmes, Richard, *Acts of War* (New York: The Free Press, 1985).

Hoseason, James, *The 1,000 Day Battle* (Lowestoft, Suffolk: Gillingham Publications, 1979).

Hoyt, Edwin P., *The Airmen: The Story of American Flyers in World War II* (New York: McGraw-Hill, 1990).

Jablonski, Edward, *Flying Fortress* (Garden City: Doubleday and Company, 1965).

Kennett, Lee, *The First Air War* (New York: The Free Press, 1991).

——. *GI: The American Soldier in World War II* (New York: Charles Scribner's Sons, 1987).

Kohn, Richard H. and Harahan, Joseph P., eds, *Strategic Air Warfare: An Interview with Generals Curtis E. LeMay, Leon W. Johnson, David A. Burchinal, and Jack J. Catton* (Washington: Office of Air Force History, 1988).

Lande, D. A., *From Somewhere in England* (Shrewsbury: Airlife Publications, 1991).

Longmate, Norman, *The Bombers* (London: Hutchinson, 1983; Arrow Books, 1988).

Lucas, Laddie, ed. *Wings of War* (London: Hutchinson, 1983).

Manvell, Roger, *Films and the Second World War* (New York: A. S. Barnes and Company, 1974).

McFarland, Stephen L. and Newton, Wesley P., *To Command the Sky: The Battle for Air Superiority Over Germany 1942–1944* (Washington: Smithsonian Institution Press, 1991).

Messenger, Charles, *Bomber Harris and the Strategic Bombing Offensive, 1939–1945* (London: Arms and Armour Press, 1984).

Mets, David R., *Master of Airpower: General Carl A. Spaatz* (Novato, CA: Presidio Press, 1988).

Middlebrook, Martin, *The Berlin Raids* (London: Penguin Books, 1988).

——. *The Nuremberg Raid* (London: Penguin Books, 1986).

——. *The Schweinfurt-Regensburg Mission* (London: Penguin Books, 1985).

Middlebrook, Martin and Everitt, Chris, *The Bomber Command War Diaries* (London: Viking Books, 1985; London: Penguin Books, 1990).

Morgan, Len, *Crackup* (New York: Arco Publishing Company, 1969).

Murray, Williamson, *Luftwaffe* (Baltimore: The Nautical and Aviation Publishing Company, 1985).

O'Neill, Brian D., *Half a Wing, Three Engines and a Prayer: B-17s over Germany* (Blue Ridge Summit, PA: Tab/Aero Books, 1989).

Overy, R. J., *The Air War 1939–1945* (New York: Stein and Day, 1980).

Paterson, T. E., *Morale in War and Work* (London: Max Parrish, 1955).

Perret, Geoffrey, *There's a War to be Won* (New York: Random House, 1991).

Price, Alfred, *Fighter Aircraft* (London: Arms and Armour Press, 1976).

——. *Instruments of Darkness* (London: Macdonald and Jane's, 1977).

Richardson, F. M., *Fighting Spirit: Psychological Factors in War* (London: Leo Cooper, 1978).

Scutts, Jerry, *Lion in the Sky: US 8th Air Force Fighter Operations 1942–1945* (Wellingborough: Patrick Stephens, 1987).

Searby, John, *The Bomber Battle for Berlin* (Shrewsbury: Airlife Publishing, 1991).

Sherry, Michael S., *The Rise of American Airpower* (New Haven: Yale University Press, 1987).

Spick, Mike, *The Ace Factor* (Annapolis: The Naval Institute Press, 1988).

Stouffer, Samuel, Lumsdaine, Arthur A., Lumsdaine, Marion Harper, Williams, Robin M., Jr., Smith, M. Brewster, Janis, Irving L., Star, Shirley A. and Cottrell, Leonard S., Jr., *Studies in Social Psychology in World War Two*. 2 vols. (Princeton: Princeton University Press, 1949).

Stokesbury, James L., *A Short History of World War II* (New York: William Morrow, 1980).

Strong, Russell, *First Over Germany* (Winston-Salem: Hunter Publishing, Co., 1982).

Terraine, John, *The Right of the Line* (London: Hodder & Stoughton, 1985).

Thomas, Roy J., *Haven, Heaven and Hell* (Monroe, Wisconsin: privately published, 1991).

Toliver, Raymond F. and Constable, Trevor J., *Fighter Aces of the USA* (Fallbrook: Aero Publisher, 1979).

Turner, E. S., *Gallant Gentlemen: A Portrait of the British Officer 1600–1956* (London: Michael Joseph, 1956).

Verrier, Anthony, *The Bomber Offensive* (London: B. T. Batsford, 1968).

Ward, Christopher, *The War of the Revolution*, 2 vols. (New York: Macmillan, 1952).

Watts, Barry D., *The Foundations of US Air Doctrine* (Maxwell AFB: Air University Press, 1984).

Windrow, Martin C., ed., *Aircraft in Profile*, 14 vols. (New York: Doubleday and Company, 1969).

Winfield, Dr Roland, *The Sky Belongs to Them* (Abingdon: Purnell Book Services, 1976).

2. Articles

Callander, Bruce D., 'Enlisted Pilots', *Air Force Magazine*, June 1989, pp. 98–101.

——. 'They Wanted Wings', *Air Force Magazine*, Jan. 1991, pp. 80–3.

Connolly, Ray, '"I don't think I was ever really frightened", Group Captain Leonard Cheshire talks to Ray Connolly', *The Times*, 21 July 1990.

Eaker, Lt. General Ira C., 'The Military Professional', *Air University*

Review, 2 (Jan.–Feb. 1976), pp. 2–12.

Galland, Adolf, 'Defeat of the Luftwaffe: Fundamental Causes', *Air University Review,* 6 (Spring 1953), pp. 16–36.

Gravatt, Brent L. and Ayers, Francis H., 'The Fireman: Twelve O'Clock High Revisited', *Aerospace Historian*, 35 (Sept. 1988), pp. 204–8.

Haseler, Prof. Stephen, 'Britannia rules – but she's enslaved to class', *The Times,* 22 Dec. 1991.

Hill, James W., ed., *Eighth Air Force News* (various issues).

Jones, Dr David R., 'The Macy Reports: Combat Fatigue in World War II Fliers', *Aviation, Space, and Environmental Medicine* (Aug. 1987), pp. 807–11.

LeMay, General Curtis E., 'Strategic Airpower: Destroying the Enemy's War Resources', *Aerospace Historian*, 27 (Spring 1980), pp. 9–15.

Ling, T. N., ed., *Bomber Command Association Newsletter* (various issues).

McCarthy, John, 'Aircrew and Lack of Moral Fibre in the Second World War', *War and Society*, Sept. 1984, pp. 87–101.

McFarland, Stephen L., 'The Evolution of the American Strategic Fighter in Europe 1942–1945', *Journal of Strategic Studies*, 10 (June 1987), pp. 198–208.

Mulligan, Timothy P., 'German U-boat Crews in World War II: Sociology of an Elite', *The Journal of Military History*, 56 (April 1992), pp. 261–81.

Nofi, A. A., 'For Your Information', *Strategy and Tactics*, 90 (Jan.–Feb. 1982), pp. 19–22.

Stafford-Clark, Dr David, 'An Hour of Breath'. *Bulletin of the Royal College of Psychiatrists*, 11 (July 1987), pp. 218–23.

Watts, Barry D., 'Fire, Movement, and Tactics', *Topgun Journal*, 2 (Winter 1979/80), pp. 4–24.

Werrell, Dr Kenneth P., 'A Case for a 'New' Unit History'. *Air Power Journal,* 39 (Spring 1992), pp. 34–41.

3. Lectures and Speeches

Culbert, David H., 'Hollywood goes to War'. Banquet Address, Tenth Military History Symposium, USAF Academy, Oct. 1982.

Blum, John M., 'United Against: American Culture and Society During World War II'. *The Harmon Memorial Lectures in Military History 1959–1987* (Washington, DC: Office of Air Force History, 1988).

Emerson, William R., 'Operation POINTBLANK: A Tale of Bombers and Fighters'. *The Harmon Memorial Lectures in Military History 1959–1987* (Washington, DC: Office of Air Force History, 1988).

MacManus, Wing Commander F., 'Flying Stress in RAF aircrew'. Lecture at the Defence Medical Services Military Psychiatry Course, 17 Oct. 1991, London.

Paris, Michael, 'The Rise of Airmen: The Origins of Air Force Elitism'. Paper presented at the Military History Research Seminar, King's College, London, 22 Oct. 1991.

Preston, Richard A., 'Perspectives in the History of Military Education and Professionalism'. *The Harmon Memorial Lectures in Military History 1959–1987* (Washington, DC: Office of Air Force History, 1988).

Zemke, Colonel Hub, 'Leadership'. Lecture to the Tennessee National Guard Commanders' Conference, 20 Oct. 1989.

4. Unpublished Papers

Boyd, John R., 'Aerial Attack Study'. USAF Fighter Weapons School, Document No. 50–10–6C, Nellis AFB, Nevada.

Gajeski, Antone E., 'Combat Aircrew Experiences During the Vietnam Conflict: An Exploratory Study'. M.A. thesis, Air Force Institute of Technology, 1988.

Gries, Charles E., 'Situational Leadership: The Key to More Effective Leadership in the USAF' Student Research Paper, Air War College, Air University, Maxwell AFB, 1981.

Jones, Dr David R., 'US Air Force Combat Psychiatry'. USAF School of Aerospace Medicine. Brooks AFB, Texas, 1986.

Lentz, Thomas L., 'Combat Leadership: 56th Fighter Group 1943–1944'. MA thesis, University of Alabama, 1986.

5. Correspondence with author

a. US Veterans

Alleman, Harry G.
Ardizzi, Peter F.
Arnold, E. E.
Badler, Bernie
Bandy, Allen J.
Barberis, Daniel
Bernardo, Alfred
Bember, John K.
Bennett, Lee N.
Bennett, Robert
Best, Lloyd G.
Beymer, Ellis H.
Blackburn, Robert M.
Borsineau, Gerry
Bowen, Robert
Bowman, Harold W.
Brandfass, Robert
Breen, Benjamin
Bryan, D. S.
Butler, John W.
Carrazzone, Gerry
Ceeley, William D.
Chealander, Allan B.
Clark, A. J.

Colquitt Jr., Alfred
Conger, Paul
Cook, Gordon
Corcoram, John
Cronin, Joseph V.
Cruver, Harry F.
Cummings, Edwin F.
Derr, Merritt E.
Doerch, George A.
Doherty, Robert
Drew, Urban L.
Engdahl, Leroy J.
Engfer, Carl J.
Feeley, Thomas A.
Ford, John C.
Framer, David
Funk, Martin R.
Gann, John W.
Gaydosh, J. J.
Gaylord, Donald A.
Goodson, James A.
Grabowski, Edward F.
Grimshaw, John L.
Hair, Thomas L.
Halm, Frank N.
Hampton, Ken

Hart Jr., Carter
Hennessy, Edward
Hennessy, John E.
Hill, James E.
Hinshaw, Hugh M.
Hoffman, Joseph H.
Hoser, Harry W.
Houser, William
Howard, Pat
Howard, Roy W.
Huff, Olen
Hutchinson, Howard
Johnson, J. G.
Jolls, Lewis M.
Jones Jr., Joe
Jones, John
Korf, Lee
Kupsick, John A.
Lantz, William F.
Latham, John L.
Lattanzi, William E.
Leftwich, Dan
Litsinger, David W.
Lockard, Chester C.
Long, Robert A.
Lotz, William H.

Maddock, Gorden M.
Matthews, Robert R.
McElvain, Scott C.
McLean, George L.
Miller, William F.
Myer, Eugene F.
Myers, Jerry M.
Nelson, R. F.
Nordin, Glenn
Nugent, Robert L.
Olmsted, Peter R.
Parker, Don
Peterson, Stanley
Pishioneri, A. F.
Podolak, Stanley J.
Powell, Robert H.
Radnofsky, Matthew
Re, Lawrence A.
Reentmeester, Lester F.
Riordan, Robert P.
Robertson, Gordon
Robison, Brice E.
Rodriguez, Louis
Roncy, E. L.
Ryan, William G.
Salvador, George
Shaffer, J. R.
Schohan, Ben
Schuh, Duerr H.
Shanker, Herbert
Shiffrin, Ben
Strong, Russell A.
Taylor, John C.
Tellefson, John A.
Thompson, William M.
Thurman, Taylor
Thorns, William M.
Trout, Ralph W.
Utley, William
Utter, Charles W.
Valenti, Jasper J.
Wasemiller, M. D.
Watson, John B.
Whitlow, William B.
Wigoda, Stephan
Wigoda, Thomas C.
Wilkinson, Sherman W.
Wilson, Charlie W.
Wilson, Curtis T.
Wilson, George H.
Wiswall, Frank A.
Woodson III, Richard P.
Wynar, Sol

Yeager, Charles E.
Yerak, Ray
Zellner, Edmond
Zemke, Hubert

b. RAF Veterans

Allen, Michael
Armit, Robert J.
Atkins, William A.
Bage, James B.
Bailey, Eric N.
Bartlett, Alan E.
Bartlett, Les
Bearns, R. J.
Biggs, Frederick A.
Booker, S. A.
Bonner, C. W.
Bridgman, Stan
Burke, W. W.
Cairns, G.
Chaffey, N. R.
Chandler, C. H.
Cheshire, Leonard
Chivers, Maxwell
Coleman, Harry
Collingwood, C. J.
Cooper, L. G.
Davies, H. G.
Davis, B. D.
Davis, Roy
Denchfield, H. D.
Dodd, Cyril E.
Down, D. E.
Duncan, G. M.
Easby, L. Y.
Ede, Les
Edgley, A. W.
Edwards, Ron
Freestone, S. N.
Furner, D. J.
Gall, Alan S.
George, J.
Glass, R. R.
Goode, R. J.
Hall, H. R.
Hawkins, D. H.
Hall, H. R.
Hart, R. W.
Hawkins, D. H.
Hay, E. L.
Hay, L. J.
Hewlett, C. A.

Hinchliffe, Peter C.
Hodgson, G. S.
Howe, H. W.
Howell, David
Jones, R. T.
Kyles, J. A.
LeMarchant, Harry F.
Mahaddie, T. G. Hamish
McCullough, Allan T.
MacFarlane, W. T.
McMillan, Fred
Mead, George
Mitchell, H. F. S.
Mosely, T. W.
Mowbray, G.
O'Hanlon, Leonard J. S.
O'Sullivan, John
Parnell, Geoff
Perks, G. D.
Pierce, E. G.
Pomeroy, F. L.
Pratt, J. R.
Pritchard, R. F.
Radcliffe, Douglas
Ratcliffe, E. G.
Reichstein, Alwyn
Reid, John
Robb, Allen S.
Robinson, J. B.
Rogers, Douglas W.
Rothwell, Geoff
Rudland, C. P.
Russell, J. K.
Saunders, Donald
Saunders, W.
Searle, H. R.
Sickelmore, S. K.
Sills, W. R.
Simpson, Arthur
Smith, James B.
Smith, P.
Spridgeon, Edgar
Street, J.
Sumter, Len
Taverner, G. C.
Vennard, R. B.
White, Kenneth P.
Williams, Denis J.
Williams, Ronald S.
Whitten, Geoffrey R.
Woodward, James H.
Wreford, A. H. C.
Yeoman, Harold

6. Interviews with author

Clark, General Albert P., USAF Academy Colorado, 30 Oct. 1991.

Milton, General Theodore Ross, USAF Academy Colorado, 28 Oct. 1991.

Stafford-Clark, Dr David, Brighton, West Sussex, 19 Jan. 1991.

Wells, Major M. L., Bourne End, Buckinghamshire, 20 April 1992.

Index

Note: Page references in bold are to Tables. References with 'n' or 'nn' are to pages of the Notes where significant further information can be found in one or more notes.